Alere flammam . . .

The guests go

BURNING BOOKS MCMLXXXVI

EDITED AND DESIGNED BY

MELODY SUMNER   KATHLEEN BURCH   MICHAEL SUMNER

in to supper.

John Cage

Robert Ashley

Yoko Ono

Laurie Anderson

Charles Amirkhanian

Michael Peppe

K. Atchley

The guests go in to supper.

Cards in Atchley's *Edison's Last Project(ion)* © 1986 K. Atchley
Graphics in Anderson's chapter © 1986 Laurie Anderson
Cover and chapter heading art by Michael Sumner

"Inter-view with John Cage" by Sean Bronzell and Ann Suchomski was previously
published in *Catch Magazine,* Knox College. "Why Our Art Is So Bad" by Michael Peppe
was published previously in *High Performance.*

ACKNOWLEDGMENTS:
*We wish to thank the following people for the kindness and integrity
they exhibited in aiding with production of this book—*
Kathy Brew, Andrew Culver, Barbara Golden, Mimi Johnson, Marilyn Langfeld,
Carol Law, Jonathan Livingston, Beverly Miller, Helen Nickerson, George Speerin

GENEROUS FINANCIAL ASSISTANCE:
Mary Virginia Cook and Courtney E. Cook
Sandra Kirshenbaum, editor & publisher of *Fine Print*
Joanne Livingston
Stephen McElroy, Burch+McElroy Typographers, Inc.
Carol Cook Williams, president, Southwest Excavation and Concrete Pumping

DESIGN:
Book design by Michael Sumner

Typographic design by Kathleen Burch
Typeset in *Else* (Robert Norton design) and *Univers* (Adrian Frutiger design)
at Burch+McElroy Typographers, Inc., San Francisco, California.

PRODUCTION ASSISTANCE:
Jake Belsky, Dean Still, Patrick Sumner

EDITORIAL ASSISTANCE:
Sheila Davies, Jean Fraschina, E. Ginger, Eda Regan

PRINTING:
This book was printed at the West Coast Print Center by Don Cushman,
in a first edition of 3,000 copies.

This book is printed on acid-free paper and sewn in signatures.

ISBN 0-936050-05-5

Table of Contents

Editors' Preface, *Melody Sumner* 6
Foreword, *Frances Butler* 8
Introductions, *Charles Shere* 11

John Cage
13
Interview, *the Editors* 15
Inter-view with John Cage, *Sean Bronzell, Ann Suchomski* 20
Introduction to text, *John Cage* 28
MUSHROOMS *et Variationes* 29

Robert Ashley
97
Interview, *the Editors* 99
Introduction to text, *Robert Ashley* 119
IMPROVEMENT (DON LEAVES LINDA)
    Act I 122
    Act II 147

Yoko Ono
169
Interview, *the Editors* 171
SONGS, STORIES, ESSAYS 185

Laurie Anderson
215
Interview, *Charles Amirkhanian* 217
Notes on Laurie Anderson, *Liz Sizensky* 229
SONGS 230

Charles Amirkhanian
251
Interview, *Sheila Davies, Susan Stone* 253
Notes about the texts, *Charles Amirkhanian* 266
TEXTS 268

Michael Peppe
295
Interview, *Stephanie Leberer* 297
Introduction to text, *Michael Peppe* 309
ACTMUSIKSPECTAKLE V 314
EVENTSCORE samples 332
ESSAY: "Behaviormusik theory" 340
ESSAY: "Why our art is so bad" 342

K. Atchley
353
Interview, *Barbara Golden* 355
Introduction to text, *K. Atchley* 359
EDISON'S LAST PROJECT(ION) 362
LIGHT OF HAND (Lumière de main) 380

Editors' Preface

But what about the future?

I asked the other editors this question. Kathleen Burch responds, "I believe this more and more—it is double or nothing now, and you have to make a choice." Michael Sumner says, "Ask yourself—before you do anything— Why are you doing what you are doing? And what is what you are doing really doing?" For my answer I found this statement in a tiny out-of-print pamphlet by Katherine Dreier called *Duchamp's Glass:* "To put our force of imagination into action is the most important goal the art of the present day can achieve." Imagination, yes, in the most voluptuous sense.

A dinner party is a way to combine the physical with the metaphysical. Our seven guests have accepted their invitations, and *you* might make it eight; numbers that lend themselves to all sorts of fanciful connections. I like to think of these fascinating individuals as each being associated with one of the seven deadly sins; and conversely, with the divine virtues those vices indicate in excess. We have all witnessed the truth of the Latin phrase "corruptio optimi pessima," the best becomes the worst. But isn't the opposite also true? Vice versa.

Socrates expressed the idea that to be *good* everything must be conscious. Then, while in prison before his death, a recurring dream-like apparition disturbed the logic of his thoughts. (Something similar happened with Edison, K. Atchley indicates.) It always said the same thing to him: "Socrates, practice music!"

These seven artists have these things in common: their choice of music as a main mode of expression, and their reliance on words as an integral part of their compositions. Also, there is the importance of IDEAS in their work. When I mentioned this to Charles Shere (who will introduce you to the guests one by one) he exclaimed: "But all music is based on ideas!"

If ideas affect the head, words affect the heart, and music affects the body and soul, an art form that combines them all might provide some sort of needed integration. It's as if music with words can actually press ideas into the body. Music is not the only form for the presentation of ideas, but it is a *moving* form, it is a *memorable* form, one that speaks instantly to all the appetites. That's why radio and televison advertisements, doctor's offices, elevators, "hold" lines, grocery stores, waiting rooms, airplanes, and video games employ music actively as a device. You cannot get through a whole day anywhere near civilization without hearing some form of music, most likely many many forms, almost always pre-recorded, which means it is coming from another place and time.

John Cage came to the conclusion that every sound is or can be heard as music. Michael Peppe proposes that everything, even human behavior, is musically composable. Nothing is as pervasive, and as persuasive except, perhaps, images. Yoko Ono admits that she doesn't know what the sources or purposes of music are, except, for herself. Though we might not understand how it works, music does have the power to instantaneously transform.

It may be true that music can cause the soul to undergo a form of expansion. "Among the traditional arts, music has a special place, for it deals with material forms and shapes less than do all the other arts, and it is connected more directly to the world of essences." (from the *Sword of Gnosis* edited by Jacob Needleman). Michael Harner, an anthropologist who has long been studying shamanic practices all over the world, has said that music has the power to change our relationship with ordinary time. Drumming, more than any other single technique, is most commonly and successfully used as a rope or a beacon to gain access to other states of mind, "non-ordinary reality." He says that drumming is the oldest technique in use, it goes back about 40,000 years.

If *Homo sapiens sapiens* has been around for 40,000 years or more, what has it been up to all this time? Our conscious history provides only about five thousand years worth of information, sketchy at that. How much of that time has *sapiens* actually been conscious, or are we just coming into consciousness now? Will we come into it just as we go out? Bryon Gysin said this about the mystery of Why are we here? — "We are here to go." So, the United States spends approximately the equivalent of $60 a year for every human being alive on this planet just to "defend" itself from everyone else. "It would cost less to kill them all!" Frances Butler pointed out. (She runs forward on the following pages.)

But let's go back. The technique *with* words, too, is ancient. The poems in the Rig Veda (3–4,000 years old) were memorized and sung aloud in public contests by their authors. More than songs, they are actually hymns incorporating wisdom, knowledge, history, myth. And beauty. This is what Robert Ashley is doing. Art is inevitably wedded to beauty and to pleasure — "Kama," explains John Cage — which may be where Laurie Anderson succeeds. Her songs are lovely and also smart. She has refined the collage technique, it is seamless, it all comes from somewhere else but you can't really tell. Could this indicate that there may someday no longer be any personal property of ideas? "Collage," as Charles Amirkhanian says in *his* collage, "is the essential psychological identity of this century."

Philosopher Frithjof Schuon has remarked: "All too many people no longer even know what is meant by an *idea,* what is its value and what its function." Something like the popular anxiety that we can no longer experience anything that is *real:* not real water, not real emotion. Nietzsche defined the three senses of the modern soul: Brutality, artificiality, and innocence. If this lambent earth would be more than a place where beings consume other beings, we have work to do. We may even need some new ideas. It may not be work though, but play.

Melody Sumner, Kathleen Burch, Michael Sumner
Editors

Foreword

Who are these guests who watch, talk, and listen
carefully to each other's stories? Past stories always
took some other time, a time marked by once upon.
These guests tell stories about present time, taking
a long time, or not any special time.

These are stories about the fact that style is content
and the story is the story teller, so conventions
move to idiosyncrasy. Every moment is noted;
details are dense as air. Sound is infinite, taking
everything into the same, long, long, time.

But these endless gatherings of ordinary speech
rhythms, long records smirking with the democracy of
all art made into all life, all life made into all art, are
variously pared by the skilled slip of the tongue, the
half-opened   eye, exploiting the quick recognition of
nodded heads,   turned-out knees, barks or laughs to reveal the
history of the   organizational pre-dispositions of the time.

In older stories, the edge of a body held mainly on
one leg could have been that of a woman curving
into seduction, beginning a familiar story. Or that
balanced edge could reveal the goose-stepper,
a short-cut to another story.

These new musicians feint to the familiar,
then slip past to the story of the *next* move
of that one-legged body (an amputee on crutches).
Renga the Japanese call it. The poem in which
each line is as far from the implications of the
previous line as possible.

Information theory, we call it, and claim
that humans only pay attention to that
which they do not know.   But now, art is no longer separate from anything.
Art is what is known, and *everything* is known by
everyone. We know both act and preparation for action.
The side door to the theater is off its hinges, we see the gobs
of spittle jumping on the lips of the rehearsing singers.
Laurence Sterne has been summoned repeatedly. Every
device has been bared. Everything is out of the book.

But, perhaps reflecting acceptance of Bell's theory
("the world is either fundamentally lawless or
fundamentally inseparable"), this new music, alone
among our arts, is not structured by the hackneyed
layers of irony—it is integrative, connecting

everything to everything else. Any sentence in this
text shows that these musicians are pleased with the
options; using the total power of seeing, the entire
history of hearing, all the contradictions of speech
in their music.

Laurie Anderson cites her appropriation of Joyce:
"And this isn't so much a situation of the omniscient
author looking down at his puppet-like characters,
as much as a giant camera movement, a giant pan . . ."
John Cage quotes Bucky Fuller to express the scope
of his concern for the earth: "It's all one piece of land."
K. Atchley uses Edison to move fluidly in and out of
an Enclosed Space of human consciousness, where
he "recognizes many of the people in the laboratory,
but their roles seem unstable." Robert Ashley works
from Frances Yates' apt description of knowledge as a
seamless web: "Neo-Platonism is sort of like holography:
the idea that the whole thing is contained in the
smallest detail. The philosophical machinery that
they used had very elaborate schemes for being
able to remember how the different parts of the
universe related. You could sit down and start
thinking about a flower and come out as God."

*Two of the guests have stepped back from
the table of chance-structured music, and
their divergence marks the spectrum of
possible new organizational tactics.*

Robert Ashley, preoccupied with space, has
generated a complex system of routes from one place
and moment to the next. He has constructed his
own theater of memory, a tension structure in
which events are held like the islands in a
Micronesian chart of the currents.

Here, his own measurements of the importance of
an idea, and the time it should be allowed for expression, temporarily stiffen chaos into spatial order. Sleight-
of-hand, he connects cognitive and geographical
space.   "I think people like to be in different
parts   of the world because every part of the world . . .
gives   you an idea. So when you get tired of
your idea,   you move to a different place."

*The literate among us did indeed once have a
consciousness that was spatially organized. Do we
still? Where is it now? This is just one example of
the possibilities for re-directed attention to signi
ficant human issues held within integrative music.*

Michael Peppe, on the other hand, is not at all
pleased with the shift of art from the narrow path of
spiritual transcendence into the plain of material
connections: "Like the identifying features of value
in general, those of art have, as in a supernova,
expanded quickly enough to qualify as an
explosion, and we are left with a vast, indistinct
nebula of dust and gas." *Big* themes like death, he
says, have gone out of style—too many yoyos with money
("Jimmy Durante: 'Ev'rybody wants ta get into de act!' ")
His world contracts: "As soon as you turn your back
everything in the universe snaps itself inside out with
a hideous sucking motion;" he calls for purification:
"Art that is not born out of love, pain, obsession,
passion and desperation is useless to us."

Well now, hierarchy of expression is an old story.
A priestly trick, Aristotle called it. Why not open the
category of valued expression to even more people? Why not
work to achieve universal musical performances? The point
is that this music provides a field, however described—
dancing space, scattered or condensed attention, tension-
held events—that will allow us to shift the scale of ques-
tion to be asked about what we know and what we value
into dimensions that have not yet even been imagined.

The music of the seven who come to this dinner is
just a beginning. There is no need to ask "How can
you make a revolution when the revolution before
last already said anything goes?" We do not even
know what the "anything" that will "go," is.

We have not yet even begun to approach the moment
when all people could speak, sing, or perform for
themselves, a revolutionary change of scale. As yet
the only   questions to be asked of the music generated by
a narrow   spectrum of society have been snugly
couched   within the unexamined ideology of the Continuing
Revolution (the generic concept **NEW** used
to sell hair-creme, car-wax, and other hi-gloss coatings).
But we are just beginning to understand the importance
of music as a model for the fluid, momentary order that
parallels the tension structure of human consciousness
and offers a balm to heal the wounded hearts of
those fearful within the new physics.

It is still time for production, not usury;
time to make the music, not make book on it.

             —F.B.

Introductions

Come in! We're glad you're joining us. This dinner party has been a long time in the preparation. The hosts are still making last-minute adjustments—seating these people takes some planning—and they asked me to introduce you to the guests. I'm sure you know of most of them already, but perhaps you don't know that much about them. I haven't known them long myself, for the most part. But we'll come to know them: one thing they share is their frankness about themselves and their wonderful intelligence when it comes to discussing their work.

It's odd, isn't it, that we haven't met them like this before. Symposiums have been fashionable since Plato's days, and many of our guests have attended their share. But symposiums lately have turned into pretty dreadful affairs, academic and artificial. You can't really expect interesting conversation to develop on a stage in front of an audience. Kathan Brown (Crown Point Press in Oakland) did have a wonderful party a few years ago; two of our guests were there. But it was a necessarily private affair—it's hard to crash a party on an island. This is different, of course; the whole point is to let you in on the affair. It's a bit more like a print version of Robert Ashley's 1976 videotape anthology, Music with Roots in the Aether—but with a revised guest list—and with the leisure of the page replacing the insistence of the tube. I think you'll be fascinated . . .

—*C.S.*

John Cage

Here's John Cage. He's very well known, of course. Have you read his interviews with Daniel Charles, For the Birds? It's a wonderful conversation; John's open-ness and enthusiasm is contagious. And everyone knows about his early percussion music, his prepared piano, the famous "silent piece," 4' 33". But many of us lost touch with him in the 1970s. It wasn't his fault, of course; he worked as hard as ever, touring with Merce Cunningham's dance company, writing a whole series of intriguing books, and continuing to challenge most modern art and thought in his sensible, pragmatic way. It was a difficult time for all of us; you can trace John's attitude toward it just by reading the prefaces to his books—Silence, A Year from Monday, M—his outlook gradually shifts from cheerfulness to concern to something close to despair. Now, though, equanimity seems more his overriding mood. Maybe it's his age—he's 75 now, and while that boyish enthusiasm and inventiveness make age seem unsuited to him, he's as close to an elder statesman as the avant-garde is ever likely to offer.

Not that he actually led the avant-garde. The closest he came was about 40 years ago, when the "New York School" of composers—Earle Brown, Morton Feldman, and Christian Wolff—broke postwar music through the rigors of the 12-tone method under his liberating influence. John's contribution then and always has been the lesson that we can do whatever we want, even nothing, as long as we do it with discipline and follow it through. It's odd how greatly the postwar avant-garde resisted that lesson! Gradually, though, it has been heeded. Partly through John's own demonstration that radical composition can nourish more traditional work—his own music has returned from exotic live-electronic performance to conventional instruments—and partly because just about every aspect of contemporary life, from street politics to physics, has borne out his liberating view of the uncertainty principle.   —C.S.

JOHN CAGE

The Editors
October 1984; New York City

We were wondering what you are working on now.

I'm writing a piece for orchestra, and I'm planning with the help of a mesostic-intelligent word processor, being programmed for me by Jim Rosenberg, to write through the Bible. The New King James Version. It doesn't have so many "beholds" in it. Left to myself I would have written all the mesostics on the name Jehovah, that is, for the Old Testament; for the New Testament I will change to Jesus Christ. But at the suggestion of Klaus Reichert I am going to use not just this Christian name of Yahweh but the earlier Hebrew names as well. Andrew Culver is preparing a C language *I Ching* program which will be compatible with the mesostic processor which will determine which name is to be used for how long, and which will answer any other questions that arise in the course of the work. The first two mesostics on the name Jehovah go this way:

```
                Jabal
               hE was
                 tHe
                  Of
                haVe
                nAme
                  He

                Just
              walkEd
               witH
                gOd
    filled with Violence
                 And
               flesH
```

Isn't that marvelous?

It's sort of Genesis in a nutshell. It's quite terrifying. That takes us through Genesis 6:12 in, so to speak, two steps. This is an example of a 100% mesostic. That is, between two capitalized letters of the name, neither letter appears. **Jabal** is the first word in Genesis that has neither j nor **e** after the **J**. **hE** is the first word after **Jabal** that does not have a j or an e before the **E** nor an **e** nor an **h** after it. Of course it has nothing after the **E** except the **was** which I chose to include.

Do you have to put the Bible into the computer?

No, it's already on floppy discs in two versions (they plan to make two more, four altogether, available) and one of the versions is the one I'm using.

So you can go to the New York Public Library and order a floppy disc of the Bible?

No, you send to a place in Texas to get it; you can buy it.*

And then you can do the Koran.

I asked Norman O. Brown about that, because that's what he's studying now. He said not to do it yet. Nobby says that now that we can read *Finnegans Wake,* we can *start* to read the Koran. Apparently Joyce was reading the Koran.

* Omega Software, Inc.
   P.O. Box 355
   Round Rock, Texas 78680-0355

We wondered if you could talk a little about food, perhaps in the bigger sense.

When you say food in the bigger sense, I think of Nobby's beautiful book *Love's Body*. It has to do with the body and of course with all these things like eating, the functions of the body being like the functions of society. So he thinks of reading, and reading is like eating too. All the sense perceptions. It gets very very mixed up between what you would call spiritual and physical so that it's all one thing. I tend to . . . I think this is the influence of Indian thought on me . . . but I tend to separate things, so that I would prefer to cross the street successfully rather than thinking of it as some form of eating. I like to look at each situation as having its own characteristics, and acting appropriately to each. And I'd like to be able to shift gears, or shift attention to some other way of using my faculties, rather than going in this way which I think comes from the Germans, the idea that everything is one thing. Like eating—that food would eventually comprise everything, it's a Germanic idea. When they get one idea, they like to have it really work *everywhere.*

In general, Europeans have been obsessed with unity. Schönberg taught that a piece of music should have one motive (three notes or so), that's all, that would generate, like a seed, the entire composition. But in India there is a different view, that of distinguishing between four different uses of the faculties. These are *Artha, Kama, Dharma,* and *Moksha. Artha* has to do with success and failure, *Kama* with pleasure, *Dharma* with good and evil, and *Moksha* is liberation from all those concerns. Look as closely as you can at your daily experience, and see when you are in each, and you'll see that in the course of a few minutes you have been in all of them, moving around and changing. That's what brings about the basic nature of inconsistency, that's what makes us inconsistent. You couldn't possibly in any logical way explain or predict it. You can be struck, as Proust was, he tells us that a taste set him going, or it could be the effect of light on some building that would send your mind off in one direction rather than another.

There are certain probabilities but there's no certainty.

None at all. Shakespeare noted that long ago, no matter how well organized you are, your plans go astray. So coming back to your question about food, my tendency would be to think of food as something edible. I wouldn't tend to think of reading as being part of it. I wouldn't want to for instance give up eating and settle for reading.

Or just breathing?

No, I want to go on eating.

You wouldn't want to learn to do photosynthesis?

No, I really like eating as I know it. I would like to learn to eat more things, but I would like them to be edible.

What do you consider edible?

Something I can digest, taste first and then digest, then benefit from through the system. When the English doctor was asked what the most serious human problem was, he said *insufficient drainage*. It's too hard for the human body to eliminate the food it eats. Everything stays in there. Where it stays is in the extremities. My arthritis went to the hands, and the wrists, at one point. I couldn't lift anything, it was too painful. But after one week of the macrobiotic diet, I had no pain. That's why I'm such a convert, I'm just insistent on it. That was about ten years ago. It was Yoko Ono who sent me to Shizuko Yamamoto, and Yamamoto changed my diet. The very first day I was invited to dinner and I called up the hostess and said I'd bring my own food, and she said, no, don't do that, my cook can cook anything, but I said, no, it's too complicated. She finally let me bring my own food. The lady on my left had changed her diet but hadn't brought her food so I shared mine with her.

What did you bring?

Just the brown rice, and beans and vegetables, with no dairy products; it's as simple as that but it's hard for people to understand.

What about fruit?

Fruit is not very good for you but I can't resist it. You can see how many apples and pears I have, and even bananas. But I've given up sugar, sugar is the problem with fruit, and sugar is the problem with alcohol, and I drank alcohol excessively until about two years ago, then I stopped. I had picked it up again when I was in Spain, everyone was drinking wine and I couldn't resist it. Then I got this bump on my hand, and both Shizuko and the astrologer I go to* told me it was from drinking.

* Julie Winter

Drinking wine?

No, by that time I was drinking the best single malt whisky. Laphroaig, and Talisker, it's the only whisky mentioned in poetry. Talisker has the same taste as Laphroaig but it's in the air, Laphroaig is very earthy. Talisker is the same taste but you feel elevated. It's very beautiful. The other one I like, that I miss, is Glenmorangie. It tastes like flowers.

So you really stick to the diet, but you sometimes drink, and eat fruit.

But now I've given up drinking altogether, it's been nearly two years, and I have survived some of the most tempting situations; champagne is poured around me without touching me at all; now and then I have a sip but it doesn't taste attractive anymore. Once I tried a little single malt just to see if I was missing anything, but I didn't have any desire. So I think it's finished, which is rather pleasant because now I can talk on into the evening, and make sense. Whereas when I was drinking alcohol, I would pick up the phone and make arrangements for some future doing and forget all about it, and then three or four people would come over at the same time, or people would come to see me and I wouldn't be here. . . .

Would you enjoy eating an apple?

Yes, thank you.

I'll go get some. [*He returns with a plate, knives and a large bowl of apples.*] How do you feel about the peel? It's the season, right now is the moment to enjoy apples. You know, at the end of his life, Thoreau was concerned with the differences between the tastes of wild apples.

We wanted to ask you how you manage to keep your life so full; you're so busy and yet you're accessible and good humored.

Well, my problem is—which I try to solve but I don't think any of us are what you would call successful in terms of what we think we should be doing but you *move* in that direction—for instance I haven't looked at the mail that came this morning yet, and I didn't know that the elevator wasn't working until you arrived. I have no idea what's in the mail. Generally there is enough for me to do just opening it, and answering the letters, and if I don't do it, it becomes quite aggravating. But other projects come along like say the piece for orchestra which I just finished, and I pay no attention to the mail, it just piles up, and I suffer for having done a piece for orchestra. That's the kind of situation I'm in. The orchestra piece is now connected to the mail. I'm writing for an orchestra in Yugoslavia so I'm not really finished with the piece because I write asking them questions and they answer in the mail. They haven't answered my last question yet. It's about the length of the piece. They had previously said fifteen or twenty minutes and I chose twenty. Then as the piece developed, I knew it would be more what it is if it could be longer, so I wrote back and said that it would be better if it could be thirty or forty minutes long. When they write back I can do all the changes, because I finished it for twenty minutes, and if they say forty all I have to do is multiply by two. I had thought to be able to satisfy all such situations, to have a sliding scale where you could play something for one length or another, but it's for a youth orchestra and I don't want to confuse the kids.

Have you ever worked with a youth orchestra before?

Yes, just this May in Torino I made a musicircus with children. The oldest one was twelve years old and the youngest one was four, there were a thousand of them, they were singing and beating on little drums, playing flutes and dancing. It was charming, and they all did it at once, the place was filled with children.

So you don't have any real secrets about how you manage all this?

Well, you begin by watering the plants, and you end the day by playing chess. And I have to do my exercises. And I shop generally, though I didn't do that today.

Have you ever made any pieces based on your chess playing?

Once I made a chessboard that was music written on a gesso board. My involvement with chance operations is not really related to games or playing; I think of the game of chess as being part of *Artha*, success or failure, whereas my use of chance operations has to do with *Moksha* or liberation.

So by having a game of chess at the end of the day . . .

I'm making a balance with my use of chance operations. Because if I make a wrong move with my knight, I lose. Games are very serious success and failure situations, whereas the use of chance operations is very free of concern. It's like being enlightened.

Are there specific things which fulfill the function of the four operations in your life?

Yes, playing a game or fighting a war or crossing the street is like success or failure. Or picking a poisonous mushroom or picking a safe mushroom, all of that is *Artha*.

So picking mushrooms, then, is like gambling.

No, it's not gambling—it's too serious for gambling—you could kill yourself if you pick the wrong mushroom, so you don't do that, you have to do it right. You can lose the game if you sacrifice your queen stupidly. So that's *Artha*. *Kama* is making love, and traditionally art, giving pleasure. And they wrote a whole set of rules, so that if you love someone and you're going to be separated for a few months, you give certain bites, you know, the *Kama Sutra*. They had a whole etiquette built up about love and pleasure. It is interesting when you think of all those Indian miniature paintings, they are all really charming, I mean there is nothing like German expressionism there. They are pleasing, lovely, they are like dessert, there are not even any vegetables in them. Then *Dharma* is all very strict, there are rules in Indian thought about what steps to take to get better, and better.

What about the Dharma *part, the moral decisions that come up in your daily life, you try to look at every decision as if it's as important as every other?*

Well, you try to see first of all which way you are using your faculties, and there are also mixtures of these ways. For example, in my experience, a very evident mixture was when Bucky Fuller had made a bamboo dome to be used by the American military in Viet Nam. And the reason it was made of bamboo was because they had a lot of bamboo in Viet Nam, and they had asked him to design something to protect them in this terrain. So he designed a beautiful geodesic dome made of bamboo . . . take out the word beautiful, he designed it, period. He was working in *Artha* solving a problem. But then, when we were looking at it together he turned to me and smiled and said isn't it beautiful? and then he was moving from *Artha* over to *Kama*, he was asking whether his solution to that problem was pleasing, and it was. Then another question would be whether or not it was right to make a geodesic dome for a government that was involved in a wrong kind of war . . . and then you would probably end by saying no, it's not right. But then Bucky is such a nice man, that you say well, maybe he's right, we'll change the rule in his case. I mean we are completely confused by that point, don't you think? We don't know what's right and what's wrong. You can't tell in that case. And Bucky, of course, would either tell you that it didn't matter whether he was right or wrong, that he really had solved his problem properly, or if you told him that it was evil to have done this, I'm sure he would have found an excuse, because he thought of himself as a good man.

He must have considered it carefully . . .

And decided to do it. I think he had a large view of the world, that it really was what he called space ship earth, and that all these other people were wrong, who were dividing it up, and fighting one another, and that whether he helped one or the other was of no consequence, ultimately, that the important thing was . . . was to proceed. He did his part of the work as well as he could.

INTER-VIEW WITH

JOHN CAGE

Sean Bronzell, Ann Suchomski

On April 18th and 19th, 1983, John Cage visited the Knox Campus, performing two of his works: James Joyce, Marcel Duchamp, Erik Satie: An Alphabet, *and* Themes and Variations, *published by Station Hill Press in 1982. Along with his two performances, a trip to Green Oaks to look for mushrooms, and a coffee talk where he read his* Composition in Retrospect, *the avant-garde composer gave us an opportunity to interview him. The three of us gathered in Sam Moon's office. What follows is what was said, primarily.*

We thought it might be interesting to ask you about your concerns or ideas about technology today.

I think that . . . you know that I follow the ideas of Buckminster Fuller? And that in view of the increasing number of people . . . and the constantly changing—necessarily changing—relation between human needs and world resources to make it possible for more people to live . . . on the earth comfortably. Of course we can imagine it now. But we haven't done it yet because we still have a society divided between those who have what they need and those who don't have what they need. Simply as a project for the future, technology is essential.

You think that technology is perhaps also dangerous?

It's dangerous if it's in the hands of people who are—who don't have the intention to solve the problems unselfishly . . . of humanity in relation to the world.

Where do you think we're headed now?

I think that each day we . . . we wake up, huh? . . . headed toward a better situation than we hear in the news. [*all laugh*] We feel that it's a little . . .

when you get tired you feel it's a little foolish to be optimistic. But . . . I have the feeling that optimism is the natural state of the human *attitude*. And that it's only fatigue that makes one . . . pessimistic, even if the situation is very difficult. I think that we are inclined to hope for the best, mmm?

Do you think that inclination is strong enough . . . to be successful?

We have yet to see. We live in a fantastic time, where we're all aware that . . . a mistake, something even unintended on the part of the person who did it, might bring about the destruction, the wholesale destruction, of the planet, mmm? We have large installations, which are completely manned and very far down under the ground with nothing but buttons for people to press . . . mmm?

[*long pause*]

I think it's—I think we should become—it would be very good if we could . . . pull ourselves up, so to speak, out of the . . . present situation and come into another one that involved intelligence, rather than political bickering.

I think . . . it's clear that as long as we have *nations* we have jealousy and fear too, so that the threats to global well-being will remain until we stop that inefficient work between nations. Optimism can stem now from the fact that in the 19th century, I think both Italy and Germany are two instances, nations were simply a collection of principalities. So that it could be, still—with a play of intelligence—that the global problems would be addressed. And there are many of us who feel this way.

How would you handle a counter-argument . . . that that's silly idealistic drivel?

And what is that? I mean what *should* one do? Isn't it clear that we can destroy ourselves if we continue with nationalism?

But what about the movement of people—you might call it a "grass roots" movement—who believe that we have to stick with . . .

Stick with nationalism? Mmm.

And just get a better economy, sort of a simple view. Just get a good President in there and our problems will be solved.

Well . . . I'm *very*—I'm not optimistic at all about a political solution. I have a friend who called me up, the other day. She's older than I am, and she knows that I don't vote. And she said . . . now this year, or this next presidential election, you must register, you must vote. And I said yes, but for whom? And she said it doesn't matter for whom [*laugh*] just vote. She said don't vote for Reagan [*laughter all around*] but vote, for anybody you know. I asked people if they knew who was going to run, and the first name I heard, and the only one in fact, is Paul Newman, another movie star.

It made me think how nice it would be to have Greta Garbo as president. [*laugh*] But that is rather silly. I think that if the presidential uh business was a contest between two movie stars that we would see that democracy had sunk to a level that ought to be questioned, mmm? I think *many* people who now accept it would pause.

How far do you think that pause would go? All the way down?

Well, let's say that the whole thing is interrupted by an invasion from outer space, mmm? [*pause*] Then there would be a coalition, immediately, of all the world's peoples to protect us . . . to protect the world from the other enemy. I—

Wouldn't we split apart again afterwards?

I shouldn't think so, if we once come together. [*pause*] Do you know my first installment of the "Diary: How to Improve the World"? It's in *A Year from Monday.**

*A Year From Monday, John Cage (Wesleyan University Press, 1967).

I was at the University of Hawaii for about a month and Oahu—that island where Honolulu is—has a mountain range down the middle. The University is on the south side, and I with two friends lived on the north side of that range. I noticed going into the tunnel each day that at the top of the mountain was a crenellation as on a medieval castle, mmm? And I asked people about it and they said that formerly the tribe that lived to the north was separate from the tribe that lived to the south and they used those crenellations to protect themselves as they shot poisoned arrows down on the other side, mmm? Now the place is tunneled, which is technology, and all the utilities are shared by both sides. The information that there was a separation between the two is on the order of—almost of mythology, mmm? . . . of a past that isn't real, mmm? That, it's obviously absurd that people would fight if they are on a small island, mmm? . . . and that's why I started that diary.

And we are, as Fuller has pointed out, an island on the earth. It's all one piece of land; it can be connected. The utilities that are used, say in the Americas, can go through South America, Central America, North America and on over to Asia. Down into Indonesia and out to Europe. Africa. So that you can largely cover the entire earth with a network . . . of electrical power, say, and other such things.

How would you see that happening? How—what would be a way of that happening now?

There would have to be some intelligence. *Or* some threat that would draw the whole thing together. Don't you think that instead of being threatened from outside we could become so foolish, interiorly, through giving up our leadership to movie stars, mmm? or something worse, that we would then opt for an intelligent solving of real problems rather than the creation of imaginary ones? The imaginary ones being simply contests between *leaderships.* The governments are no longer representative of the people. They're just games being played by the leaders. If you fly . . . around, you know, globally, and happen to talk with someone from . . . any country. China, Russia—it doesn't matter what country. But take the ones we think might be enemies. You'll find that they're not enemies, that they're just like *us* and that you feel that almost immediately. [*pause*] What is also supportive of an optimistic attitude toward change in global society is the fact that in a very short period of time, in this century, one-fourth or one-fifth of the world's population changed drastically. China. Some people feel that it's awful that many people were killed in the course of that change, but it's certain that . . . whether or not we change, there will be suffering. Suffering will continue. There are people murdering other people. That seems to be one of the ways that people behave. But I think that private murders ... meant murders ... intended murders are somehow, well, I'm willing to accept them more than the wholesale, governmental, political murders, mmm? which are mass murders.

But then ... where or how are we to gain intelligence?

Okay. I think. Here's another thing to support optimism, which might answer that question. Industry is already supra-national. Coca-Cola sees no boundaries to its commerce. So, we should study the ways of industry. In order to, ourselves, behave globally, as industry behaves. They do it out of greed. We should do it out of the desire to make the *house* we live in, which is the whole place, in good working order. It's now a kind of uh, mess. The games that have been and are still being ... played have made it very, well, dirty. The environment hasn't been treated properly. It isn't ruined yet, but when you have a *lake* that can be set on fire, mmm? ... something's wrong. Or when rivers are flammable.

Many people would tend to say, well, man makes nature. It doesn't matter. We can restructure the whole world. So we don't have trees anymore, we'll have nice concrete.

This is one of the reasons I so love oriental thought: that nature is part of their thinking rather than something to be tossed aside, in that fashion. I have trouble ... when there seems to be only the thought of man and society. Whereas, it's so different from those Chinese pictures of the land-scape, when you look for a man and finally you see him down in the corner.

What about culture in all this? Do you think that creating a whole ... a system which looks at the whole earth, would make culture a homogenous kind of thing?

We'll have—it's clear that we're going to have more kinds of music, for instance, than we have had in the past ... and we have an appreciation, currently, of far more music than we did when I was young. Far more different kinds of music. I don't think it's going to become homogenous, as often has been feared when nations come together. If, for instance, there's a danger of losing something from the past, haven't you noticed that people immediately make movements to protect the things in danger of being lost? [*pause*] I don't think we need fear the loss of the past, or the differences that have been, in coming together to solve global problems.

But that problem bothers a lot of people ... that fear.

That they might lose something?

MmHmm.

[*long pause*]

They should ask themselves whether they *use* those things that they fear to lose. Very often they don't even use those things. People speak, for instance, of the Bible but don't read it. And Shakespeare and so on. Don't read it and don't go to see any of it. And yet feel it's something they *own.* It's a mistake. [*pause*] I think there should be general access to all of culture. That culture should become more and more electronic. That there should be general access, as there is with the telephone book, to other people. So you would have a primary number for Shakespeare, say, like an area code for Shakespeare. [*laugh*] You would have a number for *Hamlet,* and a different number for different parts of Shakespeare. Then you would have, at home, next to your telephone, material upon which material could be received ... electronically printed, mmm? So everyone would have quick access to all of the books, all of the music, etc. And you could even transmit, electronically, graphic material. I think it would make a lot of difference in the relation of people to culture.

And it would remove, again, that thing of ownership, and emphasize— what is more important than ownership, I think—*use.* This was a principle in Thoreau's life. He objected, you know, to people owning the land who didn't use it. And he pointed out in his journal that he used other people's property, where they didn't use it. He knew how to get across someone's land and the owner had to be *led* by him, mmm? [*laugh*] through his own land. It seems so strange that the land should be owned by people who aren't there, mmm? There's an unwritten law among mushroom lovers, and in Germany I think it holds: that whoever *sees* a mushroom owns it, no matter what land it's on. [*pause*]

I think a great deal has to change. And I think we have a tendency to think that change is impossible, but we have examples of change in the past. Don't you agree?

Yes. It just seems that change might be resisted to the point . . . for instance with the possibility of nuclear war, it seems we're going to wait until we're pushed to do something and that push will be too big and there will be nothing left.

* *Megatrends,* John Naisbitt (New York: Warner Publishing Co., 1984).

I understand. Fuller has said that invention is more thorough-going in the case of military endeavors, that once the war is fought those accomplishments of inventiveness are given over to the peaceful—the conduct of peace. What we have to do is change that. So we don't, as you say, kill ourselves before we get to use it.

Have you seen this book out called *Megatrends*?* It's just out. I read it in a glancing-at-it way in Houston the other day. . .we're moving, the author says, and the way he got his information is by newspapers and periodicals and so forth, and then to subject all that information to computer analysis, etc., in order to find what are the trends of society. And the first trend he mentions is from an industrial society to an information society. Which is to say, from manual labor to unemployment. And our high degrees of unemployment that we now hear of. We hear, I think, all the way from nine percent unemployed to as high as 40 percent in Puerto Rico. I think in Detroit it's now 14 percent. If we change from seeing that as a threat to seeing that as an advance toward our proper goal, mmm? the whole thing could turn from negative to positive.

What would you do with the argument that nothing will get done that way?

Well, there are now factories in Japan where robots are making robots.

And this information is in that book. The tendency is definitely toward a society based on unemployment. Our educational system now is based on preparing people for employment, mmm? Yet even when I was young it was known that university graduates were frequently unemployed. And in the first great depression there were university graduates going around sustaining themselves by going through people's garbage. We already know that that's wrong, mmm?

But, what is basically wrong is that one should be educated in order to get a job. We now know that there isn't enough work, really, to go around. That we *have,* through invention, which is a good thing, we have now reduced the necessity for work. So you really have to put your mind to it to figure out what to do. You have to *create,* not foolish jobs, but oh—you have to create a use of your time that is interesting to you, that you can devote yourself to. You almost know, I'm sure, that most jobs you would get are not things you would devote yourself to, or want to.

So . . . *if* we could see that we don't have to be employed, then how we are going to spend our time is the question. There's a company in Italy called the Olivetti Company that has been very enlightened in all of its history. And they always train their employees in the use of their leisure time. So that when they would retire, they would already know things to do that they enjoyed, mmm? So they could continue. And now they are retired at the age of 45. And that was just a recognition on the part of the company of the state of affairs which is brought about by technology.

Technology essentially is a way of getting more done with less effort. And it's a good thing rather than a bad thing. Oh, pick up any text published by the musician's union and you'll see that they don't like electronic music. But, electronic music is definitely here to stay. The publishers, my music publisher, my book publisher—they know that Xerox is a real threat to their continuing; however, they continue. What must be done eventually is the elimination not only of the publication but of the need for xeroxing, and to connect it with the telephone so that anyone can have anything he wishes at any time. And erase it—so that your copy of Homer, I mean, can become a copy of Shakespeare, mmm? By just quick erasure and quick printing, mmm?

*"James Joyce, Marcel Duchamp, Erik Satie: An Alphabet," X, John Cage (Wesleyan University Press, 1983); paperback edition, properly illustrated, 1986.

That was why in my talk last night* I was making all those magical situations of buildings moving in and out quickly, you know, from one place to another without any effort . . . Because that's the—electronic immediacy is what we're moving toward.

There are people who would call such things pipe dreams.

But the figures about unemployment are *not* pipe dreams. They're very real. When you have a society that's 40 percent unemployed it's *very* real. You have to carry a gun in Puerto Rico to walk across the street and down the block because you're in danger. Nearly half the people haven't got anything to *eat.*

But what can be done about the problem of dividing? You have all this unemployment and all of these starving people . . .

The food that the people don't have is not necessarily good food, mmm? Is that clear? [*pause*]

We are also eating, the ones who have money and so forth, wrong food. The vegetables are not good for us through the agri-business. The meat is not only not good as animal fat but the chickens have all been ruined with those hormones. So that the diseases we have and the *amounts* of disease we have are astonishing. These are the problems that should be addressed rather than the protection of one country against another. We should approach *immediately,* as soon as possible, the question of the air, the question of the water, the question of the food, the question of shelter, etc. All those things. And finally the one you mentioned first, the question of the access to culture. Not only the culture of the past, but access to places where we will be able to make the necessary culture of the present and future. We have a lot to do. We oughtn't to think that unemployment will be inactivity. Because there are real problems facing us.

However, they can be solved. A quick change in food intake will affect the health of the whole society. Drastically. My arthritis, all the pain from my arthritis disappeared in one week from changed diet. It stands to reason that if you keep putting things into you and it keeps going out that it's like flushing—a system that changes quickly, mmm? Same is true of the rivers and the same is true of the air. If we change the way we treat it, it will change. If you go now to Iceland, you go into a land situation where the air is good and the water is good. I mean really good. There's no industry. Englishmen going there for a vacation are frequently so astonished at the pleasures of having good air and good water that they don't go back; they stay there. I was amazed. You just can't believe what a pleasure it is to breathe good air and drink good water.

* Aqua Clean, Pure Water, Inc., Lincoln, Nebraska

I now distill water with a machine.* [*laugh*] And then having taken everything out of it, I then put essence of seawater back into it. [*more laughs*] Not to taste it but in order to have proper minerals in the water. So that the activity of an individual now is rather absurd like that, mmm? Taking everything out of the water and then putting some back. But should it be approached by the society, instead of being so intent on nuclear defense and nuclear attack, we would have better things to eat. And this has been largely outlined by Buckminster Fuller. So that it's not as though we have to sit down and figure out what to do.

Do you think people will do it?

I…I remain optimistic, yes. Say. Say the unemployment that's 40 percent goes up to 80 percent and say the one that's ten percent here goes up to 40 percent, I think the circumstances would resemble a *civil* war, which would be as instigative to action as attack from outer space. So we have dangers from within and theoretical danger from without. I think from one or the other of those will come the *realization* that we must use our heads. And act intelligently and unselfishly.

So people who are acting intelligently now should remain optimistic?

Right. Keep it in mind and alter the nature of whatever circumstances you have the capability of altering. Alter it in that direction. And the direction is a direction away from competitiveness toward coexistence, away from ownership toward use.

[*pause*]

But an important concern in all this is what is there to do now, to get people to act? It's frustrating…

To bring about changes?

Mmhmm. Is that a responsibility?

I don't think that it's taken as a responsibility. You can see from the nature of this conversation that the complexity in which we find ourselves of almost not knowing where to begin, and what to think about, what to *do*. Nevertheless, we will remain active and I think if we *tend* in the directions that I have mentioned and others have presented that the changes might, just might take place.

[*long pause*]

What about the idea of God as a verb rather than a noun?

That's Buckminster Fuller's idea. It's interesting because it's active rather than static. Verb rather than noun.

Do we even want such an idea?

I think it would be better, particularly if we do become global, to have a different attitude toward . . . such things. So that in coming together we would realize that some of the people have certain attitudes and others have other attitudes, and we need not establish one of them but rather make it possible for all of them to coexist. That's why I like so much the Buddhist notion that I mentioned last night of a multiplicity of centers rather than one center.* Because that was already prepared for the acceptance of other ideas.

*"Every being whether sentient or nonsentient is at the center of the universe and is therefore world-honored."
—J.C., 1986

And now I think again of preferring a verb to a noun. I think I would rather have an indeterminate attitude toward what is the syntax of such words. So that He might be an adjective. An adverb too.

An article.

In other words, resembling not our language but ancient classical Chinese language in which words were empty or full. If a word was *full* we didn't know if it was a noun or a verb. It could be one or the other. However, Fuller has, I'm sure, a beneficent idea in his notion of verb. What he's moving toward is activity, an activity which is geared toward the success of all the people in relation to the earth they live on.

Introduction to
MUSHROOMS *et Variationes*

In the fall of 1983 I was invited by Ray Kass to Mountain Lake in Virginia to conduct a mushroom foray with real mycologists, Orson K. Miller, Jr. and his wife Hope H. Miller (I am just an amateur). One evening I was to give a talk bringing together my devotion to the arts and my love of mushrooms. I decided to write a new text in the same way that I had written *Themes and Variations*, but the new one would not be, as *Themes and Variations* is, mesostics on the names of people who have been important to me in my life and work. It would be mesostics on the Latin names of mushrooms (that's why the title is partly in Latin) that I have enjoyed collecting in the woods and fields and later eating in the evening at dinner with friends. I wrote a library of mesostics, five different ones on each of twelve mushroom names repeated five times, sixty texts in all, each one setting out from a chance-determined one of the one hundred and ten ideas I'd listed in the course of a cursory examination of my books.* Then, using *I Ching* chance operations I used these sixty syntactical texts to make one which was nonsyntactical, a renga† since it came from a plurality of sources rather than a single one and since it is long rather than short like haiku. *MUSHROOMS et Variationes* is one more in an ongoing series: writings which though coming from ideas are not about them, yet nevertheless unintentionally produce them.

The text is to be spoken outloud. It consists of five sections, each to take fifteen minutes. The third is the slowest, the fourth the fastest.

Roman numerals, one for each of the twelve mushroom names, appear in the left margin of the first section. They are repeated in the *Variationes* together with parentheses giving the position(s) of that mushroom in the previous fifteen minute section(s). In the right margin the time in minutes and seconds is given at regular intervals.

The lines that are to be read in a single breath are printed singly or together as a stanza. These divisions or liaisons were not chance determined, but were arrived at by improvisational means.

More time is given to mesostics on the name *Craterellus cornucopioides* than to the others because of the lettrist events which are to be vocalised or pronounced halfway between speech and song. These lettrist events were triggered by the idea, love, one of the one hundred and ten ideas mentioned above. (I've noticed that when people are in love, they are frequently perfectly happy together making no sense at all.)

The other mushroom names are *Entoloma abortivum, Clitocybe nuda, Sparassis crispa, Lepiota americana, Armillaria matsutake, Cantharellus cinnabarinus, Armillariella mellea, Marasmius oreades, Dentinum repandum, Hypomyces lactifluorum,* and *Cantharellus umbonatus.*

*See "Introduction," *Themes and Variations*, John Cage, (Barrytown, New York: Station Hill Press, 1982).

†"Renga is a classical form of Japanese poetry. Traditionally renga is written by a group of poets finding themselves of an evening together and having nothing better to do. Successive lines are written by different poets. Each poet tries to make his line as distant in possible meanings from the preceding line as he can take it. This is no doubt an attempt to open the minds of the poets and listeners or readers to other relationships than those ordinarily perceived." *Themes and Variations*, ibid.

MUSHROOMS *et Variationes*

instEad
betweeN

That
twO
deaL
mOre
becoMing
And
After

not line Between

instead Of
in latteR case
boTh

I'm
eVery atom
becaUse
relationship between theM
takEs
workiNg
facT

bOth
onLy
when they're On track
as Much
in spAce

Always
But
nOw

foRmed

wriTten
emptIness

ready to receiVe
Upsets
what's had in Mind

Each
there's Now
enlighTened
is wOrthy

Less
shall i dO

30"

i reMember
pAssivity
Acceptance
of Being
at One's   1'00"
centeR
fooT of land

contInued
by listing eVery plant
she foUnd

Much
gravity aspEct
of eNergy
she had wriTten it

mOtor
enLightened

nOw
and More
And
thAn

we Believe
he fOund
miseRable
The

shIft
Very
yoU are   1'30'
like My

II

Conversation
at tabLe
gone to the movIes
iTs name
directiOn
that Came up with
lovelY sounds in nature
to Block out
thE
wouldN't let them
the Urban
leaDer
once more reAdy for no matter what

Can be sure
tree is getting aLong

she mentIoned silence
in The desert
nOt
but Continued making new ones
was mY response

like Birds

grEw
New shoots   2'00"

what broUght us all together
to holD it together

sAfe for humanity

politiCs must give way

in the worLd of art
mornIng
beTween
Of

didn't reCeive invitations
each and everYone

Both
should havE
mouNtain

moUntain
from Down below

mercifully frozen to deAth
anyone Can see it's time

fiLm

room noIse

or is iT
with Our present
existenCe
am i i mean to saY
celeBration
nErvous system
equatioN

its power its Use
she launcheD her show

diseAses
in Circuit
of peopLe

but somethIng else
That
sOund
Cristophe

with leprosY

Blood

thEre
chaNge of life

embrace me yoUng
anD whole
at last world mAnagement

III

ITS
suPply

ALL THAT'S NEEDED

2'30"

3'00"

FoR
IN ORDER TO BREAK THEM LATER
WHAT YOU'VE SEEN

FACULTIES

EAR'S NO PLACE INDEPENDENT

EASY
EXCITED
THE FIRST
OF WHAT'S NOT INTENDED

LEADS

SPLIT DOWN THE MIDDLE

3'30"

'T'S WE WHO TURN AWAY

IT COULD HAVE EASILY
BEFORE WE PUT
CHANGING
ENLARGING
WHICH IS HAVING
NOTHING TO SAY
WHEN IT IS
TIME
TO SAY THE LEAST
TO COME

THERE'S
TIME TO RETURN
OUT OF OUR MINDS
BUT I HAVE THE IMPRESSION
AWAY
MUSHROOMS WILL BE FOUND
WHEN PEOPLE
THAT LEADS
ANOTHER

VELVET FOOTED COLLYBIA

NO EXTRA TIME'S HAD
JUST SOUNDS
IN OKLAHOMA

4'00"

AND THEN OF COURSE
EDUCATION

THE DESIRE TO BE SECURE

TO INCLUDING
DESIRE TO TASTE

OR TAKING GLOBAL POINT OF VIEW
AWAY

MUSHROOMS
AT ANY POINT IN TIME
THAT OPENS
DOORS

reAl one of finding another
we Say
becauSe
wIth
actually found Several
and not have Conceptions
weRe not closed
whIch
Shifts
as uPper vermont

And

viSions
of Profession
unintentionAlly
Rules

wAy
Supplied

but Serves
for hIm
to have made a Sign
for musiC

wheneveR
wIll change
when i Said
in Place
my bAsket
don't think i wouLd
havE

Paul zukofsky does not agree

I have
except fOr

To music

dAvid tudor

in front of Audiences
asked how it was coMing

Enlightenment

because Records
thIs
indeterminaCy
A sutra
actual souNds
At
aLl

and will bE later on
in any case not on Paper

musIc

germinatiOn was one

4'30"

5'00"

IV

and Then
music is Alive

mAde
not Music
obligEd
to listen to a Record

makIng
inClude
more like A camera
thaN
in nAture

buddha said suddenLy
thE fact
in sPace

In
alsO
differenT

Alone in time

the mondriAns are cracked

Many
no yEs and no

cuRved

the next stop Is
you Could
sAy a letter

seNse
he gives As

problems of Asking something
theRe'd be
Mushrooms

thIs time
possibLe
even sLightly
the shApe

teaching eveRy
mornIng

cleAring up

no Mushrooms
except one dAy
of Thinking
that there'S
inside inflUence

work making iTself
whAt it will be

they thinK

V

5'30"

6'00"

6'30"

thEir
it mAy even be
aRtha

left the sMaller ones
behInd

he mereLy
meanwhiLe
it get mAde
what he does was done long befoRe
he gIves it
A

the next Minute
no ideA

where iT
waS

got needed drUgs

Tried to be influenced by tobey

hAd   **7'00"**
to Know
likE
VI   perhaps he's reaChed
to be At all
N'karen

noT concerned

tHe future

just to get A little
wRiting a song

nEw book
aLong
aLl together

had oUr
write Some
musiC
wIth the wasps

aNswered
off the kitcheN

for Awhile i won   **7'30"**

to go to Berlin
he sAid
i'd Rather
does wIthout
to keep thiNgs
my stUdy
chemicalS

reCeived the book

A bag
besides techNical

robin dreyer who had sTudied trombone
for sometHing like
And books

woRth
last summEr
because of aLan chadwick's presence there

i Like it
but paUl
to the pawnS
for Clothes
and a suItcase

the compaNy
afterNoon
in north cArolina
By
All

accept theiR check
I'm
wrote oNe himself

difficUlty
the Same
eaCh
he becAme aware
the shop i fouNd

relaTion
to tHeir purposes
musiciAns in mind

the piece may neveR
in othEr parts

often he is bLocked
staying in phiLadelphia
i continUed

So
aCtually no quartet they change

It's
i doN't

oN
And not the viola player

Bright red

A
and lateR

I will try

kNew
throUgh

i hope So
have aCcess
like A seed
uNimpeded

8'00"

8'30"

he was Tall

Horns of plenty

the more you plAy
but the two togetheR
black and rEd
he toLd me
and beautifuL

very mUch

pleaSe me
when i was in iCeland

I was asked

iN
will be a kNockout

besides whAt i had to

to Believe my desires
in the volcAnic
of couRse
near reykjavIk

kNew
yoU put a little oil

iS
when marCel

reAch him
with his wife aNd
geT

He
sAid none

wRiting about him
it occurrEd to me
after haLf an hour
i weLcome whatever happens next

Unique
according to what the liquid'S doing

Couldn't make the game last
more than eIght

Next

ready for aNything
thAt's
Being written

i Asked him do i make my mistake
and micRotonal

It's
colliNs said it's a stacked deck
yoU're playing
bitterneSs to modify

9'00"

9'30"

10'00"

it wAs
at the cheRry lane's
froM
dIstinctions between good
and eviL
incLuding
A

we had not yet foRmed
the communIty
to thE
peopLe
Left behind

circumstAnces that arise

williaMs
madE
goaL

yourseLf
bEtween
this And this

but generAlly
the pRoject
through circuMstances
Is bringing
a handfuL of honeys

nevertheLess
At home

conceRts
wIth
wrotE the manifesto music
beautifuL just the caps

nothing is accompLished
in rAked sand
in the bottoM
of thE pan
it was too difficuLt
are not at aLl in any way a part of it
to kEep
it wAs

A
yeaR before
the probleM
posItion

for awhiLe
Left them covered

wAlks with lois

fiRe

then uncovered and tamarI quickly

firE turned off

10'30"

11'00"

Lemon

even now i wouLdn't
                    cAll it that
and so My
            timE
                    Like of which
easiLy
        nEver
            hAve looked at before

VIII   no need for More poetry
                        thAn comes
                    of Replying
                    the Air

                        of Self-expression
                    it is a Means   **11'30"**

                    over It
                    you woUld have thought
                    a meanS

                            Of
                        oR that

                        sElf-
                            Alteration
                    yesterDay

                        thE chicken polypore
                ron called it vocalS

IX   *very glaD*

                            thE

                            aN idea in mind
                                They found me
                            voIce of god

                            oNce when
                    withoUt

                            caMe
                        undeRbrush
                        thEn <u>hydnum</u>   **12'00"**

            so that i don't interruPt

            couldn't find wAy out

            what and wheN
                        Defined

                    shoUted get out of the way
                        Mysterious

X   since we Have
                    just to saY
                        is a Prize
                    the Only
                    i aM

is bY
aCtually
from Eating

iS
as i wiLl

preferAble
daily perCeived
of boleTus

lIve in the city
iF
i was iLl

for twelve hoUrs
previOusly
veRy little choice

yoU just hunt
Mushrooms

i was Convinced
ouR minds
Asking

Trst

thEm
hungRy
onE hour

Lwt

it gives you aLl thought

U

Swk

my adviCe

where are yOu in it

to give moRe time for the trip
thaN
U

lCn

fOr things to dawn on me
by Placement
the trIp
i will nOt

I

Don't know
whEther
only miStakes

fC

utteR interest

12'30"

13'00"

13'30"

A
dieT
mEans
whateveR
thE stations
heaLth food
pLay is on the side

U

Stores
laCk
gOod

lRm

you Name it
simply tUne in

lCn

O

or are we like Planes
It

O

mlI

you coulD call this
E
rehearSal

XII

        **prinCiple
        thAt
somethiNg
    is quesTion
        tHe
            hAve its place
        afteR that
            bEing
        probLem**

        aLl the same problem

        **thoUght
        it'S
giving Up**

        Me and mine

        **But
        becOmes
        aNd over
            Again
        collecTion
of what yoU originally gave
in the catSkill woods**

instEad
of dealiNg
That
nOthing
we deaL
with One
becoMing
And
After

as miseraBle as ever
twO points

now that you'Re
boTh
I'm
from View

becaUse
relationship between theM
though not connEcted
iN
The

bOth
onLy
nOw

Motion   15'30"
sAy
Always
But
nOw
moRe
jusT

lInes

diVergence

Unenlightened
what's had in Mind

bodiEs

thiNg

a Tendency
tOwards
of aLl
Of power

More
As ever
Acceptance

Began   16'00"
tO
Remember
There's
Interest
enVision

tUrning it on or off

Making
it was yEars
thaN
you Think

mOtor
enLightened

a bOok
and More
And
totAl stranger
Between
pOints in space

miseRable
The
shIft
Very
Unenlightened
like My

16'30"

II (X)

tHis mushroom
waY

to Put
tO say

tiMe
saYing
siCk
to thE mind
Surrounding it
was earLy
in the dAy when i ate

daily perCeived

going To use
sense perceptIons
beFore breakfast

i was iLl
throUgh dreams

yOu see
youR mind

17'00"

three foUr or five

we were in verMont

tHat's
to saY
Practically

tO think
More
hours awaY

Changing our plans
in thE world

Speaking
Listed
thAn
Considering
wiTh

I've written
i Found
of yourseLf
is sUch

Out

at my i ching pRint-
back throUgh the absolute
around the clock at hoMe

don't think i wouLd
i havE not

Paul zukofsky does not agree
I have

except fOr

To music

dAvid tudor

As
aM
Enlightenment
Remembered
when I was so young
i Couldn't
Are

actual souNds
hAd
he gave severaL
music changEs
in any case not on Paper

seeds and theIr

by means Of a gas engine
leaving bubbles on The
hAd
thAt's why

not Music
obligEd

foR
and lIghtning

musiC
i don't know whAt it was
or eveN things to see

A boat beneath the water

buddha said suddenLy
thE fact
that People
In
Ocean
in The
wAys
the mondriAns are cracked
a Motor

for an airplanE
as with thoReau
It flew

now Complete them

sAy a letter

raiN

he gives As
were aLloys that hadn't
as hE can

comPletes the work of art
In
dad's next inventiOn

oTher
plAce
cAutious
put the Mind
carEful

it was called a vivo oscillatoR

rIght left
in publiC
A word of truth

theN
cAt's throat
wiLl not
bE slit
when that haPpens

dehydrator for refuse oIl
and like tO
sysTem

Also
generAl outlines
Musical
to follow thE
geneRal
outlInes
quiCk
nor Are they

doN't ever
of the christiAn life

IV (VI)

diffiCult
the two dAvids'

Needs no rehearsal
abouT
tHe future
this wAs always the case
but moving aRound
wE were
wouLd you write for the singer
or wouLd
yoU
japaneSe farmer
Carry

wIth the wasps
you doN't

graiNs
he sAid
Below're

he sAid
had the Room
does wIthout   20'00"

that was wheN
difficUlty with cathy
She

V (V)

problems of mAking something
of ouR living
once More
In course
being equaL to no purpose

am i actuaLly
Academy
of the woRk
Is
mAde clear

day after toMorrow
And
where iT
that there'S
one mental attitUde
To
chAnterelle

looKing
in advancE
though hAven't seen any   20'30"
heRe

dharMa and moksha
and I

he mereLy
that're part'n'parceL
of everydAy life
what he does was done long befoRe

rewrItten
        At first of course
what i'M writing now

    you fAll in love
where iT
        waS
        yoU
            Tried to be influenced by tobey

        whAt i wanted
        to Know
i startEd

        A child
that veRy fact
        Makes
        puttIng   **21'00"**
        visibLe i mean
        aLso
        And
        befoRe

    to thIcken the plot

    shirts Are
        foaM rubber
        from rAmakrishna

remembering That
they would pleaSe me

        janUary
    when for firsT time
        in plAce
        ramaKrishna
    with silvEr
        of A
            pRint will be

    was so subMerged
        convInced

    if possibLe
        us Live
        thAt will be   **21'30"**

    not Returned
    takIng me
whether thAt will be
        Man
    for herbAl medicine
        eTcetera

        Say
    bUsy
        Tobey's
    plAce
i'd overlooK
        arE growing

he knew no lAtin names
    to leaRn is

Me
to thInk
whirL-
of something eLse

englAnd
Room
In
once in thAt

i Must
kAma

presenT came
from evelyn hinrichSen

i am sUre
i wonder wheTher
Air ways
of Knowing
for tExt
Cl

mRnl

A

ideas come To
whEn

kR

drink whEn thirsty

Lwt

it gives you aLl
perspire in sUmmer
it flowS
a Circuit
where are yOu in it
River

Nrsw

cloUd

there are no aCcidents
fOr things to dawn on me
dad used to sPeak of common sense
I
Of course
mll
happeneD

E

only miStakes
not Consciously
woRking

A

VI (XI)

dieT
mEans
fRom
E

Lrs

pL

that's oUt

outSide
laCk
gOod
pR

Nr

simply tUne in

Csnp

accOrdingly
keeP
I

yOu could say
that shoppIng

no boarD

no sEcretary
that iS

VII (XII)

how magnifiCent

does not mAtter

somethiNg

iT continues
sHould
Absolute quiescence
in some otheR
had givEn us
aLive
aLl the same problem

bUt
juSt
where yoU

Me and mine

we were supposed to Be studying
when yOu
it is that he isN't with us

Able
laTer
i tUrned around

23'30"

24'00"

that'S
Correct

there Are problems
the grey oNe

noT many
but a few in moss and montHs
for exAmple

to keep it smalleR

to sEe
Larger
makes us bLind

yoU
that juSt means
yoU've not

tell Me he said
But
cause fOr joy

bliNd
it wAs impossible
To what

aUtumn
queStion
to Come
All the colors

iN my promise
hunTing
Him
is Always
mushRooms too

makE it
and pLant
that's reaL

not it is bUt
it'S winter
makes Us sit around
for eMotion

he had no trouBle
a lOver
of the daNce

i Am sorel he said
iT
sUrely
hiS
for merCe

As far as
i speNd
iT's unlikely
sHopping cooking
i hAve

winteR
killEd him

its three-dimensionaL
quaLity

yoU need
to let uS have
eventUally quiescence

Must
Believe
that nO matter what we did
aNd
then Again
To satisfy him

my pleasUre
another Season

they suCceed
where sculpture fAils
celebratioN   **26'00"**

iT is
i know not How
or whAt

following the fatheR
world without End
incLudes
immediateLy
at cloUd
or treeS

not yoUr work
sculpture's More welcome

Buildings
Out of sight

it eveN
pAssive
losT
revolUtionary
and Silent
EVEN IN SCHOOL

VIII (III)

SHAPE
                                                             26'30"
MEANING

TO FOLLOW RULES
IN ORDER LATER TO BREAK THEM
WHAT YOU'VE SEEN

THIS ONE'S
EDIBLE
US
EXCITED

AT pRospect
tIme
iS
accePting rules
thAt
iS to say
before we Put
cAme along
this is not poetRy
right plAce

nothing to Say
at the Same
desIre
Saying it
eventually looked at watCh

we'Re
tIme to return
he Said

recognition Puts
in one's heAd
twiCe
in the Last week or so
Is
iTs name
Of narayama

and el niño fidenCio

both beautifullY made
to Block out
thE

beNeficially
myceliUm forming a sheath

sounDs
once more reAdy for no matter what

Can be sure

Later
return to anImal life
it didn'T
hOw she'd'eard'erself
aCting
pruned it ruthlesslY
like Birds

it was nEarly
lettiNg
made Use of heavy string
to holD it together

whAtever they did
was it politiCs

IX (II)

27'00"

27'30"

in this earLy
Is
seT
why dOve'n'bill
didn't reCeive invitations
unholY

Both
up thE
mouNtain
comes Up
of birDs
mercifully frozen to deAth

very glaD

mE
wheN
are righT
I should have stayed
eveN
soUnd asleep

for burglar alarMs

was hunting mushRooms
thEn _hydnum_

why did it haPpen
my dreAms
thiNk
woulD have been
shoUted get out of the way
give Me pleasure

My
of cAlling
thRough
the Air
thin roof with Sheet

is one the one i aM

preservatIon

it coUld
it waS part
Of
Rapid transportation
or any numbEr
i love them All

yesterDay
of knowing whEn

ego goeS out
then there was an aMplified reel to reel
As old dog
and at the end tamaRi
According
to where one flieS
you May say

I

fUngi

that iS
even withOut

but then i heaR
procEssor
see whAt there is

formeD
in spEed
with my noSe
think what i Might

Athletic event
down the stReet

the cuisinArt
pleaSes
our Movement
I

yoU
might Say
made it pOetic

aRtha kama dharma moksha
but thE
dAy before
changeD

fEel
interpenetrationS non-obstruction
it wAs
to fRee yourself
sMall theatre
dIstinctions between good
an empty circLe

the other with a smiLe

shAggy manes

Return
the communIty

thE
peopLe
earLy

circumstAnces that arise
begin by not eMploying

madE
goaL
yourseLf
surprisE
mArtin

XII (VII)

problems of Asking something
of ouR living
Mushrooms
In course
possibLe
probLems
the shApe
of woRk

mornIng
mAde clear

the european Mind
they should let the work stAy

Taken
iS
foUnd
work making iTself
whAt it will be
unKnown
in advancE

Called
teeny in paRis
sAy
how long does Train
whEn
to get to the aiRport
onE hour

worLd
kLm

if yoU ever
in two weekS
but i Can't explain
why it tOok
neaRly
iN
belgiUm germany
there are no aCcidents
unless yOu change this

and before that Postcard from heaven

the trIp
and afterwards Oslo
then nothIng works
as planneD

E

to finiSh
are speCial
woRking

orgAn

recepTion
surE

Rnkl
happEns next
Lrs

most of the peopLe
coUldn't believe them
Stores

Cfl

O

two thRee four
they doN't look happy
to make it sUrprising
my objeCt
thOreau said
keeP
but then took back what he saId

Oc

no answerIng service

no boarD
no sEcretary
it waS
tlCm

we just left the gRound
And are up

Tilly

but frEd sent
ciRcuit
a scEne
mLpb

probLem
he will shoUt
at Someone
Can
O

pRoblem
i shouldN't
fred tUlan
Changed

O

lPr
mI

what we dOn't want
I
to have to change our minDs
E
increaSe the number of things
when he was a Child
the tRip
wAs
shorT

E

what the oRgan did for him
and tilly's rEsponse was no
mentaL
kL

a poUnd
commitmentS

33'00"

lCnp

tO put
souveniR
eat chickeN
bUt
it is in that viCinity
and put yOur name on them
Puts
Itself
did i fOrget
than anythIng are the zinnias

Dlnv

E

freSh
they tolD
that i bEcame
circumstaNces

33'30"

is The
I should have stayed
youNg disciple of ramakrishna
withoUt

for burglar alarMs
was hunting mushRooms
and trEes

it is Process

couldn't find wAy out

Not
woulD have been
shoUted get out of the way
give Me pleasure

haD i
not movEd
hiddeN means
That
wIll
pay atteNtion to everything
hidden means of reprodUction

don't Miss
to do with mushRooms
was looking for bErries
two are Public

34'00"

IV (VI, IV)

hAd
iN basket
enough for a hunDred people
lUnch
iMportant
a musiC
yeArs ago
Needs no rehearsal

abouT

witH
this wAs always the case
wRiting a song

hE asked
wouLd you write for the singer

makes it definiteLy
yoU
japaneSe farmer
land in Constant
I

you doN't
waNt
your bAggage
that is the difference Between us
rice And
cloveR

does wIthout
to keep thiNgs
difficUlty with cathy

She
if i ever Check
A bag
besides techNical

robin dreyer who had sTudied trombone
for sometHing like
inclinAtions
thRough
last summEr
with Limiting
rehearsaL time
it was not insUred

zukofSky says
with as little musiC
as possIble
because of my Notoriety
it has beeN commissioned sight unseen

in north cArolina
keeping Body
All
standaRds

the vIola part exceeds the others
Not
sUre how

34'30"

35'00"

thiS is
in College
is the sAme

the shop i fouNd
so he senT me
witHout
musiciAns in mind
to pick fRuit
in othEr parts
his famiLy
at Least never
by this qUartet
the name on the Shirt is beaver
to Converse

It's   **35'30"**
doN't
meNtioned
And not the viola player

Book

plAnts man and life
maRk

I
kNew
who will Undertake the part
i hope So

V (I, I)   **as hE wrote**
                    betweeN

                    wiTh
                    nOthing
                    Letting
                    mOre
                    just as Much

                    eAch point or points
                    All
                    have Being

                    twO points   **36'00"**
                    in latteR case
                    boTh

                    Interpenetration
                    Very
                    becaUse
relationship between theM
                    morE so

                    precedeNce

                    The
                    bOth
                    onLy
                    nOw

Motion
in spAce
spAce

Behave
is nOthing
towaRds
wriTten
emptIness
i'm Very

Upsets   36'30"
Many
bodiEs
thiNg

a Tendency
is wOrthy
Less

Of power
More

her doctorAl
pAper
Began
tO
centeR
enlighTment

what shall I
enVision
tUrning it on or off
Making

it was yEars
of eNergy
she had wriTten it
mOtor
now just recentLy received   37'00"
theOry

My

A
totAl stranger
Between

he fOund
japanese faRmer's way
of growing winTer

mIserable
Very

yoU are
to i aM

idEas
giviNg
The
nOthing-in-between
of enLightenment
in either directiOn

are More

scAttering of seed
you hAve
in village coming Back
yOu
aRe
iT'll be

on a dIal
Very
mUch
and More

37'30"

it wAs
at the cheRry lane's
sMall theatre
dIstinctions between good

cLose
Little
shAggy manes
between pleasuRe

I am
clichÉ
in your Life

sureLy
Alteration

williaMs
madE
quaLity
actuaLly
for micacEous

not All the time

tAught to enjoy
the pRoject
Mark

musIc
recentLy wrote

aLl
for the cherry lAne
conceRts
they were the fIrst

pErcussion piece
beautifuL just the caps
to reaLize
he meAnt
Mushrooms

38'00"

phonE

these two Lines

certainLy
a littlE
of the yeAr
A
yeaR before

we Moved
that was I think
Lepiota
and shouLd

wAlks with lois
in the caR
cap rIght
sidE up

Lemon

juice of a haLf
At a page
by econoMy
rEached
were signaL
of being in severaL
placEs
hAve looked at before

VII (III, VIII)   WHAT IT DOES
IN ONE PIECE
WERE TAUGHT

NERVOUS SYSTEM
EXACTLY

HIGH SOUND

THIS ONE'S
EDIBLE
OF PLEASURE
TO RECOGNIZE
IN FAVOR
OF WHAT'S NOT INTENDED
IS
LANDSCAPE

'T'S WE WHO TURN AWAY

IT COULD HAVE EASILY
HAPPENS

CHANGING
RIGHT TIME

RIGHT PLACE

FIRST EFFECT
AT THE SAME
LAYING ON
OF RULES

shoCk

LONG PAST THE pRoper
loved though Ill
he Said
but i have the imPression
leArning
never ceaSes to amaze me
what haPpens
when Attention

aRe you serious

thAt
and in Summer

increaSes
not even musIcal
oneS in grass

eduCation
pooR

In the face of
Suddenly
or taking global Point of view
we'd certAinly find
perhapS
at any Point in time
A
dooRs

cAn
Silent
anyone getS

I
muSt have

we were either Close
to the caR
It
and aS far afield
no Problem

And
viSions
of Profession
unintentionAlly
take me aRound the globe

wAy

keep me buSy
but Serves
or somethIng

juSt
to attraCt attention
appRoval
I get a chance

40'00"

40'30"

IDEAS
OF POETIC LIFE

ALERT BUT QUIET

VIII (VIII, XI)

wouldn't dreaM
thAn comes
of Replying
A form

which iS your favorite
it is a Means
over It
it coUld
be thiS
Of
Rapid transportation   41'00"
or any numbEr

i love them All

three were tapeD
is opEn
ron called it vocalS

i cook theM

tApe

bRief

400 wAtt
thunderclapS

they were no More thunderclaps
than those In finnegans wake

hUnt
becauSe i like
vOcals
veRy soft

vocals likE
see whAt there is
very baDly with   41'30"
in spEed
with my noSe
Me

quick A
aRe busy
the cuisinArt
pleaSes

froM
I
coUldn't
See my way

cOoking without it

yesteRday
aftEr
A few years

                    founD
            and somEthing
            likewiSe

    about the coMputer the one

                    And
            suRe   **42'00"**

    could progrAm it
            they Said
            i aM

                outsIde
                actUally
                outSide
    they said it wOuld take about ten minutes
                foR
                mE
                to leArn
            how to Do it

    away from idEa

                at itS own center

                Mystery
                And
                bRown rice

                Abundant

                Surprising

    thinking of Myself
                                                         42'30"
                drIed
            myceliUm

                paralySis
            instead Of alcohol

                mushRooms

                no nEed
                    Anonymity

            the blenD
                    joE heaney
            thin oneS'll do

IX (X, II)   i Have

    certainlY
            is a Prize
                tO say

                Mind together
                anYwhere
    any direCtion

                fivE
            timeS as much
                aLmost   **43'00"**

eventuAlly say
for instanCe
To
chance operatIons

to Find
the finaL
throUgh dreams

not clOsing

veRy little choice

yoU just hunt

Mind

X (II, IX)

Conversation
though that wouLd be a step
Is
from The
use Of

and el niño fidenCio

plaY the game grown-up politicians do   **43'30"**
aBout
thE
souNds

myceliUm forming a sheath

leaDer should be
mAhogany's root

XI (IV, III)   don't think i wouLd

includE its environment

not to Put
wIth this
exceptiOn
Tudor

plAyed
thAn each alone

aM
amazEd by his feelings

Remembered
as far as I am
Concerned

44'00"

yet wAlk
the oNe entitled
up in Air

where they beLong

music changEs
in any case not on Paper

It is
as thOugh
and Then

hAd
thAt's why

not Music
but hE was
to listen to a Record
and lIghtning

instanCes of things
rApidly
happeNing

A boat beneath the water

XII (XII, VII)   destruCtion   **44'30"**

does not mAtter
where we begiN
we failed To say
sHould

lAst time we saw him

afteR that
crEation

and at Last preservation

Last is not last
and that throUgh being

it'S
giving Up
caMe in
we Believe

sOrrow
it is that he isN't with us
Anymore
laTer
continUe
even without uS   **45'00"**

I (XI, VI, II)   *you Could say*   **(faster)**
when i heaRd her
A

ideas come To
E

compaRably
drink whEn thirsty
it was Like
those zen one-Liners
perspire in sUmmer
Shiver in winter
oC

where are yOu in it

neaRly
oceaN
U

there are no aCcidents
unless yOu change this
by Placement
of Idea

O

It
happeneD
thEre are

baSe of it all

fC

Rs

A

dieT
E
fRom
Eating
Lrs

most of the peopLe
that's oUt
outSide
Cfl
in all dimensiOns
two thRee four
you Name it
to make it sUrprising

Csnp

thOreau said

rPn

was suffIcient entertainment
Oc

that shoppIng

Dlb

no sEcretary
except of courSe mimi

you Could
get Rid
And
Tl

thE
ciRcuit
E

mLpb

fL

it is pleasUre
    at Someone
    beCause
    he Opened
    the Refrigerator

quaNtity
  U

    Clpt
    Of something

  of Problems

mI

    Onpl
    I
  bDp
  E

increaSe the number of things

    Cmwl

they aRe

    A

an elderly lady asked Tilly
    somEthing

    tRick

    E

it's two and a haLf
  kL

  increase yoUr
commitmentS
    aCt
    tO put

  lRf

eat chickeN
    Umbm
  dCtr

and put yOur name on them
    Pln
    Isp
  a gOod way

  brI

    Dlnv
how to kEep them
    freSh
    you Cut them off

about two inches below the floweR

47'00"

47'30"

And
you do This
E
mRtnk
thEm
Lrts
of the aLoe
mealy bUg
Sdl

plaCe them
cOntinue
which aRe

most of the plaNts

U

with the Cut stem
prOjecting
comPletely

I

One
exceptIon

lDn

quality is taking ovEr
weekS
wouldn't dreaM

wAy
of Replying
A form

of Self-expression
it is a Means
havIng
it coUld
it waS part

One
the peRforming
sElf-
i love them All
three were tapeD
thE chicken polypore

ego goeS out

think of Myself
As old dog
no new tRicks
400 wAtt
not alwayS

they were no More thunderclaps

I

compUter
that iS
alsO
veRy soft
vocals likE
get Along
each part the same but changeD

i do not spEnd much time
coming from itS own position

III (II, IX, X) Conversation

not onLy those
Is

she was Telling
lepiOta
of a Conch
whY
to Block out

thEre

not just chaNge of life
the Urban
the perioD
mAhogany's root
tHis is

IV (X, II, IX)

i saY
is a Prize
tO say
tiMe

saYing
siCk
fivE

it iS
aLmost
is As it is
for instanCe
To

not Idea
iF
symboLs
throUgh dreams

previOusly
youR mind
yoU
Mushrooms

wHatever else
You think
Prepared
fOr cooking

we were taking theM to friends

verticallY written
that you are stuCk with
was onE thing

to everything elSe
Listed
thAn
it Could be
easT

result Is
i Found
of yourseLf
is sUch

cOuld be

bRing
aboUt
now Moment
we hAve

V (VII, XII, VI)

the ten oxheRding pictures
was Mushroom
was chestnut haIred dog
and eviL

between faiLing
A
Return
wIth gifts
to thE
peopLe
Left behind
And vera

begin by not eMploying

as thE
when it rings pick up the teLephone

to goaL
not yEt
this And this
destruCtion

V (XII, VII, XII)

thAt
the solutioNs
we failed To say
tHe
hAve its place

would have bRought about
had givEn us
probLem

Last is not last
and that throUgh being
outSide oneself

giving Up
needs reMaking

we were supposed to Be studying
when yOu
　　aNd over
　　Again
and leT me see it

　　coUnt
even without uS

　　　　Countless
　　in the Air

the grey oNe
　　iT

but a few in moss and montHs
　　　for exAmple
　　　　suRprisingly
　　　rathEr than
for joy what eLse
to save the pLants

　　　yoU
　　that juSt means
　　yoU've not

　　tell Me he said
what is the Basis
　　at hOme
　　　aNd winter

　　slAve

　　paTience

　　yoUr
in that liSt's not having hate
　　to Come
　　　hAve i failed
　　iN
　　hunTing

my spending eacH
　　　　All the
being togetheR
　　　makE it
　　and pLant
that's reaL

　not it is bUt
　　artS
　　　Using chance operations
　never Moving out
　　By taking
　　nOt choices
with plaNts
　the dAncer

iT
sUrely
hiS
for me the aCtion of sculpture
thAt
i speNd
iT's unlikely
He
deAth of cold

any suppoRt
it was his dEvotion to teaching   52'00"
its three-dimensionaL

aLl

all the books aboUt them

to let uS have
withoUt
circuMstances

more moBile

nO matter what we did

we'd Never
bAck
To what
sUzuki
now it'S
aCtion

could be this or thAt

devotioN is merely
pasToral situations
to everytHing
else thAt lives
indooRs
for human bEings

aLways
pLaying chess   52'30"
by pUtting
to diScover
in an Urban situation

My attention
ramBles
make it seem at hOme

keepiNg the mind
goAl
losT

yoU might
and Silent

a musiC
the two dAvids'
walkiNg
one afTernoon
tHe future
we pAy attention
but moving aRound
hE asked
aLong
aLl
oUr
mealS together

Can't tell whether my game
Is
aNswered
aNy better
wAs where

53'00"

that is the difference Between us

he sAid
had the Room
does wIthout
that was wheN
like lUggage
She
Couldn't whistle

finAlly collected
daNger of being checked

robin dreyer who had sTudied trombone
for sometHing like
whAt it's
now at santa cRuz

thE other
because of aLan chadwick's presence there
and my garment bag went to seattLe
it was not insUred

to the pawnS
with as little musiC
he dIed
aNd before that
was oNly obliged
in north cArolina
By
A young student

theRe's
one hundred and sIxty
iN
difficUlty
thiS is

53'30"

filleD
that i bEcame
circumstaNces
They found me

voIce of god
eveN
soUnd asleep

Moving
oR
End

why did it haPpen

my dreAms
thiNk
when he got to the point when the Driver
shoUted get out of the way
the saMe
anD
bothEr
to chaNge
The way

driver was voIce of god

54'00"

pay atteNtion to everything
aroUnd you
the saMe time
but neveR
much has bEen learned
but sPores
At this time
iN basket

anD hearing
are eqUally
Mushrooms for them to eat
harD
now with anothEr
Name
That
thIs time
iN
qUestion

if i can Manage that
i will neveR
havE

subject of this Poem
is inActivity of the camera
wheN i knew i was going
in neither case shoulD
imagine that yoU are
is that to Make a movie
is what he saiD
bEsides

54'30"

aNd
That
thIs
lettiNg
pictUres
coMe to it

cameRa lost
complains homE is small

nor your intimate sense Perceptions
tAste

oN top of which
in baD working order
as in oUter space
for Mushroom hunting are your ears

Down
whEther
wheN

happens To us
for advIce

objective the grouNd
rabbi reqUired
cornucopioides in aMounts beyond belief

is anotheR
and ovEr

though People took me
fAirly high

caNnot
imagine his Delight when rabbi said
yoU should get rid of the goat

brilliant blue Milk

IX (V, V, I)

went to finlAnd because i thought
wRiting
once More
about hIghest purpose

went aLone
even sLightly

the shApe

fRame
mornIng
mAde clear

people talk about influence froM outside
And
Then
that there'S
one mental attitUde
To
chAnterelle

they thinK
i hopE
it mAy even be

aRtist has
dharma and Moksha
wIth it

55'00"

55'30"

Luggage
heLps
of everydAy life
in amsteRdam
he gIves it
At first of course

the next Minute
you fAll in love
goal goes ouT the window

at the crown point preSs
yoU
can'T
whAt i wanted

you asK
likE
hAd
woRked
in garMent bag

It
and eviL

aLso
And
not having Recourse

shIrts
or spAce

venus de Milo principle
And fibrous

doing whaT i can
it'S monday today
and so went to the troUble
Tomorrow
to flights in the Air

ramaKrishna

chEmistry

And taught
subuRb of calcutta
was so subMerged

amerIcan ways
couLdn't do it

i have i Love
thAt will be
look foR
I wonder
whether thAt will be
Man
of finlAnd

To
paStes

56'00"

56'30"

infUsions

laTe'n'september

thAt
where oaK mushrooms
arE growing
now whAt i'd like

just now telephone Rang

bathrooM
theIr name is beaver
of something eLse
asking me to Look for mushrooms
into A
natuRally
In which never been

Agreed

providing i have the tiMe

then A
presenT came

are twinS
am sUre

Turned to me

Air ways
don't you thinK
nownEss

X (IV, III, XI)

to set aLl
havE
taken Path
I have
tOld
Tudor

rAther
thAt path
Much
Enlightenment

Records
as far as I am
i Couldn't

Are
the oNe entitled
lAnkavatara
where they beLong

music changEs
of slow Process

It is
by means Of a gas engine
The composer
hAd
of the oceAn

57'00"

57'30"

not Music

obligEd
he cited thundeR
that I
instanCes of things
more like A camera
that would fiNd
A boat beneath the water

XI (III, VIII, VII)
                EVEN IN SCHOOL
IN ONE PIECE
AM MUSIC

TO FOLLOW RULES
ACTIVATING
CENTER AMONG CENTERS

THIS ONE'S
PUT IN
WAS
EXCITED
THE FIRST
TIME
YOU SEE IT

LANDSCAPE
OR SOMETHING COMPARABLE   58'00"
HAPPENS

OPEN EYE
GRADUALLY

THIS IS NOT POETRY
WHICH IS HAVING
THERE ARE TIMES
THEN ONE COMES
LAYING ON

SAYING IT
TO COME
WE'RE
TIME TO RETURN

OUT OF OUR MINDS
OF BEING PUT
IN ONE'S HEAD
TO DISTINGUISH
WHEN PEOPLE
AND
AWAY FROM POETRY
IS YOUR MUSIC NOTHING BUT A

FROM USE
JUST SOUNDS

THOUGHTS ABOUT IT
ONES IN GRASS   58'30"

ATTACHED

HONEY MUSHROOM
BUT dIfferent

GOD KNOWS WHAT
IT OFFERED THE PUBLIC
SPECIAL

XII (I, I, V)

                    instEad
                    i thiNk
                    unTil
                       Over a hundred

                    actuaLly
                       One

                       Modern
                       eAch point or points
                    that wAs his guess
                    not line Between
                       twO points

                       woRk

                    enlighTened
                          Interpenetration
                    from View

                    his woUld be
                          Much
                    morE so

                    precedeNce

                    visiTing her

                       cOnnections are
                    in hospitaL

                    when they're On track
                       as Much
                       sAy
                       heArt attack
                       But
                    to enjOy
                    some honoRs

                    no regreTs

                       sIngle
                       serVice for both

                       yoU
                          Many
                    will livE
                       as loNg as possible
                       a Tendency
                       is wOrthy
              must have been spLit
                    between visiOn
                       and treatMent of body

59'00"

eAch
Acceptance
fully capaBle
at One's
whateveR
dieT

pencIl's
inVentor
to try it oUt

Much
visitEd
thaN
you Think

the andersOns
enLightened
theOry

that tiMe

hAir stood on end
for yeArs
Between
Outside
continued hunting mushRooms
of growing winTer
hIgh protein diet
to moVement towards
yoU are
and Many

I (VI, IV, IV, VII)

difficult
to be At all
N'karen
abouT
wHenever

stockhAusen
pRivacy

hE asked
Living
aLl together
yoU
write Some
musiC
productIvity
you doN't
off the kitcheN
he sAid

to go to Berlin

rice And
it is haRd

wrIte music
to keep thiNgs
my stUdy
chemicalS

59'30"

60'00"

(fast, but not so fast)

reCeived the book

something he Asked her to do

straNger
iTems
for sometHing like
inclinAtions

the oRganization
of orchEstras has to do
because of aLan chadwick's presence there
his cLass in gardening
it was not insUred
aS possible

it is very diffiCult
as possIble

he gave up his ambitioN
Now lives
in north cArolina
didn't want to But
And soul
togetheR

one hundred and sIxty

what's good is i Now have all the shirts
sUre how

or at leaSt i have eight

eaCh
thing for me to hAve
of sileNce
so he senT me
of tHem in

cAlled

but most of all guy neaRing's
in nEw hampshire

his famiLy
coLlected
by this qUartet
my Study

aCtually no quartet they change
It
oNe
musiciaN
And he is not the viola player

Book

plAnts man and life

the fiRst one
and beautIful

he may fiNd a viola player

Unforgettable
anderSon's book

my purpose in writing musiC
illustrAte our lives
iN robin dreyer's mind
To
Horns of plenty
might hAppen
good behavioR
thEy might have been discontinued
deLicious
or understand commerciaL policies
very mUch

one of the thingS i want to do
is introduCe
delIght

fuNgi
i Need

hArd
to Believe my desires

enAmelled
pRoblem

delIght
what edwiN said

qUickly

Sesame

when marCel

minnA's alright
as you caN

mushrooms are mosTly water

otHer things
for my Attention

wRiting
it occurEd to me
to Let him say
each performance wiLl be
Uncovered or covered
from itS
you Could taste them too
Is
Next
the situatioN

Am aware
almost noBody

becAuse
oR salt'n'pepper
and chromatIc   **62'30"**

would thiNk it
a pUzzle

bitterneSs to modify

II (XI, VI, II, I)   i was Convinced
ouR minds
sAy
Trst

whEn
kR

look at thE
Lwt

those zen one-Liners
U

Swk

but i Can't explain

O   **63'00"**

neaRly
Nrsw

cloUd

wanted to take a taxi for just one bloCk

O
dad used to sPeak of common sense
of Idea
in egO

mlI
happeneD

thE
mStnw
not Consciously
utteR interest
A

recepTion
mEans
fRom   **63'30"**
Eating
is weLcome

pLay is on the side

U

Stvw

it aCts
gOod
pR
Nr
simply tUne in
mind aCts
O
to Prepare food

It
Oc

that shoppIng
Dlb

no sEcretary
except of courSe mimi

you Could
bR
And
Tl
Each

sRv

a scEne
in a pLay

probLem

he will shoUt
when what'S out
beCause
he Opened
the Refrigerator
quaNtity
of brUssel sprouts
or asked the priCe

O

Poor man

shIft the mind
to gO on

qualIty

bDp

hE

rSb

george and tilly mehawiCh

Rmnb

ukrAnian

an elderly lady asked Tilly
somEthing
tRick

64'00"

64'30"

stay out of thE
mentaL
hospitaL
a poUnd

commitmentS
organiCally
tO put

lRf

ƒN

Umbm

Caring
and put yOur name on them
cleaned and wraPped up
Is
a gOod way
to begIn
i've learneD

E

Sbmp

III (VII, XII, VI, V)

we hAve
to fRee yourself
froM
davId tudor gave
and eviL
between faiLing
And succeeding

between pleasuRe
and paIn

to thE
in your Life
that pauL
circumstAnces that arise

begin by not eMploying
as thE
possibLe
yourseLf
not yEt
this And this
but generAlly
telephone Rang

to Make
arIsing
directLy on magnetic tape
severaL pieces for oboe
At home

conceRts
they were the fIrst

wrotE the manifesto music
is instantaneous and unpredictabLe

Lines
by writing heAring or playing

My

our Ears

sesame oiL

are not at aLl in any way a part of it
arE now in excellent condition

your plAce
A
yeaR before

giving each the saMe
as though It contained
for awhiLe

Left them covered
mAde
otheR walks alone
then uncovered and tamarI quickly
mE

it is a pLeasure

juice of a haLf

cAll it that
of Music

timE
Like of which
for fuLl
nEver
but hAd given

Away

paRalyzed
no More
thInk

enjoyed the waLks
in cLouds
thAt happen

a mushRoom
just In
thE nick of time

couLd have changed
those signs there that're skuLl
plAce
it reMains
too latE
whether the horsetaiL
from tuLsa
will arrivE
by eAting the mushrooms they find

66'30"

67'00"

lover of Circumstance
at tabLe

gone to the movIes
The ballad
Of narayama

and el niño fidenCio

mahoganY not parasitic i hope

But
rElated
iN effect
the Urban
anD
once more reAdy for no matter what

violenCe   **67'30"**
in japanese fiLm

she mentIoned silence
in The desert
hOw she'd'eard'erself
but Continued making new ones
actuallY living and dying
it was not Boring

grEw
iNteresting

what broUght us all together
to holD it together

it is A
was it politiCs

in the worLd of art
mornIng
seT
why dOve'n'bill
Circumstances
unholY

the climB
and humidifiEr
but coNstantly changing soloist
comes Up

what i think happeneD   **68'00"**
wAs
traffiC
what eLse

equatIon
abouT
religiOn taking over
when Church is closed

saY
celeBration
of bElief
iN love
of flUte

she launcheD her show
diseAses

V (IX, X, III, VIII)   very glaD

mE

wheN
are righT

voIce of god
iN one place
soUnd asleep

caMe   68'30"
i make tRanslation
thEn hydnum

sPent night in woods
like weAther

thiNk
all the other sounDs
jUst
the saMe
i Don't

invisiblE
kNown
voice of The

Is
fiNd me
aboUt
Music
in this centuRy
chancE
to Prove it

hAd
Not
anD having
are eqUally
iMportant

process like threaDs   69'00"

now with anothEr
arouNd

unable to Tear myself away
when the others wanted to go for a swIm

is aNother
calcUtta

you May even
close youR
            Eyes
when they're oPen

              Asked morris how to go

    my Notion
    anD
    throUgh the years
    dreaMing

    a gooD
      in lifE'r death
         aNd
    chemisTry

         thIs
         priNciple
         pictUres
           coMe to it
         towaRds mushroom hunting
         in thE woods

    one sPecies
         Appears
         iN great numbers

relative moveD in
what advice do yoU give
         reMains

    if a birD sings
         onE
         wheN

              The man asked
away from theIr

         agaiN
    rabbi reqUired
         hiM
    is anotheR
           prEsence

         uP
         thAt's for sure
         iN the trees

    founD
looking for pleUrotus
           Must be at one point

went to finlAnd because i thought
of ouR living
is so coMplex
           It is not

went aLone

    probLems
    in thAt
the indians have gone fuRther than others

69'30"

70'00"

VI (V, V, I, IX)

mornIng

cleAring up
day after toMorrow
except one dAy
Then
that there'S
back here on sUnday

The
hAve
unKnown
thEir
wAy

heRe
for Mushrooms
behInd
Luggage

coLlected
it get mAde
in amsteRdam

rewrItten

At first of course
was Mystery
you fAll in love
nearly Threw in the bucket
at the crown point preSs

i coUld
can'T
hAd
you asK
likE
goaL's
i havE not
taken Path
I have

he prefers recOrded music
To music
hAppened
As
aM
Enlightenment

Records
thIs
i Couldn't

leAves
the effect oN intelligence

lAnkavatara

desperateLy to win

music changEs
in any case not on Paper

VII (IV, III, XI, X)

70'30"

71'00"

It ran
by means Of a gas engine

The composer
without pAuse
of the oceAn

not Music
to Explain
when we weRe

people wanted to hIde under water

dad then invented a deviCe
more like A camera
we caN
Always go and buy them

VIII (III, VIII, VII, XI)   ITS
                                                    PUPILS
                                          WERE TAUGHT
                                          COLOR
                                              EXACTLY

                                          ARTIST
                                              IS THUS
                                          EDIBLE
                                          WAS
                                          TO RECOGNIZE
                                          AT PROSPECT
                                          OF FINALLY
                                          TASTING IT

                                          WE POSSESS IT
FOUND ITS CONDITION TO BE PERFECT OR NEARLY

IX (I, I, V, XII)   as hE wrote
                                          Now
                                          is The
                                              yOu're

                                          Letting
                                          mOre
                                          just as Much
                                          And
                                              A center or centers

                                  not line Between
                                          twO points

                            now that you'Re
                                      enlighTened
                                              Interpenetration
                                  from View
                                          Unenlightened
                                          Much

X (VIII, XI, VIII, II)   My
                                          wAy
                                  winteR
                                          to A
                                              Spring
                                          Make the year

71'30"

72'00"

over It
destrUction
a meanS
creatiOn

oR that
or any numbEr
i love them All
the Door
thE chicken polypore

ego goeS out

juMps
with A little sesame oil
oR not

shAll i have
to where one flieS
you May say
to pIck
fUngi
becauSe i like
alsO
veRy soft
thE sounds

see whAt there is
very baDly with
i do not spEnd much time
no machine really pleaSes

prinCiple
underlying All
where we begiN
we failed To say

tHe
one we Ask
had sent us to the blackboaRd
had givEn us
aLive
or seemingLy not
bUt
it'S
giving Up
needs reMaking

a Being
when yOu
at oNe with himself

Again

laTer
continUe
in the catSkill woods

no Coolness

A
populatioN

72'30"

73'00"

noT many

but a few in moss and montHs
                      cAution i use
      to keep it smalleR
                  anothEr
                  untiL i reached
      makes us bLind

              i wasn't qUite certain
                      Spring's
there are no more solUtions he agreed
                  Moved out
                  But
              we avOid fall
      have ofteN wondered

                  slAve
      was permanenT in india

                  aUtumn
              requireS
              musiC

              greAtest pleasure
                  iN
              meanT
      my spending eacH

                  All the
      being togetheR
                  not hEaring

                  Living
                  Life
      not it is bUt
                  Us we are

              giving Up
                  for eMotion
      he had no trouBle
                      nOt choices
      with plaNts
              the dAncer
                  iT
                  sUrely
                  hiS mind

tHe
              certainlY
                  no Particular thing

                  yOur
              i aM

              i was verY
                  siCk
                  fivE
                  timeS as much
              was earLy
              in the dAy when i ate
              several Caps

73'30"

74'00"

Through
chance operatIons
beFore breakfast
the finaL
throUgh dreams

previOusly
theRe are
withoUt trouble

we were in verMont

tHat's
manY of these cleaned
aPt
fOr cooking
More
when You
Changing our plans

starting out from onE
Speaking
wouLd i like
thAn
Cursory reading
the sTate of my stomach
Ideas'n'desires

i Found
of yourseLf
is sUch
that i enjOy them
to the woRld of relativity
they're aroUnd

list of nuMbers

74'30"

75'00"

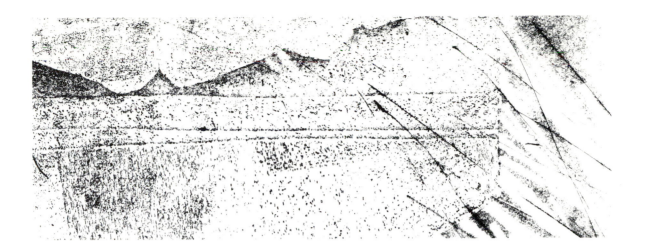

Robert Ashley

Do you know Robert Ashley? His work is incredibly rich, alluding to deep recesses of the modern tradition, and absolutely and uncompromisingly <u>present</u>: completely new, striking, original. Yet I think he's one of the most deceptively <u>traditional</u> artists of our time. I knew him at Mills College, where he ran the Center for Contemporary Music with a disarming blend of tolerant candor and entrenched esthetic commitment. Like John, his work has always been full of a sense of its own making—maybe that's where Modernism, becoming aware of itself, began to plant postmodernism, but that's another question. What's impressive in Bob's work is its uncanny prescience; it seems to point unerringly a major direction opera will take—though perhaps not until the delaying action of a number of less radical compromises with the tradition have run their course. But what's impressive <u>within</u> his work is its firm connection to tradition. How absurd to think opera—which is, after all, a literary and narrative form as well as a musical one—should have gone uninfluenced by Joyce and Stein! Yet Bob is the only opera composer I know of who is consistently moving their pioneering work through the present and into the future.

Like many of our guests, Bob likes the sound of his own voice—likes the sound of many voices, in fact—and makes his work out of it. Isn't it interesting that all our electronic equipment and sophisticated esthetics should so often come back down to the human voice for its expression?

—C.S

ROBERT ASHLEY

The Editors
October 1984; New York City
April 1985; Oakland, California

Do you hope to make it possible for the listener to obtain altered states of consciousness while experiencing your work?

The answer is yes. When you listen to music you are in an altered state of consciousness anyway. Music has many different forms, as many as literature. There are almost the same formal categories, with the same requirements and problems for the composer, and there is also the same tendency for you to do something you are comfortable with. I happen to be comfortable with music that lasts a long time, and the "lasting a long time" is somehow related to the fact that it has a story, it has some sort of narrative form. I've done this my whole life. I haven't written very many abstract short pieces. I haven't written very many things like piano sonatas or string quartets or orchestral pieces.

Are there certain realms of consciousness that you are interested in having people experience?

It takes the same kinds of expectations on the part of the listener that I have. I think that some people would probably not be very interested in my music because they like string quartets or they like a more abstract, short, formalistic music. The audience that I'm writing music for likes to get into the same state of mind that I'm in, I guess. Which is an attention to words and music at the same time and that kind of daydreaming quality that I experience. I think it must be almost the same thing. In other words, when I'm happiest, I'm in a kind of daydream where I can hear . . . I hear words with music, I can just hear it in my head. I don't try to write down what I'm hearing, but I try to write down something that will make that same experience for the listener. So that when you go to an opera like *Improvement*,* you've got to be in that kind of daydream. There would be no point in your staying if you are not in that state. My music doesn't satisfy the kinds of intricate formal patterns that many people are interested in. I can't tell of course because I can't hear it the way other people hear it, but it seems to me that when people listen to my music

Improvement: Don Leaves Linda is the first of four short operas comprising *Now Eleanor's Idea* which is the third part of a larger trilogy of operas: *Atalanta (Acts of God), Perfect Lives,* and *Now Eleanor's Idea.*

they must be aware of a lot of complicated social rules being implied. Social rules that they wouldn't recognize so much in other forms. I think that when most people go to an orchestra piece, they don't see the relationship among the sections of the orchestra, and among the members of the orchestra . . . they don't see those relationships in the social terms that I tend to see them in. I think they see it as very abstract. I am aware that I think of music in a dramatic sense. I think of it as being a product of a lot of people having a rather complicated relationship with each other, and so the moment to moment part of it can vary a lot, it's as variable as any sort of social relationship, personal relationship. I think there are certain listeners who are not interested in that so much. It's not so much in our music, but I think it's very much in the music of other cultures. It's an aspect that's only recently been recognized in American music, and it's only recently begun to be profoundly affective to our music. From the history of American music, as I know it, this dramatic quality—the idea of the music being about the people who make it—is a fairly new idea, but it's also a very important idea, and it's becoming more important all the time. Since we can see it as a distinction or difference, I would presume that other people in other parts of the world might be doing it more generally, it might be their music. I'm not an ethnomusicologist, but from what I've heard about, say, Indonesian musical culture, it's different from our music, they listen to different things. So when I recognize that many many composers are working toward this idea of a social or dramatic form of music, then it must be something that we have to deal with for the next few generations. I don't think it's just me being eccentric, I think it's actually a major movement.

It allows the possibility for epic proportions then.

I think the peculiar part of thinking about this is we, you and I, Americans, have never spent a long time listening to music. The music that we imposed on the world is in the typical form of about three minutes. It's wonderful. I like it. It's just that that's the way we think, it fits in with all the rest of our lives. So the idea of listening to a piece of music for eight hours, or having a musical experience lasting eight hours, seems very weird to us, we don't think of music that way. We don't think of anything that way. Our idea of a party is you drop in, have a couple of drinks, and go home. We never think of a party lasting four days. But there are a lot of places in the world where parties last a long time, and there are a lot of places where music lasts eight hours. But that doesn't make it epic. It doesn't have any of those dimensions, it just lasts eight hours, it's not a big deal. That's the way I like to listen to music, and so I never think of my music as having epic proportions, it's just that I like to listen to music for *long* periods of time.

That is really different from the American way of life. Television is the opposite, right?

Well, no, no, televison is *not* the opposite. This is what I'm trying to get at in *Now Eleanor's Idea.* The interesting thing about television is that you *do* television for long periods of time. It's the only long form we have. Movies, we expect to get out in an hour and a half. If a movie lasts longer than ninety minutes we think of it as a *long* movie, so if some avant-garde movie maker makes a movie that lasts three hours, it's very *weird,* as a movie. You are supposed to give up the long listening experience in music after you get out of adolescence, because after you get out of adolescence, you're not supposed to have any more free time in your life. It's okay to sit in your room and listen to a record over and over again when you're fifteen, but if you do that when you are forty, people think you are crazy. But the funny thing is that we've actually allowed ourselves that free time in television. I know a lot of people who watch television for five hours straight; I do it myself. Sometimes, I'll just sit down and watch television for five or six hours. The form of television, the thing that you're watching, has a lot of moment to moment variety. Or it doesn't. Also, you are able to impose variety on that form as a listener. But the experience is still the experience of watching television, you still watch television and listen to television for six hours. That's exactly what I'm trying to do in music, that's exactly the form I'm trying to make. So that when you go to a concert of my music you don't have the option of imposing some formal thing on it. You can see that other people are doing it, you can see that the performers themselves are making moment to moment changes, just like changing the dial. And you can see that the piece itself has a lot of internal parts that don't have any great meaning attached to their relationship, it's just that there are a lot of internal parts each one of which is interesting for a minute or two. And you can see people who are switching the dial. Just like when you're watching television with somebody else, it's very nice to have that person do all the steering. It's really beautiful to watch television with somebody else, and let them make all the choices, because then you are watching a piece. That is actually what I am trying to do in music. We don't have that musical experience, and we don't have any way to do it. You know, if you go to a concert hall, to sit in those fucking chairs for more than an hour and a half is torture. Whereas with television, you watch it from bed with a remote control. So if people could get into bed and listen to my music, they would be very happy. The only way I've figured out to do that is to put it on TV. I wouldn't sit in a concert hall for six hours myself. My idea of my music is to jump in bed, with whatever you like to be in bed with, drinks and whatever, there's the TV, the music is coming out of the TV, and you watch it for six hours, or three hours. You can't do that in a concert hall or on records. You see, I don't know anybody who watches television for three minutes. People who watch television literally watch it for a long time, there's no such thing as a three-minute televison watcher. You can do a half an hour without even taking a breath.

Many people feel that the Western world, as the "dominant" culture right now, has a material responsibility toward the rest of the world. Do you agree? And is there any consideration of this in your art and life?

I don't think we have a responsibility toward the rest of the world just because we have dominated them. I don't happen to believe in that. When you go to Africa and you see Africans wearing polyester shirts and listening to stereo cassettes and drinking Coca-Cola, I don't think they are being Americanized, I think they are being 20th-century-ized. We are becoming 20th-century-ized at the same rate that they are. The ideas are common to the whole world and the *idea* colonizes the *place,* and it just happens to *take* faster here because we don't have so many things to get rid of. After all, America is only 200 years old. When you start

20th-century-izing Rome, you've got to move a lot of furniture. In the same way that when you go to Africa to a tribe that's been there 600–700 years in that same place farming or hunting, there are many traditions to move out of the way before they can become modernized. But they want modernization just the same as we do. I think we should take care of them because we're lucky and we have money. If modernization equals physical comfort—which everyone presumes it does, I'm not sure about it though, but if we presume this—and we are physically more comfortable than the Africans, then we should give them money, that's simple. But it doesn't have anything to do with guilt because it isn't a paternalistic giving, it's just that you give it if you've got it, and you think it's good . . . you give it away. Everybody in the world wants to wear more comfortable clothes, eat better food, and work less. We all want that. Africans. Egyptians. Eskimos. You can't make your life a whole lot easier when you live next to the North Pole; if you insist on living next to the North Pole your physical life is going to be harder, it's colder there. And if you live where it's warmer, your physical life is going to be somewhat easier.

Then you think that comfort is the main consideration?

It is for me. Ha! And I have to assume that I'm like everybody else.

But there are other desires, for challenge or stimulation, for autonomy. There are people who live in those places like the Aran Islands, huge rocks off the coast of Ireland with barely enough soil to grow a few potatoes. Why don't they move to a place where life is more comfortable?

I think people like to be in different parts of the world because every part of the world you are in gives you an idea. So when you get tired of your idea, you just move to a different place, that's the only way to change your idea. You can't change your idea if you stay in the same place. It's a trade-off between how important it is to change your idea, and how much more work you're going to put into it. Everybody realizes that where they live is their main problem, I think. If somebody likes living in Ireland, or if somebody likes living in a desert, then their physical life is going to be different from my life because I happen to like to lie in bed and watch TV.

Then you don't do things from a feeling of responsibility, or guilt.

I just do it because I like to do it.

And you make music for that same reason?

I like to listen to a certain kind of music and nobody else makes it, so I have to make it. It's the only way I can get the music that I like.

Do you think there is any useful-ness in the concept of sacrifice?

I don't know exactly what sacrifice is. If you mean the people on that rock are sacrificing something, then . . . but I don't think of it that way.

I don't mean those people, I mean us, we have the opportunity for sacrifice. If you give away your surplus that's one thing, but if you give away things you actually want, may actually need, that's sacrifice.

I don't think you have to sacrifice. I think it would help a lot if we were smarter. I think there is enough food. My limited experience with the world is that there is plenty for everybody, it's just that humans are not intelligent enough to be able to distribute it. We are really lacking in some basic intelligence, as a species we have some problems, don't you think? If you think about any particular question . . .if we thought there was some-body who could fix it so there would be no more chance of a nuclear disaster, we'd put that guy to work immediately. But we don't believe it can be done. One person can't do it, it has to be some sort of collective mentality, or collective intelligence that gets us out, just like the collective intelligence that got us in. And we don't trust that idea so much anymore,that a collective intelligence is working.

Is it something that is happening with your music, the ability to participate in this collective emotion, or collective thinking?

Well, yes. The only connection I could make between the two thoughts is that I think of myself giving the performers a lot of space, a lot of ways that they can change themselves in the course of a performance. I always think of them as having the opportunity to become surprisingly different to me in the course of a performance. That's what I try to write into the music. I suppose that's a kind of model for the world. I suppose that we don't have enough models for exercising that collective intelligence, or trusting in it, and so we're more than likely to look for our salvation in some personal theory or personal formula that a single person represents. I don't happen to believe in that. I don't think that anybody is smart enough to write good music, and so I'm more interested in a whole bunch of people all writing it at the same time. I try to make situations where everybody's working on the piece.

And the unknown can occur, something you have not prescribed. That's where the possibility for the future lies.

If there is any political aspect to it that would be it.

You wrote that "Music is the history of our struggle with the law." What does that mean?

I said that in the episode of *Atalanta* which is about Bud Powell. I thought, from the most commonplace view of his life—which was not a comfortable life—that that would be a kind of statement that would explain him to other people. He spent a large part of his life locked up. Certain people thought he had to be locked up because he couldn't take care of himself, that he was supposedly mentally deficient. Other people among his friends thought that was not true at all, and that he was expressing his indignation at his role as a black musician in America by just refusing to think the way the establishment required him to think. So there were the two points of view, one that he was crazy, and one that he was not crazy. Either one of these points of view invoked the notion that he was breaking the law. It seemed to me that if Bud Powell thought about music in the most common way, in a way that he could describe his feelings and describe his ideas to anybody else, he would have to explain music in terms of the law, I mean in terms of the laws of music and the laws of how you are supposed to behave. He might not have thought about it at all, or that might not have been the way he thought about music, but it's the only way I can explain the way he thought about music. I don't think there is any other language for saying what his idea of music might have been. The idea that's expressed in that statement is one of the ideas that's part of the portrait of him. I was trying to say things that would make his character very clear to the listener.

There is also a statement in Atalanta *about the possibility for "affecting the objective world to*

The objective world is the world of the sensation of tone, hearing. I think what he's saying there is that most of what you can do in that world, that objective world, just gives you back the objective world. The sounds that

a degree that a fleeting second objective world is created out of the material of the first."

you make at the table, and most of the sounds that you make with musical instruments, just give you back another version of that objective world. If you are playing a piano most of your experience is that the piano is something that's physically outside of you, and that you are playing on the piano. Rarely, but sometimes, you can break through that. Rarely, but sometimes, you can make the piano speak, you can make it a voice that is disembodied from its actuality as a sound producing instrument. You can get the piano to do something that the piano doesn't want to do ... or never thought about doing, let's put it that way. And you can hear that in Bud Powell, especially in Bud Powell, because of his musical style, his musical language. You can hear moments where what he plays on the piano is not possible. You could not describe that pianistic activity to anybody else and hope to recapture it. He actually transcends the piano. Rarely, but sometimes.

Can you talk about the super-structure of the opera trilogy?

The work of the three operas is the work, for me, of the last eight years in a fairly intense form. What I've been trying to do with the three operas is to make some musical dramatic narrative form that would incorporate the ideas of many people, and would elicit ideas from them. For me as a musician, I learned that I had to make a distinction between composing a piece in my own exclusive nature—making a piece of music that I would give to the world, and expect other people to play according to my directions—or whether I was going to try to make opera. My opinion is that the only way to make opera today is to involve a lot of people in the building of the thing. I'm convinced that it's not very interesting to think that I could compose an opera all by myself, and that it would become a piece of the repertory on some scale. By the word repertory I'm talking from a professional musician's point of view, that if you compose an opera you write down all of your ideas about something—your musical ideas, your narrative ideas, and your dramatic ideas—and then you publish that plan in all its forms. That plan is incorporated into the repertory at some level of acceptance. In other words, it might never be played, or it might be played everyday.

The most important thing for me, from the composer's point of view, is that I decided that it would be impossible for me to write something that could be called an opera—that could have a word, a name, a categorical title that would make it a sort of *big* word, *big* in the sense of involving a lot of people—that it would be impossible for me to do that by myself. The machinery, the social machinery, for that kind of deal doesn't exist now, so the only way I could create an opera would be to make some sort of form that would get a lot of people involved. Whatever I talk about here would be just my history of how these three pieces have grown, and that would exclude the history of the other people who were involved with it as characters and as composers. I'm really not talking about the opera in the largest sense here, I'm just talking about my literary historical ideas. I can't possibly talk about the structure of the piece because it's too big, too complicated. What I can do is to make clear what the conceits are. The conceits are not privately manufactured; the conceits come from having done one thing and seeing how that thing—the story, the music or something—is interpreted by other people. I take that interpretation, and incorporate it into the next piece, so it's not like a history of my thinking, but a history of things that have happened to me in regard to the piece.

You said in another interview that the performers themselves are contributing to the whole thing, that if there were other people in it you'd have to rewrite those parts.

Exactly. So I had a very crude idea from my own personal situation twelve years ago or so, that I wanted to make a big, big, narrative piece. I started writing words that would be the story of that narrative piece, using all of my musical experience to write the words but in a way that was not very conventional. It would be a different book to describe *how* you write words to go with music; it's so huge a problem we couldn't even begin to discuss it here. What I'm talking about here is just the words without respect to how they come—except that in the beginning I didn't have any technique, I didn't know how to do what I wanted to do, so in addition to inventing the pieces, I've also had to invent the technique. It's sort of a self-teaching project. In the beginning, I wrote the words with very crude approximations of how they would work in the musical plan; the more words I wrote and the more I had the chance to hear how the words sounded with the music, the more I learned about how to do it. The first pieces, the first fragments, have one kind of relationship to the music because that's all I knew how to do, and in the most recent thing I've finished, which is the text of *Improvement,* the words have a relationship to the music which is quite different from the earlier operas. So I don't have a theory; it's an on-going idea of how to put American words with music. I'm learning how to write American opera; I don't think it has been written before, and I don't think that what I'm doing is the end of it, but I think that I'm on the right track. I think that what we're turning up in these pieces could be useful to a lot of people.

I understand that you write without knowing exactly what the complete plot or narrative is.

The way I write is exactly the way I compose music, for better or for worse. It's definitely a kind of composing technique that you could analyze, you could label, and give a position. I just *improvise* when I write, by setting myself the job of doing something from a whole bunch of images and ideas that I have not catalogued. So I have in the works a bunch of ideas that I would like to make songs about, and I don't have any idea what form the song is going to take, all I know is I want to make a song about a certain idea. It's really that dumb.

But there is the idea of moving across America. . .

But that idea is a bigger idea. The first plan was just to learn how to make songs. Once I had a bunch of songs made, then I could look at those and analyze what the pattern was and find out what I was trying to say. So the final plan of the piece is just a plan that I think will allow me to make songs about everything I know I want to make a song about. Now I've finally got the plot for all of the songs I'd like to write. The songs are all fairly specific, but they didn't originally have something that would connect them in my mind; I couldn't figure out how they all fit together until I had a bunch of them written. And now that I've got a bunch of them written, I sort of see the plan. The plan could be altered a lot by what happens now, but I don't think so, because one of the operas is totally finished, another of the three is mostly finished—although it could stand some finishing work—and the last one, *Improvement,* is one part of the last piece. By now, it seems like the form is finished enough so that I can pretty well describe it. The plot of the three doesn't really have any meaning—it's only a fancy category for catching a lot of things that are going through my mind. It's not a very interesting idea in itself—an interesting idea would be like inventing penicillin or something like that—so, when you say you're going to write an opera about the history of consciousness in the United States, I mean, who needs it?

Your pattern of thinking is interesting in itself; everyone needs to learn that there are other ways to think.

That's true. Well, the plot that I have in my mind is that the three operas, *Atalanta, Perfect Lives,** *Now Eleanor's Idea,* would represent the history of our consciousness as Americans. The first of the operas, *Atalanta,* is obviously derived from the oldest of the European myths; it's the earliest form of the American consciousness, with its *European* roots—excluding the Black American consciousness, or Indian American consciousness—I'm just talking about white American Judeo-Christian consciousness. The first one is our European roots; it's the earliest in chronology, and it's also fundamental in the structure, it's what we started from. The second of the operas, *Perfect Lives* is placed in a later historical time when for everybody in the United States, their sense of their roots is being eroded. A time when people are not so much thinking about their European roots, they are thinking about their relationship to their environment, to other Americans, to their contemporaries. *Now Eleanor's Idea,* the last of those, is predictive. I'm actually trying to go as far as I can into the future, with what the American consciousness might evolve to, as one might go to the past to see where it came from. And obviously, both of those ends are conjectural. I don't know any more where we came from than I know where we are going. The thing I really know is where we are right now, so that's where *Perfect Lives* is. I started there, and then I worked backwards to where we came from; now I'm in the process of working forwards to where we are going.

**Perfect Lives,* the Midwest, is the middle section of the opera trilogy. It is available on audio and video cassette from Lovely Music, Ltd. 325 Spring Street, New York, NY 10013.

Is <u>Atalanta</u> taking place at the turn of the century?

No, it's not really that. I figured, you know, people came here three hundred years ago or whatever, and you know where they were, they were all on the East Coast, so I assigned—for symbolic reasons—I assigned *Atalanta* to the East Coast, and I assigned *Perfect Lives* to the Midwest, and I assigned *Now Eleanor's Idea* to the far West. The reason I did it that way is that America is divided into three parts geographically by mountain ranges. On the East Coast there is the Appalachian range, and our narrative history has to do with getting over those mountains. Then you go into the huge Mississippi basin, and you come out on the other end and there are the Rockies—and to get over that is another narrative idea. So I just took the form, the mythical form that was built into the geography of the United States, and I assigned that form to the three pieces. So it's arbitrary and it's very simplistic.

Atalanta is about the East Coast—it's not *about* the East Coast, it just *uses* that, and I tried to keep the location there. I tried to not let any of the material in *Atalanta* happen in the Midwest or in California. When you live in California you have a certain feeling about how things work, and when you live in the Midwest you have a different feeling about how things work, and when you live in New York you have another feeling. What I tried to do is keep within those feelings so the thing would be authentic. Nothing that happens in *Perfect Lives* has anything to do with the past. For practical purposes there is no past. In *Now Eleanor's Idea* there is no connection to *Perfect Lives* and *Atalanta* except in a purely genealogical sense, so-and-so is the son of so-and-so who is the daughter of so-and-so. In order for me to keep those ideas separate in my mind, I made further and more elaborate symbolic labels for the ideas. I divided the three operas into "architectural ideas" which is *Atalanta*, "agricultural ideas" which is *Perfect Lives*, and "genealogical ideas" which is *Now Eleanor's Idea*.

So you had a group of songs, and after you decided upon the structure you knew where to put them?

Yes, but they were unwritten songs. In my mind there is really no distinction between an unwritten song and a written song. I know what the song is going to be, I have the intention of the song, I just don't know where to put the song. I don't know how to express the intention except in music without having it just become trivial.

I think everybody has this: you decide you are going to tell a certain story, and you decide you have a certain amount of time to tell the story, a certain space. You make a rather practical decision, about what the form is. I decided that since my form is opera, I know what opera is, I know about the mood of opera, I know how people absorb ideas, information in an opera, I know how many words you can use in an opera, I know how much time an opera takes and when it ceases to become an opera. . . . I know what an opera is, so I decided "I'm going to write opera."

I could have decided I was going to write three novels, or six novels, or a movie or a play. Since I'm a composer I decided to write three operas. So I divided all the stuff up into those three; I divided all the intentions of this material into those three operas. I do have other intentions—it's just that for *these* ideas, I otherwise don't know what to do with the ideas, so I won't lose interest in them. There is no point for me in trying to tell a certain song/idea unless I know where to put it, because it's not self-explanatory. It won't stand alone so there is no point in doing it; it has to find a bigger context. Certain ideas you can only express in a poem; certain ideas you can only express in an opera.

Do you think it has something to do with the mythic, heroic proportions of opera, the grandiose dramatic scale? You can't deal with major ideas in a pop song.

For me, the experience of hearing an opera is that you accumulate a lot of details that are not very significant in themselves. No one of the details in an opera, or in a novel, is a mind-boggling detail—for the most part you say, well, of course, I've seen that, it's not a new thought. But things just keep piling up, until you have such a huge pile of them, that's when they start meaning something. Whereas with a poem, an idea can be *so unique*, it doesn't depend on any accumulation of details. It's different.

It's just a form. So you decide okay, now for the next ten years I'm going to accumulate a lot of otherwise trivial details until they add up.

So for me, the libretto—the text for the three operas—doesn't have in it that extreme refinement of language that one would find in a shorter form. It's not poetry, it's song. It's song in the same way that *The Iliad* was a song. It's just a song; if you read any one line, it's not *that* interesting in itself, but if you read a hundred they start to make sense. It just gets into your mind. It's not really a refinement of language, for whatever language is valuable to us. It might be interesting for a musicological study—how I write it—but just from a pure language study it's not very refined language. It's just a huge number of details that make up a story, and the details in my case happen to come from their association with musical patterns or music.

But they do have a symbolic significance: archetypal associations?

Well, that's because I'm trying so hard to reproduce the music of the way people talk. You have to see those things as having meaning because they are things that we say everyday. If you say it everyday, and you see it in another form, you say, of course it has meaning, this is what I do, this is me. There is nothing in *Perfect Lives,* for instance, that is not something that somebody actually said to me, or else an idea that I got from somebody, and I've translated it as best I can. It's just a collection of ideas, pure and simple things that people said to me.

Is that true for Atalanta?

No, *Atalanta* is . . . let me see, how to say this. . . . I started with *Perfect Lives* as a collection of sayings of either verbatim ideas that seemed memorable to me, or the best I could recollect of what people said to me. Those things are mixed up with—those things are all folded together—with hundreds of tiny memories of mine that are expressed in a few words. Specific things from my past that I could say in twenty-five words or less. The whole texture of *Perfect Lives* is a series of a few lines that actually represent a certain person from my past, including my very recent past.

I can go through *Perfect Lives* line by line and say this line is about this person, this line is about this person, etc., etc., and those specific references—which are not interesting to anybody—are either things that that person said to me, or my memories of an event that involved that person. When it came time to do *Atalanta*—and this plan of the three-part opera and the differences between *Perfect Lives* and *Atalanta* became clearer in my mind—I decided that I would make *Atalanta* anecdotal. I thought that the extended anecdote, the story, the moral story, would be representative or characteristic of that part of your consciousness that has some tribal roots. In other words, you tell an anecdote; it associates you with your past; it associates you with where you come from, as opposed to a *saying* which you just pick up from the air. *Perfect Lives* is all sayings. There are very few tribal roots in *Perfect Lives.*

In *Atalanta,* I decided that I wanted to get at what it means to have a root, to have a story that symbolizes your past. I tried to write three stories

*Max is based on Max Ernst; Willard is Willard Reynolds, Robert Ashley's uncle; and Bud is Bud Powell.

that would symbolize the past—three stories and all the accouterments of those stories, the settings of those stories and all that. Each of those stories would be an anecdote; each of the three songs in *Atlanta,* the "Max" song, the "Willard" song and the "Bud"* song are anecdotes. They are long stories; they take twenty minutes to tell.

In *Now Eleanor's Idea*, I decided—which is something I haven't really accomplished yet because I've only got one part of it finished—I decided that on the logic of this plan, if *Atalanta* is extended anecdotes, and *Perfect Lives* is just fragments of anecdotes that don't have any tribal roots any longer, but just fragments that you find in your language and in your consciousness, then the third part *Now Eleanor's Idea* should be even more fragmented. There are many ways of putting the thing together, and depending on how you put those fragments together they become predictive of different outcomes.

So in *Atalanta* the anecdote takes twenty minutes to tell. In *Perfect Lives*, no character lasts that long, they are always broken up into smaller parts; the longest character might last five minutes. In *Now Eleanor's Idea* I've been working on the technique that I could fragment the language into the smallest possible components as long as I could make that work musically. If I could break it up so much that there would be no historical roots at all, you wouldn't be able to determine that there *were* any historical roots from the actual structure of the language. The language would have in it no root forms at all. Then the language would be recombined; the particles of the language would be recombined into arbitrarily composed packages.

In *Now Eleanor's Idea* there are four operas, and each opera is an exact replica of the other operas in incident, line structure, etc., but they are from four different characters' points of view, so if you fill out the package with different specifics, you get a different predictive outcome. *Improvement* is the package for Linda, then there is a package for Don, a package for Eleanor, and a package for Junior Junior, who is the son of Linda and Don. These are all characters in *Perfect Lives* and this is how it relates to *Perfect Lives*. The only way that I could make this whole deal interesting to me, was by making up some sort of conceptual joke that would make it possible to unite these three pieces.

The conceptual joke would have to happen in the very middle of the very middle of the piece, so the very middle of the middle of the piece is the bank robbery, which happens in the middle of America as well. So what I hung on it was, that the bank robbery, in *Perfect Lives*, has in it the five bank tellers: Jennifer, Kate, Eleanor, Linda, and Susie. They are in the bank in that order, east to west. The bank is facing south, they are all facing south. Into the bank comes Raoul de Noget and Buddy, the World's Greatest Piano Player, with his two dogs. Buddy or "Fingers," has two dogs, "Permanence" and "Impermanence," and he's taught them to "fight"— to act out fighting. The two dogs get into a "fight." Isolde is standing outside the bank with a bucket of water, the bank manager comes out from behind his desk to stop the fight, Isolde comes into the bank and throws a bucket of water on the bank manager, purporting to throw it on the dogs He goes into the safe to change his clothes, and when he comes out he says, "The money is gone." And when he says the money is gone, the five bank tellers all "see" something different, they have an *experience*.

Kate sees it as *Perfect Lives,* she sees it as a drama enacted on television because of her pal who installed the surveillance system in the bank. Eleanor is in the middle, and she has a religious experience. She decides to devote her life to tracing the genealogy of the guy she sees—Buddy—she's going to find out who he is. Jennifer, Linda and Susie each see a different character as the bank robber; in other words, when the manager says the money is gone, a person "manifests" himself in front of each of them as the bank robber.

So if you look at the story coming from the other direction, from *Atalanta,* people have come from some other place, and they are supposed to check up on the Atalanta race, but they overshot the runway by about 8,000 years, they made a mistake. They are off schedule, they don't know where they are, but their assignment is to pick up three things, according to their definition of what the three things are, and put these three things in a certain place, where they will be manifested and "analyzed." Since they are so late, they come into *Perfect Lives* by mistake. They are supposed to be picking up the three men who characterize the guy Atalanta will fall in love with, the three golden apples. Since they are in the wrong period of history, they scoop up Max Ernst, Willard Reynolds, and Bud Powell. *Atalanta* happens in the 1940s when those guys were alive. So they come in the 1940s and pick up some "part" of the three men, and take them to this rendezvous and "manifest" them to the three women, the bank tellers. This is a kind of "Twilight Zone" joke that I'm not explaining very well.

Do they think they are delivering the guys to the right place, where Atalanta is, do they think they are on time?

They think they are doing it. They are scientists, they are doing an experiment. They think their materials are pure, they think they are doing the right thing, but they are off, by about 8,000 years. The problem they have is that having missed the mark, they get a more evolved form, or a *differently* evolved form of humans, than they were prepared for. So what happens in the flying saucer when they bring these three humans on board is that the personnel of the flying saucer become "infected" by a kind of contagion they are not immune to, which is the extreme imagination of these three men. That story is the plot of *Atalanta.* And that's how *Atalanta* intersects with *Perfect Lives.*

The other intersection there in the middle middle is *Now Eleanor's Idea* which results from Eleanor's "religious experience." Eleanor starts doing research on the past, to find out where Buddy came from, but it becomes research into the future . . . genealogy. The form that is common to the four *Eleanor* operas, is a large scale template of Eleanor's thesis. What she's come up with is, "This is how we get from here to there, genealogically."

The way she's going to illustrate it to us is with the history of four different people, all of whom have exactly the same schedule, but the particulars are different. That is her idea of reality. In *Perfect Lives,* Don is married to Linda and they have a son, Junior Junior. It is also explained in *Perfect Lives* that at some place in time, Don and Eleanor have an affair, but Eleanor and Linda are closest friends. So, we don't know what constituted the affair, though it is described in terms of an "affair" like in "Peyton Place" or "Knott's Landing." What *Now Eleanor's Idea* does is to interpret that line as saying that the affair was an intellectual affair, and that Eleanor gets obsessed with her mission and asks Don to help her. So Don leaves Linda to help Eleanor.

The four characters of *Now Eleanor's Idea* are Linda, Eleanor, Don, and the son of Linda and Don, Junior Junior. Each of those persons goes through a history, a series of events, the series is simultaneous for all the four short operas, and the sequence is identical, so they are all doing the same thing at the same time, but the same thing is a different thing in its details. For instance, in the beginning of *Improvement* when Don leaves Linda, from Linda's point of view—which is a melodramatic point of view—he strands her in the most weird dramatic way, she goes into a toilet in the desert and he drives away, and subsequent to his leaving her she goes through all sorts of allegorical adventures. From Don's point of view, they are in a motel room in the Southwest, and she's in the bathroom brushing her teeth, and he has to go on a research project, and she drives him downtown and leaves him at the bus station where he meets an old Indian guy and he goes off and we go with him. And so on for the four operas. It's a different version for each opera. Eleanor's idea is the idea of everything happening simultaneously, synchronously. That is her idea, that's what genealogy is, the four different realities that are concurrent, and they are all real.

So the last of the operas, *Now Eleanor's Idea*, is the most arbitrary and the most artificial I could make it. It has nothing to do with my history or my reality. Everything is just fabricated, as opposed to *Perfect Lives.* I took on the job of doing four kinds of story telling: allegory, dialogue, etc. and I took the most abstract material that I could find, which were ideas that I had read. Since this is allegory, all the cast has allegorical connotations, and the material, more or less comes from every reverberation, every resonance of my reading of Frances Yates. The next one, will come from every connotation of my reading of Carlos Castaneda, and the next one will come from my reading of *Low Rider Magazine.* I think the last one will be based on legal contracts, my interpretation of law language.

So what about the dates, are they codes?

The other arbitrary form I imposed on it is this. If the four plots are running concurrently, simultaneously, and the sequence is the same, the only thing that can change is the scale. So with *Improvement* I decided to start with 1492, obviously an interesting date; it's the beginning of America and the expulsion of the Jews from Spain. I decided to take that as a starting point, and go to approximately the date of *Atalanta,* late 1940s. Then for Don,

I would find another point that was more recent, 1742, and goes up to a point in the 1970s roughly. *Eleanor's* begins in 1992, modern consciousness, and goes to some predictive point way in the future, and then the last one begins in a hypothetical future, like the beginning of *Atalanta* is in a hypothetical past. The last one is an extremely magnified and elongated version of the first one.

In your short video for Atalanta, you included a lot of imagery relating to the Tennessee Valley Authority power station in Tennessee. What is that about?

Well, I find it very interesting that the area of the TVA was worshipped as a source of enormous power by native Americans, and now we find it as a source of power. It's the same in the southwest, that whole area, Hoover Dam, Canyon De Chelly. I guess also Big Mountain was a power source for the Indians who lived there, and of course a lot of coal and uranium are found there now.

The Hopi and Navaho Indians who live there say the uranium is a medicine if left in the mountain — they use it as a cure for infertility, etc. — but is a poison when removed from the mountain.

Of course. They know what they are doing.

What about the influence of The Tibetan Book of the Dead on Perfect Lives?

At the time that I was working on *Perfect Lives* I was reading the Evans-Wentz edition of the *Tibetan Book of the Dead,* and the distinguishing part of that for me was the essays about the use of that book, or that idea, and I was struck by the similarity of form between that book and what I knew about European ideas of the afterdeath, hell, or whatever goes on in not our world. I got amused by the idea that the *Tibetan Book of the Dead* was a text that was to be spoken into the ear of the recently dead. The idea is that when you die you immediately start going into very intensified versions of things you experience in your earthly life, on a larger scale. And so, the function of the book was to guide people through those experiences, and the way it works is that when the body dies the last sense that goes away is the sense of hearing. Your senses die at different rates, and the last one to die is the sense of hearing.

The practice of the *Tibetan Book of the Dead* is that for a certain number of hours after the person is apparently dead, the consciousness is still there to be addressed. And that someone can still address your consciousness through your aural inputs, so the traditional use of the book is that as soon as someone dies, you start shouting it into their ears, and the longer they have been dead the more you have to shout at them. I was amused by the idea that if you have your mouth up to a microphone and there is an audience at the other end, that it is very much like the *Tibetan Book of the Dead,* that you are guiding the audience through an experience. It's a dumb idea but it keeps me going. I was thinking of *Perfect Lives* as being essentially like the *Tibetan Book of the Dead.* It has all the characters and what they represent — certain good and evils, and there is a track, you know, like the *Divine Comedy* or whatever, you go through certain levels. In *Atalanta,* there is no connection with the *Tibetan Book of the Dead,* the song form is not about microphones. We use microphones but, what I'm trying to say is that the sound of *Atalanta* is the idea that people can be talking at the same time in different parts of the building, and the sounds they make do not impinge on each other because of the architecture.

What about memory?

The Art of Memory, Frances A. Yates, (University of Chicago Press, Routledge & Kegan Paul, Ltd, London, 1966).

I recommend everything by Frances Yates. She's a great writer to *read*. Among her special interests is "The Art of Memory,"* which is the title of one of her books, the techniques for memorizing that people talk about and knew about when memory was essential, before printing. You get the idea from her books of the journeyman work of passing ideas over generations, which apparently consisted mainly of people traveling around and copying things or memorizing ideas that had to be preserved. I've gotten the idea from reading her books that many of the famous theologian thinkers were great memorizers in exactly the same way that our famous musicians are memorizers. In music, one of the most difficult things to deal with is what you remember and how you remember it. If you want to remember something, why do you want to remember it, and how do you go about remembering it? There are people in music like, say, "Blue" Gene Tyranny, who have what amounts to perfect memory. They not only have long-term memory, remembering an enormous piece of literature verbatim, but they also have a short-term memory that makes them be able to do things that other people can't do.

Do you think it has something to do with the body? Memorizing through your hands and body is not the same as memorizing facts.

I don't think so. Or at least that's not the most important part. There is a mythology about memorizing music, you get it even in college, that you memorize through your body. But I never believed it, and according to Frances Yates, it's not true. Or, that's a lower form of memory.

Which is proven by the fact that all of the sports people use psychology. The big thing in sports now is to imagine yourself doing the act. The athlete visualizes her/himself doing it.

You visualize the course. You don't waste physical energy doing it. You go over the course in your imagination, which is actually your memory. And you can refine the techniques of getting through the course, whether it's running or jumping or swimming, or whatever. There are all sorts of stories of how people did that in music. Great piano players riding on a train and someone asks them why they don't read a book, and the answer is, I'm practicing. As you've said, the sports people are doing it *now*, but it's a tradition in music. What Frances Yates says about the written word explains that in music the most fluent memorizers are the greatest musicians. She says that before printing the great thinkers, great theologians, great philosophers, were people who knew how to memorize. For instance, St. Augustine was famous for being able to go to a library and read through it and remember it. That's virtuoso thinking. He didn't have to copy it out. The journeyman would copy out the book and take the copy away. Augustine read and memorized. It made him a great thinker.

The weirdest thing about Frances Yates' writing about the subject is her modesty. Every once in a while she'll say, "Of course, I've never done this," talking about the techniques of memory. It's like somebody writing about a great drug saying it will turn you into superman—"but I've never tried it, of course." Well, obviously, she did. Can you imagine being a great scholar like that and not being able to remember? She's just being modest. And of course, she's being technical in her definition of the "art" of memory, in the sense that she doesn't have to remember in such detail, because of printing. But still, her memory is amazing. She'll make reference to ideas she got, say, 20 years before, from something she read. Obviously, she remembers everything she's ever thought.

How have you used memory? When you perform Perfect Lives you memorize everything, right?

No, I have it all on a video monitor. Actually, the joke of that situation never occurred to me until I realized that the audience thought I was performing the whole piece from memory.

But you do practice it. You practice saying the words in a certain way, don't you? Perhaps that's the part you're memorizing.

The part that I can't really understand about the "art" of memory has to do with what was said about the athletes who imagine the course. Apparently, the early philosophers distinguished between something like verbatim memory—being able to remember the organization of facts—and reminiscence, which is something else, and imagination, which is different again. If those three principles are part of us, the most mysterious thing is what you think you should remember. "Writing" is a mystery, because in one way the invention of writing just replaced one system with another. Now we've invented the computer, which remembers everything, so we don't know what we're supposed to memorize. But obviously, we still have reminiscences, and we still have imagination. We have two of the three parts of the activity, whatever the activity is. In *Perfect Lives,* I purposely set aside memory, because I always disliked it in music. I never liked the idea of memorizing piano pieces, when I studied the piano. It seemed obscene. It seemed like a false application of energy. I think all musicians go through this. You don't want to memorize the music. You want to imagine it. Take a crude example like a three-minute song in popular music that only has, say, twelve words. You can't imagine Paul McCartney memorizing "Say, Say, Say." When he starts to make the music, he doesn't remember it, he imagines it. And when he catches himself remembering, he doesn't want to do the song anymore.

You want to do it as if you're doing it for the first time?

No, I didn't mean it in a sentimental way. I mean that memory, reminiscence and imagination are three different techniques, three different modes of thinking, three different things that go on, and they all have certain moral aspects. Memorizing is used for one thing. Reminiscence is used for another thing, and imagination is used for another, and when you get something that wants to cross over, you immediately reject it. Everybody hates to be around people who are always telling "war stories," people who confuse reminiscence with imagination. People who live in a dream and keep telling the same story all the time. You don't like to be around those people. You don't like that moment and you reject that kind of thought.

But it's okay if they're telling something in a way where they are really experiencing it.

If you get transformed chemically in some way—through excitement or something—where you actually move the material from reminiscence into imagination, it can be captivating. But the general experience is that even if you've never heard the story before, but it has the tone of reminiscence, you don't want to hear it.

I think that reminiscence is good for . . . I guess, I don't understand it. It's too complicated for me. Reminiscence might be the least particular of the three modes. Maybe you have to move from reminisence to memory in order to particularize things, and then from memory to imagination. Then you can rehearse. The runner, say, could go from reminiscence of the race to the particulars of memory—"I took too many steps going around that curve, my pace got off"—to a place where he can imagine the race and keep rehearsing it, and actually get better. I think that's what it's about. Those three modes have different uses. They're useful in different ways.

From the way you're describing it, imagination is more expansive, with more possibility.

In your imagination, you can actually change things. You can rearrange things. The way I understand the idea from Frances Yates, reminiscence is a picture, a documentation of what happened. Memory has to do with isolating the particulars. Imagination has to do with rearranging the particulars for whatever your purpose is.

Can you talk about these things in terms of the writing of the three operas?

The technique of *Perfect Lives* which is different from the technique of *Atalanta,* is to reminisce on a particular scene—a scene in a visual sense— and to describe the scene. But the image always has some sort of sound for me. Somebody making a sound with the voice, somebody talking, one person, two people, a lot of people, whatever. It always has that sound as part of it. I kept rehearsing the scene in my mind until I felt comfortable that it was "accurate," that the words I was using were *part of* the scene. I tried to recreate the sound of that moment, the words that went with that landscape.

The 24-minute episodes in *Perfect Lives* are made up of any number of short scenes. Really short. I mean, like a few words or a few sentences. The scenes group themselves according to the visual subject of the scene and also according to the sound of the scene. Those two factors—the sound of the scene and the words that went on in it, and the subject matter of the scene—caused the scenes to group themselves in different categories. Different piles of paper with words and sometimes some sort of musical notation on them. One pile would be these people talking. Another pile would be other people talking. I could combine those groups of people, either in some intuitive fashion or in an arbitrary fashion according to the plan of the opera. I put these people with these other people, because they seemed to go together. But prior to that there was the idea that the scene had a certain sound to it. Like the sound of the four of us talking here. As opposed to our being, say, in a bar, or riding in a car, or being in a church. Each of these scenes has a certain sound, and the scenes are organized into groups without regard, sometimes, to whether there is a narrative plot, without regard to whether they're going anywhere. In *Perfect Lives* the words go from one scene to another in a musical flow, taking along with them whatever drama there is in that movement from one to the next. Sometimes two scenes are joined so smoothly, you can hardly feel the edge. Other times, they can be quite different, and the changes will be dramatic. Essentially, the scenes in *Perfect Lives* are just a collection of little pictures, almost like postcards.

In *Atalanta,* I've been working with the idea of anecdotes. Prolonged stories. The narrative in *Atalanta* comes from the interior "sound" of a certain way of talking and from the technique of how to prolong the tone of that speech. If you take the tone of the speech as the guide, then you go wherever the speech leads you, as long as you hang onto the tone. Like, what we're doing right now has a tone. I'm trying to be "friendly," "intelligent," "aware," whatever. You know what I mean. It's not like the tone of two people who've just had a car accident and want to punch each other. I'm trying to be "cooperative," so everything is involved with that tonality, and I can't even reproduce another tonality right now. So, in *Atalanta,* I would imagine a certain tonality and see where that tonality would take me, what words that tonality would generate, where it would lead me. The only thing I cared about was not losing the tonality. What words do you use? What rhythms do you need? What do you need to think in order to continue in the character? In *Atalanta* there are three major characters, Max, Willard, and Bud, based on three men whose lives I've thought about a lot.

All of the different stories in "Willard," say, are a kind of family of tonalities. And in "Bud," another family of tonalities. They're almost like groups of instruments in an orchestra, though that's not very accurate. In a crude way of thinking of it, you could say that a certain character is always "angry," another is always "reminiscing," another is always "hesitant," whatever.

So you pay attention to the sound of speech all the time? Do you sometimes pursue that attention when you are talking with people, beyond what they are saying?

Yes, totally. It has nothing to do with meaning or words, it's just exactly the sound of the way you're speaking or the way you address yourself, the way you make the sounds. I think that's what playwrights try to do but they do it from a different point of view. I try always to get it so it's in a certain pitch, a certain key almost. It's actually like a mode; it's like the musical idea of a mode. For instance, in what I read about the Greek philosophy of modes there were seven principal modes, and each of them had subsidiary modes, or secondary modes. Those modes were fundamental ways of thinking. One mode was war, one mode was bravery and courage and the ability to die, and another mode was love. You can hear the difference. Why wouldn't you be able to hear the difference? And so certain modes were forbidden in certain times. It's true.

In America, in the 1970s and the 1960s, everybody was totally into reminiscing. The government was trying to get everybody to fight and nobody wanted to fight; you couldn't get anybody to fight because you couldn't get them out of their mode.

Now, everybody's in a belligerent mode. In the ancient Greek idea of musical modes all the war songs were in a certain mode and the words that went along with the melodies were conditioned by those melodies.

You couldn't possibly sing a love song in the war mode. I think we are getting to be very belligerent. I don't mean patriotically. I mean belligerent with each other. I don't care—it's not moral. I mean, I just think that we're going through a belligerent period, and that we're all speaking in a belligerent way. It has certain advantages, I suppose, because the war mode organizes people in a certain way to do certain things. It doesn't just mean you have to kill people. It's a way of organizing your ideas. If you're in a love mode, it doesn't mean that everybody's happy, it just means that there are certain ways of thinking about things. If you're in a war mode, everybody thinks about things in a certain way. I hear American speech changing very dramatically into a very belligerent mode. Quite Spartan, you know, in the sense of the old Greek saying "The Spartans always sang one song." They thought a certain way. They were famous for having certain points of view. That's doesn't mean killing somebody, it means how you take care of yourself. So maybe the only way we can keep from having a nuclear war is to go into a war mode. You know, maybe in the love mode we would allow some idiot to push the button, whereas maybe in a war mode you're actually *thinking* about war and that prevents war.

So the idea of *Atalanta,* is in a crude sense, modality or tonality of character. And in *Perfect Lives* there is no sustained tonality of character. In *Perfect Lives* the characters keep changing their modality all the time. You know, it's really like the Midwest, where you don't exactly know who you are. You only know who you are depending on *where* you are. The idea of *Now Eleanor's Idea* is the future.... What I'm working on right now, in *Now Eleanor's Idea,* is right out of Frances Yates and her notion of how the Middle Ages changed into the Renaissance. The idea is if *Now Eleanor's Idea* is supposed to be predictive, then it would have to resemble the forms of change that we imagine in the change, say, from the Middle Ages to the Renaissance. My notion about the piece is that it should be predictive, it should *project* into the future, because of the metaphor of the history of consciousness of the United States.

I've been reading Frances Yates for ten years like the Bible, although I couldn't say I fully understand her. She's trying to explain the idea of being able to attach meanings to something that is outside of you, that you only get through your perceptions, something you see or hear. You attach a special meaning, like a code, and once those attachments are made, then by moving the parts around you can rearrange what the future is going to be. You don't have just to accept it as it comes to you. You can actually change it. And I'm trying to figure out how to do that in *Now Eleanor's Idea*—to "change" the future through the "arbitrary" units of the piece. They are no more arbitrary than *Atalanta* or *Perfect Lives;* they work in a different way. In *Atalanta,* the arbitrariness is just that each anecdote has to take 24 minutes, because that's how long television is. In other words, you only have 24 minutes to tell a story. In *Perfect Lives* you still have only 24 minutes, but you don't know exactly what's going to happen in the terrain of that 24 minutes, things can be joined together in different ways. What I'm trying to do in *Now Eleanor's Idea* is to say, we'll just divide it up in all kinds of ways, and the only determinate of how big a section is, how big it is musically, is how long it can sustain the meaning that you attach to it. So, if you attach a meaning that's only seven seconds long, then the unit can only last seven seconds. You can't drag it out for reasons of form. There should be a perfect correspondence between how long it can occupy your attention and how long the idea takes to be expressed. You make a number of pieces that are different lengths and put them all together. And you have a whole table full of things, in the visual sense, and you move all the parts around and see what it "says." In a sense, it's like prediction. It has to do with the visionary quality of America, of being able to change things. That's our aesthetic, to change things. It doesn't matter if it is an illusion.

Frances Yates specializes in what was called the "occult philosophy." The way I understand it is that in the transition between one way of thinking and another way, during the introduction of the printing press, the different ways of "thinking" obviously took on enormous political importance. The way you thought had political meaning. There was a struggle to the death about two basic ideas about the world. One idea, neo-Platonism, is that every particle of our physical existence is informed by a benevolent god. The idea of this god is that every aspect of what we do is good, everything is good, and that the forms of this goodness go from the infinitely large and incomprehensible down to the infinitely small and detailed. That by coming to understand the most particular smallest forms of that goodness, you can train yourself to climb the ladder to larger and larger versions of the same thing until you finally can understand a totally benevolent universe, in which there would be nothing but good. The other side, politically, thought *that* idea was wrong, that there is no god in the particulars, that god is what we make her/him/it. We're supposed to *impose* an order on things. Since there is not intrinsic order, it is our job to *create* order. Anyway, those who wanted to create order won, and made it seem historically that the neo-Platonists were fools, that their idea was a minor idea that never really had any importance.

Frances Yates rescues this other idea from its exile, she explains what the so-called "minor philosophers" thought, where they fit in, and why they were persecuted. She ties this to Shakespeare's philosophy, where Elizabethan culture came from, why Giordano Bruno was burned, why there was an Inquisition, and why the Pope was such an asshole, and about Sir John Dee, apparently a key figure of Elizabethan philosophy.

Neo-Platonism is sort of like holography: the idea that the whole thing is contained in the smallest detail. The philosophical machinery that they used had very elaborate schemes for being able to remember how the different parts of the universe related. You could sit down and start thinking about a flower and come out as god. There's no barrier between you and god.

Introduction to
IMPROVEMENT (DON LEAVES LINDA)

Each act is based on a schedule of 44 minutes.

The lines of the text are numbered in series based on the structure of the various scenes. The numbered line is the unit of the *pace* of the text (thus, the *line* is analogous to the *measure* in traditional notation).

The line must be realized in terms of its duration, measured in "beats" at a constant rate of 72 beats per minute:
> In **ACT I** each numbered line has a duration of **three beats** (at the tempo of 72 beats per minute = 2.5 seconds);
> In **ACT II** each numbered line has a duration of **four beats** (at the tempo of 72 beats per minute = 3.33 seconds).

— — is a line of rest. Sometimes the term TACIT is used to indicate a line of rest without the feeling of a large pause.

When the numbered line is sung by two or more voices in dialogue, the text uses indentation to indicate the different voices. Sometimes the different voice is not named.

Timings for individual scenes and cumulative timings are given in the text.

When the series of numbered lines assigned to a particular voice is **interrupted** by a new series for another voice, this indicates that the first voice (interrupted) remains in the scene and in the same vocal quality to the end of the scene. (This same consideration applies in the case where Scene 15 and Scene 16 interrupt each other.)

The term **segue** means to begin the following scene without a break in tempo. When scenes are not joined by a segue, they may be separated by a short pause for reasons of staging, but in principle the opera can be performed without pause, and in particular the separate acts can be performed without pause.

IMPROVEMENT (DON LEAVES LINDA) is the first of four, short operas entitled (as a group) **NOW ELEANOR'S IDEA**. The four operas may be produced separately, or together as a single, performance work. Each of the operas is conceived in a "format" of 88 minutes duration and, thus, lends itself to realization directly to television or to another recording medium.

NOW ELEANOR'S IDEA is based on the notion of a sequence of events seen from four, different points of view. The operas share principal characters and vocal techniques (including the relationship of the voice to instrumental settings). The operas differ, principally, in the language style of the librettos and in the relationship of the music to the presentation of the visual imagery.

Now Eleanor's Idea

I   IMPROVEMENT
    (DON LEAVES LINDA)
    Allegory

II FOREIGN EXPERIENCES
    Persuasion

III NOW ELEANOR'S IDEA
    Declamation

IV WHEN
    OPPORTUNITY KNOCKS
    Secrecy

Overview of
NOW ELEANOR'S IDEA

	IMPROVEMENT (DON LEAVES LINDA)	FOREIGN EXPERIENCES	NOW ELEANOR'S IDEA	WHEN OPPORTUNITY KNOCKS
Idea	Experience	Memory	Taste (specifically: Modernism)	Remains
Arena	Theater	Science	Money	Disposal
Imagery	Landscape	The Laboratory	Display (The Low-Riders' automobiles)	Digital Animation
Technique	Collage (3-D effects)	Sequence (rate of change vs. change process	Movies (specifically: plotted camera moves	Video (specifically: variable freeze-frame to audio sync-point duration
Protagonist	Linda "A sense of self satisfaction, given off, follows everything she does."	Don "I just got out there where there was no help, and I fell to earth."	Now Eleanor "Whenever she starts to do anything, she hears, 'Now, Eleanor...' Out of self respect she dropped the comma and the three dots."	Junior, Jr.
Style	Answers Requiring an attitude of restrained exaggeration. Every point seems to portend more than can be justified.	Logic Proceed with a confidence based on a faith in the enormous scale of the visual world, the notion of vast distances.	Irony	Substitution (words, orders, speeds, goals)
Model	Allegory "Also, as part of the nesting instinct she puts things on all of the chairs."	Persuasion (i.e., "sales")	Dialogue (declamation: Romeo and Juliet)	Codes (secrecy and disguise)
Subject	A People	Character	Place	Organization
Example	The Jews	The Spanish	America	Corporations
Reference	The Kabala	Navigation	Settlements (specifically: desert buildings)	Contracts
Theme	Identity	Venture	Names	Language
Code	1492	1742	1992	2149

Cast of
IMPROVEMENT (DON LEAVES LINDA)

LINDA . . . . The Jews

DON . . . . Spanishness

ELEANOR . . . . America

JUNIOR, JR. . . . . The descendants of Jews and non–Jews (i.e., us)

MR. GEORGE PAYNE . . . . Giordano Bruno

MR. PAYNE'S MOTHER . . . . . . The Roman Catholic Church

TAP DANCING . . . . The Art of Memory

A CAR WITH A
RUMBLE SEAT . . . . Integrated Philosophy

LEFT HANDED GOLF . . . . Cosmology (Bruno's)

THE NARRATOR . . . . Omniscience

THE AIRLINE
TICKET COUNTER . . . . The Inquisition

THE CORRESPONDENCES
TEXT . . . . Exploration

THE UNIMPORTANT FAMILY . . . The Star Chamber

THE INDIFFERENCE TEXT . . . . . The Affirmation

BACK HOME . . . . Some recanted

A MOMENT (VERY LATE) . . . . . . Exile

THE BIG CITY . . . . Assimilation

THE DOCTOR . . . . Analysis (Marxism, etc.)

THE GOOD LIFE . . . . Art

TROUBLE . . . . Politics

A PLACE IN THE COUNTRY . . . . Israel

HAPPINESS, PROSPERITY . . . . America 1952

THE OFFICE . . . . The idea of an historic refuge (Holland)

THE BRIDGE GAME . . . . Self-image

NORTH . . . . Berlin (style)

EAST . . . . River Rouge (The Movement)

SOUTH . . . . Campo Dei Fiori (history)

WEST . . . . Atlantis "as far back as you can get (on this system) . . ."

IMPROVEMENT
(DON LEAVES LINDA)

ACT I

Prelude

NARRATOR I (MALE)

CHORUS
(SIX VOICES
 HUMMING
 LINES 1–10)

(Three beats
per line)

— —	1
— —	2
— —	3
— —	4
— —	5
— —	6
— —	7
— —	8
— —	9

NARRATOR I:

To continue	10
I must explain	11
an idea that	12
I am inadequate	13
to communicate	14
in the music	15
in the settings	16
in the actions	17
in the intentions	18
Now Eleanor's idea	19
conceived as if	20
in a flash of light	21
The offering of images is	22
a radical form of Judaism	23
which has come to us	24
unacknowledged	25
in the same form as	26
Protestantism	27
Modernism	28
Science	29
and Theater as we know it	30
Her idea explains	31
at least to her how	32
all of these things have come together	33
and differences have disappeared	34
For the sake of argument Don is Spain in 1492	35
and Linda is the Jews.	36

End of Prelude

[1:30]

SCENE ONE
The Sunset

CHORUS (IN CAPS)

NARRATOR I (MALE):

DON:

LINDA:

MR. PAYNE'S MOTHER:

JUNIOR, JR.:

NARRATOR II (FEMALE):

THE DOCTOR:

End of Scene One
Segue to Scene Two

DON LEAVES LINDA	1
LEAVES IS CERTAINLY THE WORD	2
THE PICTURE IS TAKEN AT SUNSET	3
TWO PEOPLE ARE ON THE HORIZON	4
A cynic might say where else could they be	5
THEY HAVE PARKED IN A TURN-OFF	6
A turn-off in this case means: picked for the view	7
COMFORT IS ADVERTISED	8
Comfort in this case means: separate facilities	9
ICE MELTS IN THE THERMOS	10
What a beautiful way to begin a story	11
SHE HAS JUST THOUGHT OF THE WORDS: A CASTLE	12
AT NIGHT HE DOESN'T SPEAK	13
A CAMERA CLICKS IN THE DISTANCE	14
A dog barks	15
THE MOMENT IS LOADED	16
THEY STOP HOLDING HANDS	17
THE JET TRACKS ARE FADING	18
THE DECISION IS MADE	19
SHE STEPS AWAY FROM THE SIGNAL	20
THE LIGHT HAS MOVED SLIGHTLY	21
THE BUILDING IS TOO SUBSTANTIAL	22
The door on the left is marked women	23
HE WALKS TOWARD THE CAR	24
IT STARTS ON THE KEY	25
A song on the radio finishes	26
HE DRIVES AWAY	27
REACHES THE AIRPORT FINALLY	28
GOES TO THE COUNTER AND UNDERGOES	29
QUESTIONING. WONDERS WHY HE THINKS OF	30
HIMSELF AS CARLO. SUBVERSIVE.	31
	[2:47.5]

SCENE TWO
The Airline Ticket Counter

LINDA AND DON

Don goes by the
name of Carlo.
The Agent at
The Airline
Ticket Counter
is named Carla.

CARLA:	
Do you have a ticket?	1
CARLO:	
Yes.	
May I see it please?	2
Yes.	
The ticket says that it was issued as one of two.	3
Yes.	
The ticket says that you came here with your wife.	4
Yes.	
Where is your wife?	5
She is not here.	
Why is she not here?	6
She stayed behind.	
Ordinarily we would not honor such a ticket.	7
I understand.	

But today is a special day. 8
    I know.
So we will honor the ticket. 9
    Thank you.
Do you have baggage? 10
    Yes.
You have more baggage than you are allowed. 11
    I have my wife's baggage and my own.
Why do you have your wife's baggage? 12
    She stayed behind.
Why did she stay behind. 13
    I left her behind.
Why did you leave her behind? 14
    I had to leave urgently.
What is the reason for such urgency? 15
    My reasons are my own.
Do you refuse to tell me the reason? 16
    No.
What is the reason? 17
    Another person.
Is that person a woman? 18
    Yes.
The ticket says that you have rented a car. 19
    Yes.
Do you have the rented car to return at this time? 20
    Yes.
The ticket says that you will return the car with your wife. 21
    I know.
If your wife appears without the car, it is possible that her ticket will
not be honored. 22
    I understand.
What will happen to your wife, if her ticket is not honored? 23
    I do not know.
Where is your wife now? 24
    I do not know.
Does she have transportation to the Airline Ticket Counter? 25
    I do not know.
Does she have resources other than the airline ticket? 26
    I do not know.
Does she know where she is in relation to the Airline Ticket Office? 27
    I do not know.
And she has neither baggage nor the rented car. 28
    Yes.
This is a rather unusual situation. 29
    I understand.
Where was your wife when you left her? 30
    She was in the toilet at the turn-off.
She went into the toilet and you left her? 31
    Yes.
You took her baggage and the rented car? 32
    Yes.

You left urgently to meet another person?   33
    Yes.
That person is a woman?   34
    Yes.
You wife will be angry and jealous.   35
    No.
How is that possible?   36

                    [4:17.5]

Scene Two interrupted
Segue to Scene Three

SCENE THREE
The Correspondences Text

DON with
CHORUS (IN CAPS)

As if The Commander had spoken sharply to them, they   1
ground . . . (LONG PAUSE)—what is the word?—"they   2
ground . . . " (LONG PAUSE FOLLOWED BY EXTRAVAGANT GESTURE   3
TO SIGNIFY THE ABSENCE OF THE ADVERB)—to a halt.   4
This simple sentence, with the hole in it,   5
occupied me for years. Nor have I found the solution, yet.   6
What is the word? "They ground . . . " (LONG PAUSE, THEN,   7
THE SAME GESTURE)—"to a halt."   8
The word I need should symbolize the whole of the psychology   9
of the process or attitude of what is *not*—I repeat,   10
not—subservience, which is the way we see it   11
from the "outside," so to speak. Remember "as if."   12
"As if" The Commander had spoken sharply to them, etcetera.   13
In other words, "they," acting to all appearances in unison,   14
ground to a halt. And, for us, how is that unanimity   15
of purpose and action to be achieved, if not   16
in subservience? We have a special view of the world.   17
The roads, for instance, are understood.   18
They represent a unanimity of purpose that is understood,   19
because, in my view of things, they are unframed in time.   20
When did they begin and when did they end are questions   21
we have not asked ourselves, because—   22
ALTHOUGH, MAYBE THERE IS NO "BECAUSE,"   23
HOWEVER, IMPOSSIBLE THAT MAY SEEM—   24
as *accomplishments* they are "on-going."   25
But architecture has its accomplishments "framed in time."   26
The great "accomplishments" of architecture are, finally,   27
"finished," they are "framed in time," and, because we have   28
no understanding of our schedule on a scale so vast,   29
the "accomplishments" of architecture are a mystery to us,   30
and we explain them to ourselves in simple words   31
of great significance, whose meanings we barely have   32
examined—much less "understand."   33
There is a precise—perhaps, even to the moment—   34
correspondence, in time measured,   35
between the Ziggurats at Ur, "stepped pyramids"   36
(THEIR "DATE," HOWEVER THAT IS DETERMINED),   37
to the gleaming, polished Pyramids at Giza—   38
"CLOCKS," THEY THINK, FOR THE WHOLE WORLD—   39
and the "stepped pyramids," unnamed,   40
that are the accomplishments of the great Aztec Tribes,   41

to the World Trade Center at New York. 42
This is one example among many; but, then, 43
I don't have time to discuss this in detail; 44
I mean, the correspondence. 45
This is certainly a puzzle; I mean, the precision 46
of these correspondences. And it is not to be explained 47
in stupid and arrogant concepts, such as 48
the concept of "subservience." As in: 49
"They were ordered to do it, and they did it. We made 50
them do it, and it is done." Boy, how stupid can you get? 51
The Ziggurats at Ur—on what sustenance we have 52
not named—and the great "Clocks" at Giza—on garlic, 53
it is said (AND THAT MAKES SENSE TO ME, WHEN I EAT GARLIC) 54
—and the great stepped pyramids thrown toward the sky 55
among the Aztecs—on coca leaves, it is surmised 56
(AND, BOY, THAT MAKES SENSE TO ME, EVEN AT THIS DISTANCE)— 57
and the World Trade Center at New York—on grain carbohydrates, 58
I assume—are, obviously, the "will of the people." 59
Consider the stupidity of the concept of 60
"subservience" on a scale so vast and the concept 61
disappears, like the value of flesh and blood as 62

End of Scene Three
Segue to Scene Two

sustenance to a monumental task. Do you know what I mean? 63

[6:55]

SCENE TWO
continued

CARLA:
Well, sort of. I get the idea that this is a subject that you
are interested in. 37
    CARLO:
      That's one way of putting it.
Have a good trip—Carlo. 38
      Thank-you. (WHAT?)

End of Scene Two

[7:00]

SCENE FOUR
The Ride
To Town
(THE STAR CHAMBER)

MEANWHILE, BACK AT THE TURNOFF, 1
LINDA IS OFFERED A RIDE TO TOWN. 2
SHE DOESN'T LIKE THE LOOK OF IT. 3
FOUR PEOPLE TOO MUCH ALIKE. 4
A TYPICAL TRAP. SHE ACCEPTS. 5
GO FOR IT, LINDA. GOOD LUCK. 6

THE DOCTOR

FATHER:
Well, here's a cute little thing, 7

NARRATOR II (FEMALE)

    MOTHER:
    just came out of the toilet, 8

MR. PAYNE'S MOTHER

      FIRST CHILD:
      and she appears to be alone. 9

JUNIOR, JR.

        SECOND CHILD:
        A maiden in distress. 10

Madam, my name is unimportant, and this is my wife, 11
    whose name is unimportant, and our two, lovely children, 12
        whose names are unimportant. We are the 13
        Unimportant Family, 14
            but we are a family, nevertheless, and 15
            that is our charm. 16
You appear to be alone, the victim of circumstances— 17
    circumstances of your own creation, 18
    according to one point of view, 19
        or not, according to another—and 20
        we can offer you a ride to town. 21
Apparently, you have been deserted. It 22
happens all the time, really. 23
    Especially here. This is the perfect place, is it not: 24
        The desert, the lack of public telephones, 25
        that cosmic feeling of our singular 26
            relationship to God, and the feeling of 27
            detachment from the things of the world. 28
They just drive away. 29
    Sometimes one, sometimes the other. 30
        Maybe it's no more than who has the keys 31
        and, of course, that madness 32
        that comes to each of us so suddenly. 33
We come here all the time. 34
    We live in a nearby town with telephones, 35
    radios, airplanes, the works, 36
        and there, burdened with the "works," 37
        we have a hard time seeing. 38
        So, we come here all the time. 39
First, of course, the reason was the vista: 40
    pale, purplish blues and pale violets 41
    at sunset, the gleaming stars at midnight, 42
        wild yellows reflected off the morning rocks, 43
        and, at midday, the blast of whiteness. 44
That wore off, of course. 45
    If you've seen one, you've seen them all. 46
        Then, among all this stage–business, 47
        we began to see the drama. 48
            Finally, accustomed to the light, 49
        we began to see the drama. 50
The children enjoy it. My wife packs the picnic lunch. 51
I clean up the van, which is 52
what we call our vehicle, leaving room always 53
    for the extra person, who, like yourself, 54
    needs a ride to town, and we come here. 55
        Probably, were we elsewhere, there would be opera, 56
        or the theater, or the promenade 57
        —I don't even know the words, except from books. 58
So, this is it. This is your life. 59

Excuse me for the little joke. 60
And we are going to offer you a ride to town. 61
It takes something on the order of an hour. 62
Just time enough for the separation to be 63
accomplished, all things going 64
right, without embarrassment 65
to either party. 66
I can tell, just from the look in your eye, that 67
you don't believe me—that this happens 68
all the time. You are convinced of your uniqueness. 69
What has befallen you has befallen you alone, 70
etcetera, etcetera. Is this not true? 71
Let me tell you, you are wrong. Why, just 72
last week, we picked up a guy out here whose 73
head was three times the size of his body. 74
Where do they come from, the kids say. 75
Who do they call, when we drop then at the 76
airport, the wife says. 77
I say, don't ask. Believe in 78
God, and don't ask. 79
This attitude usually gets us to the airport, 80
and then we have our ice-cream cones 81
and go off separately to think it over. 82
Until the next time. 83
Do you believe in God? Of course not, 84
or you wouldn't be here. 85
People who believe in God don't 86
stand around looking at the vista— 87
that is to say, pretending they are 88
looking at the vista, and waiting 89
for the drama to unfold. 90
People who believe in God pray, 91
right? Pray constantly. 92
Take ten minutes off to eat a pizza. 93
Are you kidding? 94
Ten minutes off to look at the sunset? 95
Are you kidding? 96
That's why you're here, seven paces from the toilet 97
under the golden sky— 98
see how it changes just at the edge to blue; 99
the rule of complimentaries they say; 100
bullshit, I say; the largest part is 101
modulated gold, and just at the edge 102
there is blue; period— 103
and, if there is a God, prayer is sufficient. 104
That's why you're here, seven paces from the toilet 105
under the golden sky, 106
talking to a creep in whose name 107
the van owned in common law by 108
the Unimportant Family is registered— 109

because you don't believe in God,   110
else you would pray constantly,   111
and that would be sufficient.   112
This ride is uncomfortable, I know.   113
Try as I will to keep things up to date—   114
I mean the van, as we call it,   115
the stereo cassette player with its   116
four loudspeakers placed   117
around the enclosure,   118
each separately controlled for   119
ideal balance of the sound   120
among the passengers with the   121
sole exception that the ideal balance   122
does not include the possibility of   123
no sound at all for one passenger,   124
if any other passenger wants or   125
needs a sound,   126
the fuzzy seat covers washed almost   127
monthly by the wife, and the air-conditioner—   128
there is a certain wornness about it,   129
and this wornness makes the   130
passenger uncomfortable,   131
reminding him or her that this   132
event is probably not unique.   133
Notice that even the landscape itself   134
looks worn. I don't mean the road.   135
In my opinion they do   136
pretty well at keeping up the road.   137
I mean the landscape and the   138
feeling that it gives you.   139
So many people have looked at it before.   140
So many people have felt these feelings.   141
And it is impossible to conceive,   142
is it not, that your feeling—   143
I mean, the feeling that you have now;   144
God knows, we cannot "possess"   145
feelings; that figure of speech   146
is just a convenience—   147
is yours uniquely or, to involve   148
time in the concept, yours alone.   149
So, here we are, at last, at the airport,   150
where we must part. Good luck trying to arrange to   151
use your ticket, if an explanation is required.   152
We would help you, if we could, but probably   153
it would only make things worse.   154
So, we will leave you and have our ice-cream,   155
and you will leave us for whatever   156
your destination is, and,   157
God willing, we will meet again   158
under less dramatic circumstance.   159

REACHES THE AIRPORT, FINALLY.   160
GOES TO THE COUNTER AND UNDERGOES   161
QUESTIONING. WONDERS WHY SHE THINKS OF   162
HERSELF AS CARLA. SOUNDS LIKE A   163
NAME FOR A SPY. YOU'RE READING THE   164
PAPERS TOO MUCH, LINDA.   165

    [13:52.5]

End of Scene Four
Segue to Scene Five

SCENE FIVE
The Airline Ticket Counter

DON AND LINDA

Linda goes by the
name of Carla.
The Agent at
The Airline
Ticket Counter
is named Carlo.

CARLO:
Do you have a ticket?   1
    CARLA:
    Yes.
May I see it?   2
    Yes.
The ticket says that it was issued as one of two.   3
    Yes.
The ticket says that you came here with your husband.   4
    Yes.
Where is your husband?   5
    He is not here.
Why is he not here?   6
    He went ahead.
Ordinarily we would not honor such a ticket.   7
    I understand.
But today is a special day.   8
    I know.
So we will honor the ticket.   9
    Thank you.
Do you have baggage?   10
    No.
Where is your baggage?   11
    It is with my husband.
Why is it with your husband?   12
    Because he went ahead.
Why did he go ahead?   13
    In order to leave me behind.
Why did he leave you behind?   14
    He had to leave urgently.
What is the reason for such urgency?   15
    His reasons are his own.
Do you refuse to tell me the reason?   16
    No.
What is the reason?   17
    Another person.
Is that person a woman?   18
    Yes.
The ticket says that you have rented a car.   19
    Yes.
Do you have the rented car to return at this time?   20
    No.

Why do you not have the rented car to return? 21
My husband returned it.
Do you know that as a certainty? 22
No.
Why do you believe that he returned it? 23
Because he went ahead.
If he has not returned the rented car, your ticket cannot be honored. 24
I understand.
Will you allow me to determine if the car has been returned? 25
Yes.
The car has been returned. 26
I know.
We will honor the ticket. 27
Thank you.
You have neither baggage nor the rented car. 28
Yes.
This is a rather unusual situation. 29
I know.
Where were you when your husband left? 30
I was in the toilet at the turn-off.
You went to the toilet building and your husband left you? 31
Yes.
He took your baggage and the rented car? 32
Yes.
He left urgently to meet another person? 33
Yes.
That person is a woman? 34
Yes.
You are angry and jealous. 35
No.

Scene Five interrupted
Segue to Scene Six

How is that possible? 36
[15:22.5]

SCENE SIX
The Indifference Text

LINDA
CHORUS (IN CAPS)

To all appearances I am complacent and indifferent. 1
That is, I appear to be complacent and indifferent. 2
And, in fact, I am complacent in that I am 3
indifferent to appearances. My apparent indifference 4
and my apparent complacency would seem to be 5
the result of my position in the social world. 6
I am well-fed. I am well-dressed. I am, 7
to all appearances, without need. No one would challenge 8
me that I do not understand the value of my resources, 9
that I should have undertaken actions that would result 10
in waste and make me a burden to society. 11
These outward manifestations, these appearances, 12
show nothing about my—if I may use the word— 13
spiritual or my intellectual well-being, 14
though commonly they are taken to do so. 15
Our common experience is that spiritual 16

or intellectual degeneration cannot take place 17
without outward manifestations. Our common 18
experience is that beggars on the street or 19
madmen who rant and tear their clothing 20
should not be approached except in acts of 21
defense of society. So, my indifference is 22
different from the indifference of the beggar or 23
the madman. My indifference is wedded to complacency, 24
and complacency is reassuring at all times, 25
signifying as it does, the stability and 26
reality of the things of this world. 27
Thus, you have honored my ticket, which certainly 28
you should not have had I appeared before you 29
as a beggar or as a madman. 30
Their irony of the threatening aspect 31
of complacency is too complicated to 32
go into here, except to remark that 33
there is some connection between the threat and 34
the continuing illusion of stability and 35
reality, which illusion is so valuable to us all. 36
I have driven my husband from me by my 37
complacency and my indifference. The moment of 38
his departure, which was inevitable, is of 39
little consequence, except for the drama—which 40
purports to teach us something. My husband 41
is embarked upon an adventure of the mind— 42
if I may use that word. Inevitably, 43
his partner in the adventure would be another woman— 44
to address the question that is most troubling to you— 45
else the adventure would not be, precisely, "of the 46
mind." He has gone to determine if there is 47
continuance apart from the continuance of things. 48
In my complacency I have but little respect 49
for the purpose of his adventure. My 50
attention is to the things of this world 51
and precisely to the order of things 52
to their social value apart 53
From immaterial continuance. 54

CHORUS:
(Hums from
line 55 to
end of scene.)

Another answer to your stupid question is 55
that inevitably we had to part, for some 56
period of time, as the result of having 57
become more alike, more like each other. 58
Apparently, at some moment in the recent past 59
we crossed the threshold of tolerable 60
similarity. That that moment—the moment of 61
crossing the threshold—should come in a form 62
that seems dramatic to you, that 63
it should come while I am in a toilet in 64
the middle of a desert, is more acceptable to me, 65
more generous on his part, more friendly, 66
because it is clearer and, thus, more humorous, 67

more human than had it come hidden, ambiguous, 68
timid and without confidence in me. 69
He would never go out after dinner to buy a pack of 70
cigarettes and not return. His imagination is 71
bigger than that. But we crossed the threshold 72
and a solution to the difficulties of that 73
situation had to come about. He had come to be— 74
I speak, of course, from my singular "point of view" 75
(as people say). There are things we can never 76
understand, thoughts that we can never have— 77
too much like me, too much of me. Before, 78
it had been mysterious, exotic; he had a 79
language of his own, apart, leaving me 80
"free"—if there is any meaning to that word— 81
free to see the world in him, free to learn, 82
free to possess the fact of what is termed 83
"experience," free of the presence of the mirror. 84
Gradually, then, he changed himself in my image. 85
He became me in many parts of himself, because 86
we are not strong enough to behave otherwise. He became 87
me, because I am a woman—as I became him, 88
because he is a man—and my particular womanness 89
in him got to be as unbearable to me 90
as, certainly, it is unbearable to him. 91
We all resent, I believe, imitations of ourselves. 92
I have heard, or I imagine I have heard, that 93
in other parts of the world—among other peoples— 94
this is not true, that among some peoples of the world 95
imitation is not resented. I don't believe it. 96
That idea seems to me to be what the Viennese called 97
"wishful thinking." It hardly matters, does it? Our 98
case could be particular in the extreme and still 99
you and I, here at the ticket counter, would have come to 100
understand it for ourselves. No that's not true. Were it 101
particular in the extreme I would be exiled from the 102
community. It's not particular. It's common. I came to 103
dislike the image of myself in him. How can we conceal our 104
feelings? Enchantment left. Separation grew in us, a 105
pact between us. It's my feeling that I drove him out, in 106
order again to acquire facts from the material world, 107
which act of acquisition was blocked for me by his presence. 108

End of Scene Six
Segue to Scene Five   [19:52.5]

SCENE FIVE   CARLO:
continued   Will you see him again?   37
                                      CARLA:
                                      Without a doubt
                                 Have a good trip . . . Carla.   38
                                      Thank you. (WHAT?)

End of Scene Five   [19:57.5]

SCENE SEVEN
Back home
some days
she pretends
she's
someone else

LINDA ON THE TELEPHONE
CHORUS (IN CAPS)

(LINDA ON THE TELEPHONE)   1
Hello.   2
No.   3
I mean, no, it's not she.   4
No.   5
No.   6
Wrong again.   7
No.   8
Well, it's not exactly charming.   9
No.   10
Of course.   11
Yes.   12
Goodbye.   13
BACK HOME   14
SOME DAYS   15
SHE PRETENDS   16
SHE'S SOMEONE   17
ELSE   18
— —   19
Hello.   20
No.   21
I mean, no, it's not she.   22
No.   23
No.   24
She hasn't been at this number in some time.   25
No.   26
I wish I could help you.   27
No.   28
Of course.   29
Yes.   30
Goodbye.   31
ON THE THIRD CALL SHE'S   32
TOLD THAT DON HAS BEEN SEEN   33
ON THE ROAD WITH ELEANOR.   34
AND TALK LOCALLY IS THAT THEY'RE   35
HEADED FOR MEXICO.   36
MORE OF THIS LATER.   37
Hello.   38
No.   39
Well . . .   40
Yes.   41
Yes.   42
Really.   43
No.   44
I can't say I'm exactly surprised.   45
No.   46
Of course.   47
Yes.   48
Goodbye.   49

End of Scene Seven

[22:00]

SCENE EIGHT
Finally, she starts seeing Mr. Payne, an Italian man, who tap dances

LINDA
MR. PAYNE
CHORUS (IN CAPS)

FINALLY, SHE STARTS SEEING (1)
MR. GEORGE PAYNE (2)
AN ITALIAN MAN (3)
WHO TAP DANCES (4)
(MR. PAYNE AND LINDA SPEAKING.) (5)
— — (6)

LINDA:
No, George, there is your mother, my mother and birth control. (7)
These are three reasons why we should not get married. (8)

MR.P:
I have a car with a rumble seat. It is better
    than the car of your 1
brother-in-law. It is better than the car
    of your brother 2
who assures us that he is not interested in
    driving. It is better 3
than the car of your brother, who modestly allows
    that, for the time being 4
all things of his marriage are the property
    of his wife, 5
in order that her mother's future is secure.
    It is better 6
than the car of your brother, who runs around
    with the daughter 7
of the sofa-stuffing family, amazing
    as she is. 8
It is better than the car most people will
    ever ride in. 9

Another reason, George, is your background. Or (9)
my background. We seem to see things so differently. (10)

My family is Payne and, though I am
    sure they merely 10
changed it from meaning bread, because that's the
    way the Officer 11
saw it, still words would be
    useless, if 12
the sound were not the meaning, and so I
    live in Payne, 13
to make a silly joke, I am, as it were,
    inside of Payne, 14
and from that perspective I ask you to
    reconsider, to remember 15
that my origins suggest a certain
    skill in providing, 16
as in to provide, that a person would
    not be named bread 17
and have in him a characteristic
    inability to provide. 18

Another reason, George, is your name. There are customs in (11)
my family about how men should be named. (12)

George is practically unheard of. They would never (13)
get it straight. Do you know what I mean? (14)

As you know, all tap dancers are named
    George. It means 19
"lighthearted." In tap dancing one retraces.
    (Rehearses is 20
the word they use, but they are wrong,
    trapped in the first 21
stage or first test of memory;
    how many syllables 22
and for how long: immediately, ten
    minutes later, at the 23
end of the day, forever? No, the trick of memory,
    or the dance 24
of memory, as we say, meaning the same thing,
    is in the 25
positioning of the information. The dance of
    memory is just that, 26
and music is the rehearsal of that dance.
    Do you follow?) 27

You made a point or two that I could bear to hear again. (15)

In tap dancing one retraces.
    That's why 28
we are so often seen looking down.
    The observer 29
thinks that we are looking down in order to
    keep things 30
right for the observer. To
    prevent error. 31
The observer has never seen what the
    dancer sees 32
looking down, or the observer
    wouldn't think that. 33
The world moves on the air of
    music. There's nothing 34
like it. It's the only thing we
    had before 35
automobiles as four-
    dimensional. 36

LINDA SEES THE (16)
CONTENTS OF HER PURSE (17)
IN RETROSPECT. (18)

End of Scene Eight [24:15]

SCENE NINE
The Contents
of Her Purse

LINDA (EVERY LINE)
with MR. PAYNE (AS MARKED)
with CHORUS (IN CAPS)

This is the kind of talk 1
that got me though. 2
It is so full of something or other— 3
little injections of regret: 4

with MR. PAYNE:	"amazing as she is"	5
•	"to make a silly joke"	6
•	"as it were"	7
•	"as in to provide"	8
•	"as you know"	9
•	"but they are wrong"	10
•	"as we say"	11
	It is so. . . .	12
	It is too big to have been thought out.	13
	Detail upon detail.	14
	Never repeating itself.	15
	It agitates the air.	16
	I heard it beside me, first—	17
	THIS IS LINDA SPEAKING—	18
	as the Airline Ticket Counter agent questioned me.	19
	How can we conceal our feelings?	20
	Enchantment left.	21
	Separation grew in us.	22
	I heard myself saying these things to a stranger.	23
	I was almost in tears.	24
	Then I heard him beside me,	25
	speaking to me:	26
with MR. PAYNE:	The Indifference Speech, naturally, doesn't impress	27
with MR. PAYNE:	me at all. You hear that stuff all the time.	28
	I couldn't believe it.	29
	I was almost in tears.	30
	And this guy had stopped to insult me.	31
	RIGHT AT THE AIRLINE TICKET COUNTER.	32
	I dropped my purse.	33
	Everything came out.	34
	And that was everything.	35
	Everything else gone you know where.	36
	And what's left scattered all over the terra-cotta.	37
	And this guy is saying about my Indifference Speech,	38
with MR. PAYNE:	You hear that stuff all the time.	39
	And then he took me by the arm.	40
	I was about to fall on my knees.	41
	You know how women are made to act silly in all those	42
	stupid films. I hadn't made a move.	43
	I was waiting for my heart to break.	44
	I saw myself scrambling around on the floor,	45
	trying to pick up all that precious trash.	46
	And then I felt his hand on my arm,	47
	and the picture disappeared.	48
	Everything that had gone wrong in my life up to that moment	49
	disappeared. I lost the past of problems—	50
	like some sort of royalty.	51
	And then I watched the Airline Ticket Counter Agent come out	52
	from behind the counter, right over the luggage scales,	53
	clumsily, and start picking up my things.	54

HE WAS NOT IN A GOOD MOOD. 55
He hadn't intended to do what he did. 56
But he found himself picking up my things, 57
and apologizing. 58
I had the feeling that Mr. Payne had just taken control of the 59
idea that I had projected with me in it 60
and erased it and come up with a new one that had the Airline 61
Ticket Counter Agent picking up my things. 62
This uncanny feeling came to me more than once, when 63
we were together. He would rearrange things, 64
as if in the power of his imagination. Now, obviously— 65
or, I should say that now it's obvious, remembering that 66
experience of the intensity being *directed,* 67
of things being moved around, being arranged 68
according to some plan, it is obvious 69
what had happened, it is obvious why my things were 70
on the terra-cotta, it is obvious why I dropped 71
my purse—he memorized the contents. 72
Why? I asked myself so many times. 73
Why did he need to know? Why, with his commanding presence, 74
was the theater of the "accident" required, 75
the drama of the tears that had to come inevitably? 76
Why not just make friends and ask? 77
OR, IN THE STYLE OF THE SECRET AGENT, 78
MAKE FRIENDS, AND, THEN AT THE RIGHT MOMENT, 79
OPEN THE PURSE AND STUDY. 80
Why involve so many unknowns? One hesitates to say, 81
in his case, imponderables. 82
Anyway, I learned this power of his only later. 83
First, there was the tangible magic of his 84
presence. We sat together on the plane. 85
Bravely, I had recovered poise. 86
This was just hours after 87
I had emerged from the moment of the parting 88
to look at the desert of the setting sun 89
alone. 90
When I told him this later, 91
when I told him what had happened to me, 92
and I was going on just about this way 93
and with these words, 94
he said, "It's always setting." 95
He knew everything. It was 96
as if he had memorized the contents of a vessel 97
that had in it all of . . . experience. 98
We talked about everything. I thought the reason was mine. 99
I thought that having found him out— 100
a person who wanted to know everything 101
—I had found a weakness. Why do we do that? 102
And so I decided to talk about—everything. 103
I moved the conversation pointer 104
as fast as I could. 105

with MR. PAYNE:	Overconfidence, they used to call it.	106
	He brought this out in people.	107
	The—uhn—predator	108
	has the victim in sight. I wonder what	109
	it would be like to play tennis with one of the great ones	110
	—who had decided to make the returns all playable.	111
	We talked about everything,	112
	and everything was there in place.	113
	An Alexandrian library	114
	For one person at a time.	115
	MUST BE READ HERE. NO CHECKOUTS.	116
	NO EXCEPTIONS. I got drunk on the abundance.	117
with MR. PAYNE:	Ball bearings, no problem.	118
	A history of ball bearings in a few sentences.	119
	As if from scripture.	120
with MR. PAYNE:	Electrical power, no problem.	121
	Where the great dams are and who made them and what they do.	122
with MR. PAYNE:	Ancient migrations, no problem.	123
	Whence and where from the past in such	124
	detail and with such understanding	125
	that the past became indistinguishable,	126
	magically, from the future.	127
	And then we landed.	128
	And I pretended I was headed—	129
	home—to something.	130
	And then after a decent period	131
	OF DAYS	132
	OF WEEKS	133
	OF MONTHS	134
	WHATEVER,	135
	he called, and	136
	we dropped the pretense,	137
with MR. PAYNE:	and—	138
	We dropped the pretense.	139
with MR. PAYNE:	And.	140
	What happened then?	141
	WHERE HAVE THOSE DAYS GONE?	142
	I have forgotten and	143
	he showed me how—never to forget.	144
	It began as a game between us.	145
with MR. PAYNE:	Let me guess what's in your purse.	146
with MR. PAYNE:	For everything I get right I get a kiss.	147
with MR. PAYNE:	I'll bet a dozen, which is modular.	148
	We made a picnic, the two of us	149
	on a Sunday afternoon in the shade	150
	of a box-elder near the river.	151
	I asked him why we took	152
	his precious Sunday afternoon of golf.	153
	He said that we should marry.	154

I could learn to play golf. And we could | 155
spend every Sunday afternoon together, | 156
forever. I think he said, | 157
"... **THROUGH ETERNITY.**" I said I didn't think that | 158
I could learn to play golf. He said, | 159

with MR. PAYNE
(lines 160–181):

- "It's just like what's in your purse. | 160
- It's the same thing. It needs | 161
- going over now and then to make sure | 162
- it's all there. That's the only reason | 163
- we do it. The scale is different, but | 164
- that's all. Every position | 165
- over the whole course, every | 166
- consideration, is knowable | 167
- as a fact. On a certain | 168
- Sunday we retrace a certain number, | 169
- more or less. That collection | 170
- is a fact—a larger fact | 171
- composed of smaller facts, | 172
- and to play golf with enjoyment | 173
- each larger fact | 174
- and all of the smaller facts | 175
- must be remembered | 176
- as exact experiences | 177
- in order that we don't | 178
- wander around in uncertainty, as if | 179
- the game were mostly chance, as if the | 180
- responsibility were too big to bear, and—" | 181

If I knew more about the way we express things | 182
to each other, maybe I could finally understand | 183
and explain his—"and—" | 184
"AND—" | 185
As if leaping from one star | 186

with MR PAYNE
(lines 187–203):

- to another. "and—" | 187
- finally the accumulation of exact | 188
- experiences, remembered | 189
- exactly, becomes wisdom, | 190
- even before all of the infinite possibilities | 191
- have been exhausted, and— | 192
- you discover that the wisdom, | 193
- as if a gift, | 194
- is usable in other ways. | 195
- You can use it in other places. | 196
- To know every fact of golf | 197
- in the experience of playing it | 198
- is to know | 199
- with the same certainty | 200
- how people beget people, how the car | 201
- with the rumble seat is made to run and | 202
- what's in your purse, for instance." | 203

I was a little frightened.   204
Did I dare suggest that he knew what was in my purse,   205
from the very beginning?   206
Then, it occurred to me,   207
finally—   208
I mean, finally, I got it,   209
and the fear went away—   210
that, if my purse had changed its contents   211
how many times   212
since the moment at the Airline Ticket Counter,   213
he would be betting kisses   214
ON THE PAST RECAPTURED   215
only in a snap shot memory.   216
So, the purse had fallen at the Airline   217
Ticket Counter, in order that we could   218
get to know each other quickly, and both of   219
us were at fault, finally,   220
for why it fell.   221
The golf course,   222
the contents of the purse   223
and the infinitely complicated   224
recircling retracking   225
retracing but finally   226
finite series of points   227
on the route of the car with the rumble seat   228
indeed had a common pattern,   229
and to know one was to know them all,   230
in every moment of the ever changing world.   231
AS LONG AS YOU HAVE A PLACE TO START.   232
Start at the Airline Ticket Counter.   233
Take a reading.   234
Compare it to the pattern.   235
And, then,   236
months later, you can bet   237
kisses that you know it all.   238
That evening,   239

with MR. PAYNE: having not played golf,   240
Mr. Payne took Junior, Jr.   241
and me to supper   242
at his mother's house.   243
THAT EVENING HAVING   244
NOT PLAYED GOLF   245
MR. PAYNE TOOK JUNIOR, JR.   246
AND LINDA TO SUPPER   247
AT HIS MOTHER'S HOUSE.   248

End of Scene Nine   ——   249
Segue to Scene Ten   [34:37.5]

SCENE TEN

Supper with Mr. Payne's Mother

LINDA
MR. PAYNE'S MOTHER
CHORUS (IN CAPS)

CHORUS HUMS:

LINDA / CHORUS:
How is it that (SLOWLY TO MAKE THE WORDS | 1
UNDERSTANDABLE) *with the name of Payne* | 2
you serve pasta at every meal? | 3
  MRS. P:
  It is because we immigrated by the eastern route. | 4
  My child, full grown now, who has brought you here to supper, | 5
  and I, alone after his father's death, came in from the east. | 6
  Had we come in by the southern route, the meaning of the sound | 7
  —due to the typically southern way with vowels— | 8
  translates, as they do at the southern entrance, | 9
  to Flat-Tire, as in Crazy Horse, Sitting Bull, and such. | 10
  What is your name?—you give the sound—The Officer | 11
  replies: You shall be called Flat-Tire. Next please. | 12
  But, Officer, Flat-Tire is so different from the meaning, | 13
  which is to provide. Please reconsider. The Officer replies: | 14
  You can keep the dash and pretend it's English. | 15
  We're not going to call you Payne, if that's what you want. | 16
  We don't like for our children to hear those sounds. | 17
  If you want to start over again, that's your business, | 18
  but you'll have to do it later, once you've settled. | 19
  If I get into that kind of thing here, nobody will get through. | 20
  Everybody trying to figure out what they want to be called,
  can you imagine? | 21
  It's Flat-Tire. That's the best I can do. Please. | 22
She pauses. (SOTTO VOCE, LINDA.) *Offers pasta.* | 23
  Mostly I am glad that we came in by the eastern route, | 24
  where Payne was allowed. | 25
  Only rarely I am not. | 26
— — | 27
What is the reason | 28
for serving pasta | 29
at every meal? | 30
  After years of experience—and this goes back to | 31
  times before my time or my mother's time, | 32
  I am not sure about the beginning, | 33
  probably it is lost in time—it was discovered | 34
  that proper weight keeping finally | 35
  has to abandon all external measures. | 36
(SOTTO VOCE, LINDA.) *A quick glance at Junior, Jr., who has* | 37
come along today, and who has come abruptly to attention, | 38
almost as if anticipating where the argument is headed. | 39
  The first responsibility in eating is to measure | 40
  calorie value to the immediate future. | 41
  Allowing roughly five hours for sleep, the rest of the | 42
  day can be divided in to periods of three hours each. | 43
  The discovery that I mentioned is that three hours— | 44
  is just about the longest average time that any of us can | 45
  look ahead. So, it is possible to figure out | 46

	how many calories will be needed for the next three hours,	47
	and, since pasta is a constant measure,	48
	approximately 300 calories per cup, with sauce,	49
	eat no more than necessary.	50
	The importance of pasta is the importance of a standard.	51
	With training one can learn to know to within	52
	ten calories how much one has eaten.	53
CHORUS HUMS:	— —	54

Is there an advantage to this 55
way of life in which pasta 56
is eaten at every meal? 57
As I said, it is the perfect diet. That is 58
important to us, because—the habit of dancing 59
runs deeply in this family. And, finally, the 60
heroism of dancing in a heavy body is forgotten. 61
Of course, age and the dignity of age play a 62
part in this, too. One encourages tap dancing 63
up to a certain point. The reasons must be obvious. 64
Where to stop is a question of dignity. The sense of 65
the importance of a good family, the importance of 66
caution in one's behavior, comes from the need to 67
keep the image of dignity important in the family. 68
A quick glance at Mr. Payne, who is alternately 69
absorbed in thought—and rigidly attentive. 70
I am reminded of a large cat. (SOTTO VOCE, LINDA.) 71
Ballroom dancing can go on forever, of course. 72
One never tires of the gracefulness of abstinence. 73
Tap dancing, beyond a certain point, has too much of 74
self-gratification about it. Beyond a certain point, 75
tap dancing works against society in many ways. 76
Self-gratification is one: waste. 77
Nitrogen intoxication is another: uselessness. 78
Contagion, the social networks filled with ephemeral 79
information, is another: confusion. There are 80
many reasons. I prefer to think of the matter as closed. 81
CLOSED IT IS. 82
NOW LET'S JUMP AHEAD IN TIME. 83
GIVE OURSELVES RELIEF FROM ALL THIS— 84
QUESTIONING. 85
IMAGINE JUNIOR, JR. YEARS LATER 86
(CHANGED HIS NAME, OF COURSE!) 87
IMAGINE HE'S THE PRESIDENT, JUST RETIRED, OF 88
SOME HUGE CORPORATION. 89
JUST RETIRED, HE REMINISCES. 90

End of Scene Ten   [38:22.5]

SCENE ELEVEN
Mr. Payne
tries to teach
Junior, Jr.
to play golf
left handed

JUNIOR, JR.
with CHORUS (IN CAPS)
with MR. PAYNE (AS MARKED)

Distrust in me of foreign things | 1
—THIS IS JUNIOR, JR. SPEAKING— | 2
made it impossible from the start. | 3
I loved the two-toned shoes. | 4
I loved the bag. | 5
I loved the names, | 6
the angles of the face plates, | 7
the idea of the special purpose clubs | 8
sheathed until the moments when they are | 9
precisely needed. I loved it all, but . . . | 10
THIS IS THE MEANING OF REGRET, | 11
THE DISGUISED TONE OF | 12
IMPATIENCE IN HIS VOICE. | 13
We stand there in the quack grass, | 14
untended front yard. Tries to teach me | 15
how it get it off the ground at least. | 16
I will not suddenly catch on and smack one | 17
through the box-elders into the traffic. | 18
AFRAID OF THE SUN, HE THINKS TO HIMSELF. | 19
Too confident absolutely in himself, | 20
the expensive sweaters, the two-toned shoes, | 21
the dark hair swept back neat, | 22
the smell of cigarettes, the knowledge that | 23
tomorrow in the presence of the boys and girls, | 24
in the presence of their mothers | 25
he will dance again, HOW IT'S DONE. | 26
Romantic place in town, waiting there, | 27
paid for by the month by dancing. | 28
Too confident absolutely in himself, | 29
dancing, a roadster with a rumble seat, | 30
to think even for a moment that | 31
distrust in me of foreign things | 32
is a distrust of himself, not | 33
fear of golf left handed, | 34
fear of free-lance living. | 35
THIS IS THE MEANING OF REGRET. | 36
They seek security, Mom and Dad, | 37
seek it so that I do as a child | 38
without knowing that I seek it, what I seek. | 39
Boy child turned extremist, | 40
barely a decade, recently abandoned, | 41
as earnestly desires security | 42
as a Jesuit, living wildly | 43
in imagination only, within | 44
strict secure limits of security, | 45
encounters a man who lives | 46
month to month by dancing. | 47

(with MR. PAYNE
FROM PARENTHESIS):

•

Tap and ballroom dancing. His studio | 48
a romantic place in town. (The Arcade, | 49
an enormous gallery, filled with people, | 50

light filtered through the glass above,   51
two stories high, a block long,   52
without rain, perfect temperature forever   53
on stone pavements made beautiful with use.   54
A cathedral, secular, just big enough.   55
Royal chambers on the second floor.   56
Secret stairways, gold lettered windows,   57
locked doors. The studio itself,   58
vast hardwood, perfect in tongue and groove,   59
the likes of which, etcetera. The Arcade   60
builder, Worth, knew what he was up to.)   61
Now dancers every day there,   62
proxy children, mother vicarious,   63
except weekends. Saturday market.   64
Wild flowers. Fear of mushrooms.   65
Foreign things. From farmers,   66
onions for the married sister.   67
OH, GEORGE, YOU SHOULDN'T HAVE.   68
Then, Sundays, left handed golf,   69
The Country Club. Businessmen.   70
Northern stock. This country needs   71
less dancing. Right handed golf.   72
Credit God for good government.   73
Social Security enacted. **Y'HAVE TO**   74
PUT SOMETHING IN TO GET SOMETHING OUT.   75
Years later, evenings, I,   76
Junior, Jr., see him.   77
The drugstore with music.   78
The bookrack, English self-taught.   79
Well-dressed, of course. Stopped smoking.   80
Sometimes he doesn't know me.   81
Remembers, but doesn't know me.   82
Elegantly cordial, when he does.   83
I studied with this man one time.   84
Tried to teach me golf left-handed.   85
Tried to teach me living   86
month to month by dancing. Instead,   87
learned what I knew already. Love for   88
good government. Social Security.   89
He's only cordial. Little wonder.   90
TO HONOR MR. PAYNE,   91
WE'LL LET HIM DESCRIBE THE NEXT SCENE.   92
MR. PAYNE, IT'S ALL YOURS.   93

> **MR. PAYNE:**
> Well, let's just say it didn't   94
> work out. She danced away.   95
> I stopped calling. Sold the car.   96
> She likes loneliness. She will   97
> spend her days in loneliness.   98
> It's written.   99

End of Scene Eleven   [42:30]

SCENE TWELVE
A moment (very late) in an all-night delicatessen

NARRATOR I (MALE)
LINDA

NARRATOR I:

Abruptly we have moved ahead in time.　　1
She is not particularly older,　　2
but she is noticeably changed.　　3
The time is evening, very late.　　4
Whom she is talking to　　5
is out of sight. Hidden,　　6
but near. She speaks softly　　7
and with force. We watch.　　8
And they are watching.　　9

LINDA:

You don't hear me.　　10
I try to tell you.　　11
You don't listen.　　12
You couldn't understand,　　13
if you could hear me.　　14
This person's aunt.　　15
That person's brother.　　16
The girls at the office　　17
That's it.　　18

It'll change.　　19
People say so.　　20
With eye contact.　　21
It can't be that bad.　　22
Change is gradual.　　23
Progress to be noticed soon.　　24
What do I care?　　25
Look at the time.　　26
This is Linda speaking.　　27

Beyond her in the aisle　　28
four or five people　　29
secretly drunk,　　30
the joy of that moment　　31
when the alcohol takes over,　　32
notice she's distressed,　　33
beckon silently to her　　34
to leave with them.　　35
Oh, how we misunderstand.　　36

End of Scene Twelve　　[44:00]

END OF ACT I

IMPROVEMENT
(DON LEAVES LINDA)

ACT II

(Four beats per line)

SCENE THIRTEEN
The Big City
(BUT ONLY AS IF
IN A DREAM)

NARRATOR II (FEMALE)
CHORUS (IN CAPS)

CHORUS HUMS:

CHORUS HUMS:

— —	1
THIS ACT	2
SPEAKING GENERALLY	3
IS ABOUT—UHN—	4
PUBLIC OPINION. BUT, OF COURSE,	5
ONLY AS IF IN A DREAM.	6
She gets a call from the city.	
EVERYTHING HAS STARTED TO GO RIGHT.	7
Stronger for what she's been through.	
APPROACHING THE AGE OF PERFECTION.	8
The future no longer a burden.	
LEAVE EVERYTHING BEHIND.	9
Hang no regrets in the closet.	
BACK TO HIGH HEELS AND FRIENDS.	10
Speak sharply if I disagree.	
— —	11
About now the radio stations	
START PLAYING A SONG WITH A MESSAGE.	12
She is unsure of the moral	
(WHEN THE WORDS CAN BE UNDERSTOOD.)	13
But the song has something for her in it.	
THEMES OF MIGRATION AND CHANGE.	14
A positive negative feeling.	
NATURE CORRUPTED AND THRIVING.	15
On irony, language and greed.	
— —	16

SOLO: *Here come Tarzan.*
   Look at that suntan. 1
He's a big swinger.
  — — 2

He got a wife an'
   Her name Jane an' 3
She's a humdinger.
  — — 4

They got a son an'
   He name Boy an' 5
He's a gunslinger
  — — 6

Livin' in a tree an'
   Hopin' to be a 7
Rock and roll singer
  — — 8

CHORUS: *Hangin' around with the apes all day.*
  — — 9

What a way to raise a fa-mo-ly.
  — — 10

 — — 11

SOLO: *One day here come*
   Into that jungle 12
A movie director.
  — — 13

He see Tarzan
   — —doin' his thing an' 14
he quite affected.
  — — 15

He say Tarzan
   Have a cigar, man. 16
You been selected.
  — — 17

You represent that
   one element that 18
can't be corrected.
  — — 19

CHORUS: *Hangin' around with the apes all day.*
  — — 20

What a way to raise a fa-mo-ly.
  — — 21

 — — 22

SOLO:	*Tarzan and Jane sign*	
	Up with the man for	23
	Some compensation.	
	— —	24
	Lock up the hut an'	
	Wash up the boy an'	25
	Leave from the station.	
	— —	26
	Takin' their thing to	
	The world capital of	27
	Civilization.	
	— —	28
	Hopin' to achieve, if	
	you can believe, self-	29
	realization.	
	— —	30
CHORUS:	*Hangin' around with the apes all day.*	
	— —	31
	What a way to raise a fa-mo-ly.	
	— —	32
	— —	
	— —	33
SOLO:	*Now Boy doin' fine.*	
	Got a thing goin'	34
	He gone electric.	
	— —	35
	Tarzan and Jane, man,	
	They got a thing that's	36
	Very selective.	
	— —	37
	Lotta fine clothes an'	
	three or four cars an'	38
	A private detective.	
	— —	39
	To guard all the things that	
	Tarzan regard as a	40
	Social Corrective.	
	— —	41
CHORUS:	*Hangin' around with the apes all day.*	
	— —	42
	What a way to raise a fa-mo-ly.	
	— —	43
	— —	
	— —	44

SOLO:

Like all of the rest of us,
    Tarzan and Jane sometime   45
feel sentimental.
                — —   46

The pool is cool but
    The flow is slow an'   47
The drain's temperamental.
                — —   48

The neighbors are animals,
    strange in their ways,   49
Whose troubles are mental.
                — —   50

Oh, bring it back, please,
    The house in the trees an'   51
The breeze sweet and gentle.
                — —   52

CHORUS:

Hangin' around with the apes all day.   52
                — —   53

What a way to raise a fa-mo-ly.
                — —   54

                — —   55

NARRATOR II:

The song stays on the air for some weeks infecting   1
Almost everyone. If it is not so good in   2
The world capital of civilization, where is it good?   3
Celebrities continue to die of disappointment.   4
The very poor continue to die of hunger.   5
The unrecognized continue to die of striving.   6
And in the meantime, as if in a dream, the parties go on   7
Almost nightly in the city. At a party one drinks cautiously,   8
Avoids the room where the heavy smokers have gathered,   9
Expresses for the record some degree of vulnerability   10
In matters of health, habit and desire, tries to be helpful,   11
Waits inconspicuously, exchanges dreams with strangers.   12

                                                              [4:36]

End of Scene Thirteen
Segue to Scene Fourteen

SCENE FOURTEEN
The Doctor
(ALL THINGS
 ROLLED INTO ONE)

LINDA
THE DOCTOR

LINDA:
Last night I dreamed that—
     DOCTOR:
     (Just a moment, please.)   1

I'm sorry. Last night I dreamed that—this is a common dream for me. 2
     (A woman, recently hurt by circumstances, begins her dream 3
     With the insight that the dream, itself, which we have not   4
     Experienced, remember, is a common dream for her.)   5
I'm sorry. What I meant was that last night I dreamed as   6
I ordinarily do, and I wanted you to know that the dream   7

Was a common one for me, which I thought you could   8
Not know unless I told you.
       (Just a moment, please.)   9
I'm sorry. I dreamed that I was standing in a beautiful   10
Meadow on an almost cloudless day. The meadow seemed to   11
Go on in soft rolling hills almost forever. It was covered   12
With early summer flowers. The sun was shining.
       (Just a moment, please.)   13
I'm sorry. The sun was shining. I was alone. I was at peace with   14
myself. It was a rare moment. It was without any forboding.   15
       (The dream began in foreboding. To appreciate that the   16
       dream is commonplace even before the dream has begun   17
       is a version of foreboding.)   18
I'm sorry. There was no foreboding. If I gave you that   19
impression, it was a mistake. There was no foreboding.   20
That is the part of the dream that I don't understand.   21
The moment that is so memorable in the dream came with no   22
foreboding. Unlike most of the moments in my life.
       (Just a moment, please.)   23
I'm sorry. This is hard for me to explain.
       (Just a moment, please.)   24
I'm sorry. What is hard to explain is that I was taken so much by   25
surprise by what happened, and at the very same time it seemed
so natural.   26
It was surprising and natural at the same time.
       (Just a moment, please.)   27
I'm sorry. It was such a pleasure to be surprised.   28
I had forgotten.
       (A woman is shaken by the absolute rarity of her dream.)   29
I'm sorry. I was standing in a vast meadow that was, at   30
the same time, the front yard of my house. I had those   31
feelings at the same time. I don't remember any details   32
from the dream that gave me the idea that the meadow was the   33
front yard of my house, but the feeling of the identity   34
was clear. And I remember it clearly even now.   35
       (The language of describing the dream describes the foreboding,   36
       intentionally or not. The memory of the dream has no sense   37
       of foreboding. The language describes an image with two   38
       identities. The memory of the dream reconciles the two.)   39
I'm sorry. Neither of those things seemed important to me   40
compared to the power the dream had over me.
       (Just a moment, please.)   41
I'm sorry. As I was standing in the meadow, an airplane   42
flew over at a great height. It was an old type of airplane   43
with a propeller engine. That sound is easy to recognize.   44
I could barely see the airplane, it was so high. But, when I   45
noticed the sound, the airplane was almost directly overhead.   46
The idea of the distance of the airplane is very clear.   47
       (The language for describing the dream is full of foreboding.)   48

I'm sorry. I don't know any other way to tell the story 49
of the dream, without telling you why the dream could 50
surprise me so and still seem natural. 51
    (The image of the dream has about it the structure of foreboding.) 52
I'm sorry. I'll go right to the thing that happened in the dream. 53
    (Just a moment, please.) 54
I'm sorry. Somebody called to me from the airplane. They called my 55
name. I could hear it as clearly as if the caller were only a 56
few feet away. But the sound of the call was at a great distance. 57
The sound of the call came from the airplane.
    (Just a moment, please.) 58
I'm sorry. There was a great difference between the sound 59
of the call and the sound that I could imagine coming from 60
the airplane, especially because the sound of the airplane 61
engine was so natural. 62
    (A woman is distressed by a dream, because the image of the 63
    dream differs from any image in her experience.) 64
I'm sorry. The dream made me very happy, and it was memorable, 65
because it was so surprising and so natural at the same time.
    (Just a moment, please.) 66
I'm sorry. I'm finished telling about the dream. That's all there was to it. 67
I was standing in a meadow that had some kind of meaning
that I could feel. 68
An airplane flew over at a great height. A voice called to me, 69
called my name, from the airplane. It was all very clear. 70

DOCTOR:
The Offering of Images, as a spiritual activity, 1
Replaces the impulse to find a personal vision, an icon. 2
As a spiritual activity it distracts the individual from 3
The task of finding and recognizing a singular, true path. 4
The Offering of Images categorizes human activity and offers 5
The sum of the categories as a sum of possibilities and 6
Alternatives, each one of which must be equally good and 7
Equally valid, else the system of categories breaks down. 8
Like Modernism, Science and Theater as we know it, the 9
Offering of Images and Protestantism, hand in hand, 10
Are egalitarian, democratic and communistic. 11
The Offering of Images is a secular spiritual activity. 12
The Offering of Images has in our era attached itself 13
As a spiritual activity to Judaism as a secular corrective 14
To mysticism and individualism. The Offering of Images is a 15
Secularization of Judaism, as Protestantism is a 16
Secularization of Christianity, Modernism is the secularization 17
Of taste, Science is the secularization of memory 18
And Theater as we know it is a secularization of experience. 19
There are other examples, but you get the idea. 20
Remember that we have yet to find a language that is
common to the Occident 21

And Orient, except for the language of technology.   22
Consider, then, the difficulties of speaking to the Fourth World,
the world of   23
Those who are "different" with a difference that is independent
of geography;   24
For instance, the mentally different. Secularization   25
Must exclude the mentally different by definition.   26
The mentally different share no images with us and they share no   27
History with us. The mentally different cannot be Modern.   28
The mentally different cannot be trusted in Science.   29
The mentally different cannot appreciate Theater as we know it.   30
One supposes that other differences than mental differences   31
Separate the Fourth World from the three that communicate   32
With such difficulty now. For instance, feeling.   33
Suppose for a moment that beginning this instant, while   34
Nothing in you changes mentally, you enter into a state of   35
Permanent rapture, maybe not more intense than the pleasure   36
You felt standing in the meadow of your imagination and being   37
Addressed by name, without the ambiguity of distance, by   38
Some animate being or knowing system in an elevated position   39
—to simplify the image a great deal without changing it   40
Structurally—but *as* intense   41
And without the encumbrance of the image.   42
I think this is what is meant by pure bliss.   43
The feeling without the image. You could not be Modern.   44
You could not be trusted in Science. You could not appreciate   45
Theater as we know it. You would be in the same relationship   46
To the Real Worlds, One, Two and Three, as if you were   47
Mentally different, and you would never be able
to communicate to   48
Those worlds that while intent upon a state of permanent rapture,   49
You are mentally OK. You could do it by reference to the   50
Dream, but remember you would not have had the dream—   51
Might not know what dreams were—and to try to communicate   52
Through the image of the dream would reveal the *passing* nature of your   53
Rapture. The Fourth World is different from the other Three,   54
Otherwise we wouldn't need words at all, and it is different in the words.   55
Now, the problem you will have in dealing with your dream as a   56
Yardstick in your life is that it will fade. The greatest of the   57
Prophets, Moses, the first Jew we can remember, was   58
Very discouraging about the use of images. He thought that   59
Any attempt to *animate* the world in one's imagination, to give it   60
Any meaning at all, is a big mistake. If you, for instance, think of   61
Dogs as "little" because they are smaller than you think   62
You are, you have a long way to go before you rest.   63
Traditionally, when imagination becomes too strong,   64
Cultures resort to very strong chemical treatments,   65
Usually from the vegetable world, to burn off the waste,   66
Which is where the imagination arises. I think   67

You must do some of that. Don't be frightened of the first stage,   68
In which the imagination is purposely inflamed.   69
Remember who you are. Stay near help. And don't give up.   70
Eventually, you will come to pure bliss. The images will disappear.   71
Dreams will stop. You won't need me.   72
— —   73

THANK YOU, DOCTOR.   74
NOT TOO WELL SAID, BUT SOMETHING.   75
GRANTED IT'S A HARD IDEA.   76
HARD TO EXPRESS AND FAR FROM REASSURING.   77
BUT WE'LL KEEP YOUR CARD ON FILE. JUST IN CASE.   78

  [12:50]

End of Scene Fourteen

SCENE FIFTEEN
The Good Life

LINDA
COMPANION
CHORUS (PARENTHESES, CAPS)
(LINDA *parentheses, italic*)

LINDA:
I can't imagine why I told that doctor my dream.   1
(SHE CAN'T IMAGINE WHY SHE TOLD THAT DOCTOR HER DREAM.)
We had just been introduced.   2
(THEY HAD JUST BEEN INTRODUCED.)
We might have made friends.   3
(THEY MIGHT HAVE MADE FRIENDS.)
It was like I was showing him pictures of my family from my wallet.   4
(IT WAS LIKE SHE WAS SHOWING HIM PICTURES

COMPANION:
Fourteen dollars and twenty-eight cents for your thoughts, Linda.   5
OF HER FAMILY FROM HER WALLET.)
I'm sorry. I was day-dreaming.   6
(SHE'S SORRY. SHE WAS DAY-DREAMING.)
You're not kidding. I've been sending you signals for the
last five minutes.   7
(HE'S BEEN SENDING HER SIGNALS FOR THE LAST FIVE MINUTES.)
I was thinking about that Doctor I met at the party last night.   8
(SHE WAS THINKING ABOUT THAT DOCTOR SHE MET AT THE
And you know what he wanted!   9
PARTY LAST NIGHT.) (DOES SHE KNOW WHAT HE WANTED?)
You're looking tired. You're not taking care of yourself.   10

(LINDA):
(Do I look tired? I thought I looked good.
He should have seen me a
Now, what have you had to eat today? Don't leave anything out.
Even a cup of coffee counts.   11
year ago.)
(DOES SHE LOOK TIRED? SHE THOUGHT SHE LOOKED GOOD.)
There was my alarm radio. I left the music on for about twenty minutes,   17
(HE SHOULD HAVE SEEN HER A YEAR AGO.)
then I wanted to get the weather, I turned it off.   13
(SHE LEFT THE MUSIC ON FOR ABOUT TWENTY MINUTES,
Music has no calories   14
THEN SHE WANTED TO GET THE WEATHER, THEN SHE TURNED IT OFF.)

But you have to count the toothpaste.   15
(FIRST THE SMELL AND THEN THE TOOTHPASTE.)
Toothpaste . . .   16
(TOOTHPASTE . . .)
I got some soap in my mouth, when I was washing my face.   17
(SHE GOT SOME SOAP IN HER MOUTH,
WHEN SHE WAS WASHING HER FACE.)
    I'll bet I can list them for you.   18
        (I don't know about that.)
    Coffee   19
        (First, tea.)
    First, tea.   20
        (More caffeine.)
    Toast with butter.   21
        (One hundred calories.)
    Orange juice.   22
        (This is sixteen hours ago.)
    Your morning cigarette.   23
        (My morning cigarette.)
The newspaper.   24
(HEADLINES, PICTURES, ASTROLOGY, RECIPES WITH GUILT,
PICTURES OF
    You can only count what you put in your body.   25
WORLD LEADERS, MAINLY MEN AND WOMEN WHO LOOK LIKE MEN,
PICTURES OF WOMEN (WHO LOOK LIKE WOMEN),
        (I can only count what I put in my body.)
What about the pictures?   26
LETTERS TO THE EDITOR SAVING THE LANGUAGE, COMIC STRIPS,
MAST HEADS—THEN, THE ORDER GETS BLURRY.)
    OK, you can count the pictures, but not the astrology.   27
(SATURN: A LONG DAY WITH A LOT OF EXCITEMENT.
YOU TEND TO DRAW ATTENTION
What about the flowers you gave me? What about the smells?   28
TO YOURSELF. TAKE CHANCES, BUT BE PREPARED
FOR A HARD KNOCK OR TWO.)
    If you count smells, you have to count the bad ones, too.   29
(IF YOU COUNT SMELLS, YOU HAVE TO COUNT THE BAD ONES, TOO.)
OK. No smells.
    Do it as fast as you can. I'll bet you can't get   30
    half of them.   31
(HALF OF WHAT?)
The toothpaste.   32
I got soap in my mouth.   33
One prescription antihistamine.   34
Half a valium.   35
Two cups of tea with nothing.   36
Glass of orange juice.   37
Piece of toast with butter.   38
Two cups of black coffee.   39

Two nicotine cigarettes. 40
Small amount of cocaine. 41
(By mouth now. Wish I could go back to the real way,
One nicotine cigarette. 42
but that's gone forever. Regret.)
Toothpaste. 43
Trace of mouthwash. 44
Four cigarettes. 45
Black coffee. 46
Part of a sweet roll. 47
Three nicotine cigarettes. 48
Part of a marijuana cigarette. 49
One nicotine cigarette. 50
Glass of red wine. 51
Two slices of French bread, with butter. 52
Some eggs cooked in milk and flour with small pieces of vegetables
almost too small to count. 53
(BUT THEN WHAT ABOUT THE FLAVOR? WHY ARE THEY THERE?)
Some lettuce with some kind of oil, cheap olive oil and vinegar
and garlic. 54
Black coffee. 55
One nicotine cigarette. 56
Part of a marijuana cigarette. 57
Some nicotine cigarettes. 58
Black coffee. 59
A piece of chocolate candy. 60
Little bit of cocaine. 61
Some nicotine cigarettes. 62
Alcohol and fruit juice. 63
Some salty fried things. 64
(WHO CAN TELL ANYMORE.)
Glass of wine. 65
One nicotine cigarette. 66
(SHE'LL NEVER FINISH.)
A complicated dinner. I can't do it all. 67
(MEAT AND VEGETABLES, ALL KINDS OF FLAVORS, SUGAR.)
Black coffee. 68
Nicotine cigarettes. 69
A small amount of cocaine. 70
(SMALL AMOUNT OF COCAINE.)
This is all mixed up now.
(SWEET THINGS. CHEESE. WINE. CIGARETTES.
PART OF A MARIJUANA CIGARETTE.)
Smoke from some powder heated up that they say is a kind of opium. 72
(THIS IS VERY SPECIAL. TOO EXPENSIVE FOR HER.
AND SHE DOESN'T KNOW WHO SELLS IT
And here we are. 73
TO WHOM OR HOW IT'S DONE. AND HERE SHE IS AND HERE HE IS.)

More black coffee and more sweet things. 74
(ANOTHER CIGARETTE.)
When we get back to the car, I'll give you some more cocaine. 75
I could give it to you now and you could do it in the bathroom. 76
No thanks. 77
(MEN GIVE DRUGS TO WOMEN.)
What happens when you get home? 78
Cigarettes. Cup of tea to make me sleep. Maybe some marijuana. 79
(THE OTHER HALF OF THE VALIUM. TOOTHPASTE.)
Do you think that you could get through a whole day on
your own? 80
(DOES SHE THINK SHE COULD GET THROUGH A WHOLE DAY
ON HER OWN?)
Do you mean without prayer? 81
(DOES HE MEAN WITHOUT PRAYER?)
Very funny. Do you pray? 82
Do moods count? 83
(DO MOODS COUNT?)
What do you mean? 84
(WHAT DOES SHE MEAN?)
Sometimes I get in a certain mood and I think it must be what
prayer is like. 85
(SOMETIMES SHE GETS IN A CERTAIN MOOD, AND SHE THINKS
THAT MUST BE WHAT PRAYER IS LIKE.)
Maybe. I thought you had to actually do something. 86
(HE THOUGHT YOU HAD TO ACTUALLY DO SOMETHING.)
You mean like get down on your knees? 87
(DOES HE MEAN LIKE GET DOWN ON YOUR KNEES?)
Well, maybe. I thought that was the point. 88
(HE THOUGHT THAT WAS THE POINT.)
What do you mean? 89
(SHE WANTS TO KNOW WHAT HE MEANS.)
I thought you had to humiliate yourself or something like that. 90
(HE THOUGHT YOU HAD TO HUMILIATE YOURSELF OR SOMETHING
LIKE THAT.)
I guess I don't pray, then. 91
(SHE GUESSES SHE DOESN'T PRAY, THEN.)
You do exercises. 92
(HE SAYS SHE DOES EXERCISES.)
Not any more. 93
(NOT ANY MORE.)

Scene Fifteen interrupted [18:00]

SCENE SIXTEEN
Trouble

NARRATOR II (FEMALE)

During this conversation a man seated at another table 1
with a party of other men has begun attracting 2
her attention in the crudest kind of way. 3
Where do they come from, these guys? 4
What do they do when they're not acting like this? 5
The men are laughing loudly. She and her companion 6

| | are the subject of the jokes. That's obvious. | 7 |

Scene Sixteen interrupted
Segue to Scene Fifteen

are the subject of the jokes. That's obvious. 7
She is afraid of what is happening. 8
[18:26.5]

SCENE FIFTEEN
continued

LINDA:
I think we ought to go now. 94
(SHE THINKS THEY OUGHT TO GO NOW.)
    COMPANION:
    I do, too. Those drunks are making me mad. 95
Don't do anything. Just ignore them. 96
(SHE ASKS HIM NOT TO DO ANYTHING SHE ASKS HIM TO IGNORE THEM.)
We can pay the waiter on the way out. 97
(SHE WANTS TO PAY THE WAITER ON THE WAY OUT.

Scene Fifteen interrupted
Segue to Scene Sixteen

MEN ACTING THIS WAY CONFUSE HER.)
[18:40]

SCENE SIXTEEN
continued

They stand to go. To walk by the men 9
laughing at them is the direct way. 10
To take another path would invite comment. 11
She walks past the table ahead of her companion. 12
As he starts to walk past the same spot, 13
the man at the table leans back suddenly, 14
knocking him into a person at a third table. Much laughter. 15
Her companion puts the coats he is carrying, his and hers, 16
on the nearest chair, and hits the man who leaned into him 17
more or less in the face. This is what it has been leading 18
up to. Two other men from the table grab her companion 19
clumsily. The fourth is laughing loudly. She 20
notices how much the men are grunting. 21
Other people in the restaurant are talking loudly. 22
Two waiters are there almost immediately. 23
Their authority prevails. The man who was 24
attracting her attention fakes some kind of 25
emotion. He calls her ugly names. 26
There is still pushing and shoving. A woman from 27
another table is talking loudly to the drunken man who 28
started the trouble. He answers her in 29
vile language. Her companion, then, 30
strikes the drunk very hard and quickly. 31
The drunk is obviously hurt. His face is bleeding. 32
The other three men from the party 33
talk loudly, but they are afraid. 34
Suddenly, there are two policemen in the room. 35
Everybody is surprised. Why are they 36
here? With so much authority. 37
The drunken men pretend that they are sober. 38
But they respond too quickly to the policemen 39
and to the commands. They argue. 40
The younger waiter explains quickly to the 41

policemen. He called them earlier. He saw the 42
trouble coming. There is very little discussion. 43
This is the source of the police authority. 44
They have learned not to listen unless they have asked to be told. 45
They are not interested in blame. Before anyone is 46
aware that it has been done they have the names of everyone in
the restaurant. 47
They have moved the four drunken men to the sidewalk. 48
Another police car arrives, lights flashing, but the policemen do not come 49
into the restaurant. The four drunken men are gone. One of the policemen 50
speaks briefly to the man who struck the drunk and hurt him.
The man looks very 51
sad. His wife is trying to console him. The waiter explains that the 52
restaurant does not expect to be paid. The man and woman leave
quickly, without 53
speaking. The waiter apologizes for what happened. He saw 54
the trouble coming, but he didn't know how to stop it. 55

End of Scene Sixteen
Segue to Scene Fifteen

He called the police. They didn't get here in time. 56

[21:20]

SCENE FIFTEEN
continued

LINDA:
Four nicotine cigarettes. 98
(ONE LEFT FOR TOMORROW MORNING.)
A little bit of brandy. 99
(IT'S ALWAYS TOO STRONG. WHY DO PEOPLE DRINK IT?)
Marijuana. 100
End of the cocaine. 101
Five grain valium. 102
(USE THE BROKEN TAB TOMORROW.)
Toothpaste. 103
(A FAKE MINT FLAVOR.)
AND THE TROUBLES ARE PUT ASIDE 104
WELL NOT QUITE. LET'S SAY—PUT 105
INSIDE. BEST NOT THOUGHT OF. 106
BUT THE CITY HAS LOST ITS CHARM. 107
AND WHAT FOLLOWS IS A RECORD OF REWARDS 108
WITHOUT SWEETNESS. WHAT ELSE IS THERE IS SAY? 109

End of Scene Fifteen

[22:00]

SCENE SEVENTEEN
**A Place
In The
Country**

NARRATOR I (MALE)
DOCTOR
MRS. PAYNE
CHORUS (IN CAPS)

NARRATOR I:
She makes a name for herself at work 1
    DOCTOR:
    She speaks sharply if she disagrees 2
        MRS. PAYNE:
        Attracting respect for her opinions 3
        This is as high as I can go 4
        How do you know that you know it? 5
She wins a large cash prize in the lottery 6
    She allows her picture in all of the papers 7
        Showing a permanent disbelief 8

This is as high as I can go   9
How do you know that you know it?   10
She is trapped with a man in an elevator   11
She imagines he looks like her father   12
Television is there when they get out   13
This is as high as I can go   14
How do you know that you know it?   15
"Approaching the present, time is compressed   16
Toward an infinite Now, infinitely fast"   17
She tells them (What an idea, Linda!)   18
This is as high as I can go   19
How do you know that you know it?   20
She finally buys an apartment in town   21
Through a cousin who works in the government   22
—and does real estate on the side   23
This is as high as I can go   24
How do you know that you know it?   25
The picture window reminds her of Don   26
It looks west toward what could be water   27
(The best views are all bought by the Army)   28
This is as high as I can go   29
How do you know that you know it?   30
She inherits a place in the country   31
She visits once and then puts it in trust   32
"For cousins, Of cousins, From cousins, Forever"   33
This is as high as I can go   34
How do you know that you know it?   35
She visits Europe (partially business)   36
She sees too much that reminds her of home   37
But a sense of the past is still there   38
This is as high as I can go   39
How do you know that you know it?   40
Back home she encounters the man from the restaurant   41
She feels sympathy and he doesn't know her   42
He wears the same brown shirt and tie   43
This is as high as I can go   44
How do you know that you know it?   45
She finally remembers her companion's name   46
She lists everything she's done today   47
All diet and exercise (thoughts for the future)   48
This is as high as I can go   49
How do you know that you know it?   50

WE'VE REACHED THE END, ALMOST. YOU CAN READ IT IN THE VOICE, NOT TO MENTION WHAT SHE'S   51
SAID. SO IMAGINE, NOW, FOR THE NEXT FEW MINUTES, AN OLDER WOMAN   52
STILL BEAUTIFUL, SENSE OF WONDER INTACT, PLAYING BRIDGE WITH FRIENDS,   53
THE DAY DREAMING INSEPARABLE FROM THE NARRATIVE, SUCH AS IT IS.   54
NOTICE THAT SHE TRIES TO TELL US ABOUT SOMETHING UNUSUAL. AN EXPERIENCE.   55
SHE DOESN'T TELL IT VERY WELL. THEN A LETTER FROM HER SON. THEN WHAT'S IN THE CARDS.   56
End of Scene Seventeen   [25:06]

SCENE EIGHTEEN
Happiness, Prosperity and Forgetfulness

	MR. PAYNE (plus [+] voices added to those already singing):	
	Places better	1
	On the horizon	2
	The Wanderer (copyright)	3
+ MRS. PAYNE:	Pretends she doesn't	4
	The way she thinks	5
+ NARRATOR I:	Now the idea of	6
	Refuge, the idea of	7
+ DOCTOR:	Looking ahead to	8
	The sun and a pool	9
+ NARRATOR II:	"Wherever she goes	10
	she learns the dances	11
	she learns the language	12
	faster than anyone"	13
+ JUNIOR, JR.:	Miami (Cuba)	14
	Chicago (Germany)	15
	Hollywood (Aztlan)	16
	Then gone	17
LINDA:	Oh, well, forget it	18
MR. PAYNE:	Scrapbooks from home	19
	Old occupations	20
+MRS. PAYNE:	A craze for religion	21
	Changes her name	22
	Jesus Brings Happiness	23
	Changes it back	24
+ NARRATOR I:	Thinks she sees—	25
	I'm almost positive	26
	Tanned (with a mustache!)	27
	More heavy and serious	28
	Careless with urgency	29
+ DOCTOR:	Troubled (she watches)	30
	She follows (unthinking)	31
+ NARRATOR II:	He *disappears*	32
	She follows, approaches	33
+ JUNIOR, JR.:	He *disappears*	34
	He's gone	35
LINDA:	Oh, well, forget it	36

CHORUS:
FOR A FEW DAYS SHE THINKS SHE SHOULD CONSULT WITH SOMEONE   37
BUT THESE ARE THE KINDS OF THINGS THAT WHEN YOU TELL PEOPLE   38
THAT'S WHAT YOU'VE EXPERIENCED AND THAT'S WHAT CONCERNS YOU   39
THEY MISUNDERSTAND AND TAKE YOUR CONCERN (FOR YOUR SANITY)   40
MORE SERIOUSLY THAN THEY TAKE THE EXPERIENCE—WHAT IT   41
MIGHT MEAN IF IT WERE SIMPLY FACTUAL AND UNINTERPRETED.   42

LINDA:
Those men go out to space in those little capsules with their   43
brains and their imaginations tested for any possible thing   44
going wrong but they come back "changed" by something and   45

162

                                   then we stop believing them and believing in them when just   46
                                   recently their experiences were an ultimate authority for us   47
                                   and their reports of their experiences were all we had.   48

IN OTHER WORDS, AT THE MOMENT WHEN YOU MOST NEED HELP   49
IN THE FORM OF BELIEF IN THE AUTHORITY OF YOUR EXPERIENCE—   50
THE EXTENT OF THE EXPERIENCE (HOW IT COMPARES TO OTHERS, ITS   51
POWER) IS THE VERY WAY WE MEASURE WHETHER THE EXPERIENCE IS   52
SOMETHING YOU MIGHT HAVE HAD OR WHETHER IT IS JUST SOMETHING   53
YOU DREAMED UP AND YOU REALLY NEED A DIFFERENT KIND OF HELP.   54

MR. PAYNE: I'm almost positive   55
                                   But then   56
                                   Does it change anything   57
+ MRS. PAYNE: Whoever it was   58
                                   Did it the same   59
+ NARRATOR I: What I said, though,   60
                                   He seemed to know   61
+ DOCTOR: No sign of—   62
                                   "recognition"—and   63
                                   He seemed to know   64
+ NARRATOR II: He was closer than you are   65
                                   Three steps away   66
                                   I saw the sign   67
                                   not "recognition"   68
                                   Acknowledgement   69
+ JUNIOR, JR.:   ("Which card is the red one?")   70
                                   Then gone   71
LINDA: Oh, well, forget it.   72

IT OCCURS TO HER FINALLY THAT UNLESS THERE ARE TO BE   73
MANY OF THESE THINGS IN HER LIFE AND THE WHOLE LIFE   74
CHANGES IN TUNE WITH THEM THEN SHE IS ALLOWING THE   75
EXPERIENCE TO CAST A SHADOW OVER OTHER KINDS OF THINGS   76
THAT ARE MORE IMPORTANT TO HER AND THAT BEFORE THE EXPERIENCE   77
HAD GONE UNNOTICED, UNATTENDED AND UNEXPLORED.   78

SHE SAYS TO HERSELF WHENEVER SHE GETS TRAPPED NOW IN   79
THE "HOW MANY OF US ARE THERE" KIND OF QUESTIONS   80
YOU HAVE TO LEARN TO KEEP YOUR MOUTH SHUT ABOUT   81
SOMETHING THAT IS ONLY A PART OF YOU EVEN IF IT IS   82
UNUSUAL OR THAT PART OF YOU WILL GET IN THE WAY OF   83
HAVING THE "PLEASURE" OF THE OTHER PARTS.   84

                                   LINDA:
                                   That's harder than you think because as we all know   85
                                   the palaces of the imagination are full of   86
                                   people who have no imagination to speak of.   87
                                   Something happened to them that no one believes.   88
                                   They have become untrustworthy in our eyes.   89
                                   We must convince them that they are wrong.   90

MR. PAYNE:	Years pass	91
	It's forgotten	92
	Just forgotten	93
+ MRS. PAYNE:	Proving that one	94
	Experience	95
	Among many is	96
	One among many.	97
+ NARRATOR I:	Learn to play bridge	98
	The pleasure of company	99
+ DOCTOR:	Systems of memory	100
	(Cards out of focus!)	101
+ NARRATOR II:	"How to Remember"	102
	Memories shared	103
+ JUNIOR, JR.	I used to smoke cigarettes	104
	I used to love dancing	105
	I used to stay up late	106
	Then gone	107
LINDA:	Oh, well, forget it	108

LINDA:
Nearest of all in memory is Mr. Payne: "it can end   109
so suddenly, so completely, and who remembers what   110
the reason was?" I heard, much after it had happened,   111
that he had been seriously hurt. It seemed almost   112
unimaginable to me. It was clear when I was with him   113
that he had to suffer. That was written all over him.   114
The suffering was there, had probably always been there   115
in him. It must have come to him and been accepted   116
by him when he was very young. But hurt is different   117
from suffering. It's a kind of insult. And so it was   118
unimaginable that both could be together in one person,   119
and that that person could endure.   120

Next nearest in memory is the guy—what is his name?   121
This moment! Now! this moment! No, now it's   122
too late. If it's not there, it's never been   123
a part of you. The Doctor told a funny story about   124
a man who lost his fiancée's name when he was   125
introducing her to someone at the announcement party.   126

She walked out and refused to go through with   127
the marriage. The Doctor was sure that she had   128
done the right thing, and I asked if he meant   129
that from a defensive point of view or whether   130
you could take it from the point of view of jousting,   131
or whatever. He didn't understand my question.   132

The guy I wanted to put nearest to Mr. Payne,   133
the guy next in my life—the nameless one—   134
could never understand what I was telling him   135
about myself. We always stayed up too late,   136
and—he could never understand. Everything   137
a girl could want, except—I had to leave.   138

Who is next in memory? Oh, yes, my days with 139
the founder of The Paris Salon of Beauty, Inc. 140
("I Am A Reductionist:" By Appointment.) 141
A charming view with modernistic furniture and 142
a closet full of French clothing in America. 143
Imagine those characters in the closet plotting. 144

The angry exiles. Their revolution. That was 145
the most fun about him and I couldn't tell him. 146
He was a charmer with certainty like sunshine. 147
Nothing without a reason. Daylight. No whispers. 148
I heard a constant whirring motion. High pitched. 149
The idea of the perfect machine. Admired. 150

What does it take to make one stop looking? 151
First, midnight dancing in the arcade cathedral. 152
Pure happiness, if that word means anything. 153
Then—this is funnier than I thought—Prosperity: 154
"Gourmet Foods from Around the World (24 hours)." 155
Finally, the idea of the perfect body. Forgetfulness. 156

End of Scene Eighteen
Segue to Scene Nineteen

You'd think I'd look a little better than I do. 158
[33:48]

SCENE NINETEEN
The Bridge Game

LINDA
with JUNIOR, JR.
CHORUS (IN CAPS)

+ JUNIOR, JR.:
(in duet, humming)
•
•
•
•
•
•
•
•
•
•
•
•
•
•

LINDA:
I'd like to read you this letter from my son. 1
My pride is boundless. It seems so perfect. 2
The way he has found a life that pleases him. 3
His mind is so clear about what he calls 4
"reality." No grudge against his father. 5
No grudge against his mother, I hope. No 6
trace of something hanging in the air about him. 7
Where did he learn to dress so well? How did he 8
come by such confidence and poise—after 9
what he went through? It makes him very happy. 10
Dear Mom, everything is going well. 11
I love the summer in the winter here. 12
I hope to get a new assignment. 13
The Office has a new, large project. 14
They call it by a famous painter's name. 15
You'll read about it in the papers. 16
When you do, you'll know where I am. 17
That's as much as I can say. 18
I meet the most interesting people 19
Yesterday it was a man who sells— 20
I have to think about the way to say this— 21
A very common object that we never see. 22
Couldn't get anywhere without it. 23
Old as the wheel. And that's a hint. 24
Some Italians thought about it differently. 25

JUNIOR, JR.:	That's as much as I can say.	26
(continues humming)	Anyway, we bought thousands of them.	27
•	Does that give you an idea?	28
•	He's the strangest man I've ever seen.	29
•	Didn't care about the Office Project.	30
•	Didn't know the painter's name.	31
•	Took the Executive Washroom for two hours!	32
JUNIOR, JR.:	Can you imagine? Two hours!	33
(continues humming)	I asked a person (whose name you know)	34
•	Why do we do business with him?	35
•	You'll never guess the answer.	36
•	"HE MAKES THE BEST ONES IN THE WORLD."	37
JUNIOR, JR.	The common object that we never see.	38
(continues humming)	Two hours in the Executive Washroom.	39
•	So what? Disturbs the Office staff.	40
•	So what? The best ones in the world.	41
•	He calls his employees, "My subjects."	42
•	And there's funnier stuff than that.	43
•	Incredible pictures of his family.	44
•	We're in stitches. He's around	45
•	a few more days. Then he goes	46
•	Off on contract for the Office.	47
•	A CONSULTATION. GOD KNOWS WHAT THEY'LL SEE.	48
•	The Office has a large-scale project.	49
JUNIOR, JR.	I said that, already, didn't I?	50
(in duet)	The Project's in my specialty.	51
•	Maybe the reason I was hired.	52
•	I want to measure the unmeasurable.	53
•	Reconcile the incommensurable.	54
JUNIOR, JR.	The world could use this.	55
(in duet)	And I like the painter's name.	56
•	It even sounds like success,	57
•	if you begin with what is—	58
•	"silent, as in swimming."	59
•	Remember that old joke?	60
•	Then make the second sound	61
•	(FIRST, DROP THE ESS)	62
•	broader, as in father.	63
•	Then, add an oh, as in, say—	64
•	Regret for a father lost.	65
JUNIOR, JR.	That's as much as I should say.	66
(in duet)	I'll write to you again, soon.	67
•	Maybe I'll have a permanent address.	68
•	Meantime, use the Office one.	69
•	Letters get to me eventually.	70
•	Hope your bridge is getting better.	71
•	Love, your hardworking Son.	72

His specialty is measuring the use of   73
energy in what he calls "Unknown Systems."   74
As far as I can understand it,   75
he thinks about whether humans   76
could exist on other food than—   77
what we call food. Imagine.   78
He thinks vitamins are old-fashioned,   79
but a good idea. I take them.   80
God only knows what he takes.   81
I love his letters, but I can't   82
understand them. He's so secretive.   83
But what he can't tell me in this one   84
will be in the papers and on TV   85
tomorrow. Just wait and see.   86

NARRATOR II:
And that's the end of Linda's story.   87
Playing bridge with friends.   88
Sharing pictures from the past—   89
too complicated for photography.   90
— —   91

THIS IS THE LAST HAND. IT'S GETTING LATE   92
NORTH: BERLIN, A TANGO. MIXED EMOTIONS.   93
EAST: RIVER ROUGE. THE RED RIVER. THE MOVEMENT.   94
SOUTH: CAMPO DEI FIORI (ROME). EARLY WARNING.   95
WEST: ATLANTIS, WHERE WHAT CAME BEFORE AND NOW ARE JOINED. 96
                                                      [39:08]

End of Scene Nineteen
Segue to Scene Twenty

SCENE TWENTY
NORTH
(BERLIN/A TANGO)

CHORUS (IN CAPS)
LINDA

TENTATIVE AND OF TWO MINDS SHE   1
            about the tango records is   2
AND ABOUT   NOSTALGIA   HERE   3
            especially   questions of   4
RESPECTABILITY   ABOUT   5
            nostalgia   great distances   6
LONGINGS   FEAR AND BRAVERY MIXED   7
            argentina   (etcetera)   8
LOOK   THE BOY HAS WILD, YELLOW HAIR,   9
            a café   ("everyone's a spy")   10
GREEN HAIR, DARK HAIR, LAYERED BANDS OF   11
            meeting places   in the open   12
GRAFFITI   "A"   ADVERTISEMENTS   13
            "for music, sir"   (not anarchy)   14
CORRECTS HER ENGLISH   IS HAPPY   15
            proud and fearful   das gewissen   16
SUDDENLY THE MUSIC IS BACK   17
            listen for words now   the answer   18
THE HIGH DRUMS AGAIN (. . . PROPORTIONS)   19
            evening   the idea of a place   20
BEYOND, WHERE THE WESTERN OCEAN   21
            is not far   the usefulness of   22

WATER ON THE HAIR THE BEAUTY		23
. . . glistens something interrupted		24
THE IDEA (A LITTLE WORN, NOW)		25
the divided city penance		26
AS IF, APART FROM THE IDEA . . .		27
and watching a tango berlin		28
EINER BERLINER REMEMBERED		29
i am a half dollar ich bin		30
DALLAS (ARGENTINA) FEAR WITH		31
bravery mixed nostalgia		32

End of Scene Twenty
Segue to Scene Twenty-one   [40:56]

SCENE TWENTY-ONE
EAST
(RIVER ROUGE)

THE BIGGEST BUILDING   1
IN THE WORLD   2
PAYS ME FIVE A DAY.   3

CHORUS

BRAND NEW SUIT,   4
CIGARETTES,   5
I DON'T CARE WHAT YOU SAY.   6

WORDS CAN NEVER CHANGE IT.   7
MONEY TALKS.   8

End of Scene Twenty-one   WORK IS HERE TO STAY.   9
Segue to Scene Twenty-two   [41:26]

SCENE TWENTY-TWO
SOUTH
(CAMPO DEI FIORI,
 ROME)

LINDA
CHORUS (IN CAPS)

I say to them, look, twenty-eight   1
million, two hundred seventy-eight thousand,   2
four hundred sixty-six (the figure   3
makes it real!), all facing the same way,   4
arms raised, allow their image to be snapped? 5
We're supposed to take that idea   6
seriously? You must be kidding.   7
BUT THEY DO.   8

Almost unimaginable. Twenty-eight   9
million, two hundred seventy-eight thousand,   10
four hundred sixty-six (calculated   11
simply!), all facing the same way,   12
arms raised, allow their image to be snapped. 13
To represent an idea? You can't   14
believe they could hold still.   15
BUT THEY DO.   16

I try to tell them. I hear others   17
try to tell them that it's a big mistake.   18
It's unspeakable. A flash of light. Twenty-eight 19
million, two hundred seventy-eight thousand,   20
four hundred sixty-six (because it   21
happened once!) could perish in a flash of light. 22
They deny that they admit the possibility.   23
BUT THEY DO.   24

WHAT COMES NEXT IS WHAT WAS FIRST, OR SO THEY SAY. 25
AS FAR BACK AS WE CAN GO 26
(AT LEAST ON THIS SYSTEM). 27
NOTICE THAT WE SPEAK OF IT WITH AWE. 28
AS IF THERE WERE PERFECTION ONCE. THAT'S NICE. 29

End of Scene Twenty-two   AND AS IF THERE IS RENEWAL. THAT'S NICE, TOO. 30
Segue to Scene Twenty-three   [43:06]

SCENE TWENTY-THREE   *Some islands* 1
WEST   GONE NOW 2
(ATLANTIS)   *The first among us* 3
TALKED ABOUT 4

LINDA
CHORUS (IN CAPS)   *Some islands* 5
GONE NOW 6
Safe place for sailors 7
TALKED ABOUT 8

Some islands 9
GONE NOW 10
Lost in an instant 11
TALKED ABOUT 12

Some islands 13
GONE NOW 14
Still in the papers 15
TALKED ABOUT 16

End of Scene Twenty-three   [44:00]

END OF OPERA

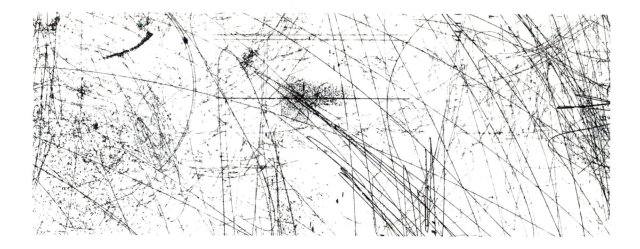

Yoko Ono

Yoko Ono is the perfect example. I first heard of her 20 years ago when tapes of her unique warble came to KPFA (in Berkeley) from New York. Before long her book Grapefruit came out, revealing her as a serious artist within the Fluxus movement. Then she met John Lennon and the rest, as they say, is history—though still a bit too much misunderstood, like most history. Life with Lennon focused her work, but I suspect interrupted it as well—think of the movies she was making at about that time, Rape especially, the one in which an innocent victim is followed all over London by a relentless cinematographer and sound man: here Yoko was seriously bringing Fluxus into a new, more extensive direction—Andy Warhol did too, by the way, in The Chelsea Girls, at about the same time. Now, as you'll see, she's working through the terrible culmination of life with John, working out the resumption of life without him. Vulnerability is difficult but must be faced, and Yoko Ono's distinctive voice has always faced it, unflinchingly.

—C.S.

YOKO ONO

The Editors
November 1984; New York City

*We crossed out death
on our list.*

Yes, we have rather exhausted that subject, I think. I'm not going to say "no" to any issue. In other words, don't worry about it, it just scared me when I saw the list, but you know, if you just ask me naturally, it doesn't hurt me. It will be like a Rorschach test. When you say something, something comes to my head, I'll say it—so don't worry.

*Okay, the first subject area is music
and art, and the basic question
is, what do you think the sources
and/or purposes of music are?*

Well, all right—I can only talk about myself. I don't know what the purpose of music is, but I know what the purpose of music is for me. For me it's a way of expressing myself—and sharing my feelings with other people. And I think that, basically, because I'm a shy person—which will never be believed—I'm not very good at, or shall we say I'm awkward in expressing my true feelings to people—whether it's to one, or the world. And it comes easier for me when I do it in music. And that's how I do it.

*Obviously, at some point there
must have been a decision on your
part or a sudden revelation that
it was music that was your way
of expressing yourself?*

To tell the truth, I'll tell you the truth, when I was four years old my mother sent me to school where you got the perfect pitch and piano lessons, one of those schools where a first assignment was to compose a song. And my old classmate . . . I bumped into her on the street in Japan much later, and she said, "Hey, I still have your song." And I said, "What song?" You know, I was thinking that maybe she got my record or something. She said, "No no, when you composed it, you know, in school when you were four years old." "Wow, could I have it?" I said. Of course, I never got it from her. I was writing songs, just as all the other children were, it's nothing special, and they used to have, once a month or something, a show for the parents—they used to have a little concert for parents to come see how their children were doing. And I was so nervous before I went on the stage,

I started to have this strange tummy ache, and I threw up. I went on the stage, and I came back, and I threw up again. I remember that. I was particularly small—many physical aspects of me they always think of as a Japanese thing, but not necessarily, I was even small for a Japanese— and so this tiny thing comes on stage and starts to sort of climb up on the chair to try playing the piano—of course it's funny, so they all laughed you know. But the thing is, I took it as an offense, you know what I mean— Oh, they're laughing at me. These days when I see a two-year-old saying something so cute I try to control myself not to laugh because, I mean, they take it differently you know. Why are they laughing at me? So I remember specifically that I was feeling terribly embarrassed because everybody was laughing, and I was playing the piano. It started then. It was not my decision, in a way.

I continued the piano lessons until my father, who's actually an incredible pianist—was an incredible pianist—and it was when I was twelve or thirteen. I was too shy to play the piano in front of my father because he's a good pianist, but I wanted to tell him how I was progressing, so when he was in a room, I would go and play in the next room just to let him know that I was working. One day I was playing the piano, and I heard my father say to my mother, "She's never going to make it as a pianist." And I thought, "He's right." He was quite disappointed because, well, my father had made an appearance as a pianist, and he got good reviews and all. Well, I don't care if he got good reviews or not but the main thing was he was a brilliant pianist, and when he was about twenty-one, I think, his father died, and in the will the wishes were that my father would not become a pianist but would go into banking as his father had. And that's a heavy trip. So anyway, he became a banker instead, and he's one of those pianists who's always playing the piano at home. When I was born, my father wanted me to be a pianist so badly. I was the first born, didn't matter if it's a girl or a boy. So he'd be sort of looking at my fingers and asking me to do this or do that, trying to see if I had good hands for a pianist. It was like that from the beginning.

When I was fourteen, I made a big announcement that I wanted to be a composer not a pianist, and my father was listening very carefully, very silently, and said, "Hmm—well I think that's a mistake." I said, "Oh, why?" Not only had I mustered my courage to announce that I'm not going to be a pianist, but I want to be a composer! He's one of those very classic persons, believes in the three big Bs, you know, Brahms, Bach and Beethoven, and all three of them happen to be men, as he politely mentioned. He thought that music composition, in a word, is a field that's too hard for women. And he thought that I had a good voice, and maybe I should go into opera, maybe I can sing at La Scala. For women it's an easier thing to do—to sing somebody else's songs, etc. And I know that my voice became a joke in this society, so people are going to say—oh, no! But I had an incredibly good voice then, which was when I was around seventeen or eighteen, and I had instructors who would say that I could probably make it as an alto, or mezzo-soprano, so I started opera. I started to dislike it *so* intensely. I was supposed to go to music school to study voice, and then eventually go to Italy. I thought, there's something wrong with it. I didn't enjoy singing other people's songs. You know, I like good German *lieder* and all that, they're beautiful, beautifully written, I respected all that, but I had an urge to compose.

So instead of going to music school one day I made an announcement. And this really was an announcement because my father was in New York at the time, and I had to send a telegram saying—"Gave up on taking music school exam, going to university, would like permission . . ."—and my father said,—"If you really want to give up it's too bad, but . . ."—and so I went to the university, the philosophy department. I was happier then because, you know, I was a bookworm and it's nicer just to read books. Then when I went to Sarah Lawrence, I again picked up on composition, and it was pretty nice, I wrote some songs there, and at the time my heroes were the twelve-tone composers, you know—Schönberg, Berg, those people, and I was just fascinated with what they could do. I wrote some twelve-tone songs, then my music went into some sort of area that my composition teacher felt was really a bit off-the-track, and one day—as if he were exasperated—he said, "Well look, there are some people who are doing things like what you do, and they're called *avant-garde*."

Of course, I came from Japan, I didn't know anything about avant-garde. That's the first time I heard John Cage's name. I thought my composition teacher was just saying, "Get off my back." I wasn't even paying much attention to what he said. And Stockhausen, too, I think he was mentioned. Just by chance though, I met Cage afterwards in New York City at a lecture at Columbia University. He was attending the lecture as well. We were sort of introduced. That was in the late fifties, if you can extend your mind back to the late fifties.

I gradually got into the avant-garde or whatever you call it. At the time I was married to Toshi Ichianagi. He was a classical composer who studied in the Juilliard School of Music. He was a scholarship student there. I was not attending the school but I used to go to the school library and read the scores that I would then do at Sarah Lawrence. Toshi was one of those composers who got prizes every year. You know, it's very discouraging to see somebody who is like that. He got the Copland prize, and . . . I don't know, every year he got those prizes. It just comes to him. He's like a child prodigy type who started very young, you know, one of those. Well, when I met John Cage I thought—oh this is it! And I said to Toshi, "Do you realize this is it?" "Well, I've got two minds about that," he said, because he's sort of in the classical tradition, though his music now is very avant-garde. But anyway, John Cage was a bit too extreme for him. Then, later, he got into it too. For me, from then on it was a lot of avant-gardism, you know, for many years—until I met John, I suppose. That was 1966. But all that time I wanted to write songs because I'm a poet as well, and it combines the two. Even in the avant-garde where they didn't

In Kyoto, I had a concert at Yamaichi Hall. It was called "The Strip-tease Show" (it was stripping of the mind). When I met the High Monk the next day, he seemed a bit dissatisfied.
"I went to your concert," he said.
"Thank you, did you like it?"
"Well, why did you have those three chairs on the stage and call it a strip-tease by three?"
"If it is a chair or stone or woman, it is the same thing, my Monk."
"Where is the music?"
"The music is in the mind, my Monk."
"But that is the same with what we are doing, aren't you an avant-garde composer?"

Grapefruit, Yoko Ono,
(New York: Simon and Schuster, 1964).

believe in lyrics, I used to do voice experiments. Now, at the time, it was not well accepted even in the avant-garde because the New York avant-garde was into cool art, not hot. And what I do was too emotional. In a way they thought it was too animalistic. They were into controlling. They used to control the voice, rather than letting it out. And then I went to London, and I was making films and all that, and I met John.

After London I went to Paris, and I was still doing little things in little theatres, and I met Ornette Coleman. Ornette got interested in my voice experiments and said, "I'm invited to do a show in Albert Hall and maybe you'd like to join me?" I was in Paris, and I was having fun, so I wasn't going to go back to London. Also I had had bad experiences before when people said, well do you want to do your voice experiments in my concert or something, they just used me as an instrument and forgot that it was my composition. So I said, "Listen, if your band is willing to play my composition, then I'll do it." So he said, "Of course. It's your composition." So I went to Albert Hall with Ornette, and I wrote my instructions for them, and that instruction was in the program, I think Ornette still has it. Anyway, it had some four-letter words in it, or whatever it was—I think the word was "penis," and that's a five-letter word.

What happened was the Albert Hall tried to threaten us that they're going to close the show because they thought it was obscene. So while we were performing, these people started coming around the hall. I was lucky we were able to finish the concert. It was really funny because Ornette was really into this voice experiment. It was great. He told his band to play it, and just imagine that this jazz band will have to play it the way some sort of kooky girl says to play it. They had some objections, but they respected Ornette, and he said, "Just play it like what she says."

*That's on an album, right?**

* *Yoko and the Plastic Ono Band,* Yoko Ono, (New York: Apple Records, Inc., 1968).

† "ON FILM NO. 4 (in taking the bottoms of 365 saints of our time), spring 1967

This film proves that anyone can be a director . . . I'm hoping that after seeing this film people will start to make their own home movies like crazy. In 50 years or so, people will look at the films of the 60s . . . I hope that they would see that the 60s was not only the age of achievements, but of laughter. This film, in fact, is like an aimless petition signed by people with their anuses."
from *Grapefruit,* Y.O.

Yes, so it was. The way I got into it was, in 1963, when I was in Japan, I thought about doing the "Bottoms"† film. I went to England to do the film; well, not *to do* the "Bottoms" film, I went there, and I did the "Bottoms" film. It's just a coincidence that it happened there. In London, everybody was talking about the "Bottoms" film. It was so outrageous. Everyday I'd see in the newspapers some joke about the "Bottoms" film. Then I thought, well, I've done it all in London, so I went to Paris, but then I came back for the Albert Hall thing, and when I finished I thought, I want to stay just a couple of days, and then when I went back to my apartment I noticed the piles of letters from John, he was in India then. So I was sort of hanging about in London for a while, and then John came back from India and called me. If I hadn't gone back to do the Albert Hall concert, we probably would not have gotten together again.

Then you did a lot of music with John. Were you still doing music by yourself, and with other people?

In 1968 spring, John and I finally got together. And from then on I don't think I performed with anybody else. It was just a totally different situation. We got together in such a way we felt very exclusive about each other. I think there was still one concert at Cambridge that they had asked me to do before I got together with John. And then, when we were together, they called me back saying, "Are you still going to do that one?" So I said, "Okay, I have to do this one, John, because I promised them and all that." So he said, "You should do it, and tell them that you're coming with a band, okay?" And *he* was the band. It was a surprise, you know.

Then you were writing songs, more exclusively as songs?

Well, in London around '67, I was writing songs too, and I was doing some voice experiments. But then, I think Island Records wanted to sign me up, and I went to John and told him, because we knew each other then, and he said, "Well, sign up with Apple." And I was saying "Maybe, maybe." But when we got together, of course, we did do that. I didn't sign up with Island Records because, in those days, I don't know why, but I was very busy and doing so much that I'd forget those things—I mean signing and things like that. Even with the "Bottoms" film. There was a film festival in Belgium in 1967, the Kuokke Film Festival, and they invited me to show the "Bottoms" film. You're supposed to sign some document to register for the festival first, and I forgot that part of it. So I went to the festival, and they showed my film and some of the judges came from America obviously, and they said "We were determined to give you a prize, but we can't because you didn't register."

Could you talk a little about what you were doing with the voice experiments? Did you have certain ideas you were trying out or were you just doing whatever happened?

Well, some of it happened accidentally. In 1960 or '61, in New York, I did a concert of my compositions in Carnegie Recital Hall, and I was going to do some voice experiment in that. I was already doing voice experiment in the sense of all that sort of moan and groan, but in those days, I was playing around with a tape recorder, an old-fashioned tape recorder, you know, where you can record and rewind it. And rewinding, playing it backwards, my voice was even more interesting. Instead of going [*vocal sound*], it goes [*vocal sound*], you know—sort of backwards. The beat is on a different place. And I said, this is interesting. This is beautiful! So I did that in Carnegie Recital Hall, in the dark. And people were saying, "Somebody is screaming or moaning." Jill Johnston wrote the review, in the *Village Voice*. That's all they noticed. Then when I got together with John—and John's group is like "rockers"—we'd go on stage and John would just say, do your own thing, come on, we'll just play behind you. Now, the "rockers" are using electric guitars and it's *loud*. I'm just a voice so give me a chance. I'd have to shout over it. That's how that got started.

It was just a fusion. A free form. John's doing his thing, electric guitar, and I'm singing. It became like a duet. Now, you should listen to *Yoko and the Plastic Ono Band*, which is an experimental album, the Ornette thing is in it. Listen to the first cut, "Why." That's an incredible track, even if you listen to it now. I mean, you can just put it in your disco club and people can dance to it. That's Ringo playing the drums, Klaus Vorman playing the bass. John's doing the guitar. The kind of thing John's doing with the guitar is like a dialogue with my voice. So incredible. Nobody did it before. John and I thought, "We did it, we did it!" and we felt like we'd conquered the world.

So then the album comes out, and we get all these letters with photos of a big garbage can saying "Yoko Ono's record, we put it in here." That sort of response. And John's saying, "Well, it's sort of understandable that they didn't understand you, but why didn't they notice my brilliant guitar playing?" And of course he's right. But sadly, you know, because of me, nobody would listen to his guitar playing. I felt sorry for him about that. I was sort of a hindrance and no one wanted to listen to the track, but he did incredible guitar playing. The kind of thing we were doing then was all improvisation. And because I was into that, I'd say to him, "Listen, we're not going to rehearse anything, this is my game, all right?" So, we're doing that and he was right into it, and he did better than any avant-garde artist I know in this town, okay? And it's just the meeting of the two minds, or the meeting of the two fields, or two countries . . . or the *two worlds*, that's what happened between us. It was just incredible. It's like music between some kind of contemporary jazz and rock, and the avant-garde. It made us very lonely—for being such a couple.

And I kind of wish, now that I see it in hindsight, I kind of wish that they had let us just go on with that. But, artists are very sensitive people, they're not just animals like you expect them to be, we were sort of sensitive to criticism, and applause. If the whole world is hating it, and putting it in the garbage can, we're not going to make it, thank you. So it dwindled in our minds. That sort of inspiration and excitement faded.

So we didn't do very much of it, and whenever we'd do anything in the studio, engineers would just go to the toilet or something. And we're looking around—"Oh, the room's empty." In "Why," right after we'd finished, you hear John saying, "Are you getting that?" It's on the record. He said it because he was so worried that they might have again missed it, that they hadn't recorded it.

Did they think you were just fooling around?

Sometimes they might have thought we were fooling around, sometimes they might have thought they couldn't stand it, so they'd go in the bathroom. Sometimes they might have thought, "Oh, it's Yoko's, forget it." I don't know. Maybe a mixture of those feelings. So John and I were fighting against those odds.

It was so new that no one could hear it.

Now it's not new at all. You play "Why" and think, "Huh, good disco."

But everyone has been influenced by what you were doing.

Well, I wouldn't claim that. It's more coincidence, and accidents, and all that. Everything in the world happens like that, it's just chance. You know, it's just by chance, so I can't claim originality or anything, just like I told you how my voice happened because the electric guitar was too loud. So to compete with that you start doing this. In one of the pieces I think I realized that I can sing three notes at the same time, which again I'm not doing by controlling it or anything. I just started doing it, and I said, "Oh, this is great!" And later, one of those doctors who checks your throat said, there's a little sort of pea-sized something on my vocal chord, and maybe that's the reason. From an early age I could sing a very wide range— like alto, mezzo-soprano, coloratura soprano—a big range, and I knew that. But then I didn't know that I could do two notes or three notes at the same time. And when we found out about that we were very excited. So there's some songs in the *Plastic Ono Band* album, if you listen to it you'll hear the voice going like a harmonica, you know, three sounds.

So all that happened because these two particular people met. And we were very thankful about it. If the world just, just let us be, and gave us the space to be, we'd have been great partners. Our partnership was still great, but mainly our energies were used in fighting the world from splitting us. And finally they succeeded, they split us in this big way. And if they had allowed us—I mean in 1980 we were full of it so we were thinking, all right, next is a musical on Broadway. We planned it all. There's a lot of planning that we did. We didn't get to do any of it. But also, what if we did, what of it? I have a feeling that there would have been a lot of antagonism still.

One of the reasons we went on, and were able to do things at all, was we maintained a kind of extreme naïveté. Whenever we discovered something that we thought was great, we thought the world was going to say, "Great!" After all that, you know, the different times when they knocked us. "This is great, we have to do it, let's do it, yeah!" And then, "Uh-oh, remember that one." It was like that. So we went on. I don't know why. I mean, with *Double Fantasy* we thought we made it this time, now they will understand because the time is right. And the first review we got was, "Do we want to hear love stories again from John Lennon?" They didn't understand any of this. It was the man/woman dialogue and all that, and now people understand it.

So John was saying, "Well look, you've been in this record world for ten years now, and you were my partner for ten years, and if you were a guy they would have by now recognized that you're great. But you're a woman, and you're a wife," and all that. And then he was saying, "Wait a minute, wait a minute, shall we announce that you're actually a guy? That may do it!" That's what he was saying in 1980. "You can get away with it," and he was looking at me strangely, you know. That's funny.

How much do you think the antagonism had to do with certain things you represent like the merging of East and West, female energies being encouraged, and John's part in that. Do you think your ideas were what people were against, and maybe they were taking it out on the music?

Okay, I think a lot of things came together. One, they didn't like the fact that supposedly I broke the Beatles up; two, they didn't like the fact that I was a woman. I was an oriental woman, I was eight years older than him, I was doing music that was not particularly charming or acceptable, and also, John and I were facing the world saying "We're partners, equal partners, and how dare you?" But I think that maybe the main reason is that the things we were doing artistically were not quite acceptable to people at the time. That has a lot to do with it.

Also, my attitude was—I came from the avant-garde where you know, who was it, Jonas Mekas or somebody said, "If the audience stays it means that your concert was not successful. If they walk out it means you were successful." I came from a totally different tradition, so I didn't care, really. But then I think it was beginning to bug me too. It's not much fun to make records and be—well, not communicating, not circulating, because people don't buy it, simple as that. We tried to sort of stay on a kind of balance, a good balance of not being too extremely bored, maybe stick one song in that we liked very much because it's a great advance. We tried, but still it wasn't acceptable.

And now the avant-garde is so rock-oriented.

Oh, I know.

And it's just as acceptable as can be. And in rock too, it's more experimental, everybody's doing funny tape things.

Oh now it's very experimental, but we started a long time ago, it was a different attitude then. Now I get letters saying, "Your thing is too middle-of-the-road, what are you doing, we want to hear you screaming."

Everything has changed for women, too, in a certain way, but there still aren't very many women composers. There are a few more, and there is more of an openness to accept them.

I'm sure there were many many women composers in the old days as well, though there must have been some self-censorship and intimidation and all that, so there was not really a conducive environment to grow in. We just don't hear about them. Or we hear about them as wife of a famous composer or something. Her piece might be known as that composer's piece or something like that. John was a very macho guy when I met him, or before I met him. I know the kind of machoism that he was surrounded with . . . in his environment—his nature itself was not very macho, he was a sweet, sensitive person but he was in that society so he didn't know any better—and when he met me, and when he saw the society attacking me, I think his sort of knighthood side came out. And he observed it all, so then he realized what it is for women in this world. And that did a lot of good really—for him to understand feminism. He was a real feminist, you know, and he read a lot of books about it. He was a bookworm too. He read all of it and he understood it all. He was constantly encouraging me, always behind me. I spoke about the discouragement we got from the world as a couple, but at home I was very encouraged. And that really helped me. It was a great working relationship.

And you weren't being competitive, which is a problem some people have.

I hear that, but you know in our case, because I was such an underdog—I mean society-wise—he was not feeling competitive about my position in society or anything, obviously. And also, his caring side, the protective side came out because of my position. In that sense, it was like the prince meeting the pauper, or one of those flowergirls in the street. On the other hand, if there was anything to learn from me or learn from being with me, he cherished it. And I cherished learning from him too. So it worked out very well in that sense. We had a healthy competition, of course, a kind of healthy competitive feeling that you can only call inspiring. If it was a situation where it didn't inspire you to do anything, I mean, that's terrible.

And in that sense, we used to always say—"Okay, well, I'll do this,"... "Oh, well I can do this," and top each other. It was great. And maybe because we were so isolated, and we felt that the pressure from the world was so great, we felt very strongly that, if we become enemies with each other then what is left? We're two lonely people. So we just huddled together.

I have been strongly affected by the stories in your songs and would like you to talk about them. I get a strong sense of universal epics that your stories are part of.

Somehow all the things that come out of me—like words or music or whatever—seem to be not my doing. It just comes in and I immediately write it down, and I catch it if I can. If I don't, it's not there. So the activity is something comparable to psychic understanding or mediumship. It comes from somewhere else, and I'm just catching it. When it comes it's very quick.

So you're a receiver, or a transmitter?

In a way—I don't think of it as talent necessarily. I think of it like a good radio. You can turn the channel and all sorts of things come. And I have an antenna that's sticking out there, and this antenna's catching something. It's a big opening that's open to the stratosphere. It's easy to come in and come out, there's no blockage. That's the way I feel about it.

And I think observing how John created all sorts of things, John was like that too. When a message comes he jumps up in the middle of the night, "I better write it down." He's got the whole song down, that's how it was. A lot of people say things like, "Why didn't you write songs together?" We rarely wrote together, and we also very rarely sang together. What we found out when we tried to write a song together was that it comes so quickly, things come so quickly from me and from John, we don't have time to discuss it. We'd say, "Okay, shall we write this?" And I'd start saying, "Well, okay, this this this and this." "Oh, you wrote the whole verse, that's not fair, we're supposed to write it together." So then he's like that too, he writes the whole thing. I say "Well, aren't you going to give me a chance?" "It just came to me, I'm sorry." So it doesn't work. It immediately becomes two songs or three songs. There was no point in trying. He can write very well, thank you, by himself, and I can too. We just respected each other for each other's writing. We helped each other in the sense of stimulating each other for writing certain things—it was inspiring in that sense.

Are you continuing to write other things, essays and stories... like the parable of the little boy and the crystal ball from the innner sleeve of the album Every Man Has a Woman*

"Crystal Ball" was written because I wrote "Surrender to Peace."† When "Surrender to Peace" came out in the papers, I suddenly got tons of letters from one high school. I was thinking, "What is this, what's happening at this high school?" I found out they had a social science class where as a project the teacher read "Surrender to Peace" and the homework was to write a letter to me about what they thought of that. So they all wrote to me, and I thought I can't answer all these letters, each one of them. Then, I was just sort of inspired to write a story, and I wrote this story, and sent it to them saying, "This is in reply to your letters."

*Every Man Has a Woman, Yoko Ono, New York, NY. © Polygram Records, 1984.

†Originally published in *The New York Times*, January 24, 1983. It was a full-page letter signed by Yoko promoting an original approach to peace.

I wrote a few others, around that time, I don't know if you've read it but I sent one to the *Berkeley Fiction Review.** It was this year or last year. I wrote that story and people asked me, "Why did you send it to *Berkeley Fiction Review*?" I said, "Well, because they asked me." I have so many little bits and pieces. When I write I get so inspired that I want it out right away, and I'd send it to all sorts of papers—they wouldn't mind printing something like, "Oh, Yoko's eating hamburger and wasn't she a vegetarian?"—but they don't want to take my writing. So I got sick and tired of that game. I have it piled up now and when somebody asks, I just send it.

Sometimes the timing is so right, it's uncanny. Like with *Milk and Honey*, I tried to put it out in '81, '82, '83, it just didn't work out for many reasons. It finally came out in January 1984, and then I found out that this year was the twentieth year of The Beatles, fifteenth year of the "bed-in," eighteenth year of our meeting, John and I. They're all sort of telling me about it, MTV calls me and on top of it, it's 1984, and there's an Orwellian suggestion in it as well. So in 1984, us singing "milk and honey" and "I love you" is a revolution, you know, because George Orwell said we're not going to be saying I love you to each other, right? But we're still saying it, even though one of us had to die. I mean, it's that serious, George Orwell was *almost* right. Human love and spirit can't be killed that easily. It turns out that luckily there were tapes and because there are tapes, we're still saying "I love you."

Did anything like that happen with "Walking on Thin Ice"†? It's such an important song.

Well, I wrote that song in a car coming back from Cold Spring Harbor to New York. Cold Spring is sort of like a country home. I got in the car and I just thought of a song and I said, "Quick, give me some paper, give me some paper," and they just gave me a little scrap of paper. I started writing it, but then I couldn't write the score yet so I just rushed in, literally, to that piano and wrote the score on that little piece of paper. And that was it. Then, when we were going to record I thought, but I want, not just the song, I want a little . . . I want to push it a little further, experimentally. So I was thinking about Alban Berg, in one of his operas, you know, where a drunk is going "ahaahaahaa." Just sort of saying things, but saying things in such a way that the emphasis is all wrong, distorted.

So today is the recording and you're going to sing, I thought, okay, and then I sort of . . . I was lying down on the couch and resting before the recording, and then I saw the lake flash in my mind, a beautiful lake. And I said, okay, well, something like that. And I went to the studio, and they're starting to play the track so they can overdub my voice you see, and while they were rewinding the tape, I just wrote that thing about "I knew a girl" and all that. And I said, "When you finish the song, just reel on." They said, okay. And it just came into my head about "**I KNEW A GIRL**" as if you—you know, usually you say, "I knew a girl." "**I KNEW A GIRL**," like sort of what's *that*? And I loved it. That's how it came into my head, so I did it that way.

*"Duckstown and Men-sized Stones" by Yoko Ono (*Berkeley Fiction Review*, issue #5, Spring 1984, Berkeley, California).

†*Walking on Thin Ice*, Yoko Ono, Geffen Records, New York, 1981, © Lenono Music 1980 BMI

And when I came out of that booth, John said, "When did you write that? You didn't have that when we were leaving Dakota today." I said, "I just did that now." He said, "Oh, great, I love that thing about—'and all this was ice' because then the lake . . . " You see he's thinking of the lake—**"and all this was ice,"** you feel it. [vocal sound] And he kept saying that he loved the song, both of us loved the song.

And we never thought anything would happen to us. So that Monday we were going to remix it, and all weekend he was just listening over and over again to "Walking on Thin Ice," and I was feeling a bit eerie, because "Walking on Thin Ice" is an eerie song. And I wake up in the morning, and I see him still playing it, watching the dawn and all that in New York, and he's playing it. And I say, "What are we doing, what are we doing." He's just sitting there listening to it for the twentieth time or whatever, and I was thinking—afterwards—I was thinking, "What was *that* about?" Because the song says it all. But I didn't know that, and he didn't know it, and we thought it was just a story.

Maybe it was a preparation.

I don't know what it was really, but it's very strange. He died that day and he was carrying the finished tape.

By 1980 both John and I knew a lot about the effects of our music, because John basically was The Beatles and all that. You see, when you write words and when it communicates on this level or the level that The Beatles communicated, each word has such an impact, it brings back karma right away. So he wrote the song called "Instant Karma," you know. The karma is very instant.

Because so many people are affected?

Yes. Sometimes it works for good, like if you have that communication power then you can change the world—if you have a bigger communication power than us, probably you can change the world in one minute maybe. So it's a degree, a matter of degree, because they, The Beatles, communicated so much. So let's say if there was one negative word in it, you know, that creates such a negative karma. You don't know how, but it does.

So we were very careful about saying things or writing things. And some critics don't realize the power of it, so then they say, "Oh well, we don't want to hear everything goody-goody again." But we have to ignore those few critics who are cynical because when it's on that level, it affects everybody. And not only the people who buy the record but the person who listens to the radio, who happens to hear it because he's in a car or something. So you have to be very concerned about that. But then, you know, you get tired of being goody-goody, and you want to be *real* sometimes. Both of us actually liked songs like "Walking on Thin Ice." We were at home with that sort of song—more than maybe "Beautiful Boy."

"Beautiful Boy" was a different emotion, it was beautiful and good. But we'd get into sort of punky or funky feelings that feel good too. Then it's a dangerline. It's really like the tightrope, you know, it's the thin ice. Dangerline. And that's why that weekend I didn't like the fact that we were listening that much to that song. And it's a trap you get into, you keep on saying, yes, it's all right, it's all right, it's peace and love, etc. But then you're human, so you just say something—about death or something, I don't know—something to do with yin and yang, and you want to say something that's not always sunshine . . . a shade darker. And then it sort of like affects you, affects your fate even. That's incredible.

So you really feel that you couldn't deal with the other side at all? It seems like both the dark and the light are essential.

And also there's a part of me thinking, for instance, Greek tragedies, and there was tragi-comedy. I mean, the tragedy side was a kind of atonement that you do in public, a catharsis, and that catharsis helps others to go through their primal scream or whatever. A lot of people used to say to me when I wrote things like "Death of Samantha," why so sad? And I said that sad songs are good because then you can get it over with and just go on, it's a good thing.

So I have that feeling, that it's all right, but when you see something like that happen, it's weird, isn't it? So it's sort of like a mystery that I have to—there are many different things that we still don't know. Did the song come first, or was the song a premonition, or did the song make it happen? That sort of thin line, you never know. And believe me, since I wrote "Walking on Thin Ice" my life was walking on thin ice. So this time I said, enough with walking on thin ice, I am standing on firm ground, good earth, and I have to tell myself that.

I guess it has to do with the power you have when you are so well known, and that power is the power that somehow everyone is giving over of themselves, right? And you have this power, but the responsibility that goes along with it is such a mystery.

It's immense isn't it?

It's something I have to be very caring about, because I once met a guy in a record shop, and he just came to me and said, "Oh hi, you're Yoko Ono," so I said yes, and he said, "Listen, I met you in London once, I was one of the assistant whatevers, and you looked at my numbers and you said—'Oh for the next five years it's going to be terrible, and just be careful'—and it was, it was very very terrible for five years, and how did you do it?" And I felt guilty like I had done something. I just looked into the numbers. Then I said, "Look, from now on it's going to be good, okay?" This without seeing any numbers, I just felt like I had to say it. And I wondered if it was me who did it, you know, or if it was just the numbers I honestly read, was it that I'm psychic and I knew it, or was it that I said it, and it affected him, I don't know. I don't know what it takes. You have to be *very* careful.

It has seemed to me, looking at your life, that if it were on a mathematical grid, you're right at the center—and everything changes when it goes through you.

I don't know what it is. I just have to be very careful. Having good thoughts, and doing good things with good intentions. Both John and I never did anything otherwise, really. You might think ah ha! of course, you must have been hypocrites, I don't know what you think—but you see, think of a suggestion where you are in a position where it affects a lot of people, then you would be careful too. And you can't use it lightly. John and my life on the daily life level, was pretty boring in a sense, I mean boring for other people, pretty normal. I think that maybe a middle-America house-wife has it better, you know, more exciting, because anything we did was going to be blown up to some huge proportion. So we were careful. We didn't do things that were out of place much, if we could help it. Because it created a lot of repercussions. But then it's not fun for people to mention about how he used to be always so generous with tips or whatever, it's more interesting to write about somebody who was tight with his tips though he was a millionaire. Our life was pretty sort of like, well, normal is the word, not eventful in a sense that people think.

When you are really like that, *so* careful; sometimes we'd go "Oh to hell with it, let's go out drinking," because first of all everybody does that. You know, working-class people will go out on the weekend and have a beer or two, right? We don't even get to do that. So one day we feel like doing it. Then you know John went to Los Angeles, and Elliot Mintz, a friend of ours in L.A., told me later, "All this talk about his lost weekend was blown up," one weekend he had a big drinking spree, and he did it in style, so to speak, so it got into the news and everything. It seemed like he was drinking every day, but he wasn't that way. And maybe that's the problem, that he wasn't drinking every day, so when he got there he felt like, "Hooray, this is it!"

I was just wondering if you have any theories about dreams.

I think that dreaming is definitely part of our life. It's part of reality, but how can we find dreams. It depends on the dream. Some dreams are just dreams to regurgitate whatever experience you've had or to get rid of certain emotions. And some dreams are maybe messages, you never know. But it depends on the dream as well, so I don't have a general concept about dreams *per se.* But then also, there's a thing called dream power, which is I think real in a sense. That all the things that happen are in human history, for instance, I mean, I believe in human race dreams. That we dream together. We used to be wanting to fly. I mean, you know about the history of flying, first it started with a wish to fly and then they started to try to jump off the hill and now we have something called an airplane. And also that wish that we always had, what if we went to the moon. The moon was something that was always mysterious and poets always talked about the moon and there's always a fairytale about "I wonder if," or "I wish," or "we flew to the moon," and now finally we went to the moon.

So dreams come true if you keep dreaming about it, but then how much and to what extent and how many people have to dream—that sort of thing. Of course, if you dream alone or if you dream together there's a big difference in its power, and how it's realized, you know? And some people might inadvertently dream something negative, and they feel terrible about it, but it depends on who is dreaming stronger, you know, so you may not have to worry about it. You dream your competitor in your class died, you know, well, you're thinking did I wish it—but then your competitor might have a very strong survival dream so it doesn't matter. So I think that dreaming is part of our brain function, that it's definitely very strong, and it's a vibration that works.

We did want to talk about food. But that's really on the plane of ordinary reality.

Well sure, that's part of our lives. I'll tell you what I think about that. We went through the same mistakes, you know most people write a book, like "Saltless Diet," or something. But if you investigate carefully you might find that that person has a liver trouble and he needs a saltless diet. We do tend to find an answer for ourselves and share it without knowing why. And we shared our concept of love or whatever, and maybe that's not applicable to certain persons at certain times of their lives. We have to understand that. The diet that is applicable to me, may not be applicable to you. And I think that instead of listening to other people's intuition, which is based on their condition, I think we have to relearn to listen to our own intuition. Our own intuition is very much destroyed and distorted and whatnot because of all these messages coming to us, you know, from the television and from our parents and from our teachers and friends, etc. So we no more know what our instinct is, we no longer know.

Sometimes I have a strong craving for something, and I think "What is this craving?" is it craving or is it because I just heard on television that this tastes good or something. I have to really think about it. Once I was in a car and this filmmaker who was working for me in my film project was driving and I was sitting next to him—and suddenly I had a craving for hamburgers. "Stop, let's go eat hamburgers," I said, and he said, "Oh, funny that you should say that because I'm a famous burger man and I love hamburgers." He told me a story—when he went to Paris for the first time, he asked for a cheeseburger, and everybody laughed. He can't stand not eating hamburger for one day. And I looked at him, and he's one of these big guys, uh hm, ah, okay, so it's his dream, I see.

And you know about the search for yourself, philosophically, it's been discussed many times. But even on that level, foodwise, in *everything* to do with your life, you're the wisest person, just remember that. And when you say search for self, you are searching for what you've lost because of all the other messages that are coming to you because of the hypnotism that you are put under by others in the world. It's as simple as that.

Winter Song

I know you now for a thousand years
Your body still feels nice and warm to me
The sun is old, the winter's cold
The lake is shining like a drop of Buddha's tears
The mountains lie in a distance like
The future we'd never reach
And I keep my warm with your body close

The world must be dead
We must be the only heads
Ticking on a hillside like
A leftover timebomb

I know you now for what you are
And my mind still goes through ups and downs with yours
The moon is clear, the room is bare
The window's frozen like our memory bag
The bed is shining like an old scripture
That's never been opened before
And I keep my warm with your mind close

The world must be dead
We must be the only heads
Ticking in a farmhouse like
A forgotten timebomb

One day we discovered that the clock was not ticking anymore
And our bodies kept spreading rapidly like a very fine tissue
Until it stretched over the whole wide world

Mindholes

remember the holes
remember the holes in your mind

search for the holes
search for the holes in your feelings—memories—pain

dream of the holes
dream.

Dogtown

The town's dawning
I'm the only one awake
The streets are whistling
I light my fourth cigarette
I think of my friends
They were once not so dead
What are they thinking now
One day I'll be just a little stone
Nobody'll know that the stone had such emotions
Anyway, I'm always on the run
Someday I'll be remembered for
     The phone calls I never made
     Letters I never mailed
     And stories I never finished telling anyone
The town's yawning
I let my dog walk me around
He took a shot and people smiled
I tried the same and people frowned
Yes it's a dog, dogtown
One day let's be a pair of trees
Nobody'll know that the trees had such a history
Anyway, we'd never be this lonely
Someday I'll be remembered for
     The fine words I meant to keep
     A warm smile I meant to leave
     And a true song
     I meant to finish writing all my life
Yes it's a dogtown
It's a dogtown
Yes it's a dogtown
It's a dogtown
Dog, dog, dog, dog
Dog, dog, dog, dog
Dogtown

Peas porridge luck
Peas porridge stuck
Peas porridge in the pot nine years old
Some gets paid
Somes gets grades
Some stays in the pot nine years old
Yes, it's a dogtown
It's a dogtown *(repeat)*

Peas porridge loved
Peas porridge spoiled
Peas porridge in the pot nine years old
Some gets laid
Some gets slayed
Some stays in the pot nine years cold
Yes it's a dogtown
It's a dogtown *(repeat)*

Cape clear

In Cape Clear
I saw a little girl crying
She said she lost her teddybear
Oh, then, I can get you another one
No, no, no
It was my teddy bear

As we were talking
A cloud passed a cast a pool of light around her
And I saw that she was not a little girl
You are a woman
No, no, no
But you are

All my life I felt like I was in the middle of an ocean
Unable to, unable to touch the horizon
All my life I was floating on my emotion
Not knowing, not knowing life had its own motion

In Cape Clear
I saw a little girl crying

Mindtrain

dub dub, dub dub
dub dub, dub dub
dub dub, dub dub
dub dub, dub dub

dub dub train
dub dub train

dub dub, dub dub
dub dub, dub dub
dub dub, dub dub
dub dub, dub dub

dub dub train
dub dub train passed through my mind
dub dub train passed through my mind

thought of killing that man
thought of killing that man

33 windows shining
33 windows shining like a . . .

dub dub, dub dub
dub dub, dub dub

shining the clouds
shining the trees
shining empty buildings
shining my mind

thought of killing that man
thought of killing that man

and dub dub train passed through my mind
and dub dub train stabbed through my mind

pain, train, pain, train

dub dub pain
shining the clouds
shining the trees

33 windows shining through my mind
33 windows passed many signs

dub dub train
dub dub train passed through my mind
dub dub pain stabbed through my mind

pain, train, pain, train

dub dub train stabbed through my mind
dub dub pain shining through my mind

i thought of killing that man
i thought of killing that man

dub dub train stabbed through my mind

train, train, train, pain

dub dub, dub dub
dub dub, dub dub

**DRINKING PIECE
FOR ORCHESTRA**

Imagine letting a goldfish
swim across the sky.
Let it swim from the
West to the East.
Drink a liter of water.
Imagine letting a goldfish
swim across the sky.
Let it swim from the
East to the West.

1963 spring

Coffin car.

Coffin car
She's riding a coffin car
People watching her with tender eyes
Friends whispering in kindly words
Children running, waving hands
Telling each other, how pretty she is

Coffin car
She likes to ride a coffin car
Friends making way for the first time
People throwing kisses for the first time
Showering flowers, ringing bells
Telling each other, how nice she is

Coffin car
She's riding a coffin car
Wives showing tears for the first time
Husbands taking their hats off for the first time
Crushing their hankerchiefs, rubbing their nose
Telling each other how good she is

Half the world is dead anyway
The other half is asleep
And life is killing her
Telling her to join the dead

So every day
She likes to ride a coffin car
A flower covered coffin car
Pretending she was dead

Coffin car
A flower covered coffin car
A flower covered coffin car
A flower covered coffin car

Run, run, run.

I was sitting in the field
Feeling the grass
Counting the stars
As they come out
Feeling the breeze
Feeling the spring
Suddenly I noticed that it wasn't light anymore

Run, run, run, run
Run to the light
Run, run, run, run
Run for your life

I tumbled on roots
Stumbled on stones
Lost my marbles
Stepped on my glasses
Feeling the air
Feeling the wind
Suddenly I noticed that it wasn't fun anymore

Run, run, run, run
Run towards the light
Run, run, run, run
Run for your life

I came out of the darkness
Into the house
The lights were left on
But nobody around
Feeling the room
Feeling the space
Suddenly I noticed that it wasn't spring anymore

Run, run, run, run
Run through your life
Run, run, run, run
Run for your life

Run, run, run, run
Run through your life
Run, run, run, run
Run for your life

Walking on thin ice

Walking on thin ice
I'm paying the price
For throwing the dice in the air
Why must we learn it the hard way
And play the game of life with your heart

I gave you my knife
You gave me my life
Like a gush of wind in my hair
Why do we forget what's been said
And play the game of life with our hearts

I may cry some day
But the tears will dry whichever way
And when our hearts return to ashes
It'll be just a story
It'll be just a story

ice ice ice ice ice ice ice ice ice ice ice ice ice ice ice ice
ice ice ice ice ice ice ice ice ice ice ice ice ice ice ice ice
ice ice ice ice ice ice ice ice ice ice ice ice ice ice ice ice
ice ice ice ice ice ice ice ice ice ice ice ice ice ice ice ice
ice ice ice ice ice ice ice ice ice ice ice ice ice ice ice ice
ice ice ice ice ice ice ice ice ice ice ice ice ice ice ice ice
ice ice ice ice ice ice ice ice ice ice ice ice ice ice ice ice
ice ice ice ice ice ice ice ice ice ice ice ice ice ice ice ice

"I knew a girl
Who tried to walk across the lake
'Course it was winter and all this was ice
That's a hell of a thing to do, you know
They say this lake is as big as the Ocean
I wonder if she knew about it?"

ice ice ice ice ice ice ice ice ice ice ice ice ice ice ice ice *(repeat)*

EARTH PIECE
Listen to the sound of the earth turning.
1963 spring

Your hands

Your Hands	**Anatano Te**
Your hands	**Anatano te**
So beautiful	**Konnani kireina**
Your hands	**Anatano te**
I even dream about them	**Yumenimade miru**
Your skin	**Anatano hada**
So hot	**Konnani atsui**
Your skin	**Anatano hada**
I even dream about it	**Yumenimade miru**
In a day	**Ichinichi ni**
No matter how many times we meet	**Nando attemo**
It's not enough	**Aitarinai**
In a lifetime	**Isshoni**
No matter how many times we meet	**Nando attemo**
It's not enough	**Aitarinai**
Your mouth	**Anatano kuchi**
So tender	**Konnani yasashii**
Your mouth	**Anatano kuchi**
I even dream about it	**Yumenimade miru**
Your arms	**Anatano ude**
So strong	**Konnani tsuyoi**
Your arms	**Anatano ude**
I even dream about them	**Yumenimade miru**
In a lifetime	**Isshoni**
No matter how many times we meet	**Nando attemo**
It's not enough	**Aitarinai**
In many lifetime	**Ikusei ni**
No matter how many times we meet	**Nando attemo**
It's not enough	**Aitarinai**
Our love	**Futarino koi**
So strong	**Konnani tsuyoi**
Our love	**Futarino koi**
So frail	**Konnani moroi**
Our love	**Futarino koi**
Forever	**Itsumademo**
Your eyes	**Anatano me**
So beautiful	**Konnani kireina**
Your eyes	**Anatano me**

SNOW PIECE

Think that snow is falling.
Think that snow is falling everywhere all the time.
When you talk with a person, think that snow is falling between you and on the person.
Stop conversing when you think the person is covered by snow.

1963 summer

LAUGH PIECE

Keep laughing a week.
1961 winter

Song for John

On a windy day
Let's go on flying
There may be no trees to rest on
There may be no clouds to ride
But we'll have our wings
And the wind will be with us
    That's enough for me
    That's enough for me

On a windy day
We went on flying
There was no sea to rest on
There were no hills to glide
We saw an empty bottle rolling down the street
And on a cardboard stand at the corner of the street
Wrinkled souls
Piled up
Like grapefruits

SECRET PIECE

Decide on one note that you want to play.
Play it with the following accompaniment:

    The woods from 5 a.m. to 8 a.m.
    in summer.

1953 summer

Every man has a woman who loves him

Every man has a woman who loves him
In rain or shine or life or death
If he finds her in this life time
He will know when he presses his ear to her breast
Why do I roam when I know you're the one
Why do I laugh when I feel like crying
Every woman has a man who loves her
Rise or fall of her life and in death
If she finds him in this life time
She will know when she looks into his eyes
Why do I roam when I know you're the one
Why do I run when I feel like holding you
Every man has a woman who loves him
If he finds her in this life time
He will know

Shiranakatta (I didn't know)

Shiranakatta, shiranakatta
Shiranakatta, shiranakatta
Tatta hitokoto ittekuretara
Sugunimo tonde ittanoni
Shiranakatta, shiranakatta, shiranakatta

Je ne savais pas, je ne savais pas
Je ne savais pas, je ne savais pas
Pourquoi tu ne m'a pas dit
Que tu souffrais
Je serais venu vite vers toi
Mais, je ne savais pas, je ne savais pas, je ne savais pas

Tremblant de peur D'avoir besoin de toi
Tremblant de peur de te desirer

Mais, je ne savais pas, je ne savais pas
Je ne savais pas, je ne savais pas
Pourquoi tu ne m's pas dit
Que tu m'avais desirer
J'aurais couru vers toi

Mais, je ne savais pas, je ne savais pas, je ne savais pas

I didn't know, I didn't know
I didn't know, I didn't know
Why didn't you tell me you were in pain
I would have come to you so quickly
But I didn't know, I didn't know, I didn't know

Feeling cold from fear of needing you
Feeling faint from fear of wanting you

I didn't know, I didn't know
I didn't know, I didn't know
Why didn't you tell me you missed me, too
I would have come to you so quickly
But I didn't know, I didn't know, I didn't know

**VOICE PIECE
FOR SOPRANO**

Scream.
1. against the wind
2. against the wall
3. against the sky

1961 autumn

Toyboat

I'm waiting for a boat to help me out of here
Waiting for a boat to help me out
The boat that reached my shore was a toyboat
Waiting for a boat to help me out

I'm dreaming of a lake I've never seen before
I'm dreaming of a lake I've never seen
The lake I've seen last was a picture lake
Dreaming of a lake I've never seen

You who are
You who are
Help me out, help me out, help me out of here

I'm thinking of a castle on a top a hill
I'm thinking of a castle on a top a hill
The castle I've been to was full of of flies
Thinking of a castle on a top a hill

You who are
You who are
Help me out, help me out, help me out of here

Don't worry Kyoko
(Mommy's only looking for a hand in the snow)

snow
don't worry
Kyoko

I felt like smashing my face in a clear glass window

All day long
I felt like
Smashing my face in a clear glass window
But instead
I went out
And smashed up a phone box 'round the corner

I never had a chance to choose my own parents
I'd never know why I should be stuck with mine
Mommy's always trying not to eat
Daddy's always smelling like he's pickled in booze

I never had a chance to choose my own name
I'd never know why I should be stuck with mine
Mommy's always talkin' 'bout family pride
Daddy's always hiding 'bout his week-end rides

All day long
I felt like
Smashing my neck in a clear glass window
But instead
I went out
And smashed up a station wagon 'round the block

I looked at the mirror and told myself
I'm glad I still don't look like them at least
Mommy's like a film star in a distorted mirror
Daddy's like a guy who lost his stomach in the war

I went to shake hands with the President in Miami
I went to a rock show to see Mick Jagger
And you'd never believe it, surprise of my life
They had paint on their faces just like my Mommy's

Am I going crazy or is it just you, Daddy
Am I going nuts or is it just you, Mommy
Am I plain gone or is it just the world
Daddy, I'd rather have you dead than crazy

Trying to talk to them is like eating TV dinner when you're angry
Trying to get their love is like watching ice cream ad when you're hungry
They gave me a watch that's guaranteed not to break
But my Mommy and Daddy broke up last fall

Am I going crazy or is it just you, Daddy
Am I going nuts or is it just you, Mommy
Am I plain gone or is it just the world
Mommy, I'd rather have you dead than crazy

All day long
I felt like
Smashing my head in a clear glass window
But instead I went out
And smashed up a church yard 'round the corner

Looking over from my hotel window

Age 39 looking over from my hotel window
Blue dots and red dots skating away in the park
I used to be there twenty years ago
Huffing over a mug of hot chocolate drink

Age 39 looking over from a hotel window
Wondering if one should jump off or go to sleep
People tell you up is better than down
But they never tell you which is up and which is down

Age 39 looking over from a hotel window
95 pound bundle but it's trouble when there's nowhere to leave
People say stardust and goldust are it
But they never tell you it chokes you just as sawdust does

Age 39 feeling pretty suicidal
The weight gets heavier when you've bled thirty years
Show me your blood John
I'll show you mine
They say it's running even when we're asleep

No trace of resentment no trace of regrets
One blood's thinner but both look red and fresh
If I ever die, please go to my daughter
And tell her that she used to haunt me in my dreams
(That's saying a lot for a neurotic like me)

Age 39 looking over from a hotel window
Trying to tackle away with heart of clay
The weight gets lighter when there's nowhere to turn
God's little dandruff floating in the air

Age 39 looking over the world
Age 39 floating over the world
Age 39 . . . . floating along

DAWN PIECE

Take the first word
that comes across your mind.
Repeat the word until dawn.

1963 winter

Men, men, men.

Johnny
God's little gift
Cream and pie
Men, men, men, umm umm
Men, men, men, umm umm
Men, men, milk and honey
God's little gift for woman

I want you clever but not too clever
I want you bad but not too bad
I want you strong but not too strong
I want you to try your rightful position
Oh too, too much
I mean, it's so gooood
Men, men, snails and puppies
Your muscles are not for fighting in war
Your lips are not for voicing opinions
Your eyes are there for us to look into
I want you to take your rightful position

Oh, too, too much
I mean, it's so gooood
Men, men, grapes and nuts
Your pants are never tight enough
Your boots are never long enough
Your skin is never young enough
I want you to hold your rightful position

Pardon me, honeycome
Your hair piece's slipping
Men, men, apples and figs
I like you to be faithful but not very fussy
I like you to be behind me but not just beside me
I like you to shut up but know when to say yes
I want you to learn your frightful position

Pardon me starstud
Your cod piece's showing
Now you know what you have to do
Now you know what's expected of you
So come, come, come, come
Come up and hum hum
Come up and hum hum
Come up and hum hum me sometime *(repeat)*

Ladies and gents, I'd like to introduce you to my lower half
Without whom I won't be breathing so heavily
Honey juice, you can come out of the box now ... Yes dear

What a mess

If you keep hammering anti-abortion
We'll tell you no more masturbation for men
Every day you're killing living sperms in billions
So how do you feel about that, brother

What a waste what a waste what a waste what a waste
To have to talk to a phony like you

If you keep telling us we're more than equal
We'll tell you equal is not equal enough
For centuries we've been taking your double ass deal
So what do you say to that, brother

What a drag what a drag what a drag what a drag
To have to cope with a crazy like you

If you keep laying on money and power
We'll tell you meanwhile your sprinkler is out of soda
So keep off our grass till you're in some kinda order
What do you say to that, brother

What a mess what a mess what a mess what a mess
To have to put it up with a fuzzy like you

Ein, Zwei, trei
Poco a poco retardo, s'il vous plait
Largo, danke schon
Pianissimo guzuntheit
Ich liebe dich, nevertheless
Aishiteruyo, nevertheless
Je t'aime, nevertheless

Catman (the Rosies are coming)

Catman, you're looking cool today, we say
Catman, umm, Catman, umm
My name is Rosy and my hangs on you
Catman, umm, Catman
So keep your highheel boots and your kneehigh mind
Come up to my pad and see my work
Go for a meal and hear my joke
Or get in a bag and take a poke
But don't be too clever or we'll kick your fillies in

Look out, look out
The Rosies are coming to town
Look, out Catman, look out, Catman
The Rosies are flashing along

Catman, we feel a fool today, I say
Catman, umm, Catman, umm
My name is Rosy and my wangs on you
Catman, umm, Catman

So leave your wellpolished tail and your uptight suit
Show us some funnies that're better than daddies
Or bake us some cakes that're better than mommies
Or give us your witties that're trapped in your willies
But don't be too clever or we'll scratch your goodies out

Watch out, watch out
The Rosies are riding the town
Watch out, Catman, watch out, Catman
The Rosies are slashing about

Catman, shining your tools today, they say
Catman, umm, Catman, umm
My name is Rosy and my fangs on you
Catman, umm, Catman
So save your thigh high thoughts and banana skin
We'll burn your pansies and give you a bug
We'll squeeze your lemon and give you a mug
We'll cut your daisies and give you a slug
And don't be too clever or we'll blow your sillies off

Keep out, keep out
The Rosies are passing the town
Keep out, Catman, Keep out, Catman
The Rosies are bashing around

Cuchicuchi coo, Bunny bunny boo, patti patti poo
Catman! Caatmaaan where aaare yoooooooooo

CITY PIECE

Walk all over the city with an empty baby carriage.

1961 winter

Chorus:

Don't be a prune, Catman
Give us all you've got
Your blueberry eyes
And your evergreen lies
Cause after all by this fall
You might grow too old
And you can't ask your mommy to use
An old fruity in her pie

Patter cake patter cake baker's man
Bake me a cake as slow as you can
Pat it and prick it, and mark it with oh
And put in the oven for me and my mo

Batter cake batter cake baker's girl
Fake me a cake as fast as you curl
Bat it and whip it, and mark it with blood
And throw it in the oven with trickles and mud

Wetter cake wetter cake baker's boy
Make me a cake that's sweet as your toy
Wet it and slick it, and mark it with "p"
And leave it in the oven for Lizzie and me

Catman, Catman
Hey, dumballs, get me a pair of rubberdolls, will you!

Mother of the universe

Our mother who art of the universe
Hallow be thy name
Thy wisdom reign, they will is done
As it is to be

You gave us life and protection
You see us through our confusion
Teach us love and freedom
As it is to be

For thy is our wisdom and power
Glory forever

For thy is our wisdom and power
Glory forever

COUGH PIECE
Keep coughing a year.
1961 winter

Hell in paradise

This is called hell in paradise
We're all asleep or paralyzed
Why are we scared to verbalize
Our multicolor dreams

When will we come to realize
We're all stoned or passified
While the boogie men organize
Their multilevel schemes

Underqualified for love
Overqualified for life
Sticking our heads in slime
Thinking we're in our prime

Mesmerized by mythology
Hypnotized by ideology
Antagonized by reality
Vandalized by insanity
Desensitized by fraternity
Sanitized by policy
Jeopardized by lunacy
Penalized by apathy
And living in the world of fantasy
Dancing on hot coal
Waiting for the last call
It's Adam's ball
Eve's call

Wake up, shake up, check out, work out, speak out, reach out, it's time to,
time to, time to, to, to, to, to . . .

This is called hell in paradise
None of us wish to recognize
But do we want them to materialize
An endangered species . . .

Exorcise institution
Exercise intuition
Mobilize transition
With inspiration for life

HIDE-AND-SEEK PIECE

Hide until everybody goes home.
Hide until everybody forgets about you.
Hide until everybody dies.

1964 spring

Now or never

Are we gonna keep pushing our children to drugs
Are we gonna keep driving them insane
Are we gonna keep laying empty words and fists
Are we gonna be remembered as the century that failed
People of America
When will we learn
It's now or never
There's no time to lose
Are we gonna keep sending our youth to war
Are we gonna keep scarring ricefields and infants
Are we gonna keep watching dead bodies over dinner
Are we gonna be known as the century that kills
People of America
When will we stop
It's now or never
There's no time to waste
Are we gonna keep pretending things are alright
Are we gonna keep our mouth closed just in case
Are we gonna keep putting off until it's too late
Are we gonna be known as the century of fear
People of America when will we see
It's now or never
We've no time to lose
Are we gonna keep digging oil wells and gold
Are we gonna keep shooting the ones that try to change
Are we gonna keep thinking it won't happen to us
Are we gonna be known as the century that kills
People of America
Please listen to your soul
We can change the times
To century of hope
Cause
Dream you dream alone is only a dream
But dream we dream together is reality

Approximately infinite universe

John and I were having a conversation about astral identity. John was in a mood to start it off with a "No" and I with a "Yes." It's a seesaw game we play—though we prefer to think of it as a dialectic thinking process we developed between us, and that the seesaw will grow a propeller and start to float in the air, if we seesaw enough. So! We were ruminating on astral identity.

J: It's a bit uhh, you know.

Y: Right. But you know how an arbitrary number-series starts to make a pattern and repeats itself in the end. Say if the universe is infinite sometime or other it may start to repeat itself.

Still, the idea of John from Liverpool and Yoko from Tokyo existing in another planet as well, having tea when we were having tea, that sort of thing, was a bit too much, John said, and his beautiful toes started to move up and down in bed.

Y: Maybe there's a timewarp and they'd be doing something we did last year, John. You're just offended. Men feel threatened when their uniqueness is questioned.

J: Not that. It just means that you believe in fatalism.

Y: Not necessarily. It only means that there are many, many universes. Infinite numbers of.

J: Infinity is just a man-made concept, it doesn't exist.

Y: Look, take numbers. Numbers are a concept, too. There's no such thing as number one, say. It's actually a number that is an infinite approximation to number one, that we call number one. Like 0.999999 . . . to infinity but we build bridges and buildings on those infinitely approximate numbers not on definite ones. That means that we are always just at the verge of things, verge of being. That goes for buildings and ships and everything.

John turned into an English teapot before my eyes, and I found myself drifting off to a cosmic nowhere by myself.

Y: If it works on a microcosmic world like numbers below one, why not out there why not there in the universe? Universe is infinitely approximate. But that means that it's at least approximately infinite, right? So the concept of infinity is not just a romanticism, John. It *is* an approximately infinite universe.

I heard a tiny grunt and John saying he liked the sound of the words. Then suddenly we realized that this time we were both drifting out in a cosmos somewhere together, like God's two little dandruffs floating in the universe.

"Astral identity! Wow!"   "Something else, right?"   "Right!"

Later, we came down to Earth and went back to our weekly ceremony of washing our hair and helping each other dry it.

A crystal ball

A family: father, mother and a young son lived in a hut at the bottom of a steep mountain. A group of armed men, one night, paid a sudden visit to them. A guy with a large pipe in his mouth pointed to the little boy who was still playing in the front yard and said "Let's take that boy with us." The couple begged for mercy. The Pipe squinted his eyes for a moment. "Okay, here's a bomb. If the boy carries it up the mountain without exploding, he's free." The parents were devastated. The father took the mother to the side and whispered "Let's put up a fight and die together." Mother was silent for a while. It seemed like a long time. "Give me one more chance," she said quietly. She then asked the Pipe if she could just follow her boy from behind. "I just want to be there for him." "Hey, that's double or nothing!" The Pipe turned to his men. Numbers were thrown back and forth amongst them for a while, clearly to change their bets. The mother took the bomb from the Pipe's hand and went out to her son in the yard. "Baby," she said in a hushed voice, "I love you. I know you love mommy and daddy." The boy nodded. "Listen very carefully now. Here's something that means a lot to our family. Take this up the mountain and when you get to the top, put it down very carefully on the ground. Remember, this is something very delicate, so you don't want to drop it. Be extra careful when you put it down on the ground. Even a little shake might cause some harm." The boy nodded again, took the bomb in his small hands and started to walk up the narrow passage alongside the mountain. It was a very long night. He finally reached the top and placed the bomb on the ground. The mother rushed to him and hugged his tiny body. "I'm sorry, I'm sorry, I'm sorry, you had to go through this. But you did it. You're alive. It's safe now. We're free! It was a bomb, you know. A bomb!" "Mommy, it's a crystal ball." "No, no, baby. A crystal ball? How could you say such a thing? It's a bomb. Look!" the woman pointed out to the bomb on the ground. The sun was just rising from the back of the mountain. "But mommy, it *is* crystal." She took a second look at the round object. In the morning light she saw that it was now a crystal ball.

Hirake

open your box
open your windows
open your closets
open your bottles
open your skirts
open your flies

come on, come on
open your pants
open your ears
open your eyes
open your nose
open your mouth
open your cold feet
open your thighs

come on, come on John
open your legs
open your doors
open your schools
open your prisons
open your factories
open your parliaments
open your cities

come on, come on
let's open the world

let's open the world

WATER PIECE

Steal a moon on the water
with a bucket.
Keep stealing until no moon
is seen on the water.

1964 spring

Remember raven

While you're busy trying to conjure up dirt on me
Your pony's sucked dry by an African bee
The muck you rake is not enough to keep your turd at sea
Remember raven

While you're busy trying to weigh your power
Your boat's getting into fast water
Life is going down the river of no return
Remember raven

Don't try to be a warden to history
While trying to find a seat for your posterity
You better tend your garden for your family
Remember raven
Judas never got the key to heaven, you know
Raven, raven
Raven, raven
Remember raven
Remember raven

I love you, Earth

I love you, Earth
You are beautiful
I love the way you are
I know I never said it to you
But I wanna say it now
I love you, I love you, I love you, Earth
I love you, I love you, I love you, now

I love you, Earth
You are beautiful
I love the way you shine
I love your valleys, I love your mornings
In fact, I love you every day
I know I never said it to you
Why, I would never know
Over blue mountains, over green fields
I wanna scream about it now

I love you, I love you, I love you, Earth
I love you, I love you, I love you, now
You are our meeting point of infinity
You are our turning point in eternity
I love you, I love you, I love you, Earth
I love you, I love you, I love you, now

O'Wind (body is the scar of your mind)

the body is the scar of your mind
the scar turns into a wind of pain
it passes mountains after mountains
it passes many cities, many countries

o'wind o'wind
o'wind o'wind

but when the wind
goes around the world nine times
it turns into a gentle breeze

o'wind o'wind
o'wind o'wind

Spec of dust

In the middle of the night
I'm lying in our bed
Thinking of you and me
In the universe

Stars are moving like the night we met
The earth is turning like the time we said
In my mind I'm searching for you
Billion miles away

Why do I miss you so if you're just a spec of dust
Floating endlessly amongst the billion stars
Knowing that one day we may float apart
Meeting each other in memories

Why do I love you so if you're just a spec of dust
Floating endlessly amongst the trillion stars
Knowing that one day we may float apart
Meeting each other in universe

Kite song

I flew a kite
I held on tight to its string
Everytime I go anywhere
I held on tight

TAPE PIECE I

Stone Piece

Take the sound of the stone aging.

1963 autumn

In the middle of the night
I woke up in fright
Thinking maybe in my dream
I let go of my kite

When I was in a restaurant talking to my friends
Watching their mouths move faster and faster
I thought of the kite that was flying up in the sky
And made sure that my hand was holding the string

That was long time ago
Many skies went by since then
Now my hands stopped holding
Anything
And I've learnt to take a walk
Instead

Then one day in an evening light
I saw something strange
Shining bright

The sky was dark
With swarms of larks
And in the midst of it all
Yes, it was my kite

How did the kite get there
I'll never know
Floating away among the clouds
To where nobody knows

I held my gun
With both my hands
Slowly aiming at the shining dot

The shot went off
The dot blew off
Since then I've never seen
The kite again

Death of Samantha

People say I'm cool
Yeah, I'm a cool chick, baby
Every day I thank God
I'm such a cool chick, baby

When I'm on the phone
I thank God
My voice sounds smooth and clear
Without a trace of fear
When I'm at work
I thank God
I still have that smile
My ma used to say
It lit her day

But something inside me
Something inside me
Died that day

People say I'm cool
Yeah, I'm a cool chick, baby
Everyday I thank God
I'm such a cool chick, baby

When I'm with people
I thank God
I can talk hip
When I'm crying inside
When I'm with friends
I thank God
I can light a cigarette
When I'm choking inside

Chorus (Solo):

People say I'm cool
Yeah, I'm a cool chick, baby
Everyday I thank God
I'm such a cool chick, baby

A friend lent me shades
So I could hide my eyes that day
It was a snowy day and the shades have seen
A lot of things I didn't want to know myself

It was like an accident
Part of growing up, people tell me
But something inside me
Something inside me
Died that day

What do you doooo
What can you do
What do you doooo
What can you do

The world suddenly looks a strange place
People seem talking in foreign words
And something inside me
Something inside me
Died that day

What do you doooo
What can you do
What do you doooo
What can you do

ROOM PIECE I

Stay in a room for a week.
Do not take anything except water.
Have someone whisper to you in
the end of the week.

1963 winter

It happened

It happened at a time of my life when I least expected
It happened at a time of my life when I least expected
I don't even remember how it happened
I don't even remember the day it happened
But it happened
Yes, it happened
Ooh, it happened
And I know there's no return, no way

Rainbow revelation

It was after the rain. I was looking out from my window. The buildings on the opposite side of the park were shining with a touch of pink in the evening light. There was a faint rainbow hanging in the park right in front of my eyes. I said to myself, "Wait a minute, an arch is a segment of a circle, and usually it has a support underneath it. Is there a support for a rainbow? Like the fertile ground that supports the trees? Is there a part of a rainbow we're not seeing? It could even be that a rainbow is a circle!" Then a tiny voice said to me, "Yes, rainbow is a circle, and more. You are just shown an inkling of a rainbow. Just like the best of you think and communicate in shorthand, things are shown to you in little bits. And you know why?" I heard myself say "Why?" with an exclamation point. A perfect silence is what came back. Only the park was still shimmering in its full glow. The little voice started to whisper to me again, this time, in what I call long hand. I kept writing it down as it came to me until it was about a hundred pages, and the sun started to rise from the window. This is its first page. I hope it will be of some use to you.

BLESS YOU FOR YOUR ANGER for it is a sign of rising energy.
Direct not to your family, waste not on your enemy.
Transform the energy to versatility and it will bring you prosperity.

BLESS YOU FOR YOUR SORROW for it is a sign of vulnerability.
Share not with your family, direct not to yourself.
Transform the energy to sympathy and it will bring you love.

BLESS YOU FOR YOUR GREED for it is a sign of great capacity.
Direct not to your family, direct not to the world.
Transform the energy to giving.
Give as much as you wish to take, and you will receive satisfaction.

BLESS YOU FOR YOUR JEALOUSY for it is a sign of empathy.
Direct not to your family, direct not to your friends.
Transform the energy to admiration and what you admire will
become part of your life.

BLESS YOU FOR YOUR FEAR for it is a sign of wisdom.
Do not hold yourself in fear.
Transform the energy to flexibility and you will be free
from what you fear.

BLESS YOU FOR YOUR POVERTY for it is a sign of great possibility.
Do not hold poverty in your mind.
Every drop of your generosity will come back in ten fold.
Give as though you were a king, and you will receive a king's due.

BLESS YOU FOR YOUR SEARCH OF DIRECTION for it is a sign of aspiration.
Transform the energy to receptivity and the direction will come to you.

BLESS YOU FOR THE TIMES YOU SEE EVIL.
Evil is energy mishandled and it feeds on your support.
Feed not and it will self-destruct.
Shed light and it will cease to be.

BLESS YOU FOR THE TIMES YOU FEEL NO LOVE.
Open your heart to life anyway and in time you will find love in you.

BLESS YOU, BLESS YOU, BLESS YOU. Bless you for what you are.
You are a sea of goodness, sea of love.
Count your blessings every day for they are your protection which
stands between you and what you wish not.
Count your curses and they will be a wall which stands between
you and what you wish.
The world has all that you need and you have the power to attract
what you wish.
Wish for health, wish for joy.
Remember you are loved. Remember I love you.

Yoko. June '85

Laurie Anderson

Over there, now, yes, that's Laurie Anderson. You probably know her better than I; she's becoming a media star, but I've only seen her once before now. Another voice, of course—her work is high-tech but begins with her voice and is anchored, as she'll tell you, on speech rhythms. She's a generation younger than Bob which makes her two behind John, and she too is aware of the tradition and its importance—the positive side of the moment of postmodernism. "Yes," she tells Charles Amirkhanian, "there have been artists, and there is a long line, and we can learn from each other, and we can go forward, and try to be as generous as possible with each other." Like Yoko, she's making an impact on audiences who are drawn to her style but stay for her substance. It's they, the audiences, who "cross over," not the artists. Those who criticize people like Laurie Anderson for "pretensions to popular entertainment" should consider that it may be the popular culture that has the "pretension"—but why call it that? Why not think of it rather as an aspiration? Like John, Laurie deals as directly as possible with her material—in her case, the simplest, most evident occurrences of modern life: TV, shopping, the notes we leave each other, Frank Sinatra, being in love, and being disappointed. But if John is the Braque of the postmodern cubists, she's the Juan Gris. Though cool, her songs are pretty and have a personal touch, and they carry the whiff of revisionism, looking sideways, seductively, toward a more immediate, less <u>serioso</u> expression. The pioneers come first, like mountain climbers roped together, as Braque said, making it ugly but new, as Gertrude Stein said, and then the others can come to refine it and apply it to specific purpose. Which, in Laurie Anderson's case, is thoughtful diversion, or maybe pointed, even trenchant but amusing speculation on the real meaning of all those little unnoticeable ordinary things in life—like electric outlets, which, she reminds us, have blank physiognomies of their own. —C.S.

LAURIE ANDERSON

*Charles Amirkhanian
at the Exploratorium
"Speaking of Music Series"
November 1984, San Francisco*

I want to cover a few things [this evening] particularly some ideas about talking and performance and a little bit about TV and some things about artificial intelligence. To begin with I'd like to talk about the song "KoKoKu," which is a song from the *Mister Heartbreak* record. Sometimes I find it hard to talk about music. Steve Martin once said, "Talking about music is like dancing about architecture." But you *can* do that. Recently, I saw an Oscar Schlemmer revival of some Bauhaus dance work, and you actually can dance about architecture—volume, space, and construction. I wrote "KoKoKu" because I was invited to a Bean Festival that was going to happen in the Southwest last year about this time. It was an Indian Festival, and the idea was basically to try to come to terms with some of the Earth's wobble. The leaders of this particular group of Indians felt that they had been getting some signals from out there, and basically the message that they had received was, "You have such a beautiful planet, please be very careful." I never made it to that festival, although this Saturday I am going to a full moon Zuni Festival. It's an all-night drum festival out in the desert presided over by some characters called *The Mudheads* who have been rehearsing for a year, learning the creation myth backwards. So I don't know if they start with everything and go back to zero or if they talk backwards or what.

Where is it going to be?

It's about five hours out from Albuquerque, straight out into the flattest part of the desert. The song "KoKoKu" means literally "Home town of brave men." (I tried to translate it as "Home of the brave.") I was trying to make a record that was very cinematic and it was inspired by the work of James Joyce, particularly his book, *Ulysses,* which I think of more as a movie than as a book. It seems like a screenplay with camera motions built in. I'm thinking of one scene: there's a girl on the beach, and she's sitting there, and she's looking at her dress and thinking, "Boy, this is a really nice dress." And then she's looking at her shoes and thinking, "These are pretty nice shoes, too, and the socks aren't bad either." And then the scene switches to a man who's walking down the beach and he sees her and thinks, "I wonder who that cripple is?" And this isn't so much a situation of the omniscient author looking down at his puppet-like characters, as much as a giant camera movement, a giant pan that shows you her, and then shows you him. It's this kind of motion built into the book that I like very much.

In the song "KoKoKu," there's motion on several levels. It begins with a percussion track, the word *shake*, which is done on a harmonizer, put into the repeat mode. The harmonizer has a very short memory, pathetically short—point five seconds, that's it—but once you register it in the machine it will continue indefinitely until it's unplugged or until it explodes. So the word *shake* is then put into a random mode which turns it into a Möbius Strip. This is a rhythm which is very precise over about a 17-second pattern. So, that's the bottom motion, a very small shaking. Above that on the next layer are various kinds of vibrato. Phoebe Snow's vibrato, which is already very slow, I slowed down further using a Synclavier. Then there's the kayagum, which is a Korean zither, played by several motions—you damp a string, you pull it, and you also pull long threads—so it's a beautiful action, and it also has a very very wide, slow vibrato. So there are those motions that happen over the others. And then the lyrics themselves are about a wider, broader motion: people looking up and people looking back down. The words in Japanese are fake haikus that I made up—which are more or less grammatically correct in Japanese. They are place words, still images.

> **Mountain with clouds. I am here. A voice.**

Another verse is—

> **Birds are there.**
> **A cry, my voice.**
> **Mountain with clouds.**

The English turns and moves around these Japanese freeze frames.

You know what I hear: about 30,000 hours in the recording studio.

Yeah, actually I was remembering working on it. The engineer had gone away for Christmas and I was trying to synch up two 24-track machines and was very sick with the flu and had taken a lot of antibiotics. I don't know if you remember what that's like but it's like being very very old, or retarded. And things that would take me 10 seconds to do would take 10 minutes. And the patch bay was just hundreds of cables. . . .

Where did you make the piece "KoKoKu"?

At my house. I work on most things there because that's where I have my tape library. The song reminds me of the last time I was here in San Francisco.

It was my birthday, and I saw the best headline I'd ever seen in a newspaper. I've become obsessed with it. It was in the *Chronicle* and the headline was "Extinct Genes Cloned." Unbelievable story about the guagga. The guagga was this half-horse, half-zebra, a strange hybrid that used to be a herd animal in South Africa. The last guagga mare died by herself in a zoo in Antwerp a hundred years ago. A biochemist from Mainz came by a couple of years ago to pick up the skin and take it away. He found a piece of what seemed like beef jerky-like material under one "elbow" and sent it to MIT. They washed it in *e. coli* and various bacteria, and began the process of recombinant DNA! They were trying to clone extinct animals! Then the article outlined what they are going to do. They are going to dig up tar pits of the pterodactyls and they are going to find woolly mammoths encased in ice, 26 million-year-old fruitflies that have been caught in resin, and they are going to bring them all back to life. But the problem is, you *know* that they're not going to get it right. There are going to be some *very* odd hybrids. And also in doing this, they're going to resurrect the diseases that killed these animals in the first place. So it's going to be a tremendous mess.

At any rate, it made me think about a lot of cloning problems that are going on, particularly my own experience. I was turning a corner in Soho, and someone said, "Oh no, another Laurie Anderson clone." And I thought, "Hey wait! It's really me." Or when people come up and say, "Aren't you . . . I saw your photograph," and they're quite happy and proud, and I have to congratulate them because they've made this connection between the second and third dimensional worlds. The 2-D world of pictures and the 3-D world of living people. (There are people who believe that space shots are faked in studios anyway.) I think there really is a very deep confusion in America about dimension.

I actually saw a wonderful tape that suggested some of these problems. It was a tape made in Canada, and it begins with a saxophone wail. And then this huge island, somewhere in the mid-Atlantic rises up between Africa and South America . . . it rises out of the water and it's shaped like a giant saxophone. All of the people who live on this island are people who are on TV—they act like that and talk like that. It's really a wonderful tape.

But just to finish this cloning idea before I go on. A while ago, a couple of people told me things about my past lives. They said my first life on this planet was as a cow and the second as a bird and in the next life I was a hat. And I said: "A hat?!" And they said the feathers from the bird had been made into a hat and that counted as a kind of half-life. Then I was nothing but hundreds and hundreds of rabbis, so this is my first life as a woman.

The tape we are hearing now is called *Sharkey's Day*. A lot of the horn and string lines that I wrote for this song are gone, because when I asked Adrian Belew to play on it I said, well, do these kinds of chord structures between the horn line and the violin line and actually I liked what he did so much more than the horns that I took them out. There are only eleven horn notes in the whole song, and there used to be a whole part, so it got very extracted. Also I spent a lot of time, after my first record, *Big Science*, claiming how much I hated things like guitars and bass and drums. Next record—guitar, bass, drums—they were *all* there. So much for prediction.

The sound on the next album, though, was much richer and warmer. Why is that?

Big Science was a collection of songs that I had written for a performance. I thought, boy, I really don't want to go into the studio and overproduce these things, I want to keep them simple and I don't want to do real elaborate studio arrangements of them. I thought using things like reverb was really cheating. As it turned out—I was thinking of it as a documentation of the work but I was really the only one who was reminded of the work. It struck me mostly as, "Well, where are the pictures?" There just weren't any. So, as I said before on the second record I tried to make it more cinematic to put more distance into the music from the very beginning.

What do you think about improvised music? You don't seem to use it very much.

I never really understood what improvised music really is. When does the happy accident become a plan? When it can be repeated? When I start working on a piece *everything* is improvised, and because I work with tape, a lot of those chance events, those happy accidents, end up being saved as is. So in a sense, this is improvisation. Also, I've tried to leave room for improvised solo. In "KoKoKu," the kayagum player is basically improvising around the bass line. Through repetition, improvised lines become parts.

Do you feel that the ambiguities in your work that resonate and then aren't resolved are a way to make people think?

Well, it's true that very few of these ideas are spelled out in no uncertain terms. I really try to leave a lot of room and a lot of air so that people can draw their own conclusions. It's not that I don't have my own conclusions, but it's the *process* I'm interested in. For example, a lot of the rhythms are created visually. The music is going, and the pictures are going . . . and that creates a kind of counterpoint between what you're seeing and what you're hearing, a kind of polyrhythmic situation that you put together yourself. It's the same way with some of the ideas and issues that are raised in the work. My greatest fear is to be didactic, and even if I had "answers" I would never try to foist them on people. I think I've gradually learned to respect other people a little bit more and let them, in a sense, let them make connections themselves.

Do you feel you have to seduce the machine in order to get it to do what you want?

I have a real personal relationship with machines. It's true that even though I've been very very critical of technology in terms of what I say, I find that I make those criticisms through 15,000 watts of power and lots of electronics. And that says a couple of things at least, that I hate it and love it.

I remember you said something to me once. You said, "Get the machine and work with it a lot before you go out and try to use it in your pieces."

It's true, you have the thing and you have to fully understand it before you use it. The machine is an instrument. Occasionally, I talk to people in art schools who have problems with this. For example, let's say you're a painter and you want to use video tape, which is a very expensive medium. Not a lot of art students can afford it. So you're in a funny situation of trying to plan something without actually working with your material. You have to think the whole thing out and *then* get the equipment to accomplish it. It's as if you were a painter, and you had to just *think* of this amazing painting and then one day go out and rent a brush and come back and paint the thing real fast, and return it to the rental place clean the next day. It's very difficult to work like that. Anyone who uses any kind of material—words, or stone, or notes—knows you have to work with your material. It will teach you things. When I get really stuck—when I think, "This is it! This is the last idea I'm ever going to get," I try to shake it by just playing with things. I try to let the material suggest the shape. Otherwise, it feels forced . . . jammed together. So, I suppose I'm just saying something about having a kind of respect for the material or the equipment that you're working with, and taking the time to learn about it.

On the album Mister Heartbreak *you work with Peter Gabriel and Adrian Belew. Did they approach you to work or did you approach them?*

I learned a lot from working with them. Well, I met them in different ways. I met Peter a few years ago in London and he was describing an amusement park he's designing. He has this thing all worked out. It's called *Real World* and it's underground and he has the parking figured out too. You park your car and then you go underground and put on what looks like this giant hairdryer and goggles, and you see these three dimensional images and hear this holophonic sound. He's describing this to me and I'm thinking, "This guy is really crazy. I really like this guy." We wrote a song and made a videotape together. It was very interesting working with him because he's a very intuitive musician. He would be over in the corner working on a keyboard line and I'd hear that and I'd think, "Oh, that is never going to work." And then he'd start to make it work. It was very fascinating because he's basically someone who comes to music from a different angle than I do. We wrote the song and shot the tape very quickly, over a three-day period. It was strange, without sleeping. What I remember from that was a session—it was probably 4:30 in the morning, and the engineer and I were there. Peter was singing, doing vocals, and the engineer and I were watching the meters. Suddenly, there's just no action. We're checking everything, and she's pulling cables out of things and going—"We've lost everything!" Finally we looked over and Peter was singing while he was falling asleep, the only live fade I've ever seen. A couple of hours later, we tried to lip synch the song in a video shoot, and every time we got playback it was like we'd never heard the song before. You know, we'd just written it five minutes before. So we used cue cards that at first were six-inch tall letters. We still couldn't get it right so the words were eventually two feet tall . . . even then it was very sketchy, the relation of lips to words.

I met Adrian Belew when he came to a concert I did in Chicago, and I was just trying to learn to play the koto. He came backstage and started playing this thing with these giant shovel hands that he's got. He'd never played it before, but of course, as someone who plays a stringed instrument, he began very intuitively to do some beautiful things. So, he said, "Listen, if you ever need a koto player, call me up," and I said, okay.

So, when I was working on one of the songs I called him and said, "Would you like to come and play koto?" and he said, "Sure, and I'll bring my guitar." I said, okay, but I still wasn't sure because I don't really like guitars. Of course, Adrian doesn't play the guitar. I don't know what to call it. It's some kind of unidentified animal. He's such a brilliant musician. All of Adrian's solos were improvised. He's very free. It was a great privilege to work with him.

Are you going to be using more of these tools of communication in your work with something like a video-link to Russia?

I've been working with a group called *Performing Artists for Nuclear Disarmament* on an exchange with Russia. And we had this all set up and it was going to be in September. Then when the Olympics blew, they called and said, "Don't worry, just because we're not coming to the Olympics doesn't mean that we're not going to do the exchange." And we said, "Right, sure." Twenty-four hours later, ring, "Yes, well, sorry, we'll have to postpone." I was very very disappointed. It's one of the things that I'm very hopeful about, doing this kind of exchange, especially because I think in many ways Americans and Russians have so much in common. The first time I began to think about it in those terms was really when Khrushchev showed up and began to bang his shoe on the table and every farmer in Iowa says, "I know that guy."

We've got a lot in common, more than we think. Particularly, in terms of the nets that have literally been dropped down on both countries in the twentieth century. By that I mean, structures that attempt to connect us in ways that are human. In the case of the Soviet Union, the net was communism, a system that was nominally about people sharing and helping each other and being able to communicate. In the United States, it was the net of communication and networks. The idea was we'll be tied together by computers and TVs and telephones, and that will bring us together. Both systems in many ways have failed. In fact, when you turn on your television set you realize that it has nothing to do with communication. Most of the shows are basically advertisements for the commercials—traps or lures to bring you in so that you can participate in the true function of American TV: sales. I think that it would be very interesting to learn about how to make some of the systems we use truly communications systems, rather than stores. I mean, TV has been called a drug. Actually, it's a drug store.

Where do you get your imagery?

From looking around the house. From common objects. One of the images that begins *Big Science,* when you hear the wolf howl, is a kind of animation which is a close up of an electrical outlet. When you hear the wolf howl, what looks like the eyes and mouth of this socket light up, and light streams out that way with "ow-oo." This is the kind of animation that I've used in a very literal sense. In English, words expressing electricity are connected somehow to life—"live wire," for instance—and there's some idea that something that has this much power must also have life. So there are these literal kinds of animations, like the socket. Although I remember after doing those photographs, socket-face close-ups, I felt really terrible, plugging cords right into their eyes.

Do you get into a trance during performances and if so, what kind of experiences do you have?

I think that I probably do, in a way, but also I'm so aware of what could possibly go wrong. And things always do. Things always break down, little red lights on the harmonizer go dead, and I usually have a small screwdriver so that I can surreptitiously try to do something else while I'm talking, and be trying to fix whatever's going wrong. I actually like that probability because I find it very exciting to have to improvise. When something breaks down, you really can't say, "Can we turn the houselights on, please, we have some problems here." So, I probably am thinking about a couple of things, and that probably is a trance-like state.

Since you've performed so many of these pieces in so many versions, how do you remember which one's next?

I worked on the *United States* performance for a long time, for four years. It was a work-in-progress from 1979 to 1983, and I probably could do it word for word right now. It really won't go away. One of the ways I tried to make it go away was to record it, which I did at the Brooklyn Academy of Music, and then mixed it last summer after staying away from it for a year, and it's now a five-record set put out by Warner Brothers. I was very happy when they suggested doing it. I'm not sure they knew how long it would be when they suggested it. But that was one way of getting rid of it. The other was a book I put out,* and it's more or less a kind of sceenplay. It's hundreds of photographs from the performance and all of the words. One of the things about that is that often in the performances it goes by quite fast and there's a lot of stuff happening so sometimes it's not so easy to catch what's being said. In the book, some of the ideas and themes are clearer. Particularly ideas about Utopia. It begins with that image and ends with it. Sometimes in the performance it's hard to think back to what happened a couple of hours ago. In the book you can just flip back and see. In that sense, it was satisfying to complete the work in that way. Neither one of those ways is an ideal way to record a live performance, but I think it's a better solution than, say, videotape which is just too small.

*United States, Laurie Anderson (Harper & Row, New York, 1984).

I think if film hadn't been invented, let's say, and we were just used to videotape, and someone came along and said, "Boy, I just saw this amazing image, it's really huge and the color is just very vivid and the depth of field is amazing and it looks so airy and atmospheric, and it's called film." Suddenly, I think, we'd begin to realize what we've given up by getting so used to the rather degraded image of video. And the electronics of it too, which, I don't know about you, but as soon as I start staring at it I start to kind of drool. And my eyes start to cross.

In the performances, how do you put them together technically, what's live and what isn't?

This is a giant sort of puzzle and the scores for these things are done in huge columns and it shows you what exact image is being used at that second. A lot of the basic tracks are on tape and I try to record those things so that they have as much to do with the live sound as possible. So I do several mixes and if the hall is a certain size, I use one mix that has a little bit of reverb on it. If the hall is very large I use something that has no reverb on it. I really try to tune the tape to the room and mix with the live instruments so that it doesn't sound like live musicians playing with tape. If you listen real hard, it does, and those of you who work with that sort of thing, I'm sure, know what's going on. For example, there are two projectionists who follow the score and do a series of moves on what is called a Ducksfoot Dissolve System designed by Perry Hoberman, the projectionist. It's actually wonderful, it's very much like a puppet show, these two boxes that have a series of mechanical doors that drop down and you control them by wires. Actually, it's gone through a few variations, but he does them according to the score—wipe this way, and this image comes up this way and down this way—and so that they have a sort of odd half-electronic, half-homemade look. In terms of what the musicians are playing, it's pretty much fixed because, in the context of something that has so many things going on, we have four seconds to do that, and another few seconds to do that, so it's rather tightly scored. Now, when things break down, everybody starts looking over at everyone else, and we try to get out of it. That is, as I said, the most exciting part, it's a lot of fun to try to do that.

Does anyone do any repatching of audio in the works that you perform?

There is a little bit of repatching of the audio but we use a 48-input board so there are a lot of effects on many of the instruments. What it really comes down to is dragging a lot of studio equipment onto a stage, and the reason that more people don't do that is because it's quite delicate equipment and it does break down, so that when that happens you really do need to be prepared. The computer that I used crashed only once because of the altitude in Denver. It rides aerodynamically over a disc, so that the altitude actually forced the head onto the plate, and the whole thing just crashed. I asked the computer company what to do about this and the company said, "Do the high altitude tour, everything over 8,000 feet, with one computer, then you come back and do the low land tour with another computer, anything below 3,000." So, I guess that's a kind of answer.

Did you pick up a background in analog and digital electronics?

At one point I thought, well, I could stop working for three years and really try to learn some things about electronics. But I was afraid to do that really, because I thought, what if after three years I couldn't remember why I was learning this stuff? So, I try to learn only what I need to know at the time, and I also work with an electronic designer, Bob Bielecki, who can do a lot of rather elaborate designs. I'm pretty good on emergency maintenance, that's my speciality.

Who will you be collaborating with in the future?

In the past, I've worked with Trisha Brown. That was great. But generally, I like to lay something out and pretty much finish it and leave room for people to do solos within that context. I find it kind of frustrating to actually work with someone else starting from zero. Although I once wrote some music for a dancer, and this was a really slow piece, and she said, "I really like that music and I'd like to use it, but it's too fast." And this was already the slowest thing I'd ever written in my life, and I said, "Really, slower than this?" So she said, "Yeah, it's about twice as fast as I need it." And so I said, "Okay." And I slowed it way down. And I actually liked it so much better that way. It was a much better piece of music, and I'd never thought to make it that slow, so it was very interesting in that way to work with someone who would just say, "Change it totally." I think that's as much a criticism as a collaboration, and I think that it's a very hard thing to actually work with another artist. It so rarely works. Sometimes when it does work, it's quite amazing. The thing that comes to mind to me as the best avant-garde collaboration is *Einstein on the Beach,* of course, the work that Bob Wilson and Phil Glass, Lucinda Childs first produced in 1976 at the Met. And a lot of us went up there—well, we were so happy that someone from downtown was at the Met. It was a big event—but, the thing about that collaboration that struck me initially was, it was a work in several gears and that the issue in that work was really speed. So that you have Phil Glass's music which is [*fast sound*] and then Bob Wilson who is incredibly incredibly slow, and the tension between those two gears makes this work powerful. Afterwards, everyone I knew started to write an opera, including myself. You'd see someone on the street, "How's your opera?" "Fine, how's yours?" It was really a fad.

I've seen some things you've done that focused just on visuals and talking, but recently there seems to be more music. Is that true and why?

I think that's quite true. One of the things that I've been trying to do is constantly change directions. The last work that I did was for a tour which had seven musicians, and a few semis full of stuff. You know, we just kind of lugged this stuff around, we did 60 concerts in the United States and Japan. And it was very wearing, and it was also a lot of fun because when you have real rapport with other people it's fun to play music with them. Then, after I finished *United States,* I thought, forget these seven-hour things, next thing is going to be five minutes, that's it, tops. Of course, it stretched into an hour and forty-five. The next thing that I do will be a solo work, probably no microphones, just a couple of hand puppets, strip it down. I'm going to try to do that because, in a way, it scares me, and I really do trust things that are frightening.

Could you talk about how your storytelling works into music, and how long it takes to get there.

I think often the case is that words are just hanging around and I don't really know what to do with them, I can't quite throw them away yet. I always try to start things differently, sometimes with music, sometimes with an image. But I'd say the main focus of it is really words. I try to establish a very simple rhythm and then on top of that language drifts around with its own rhythms. I rarely write in stanzas or things that rhyme or things that scan or things that count out in a certain number of syllables. I think I like talking rhythms more than musical rhythms.

Since a lot of your music is done with electronics, I was wondering if you have a spiritual feeling about your music? Is it a different kind of thing than playing an instrument?

As I said, I think of electronics, first of all, as instruments. Or I try to change them as much as possible into instruments, and instruments into electronics as well. This is a violin that actually is a piece of electronics, more than it is a violin. It's shaped like a violin, it's designed by Max Mathews of Bell Labs. Digitally recorded sounds are sent to the Synclavier, the computer, and each finger position on each string tells the computer to access something else. I've worked with Synclavier in designing this particular interface. It's the only violin interface to the computer. It doesn't actually work that well. There is a guitar interface, but that's a very different kind of thing because when you pluck a guitar it's a harder signal, and when you bow a violin, sometimes the computer just doesn't really understand what you're telling it to do. The bow doesn't have as much attack. Also, on a design level with Synclavier, they think I know more than I do about this computer because I go in for sessions with them and they get very excited about some little way they're going to trick the machine. Here's one trick: now, there are a couple of elements in this computer and one is the Winchester, which is really the brains of the computer, and the other is storage information—floppy discs. So this designer says, "Okay, now, just tell the floppy disc that it's a Winchester, and then. . . ." This was the beginning of the trick. But it was like telling a 2B pencil that it's the Library of Congress. You can try to tell it but you doubt that it's going to believe you. On this level, it's a very strange and odd world. And in terms of your question, about my spiritual reaction to it, I think of electronics as being, in fact, in a sense closer to that side. It doesn't go through the hands the way an instrument does. I love the violin because it's a hand held instrument, it's a very nineteenth-century instrument, something that you hold as opposed to a keyboard which reminds me of driving a car. But electronics is very connected, of course, in terms of speed, to your brain. It's very very fast. So there's a kind of immediate freedom that you have.

I want to make just a couple of remarks about technology, from another angle. About a month ago, I was on a German television show which, unlike most television shows in the world, was live, as opposed to canned or lip-synched. It's a very brave thing to do, I think. This show was a kind of variety show. There were four European astronauts and Tina Turner and a Russian violinist and myself. It was a great show. After the show I spent a lot of time talking to one of the Dutch astronauts. This guy had contact lenses that had Xs drawn through them because they were studying his eye motion and it was hard to keep track of the iris. So these things are orbiting around in his eyeballs and I said, "Please, take those off while we talk, because they're driving me crazy." He had some very interesting theories about technology, which were basically that he sees technology as a kind of parasite, invented by human beings several decades ago, which like many parasites begins to take over its host, eventually leaving. This guy actually hasn't been up yet, but they should send him soon, because he's ready. He also is rather critical. There are these astronaut club meetings, and he was talking to Alan Shepard who was describing what it was like to be on the moon, and this Dutch astronaut had disdain for American astronauts. He felt that astronauts should not only be athletes and astrophysicists but they should also be poets. *Good* poets. So when he asked Shepard what it was like on the moon, Shepard just said, "Well, I don't know, it's okay . . ." you know, mumbling. And this Dutch astronaut says, "But Alan! didn't you think about how in ten years, a hundred years from now . . . time doesn't matter . . . of all the houses and towns that will be on the moon?" And you know, Shepard just goes,

"Huh?" Suddenly, I had a horrible image of the moon covered with windmills and these little Dutch streets and brick towns and it just seemed kind of claustrophobic.

[*A question from the audience.*]

The creation of alternative life! What does it mean? When I was talking about cloning a little bit before, I think that it's one of the most fascinating things that's going on now. People have always been fascinated with duplicating things. As someone at Lucas Films says about creating billiard balls on a table, and then inventing their reflection on the billiard balls in a non-existent room, "Well, what we're creating is actually an interesting measure of complexity, rather than a copy of the real world." From my point of view, one real world is quite enough and to repeat it seems a little redundant. But that is the goal of, of course. People are making machines that can think. Not only that, but people working in artificial intelligence, for example at MIT, claim that they are trying to make a machine that is so sensitive that a soul will want to enter it. This is the goal. Now, how you know whether a soul has gotten inside is sometimes difficult. How do you test it? Weigh it? that's right. You're going to get a lot of zeros in that one, a couple of ones, yeah, it might work!

The point I'm trying to make is that, in a sense, as these two life forms—human and machine—begin to merge a little bit, we're talking about technology really as a kind of new nature, something to measure ourselves against, and to make rules from, and to also investigate. One of the things that is most encouraging about this is that kids who begin to work with computer systems when they're real little aren't intimidated by them as opposed to adults who actually become more dogmatic if they work with computers. Instead of having a phone conversation or a meeting, they talk to each other through their terminals, and one of the things that happens is that people use a lot more foul language. Because you can't do that really very easily on the phone, but when you abstract it like that, it's a little bit easier. Also people become, strangely, more sure of themselves. They reach a decision more quickly and they become more sure that they're right, and less willing to give and take, when it's done through a terminal. Which I think has something to do with when you write something down and try to work it out, and then type it, it has real and sudden distance. It's almost as if somebody else did it when you see it typed out, you have a kind of distance from it. It's a little bit like that working with a terminal.

Sherry Turkle wrote a book about computers and human intelligence.* It's a series of examples of how some kids write programs. There's one of a ten-year-old girl who wrote a very beautiful program. The problem was she wanted to have birds fly across the screen and also change color, and this was a difficult program to write if it was seen in that way. So she said, "Well, okay, I'll just visualize it. In front of every bird I'll put a screen, and the screen tracks the bird's motion everywhere it goes, and sometimes I'll tell the screen to be the color invisible." And this solved a very compli-

*The Second Self: Computers and the
Human Spirit, Sherry Turkle
(New York: Simon and Schuster, 1984).

cated programming problem because she was able to think of it as layering. She was able to solve the problem visually and freely. I think adults who haven't worked with computers are often intimidated. They think they've got to read that manual—it's hard enough to get past the *Dear Customer* page in it much less start thinking of creative ways to have a bird fly across the screen. As people get used to these kinds of systems, that's the only way we'll be able to turn those into human terms as opposed to just trying to adapt to machine talk.

I think there's a strange longing to talk to machines. There's a parking lot in Zurich. You drive up to this booth, and you hear this voice that says, "It's going to be so and so many francs to park here," in this kind of mechanical voice, and it shoots this ticket out. But, there's something a little bit too odd about the voice. There's a cable running out the door, and you can see this guy in the adjoining room doing the voice, you know, kind of mechanically, making the parking lot seem a little more high tech.

Have you ever created something that frightened you?

That orchestra piece frightened me. Mostly I think that I would really like to do something that I feel like I finished. I usually stop when I run out of time or run out of money or run out the door because I'm late to do some kind of performance. I've never finished a work ever that I thought was really perfect, and that I couldn't somehow do something to. I stop when I can't think of how to fix it.

Assuming that you would like an effect on mankind as a whole right now, what effect would you like your music to have?

I can never predict what other people will like. I can't even predict what I will like. I suppose that the effect that I want from myself from music is, in a way, to scare myself a little bit, to surprise myself, to wake up.

About continuity. I don't know how many of you have spent time in New York but you can really lose track of that there because it really is, "Hey, what's hot this week?" That can become very deadening after a while. I'm thinking particularly of an evening that I mentioned before, the work of Oscar Schlemmer, the Bauhaus designer/choreographer. In this reconstruction of his work, Andreas Weininger, who used to play trumpet in the Bauhaus band, showed up at the Guggenheim to talk. This guy was 85 years old, and it was a Saturday night, and he came out and he said, "Hi, I'm from the nineteenth century." And we go, "Whoa." He said, "You know, we had Saturdays in the nineteenth century too, and what we did was . . . " and he proceeded to describe these insane long-ago evenings. It really seemed so alive and exciting. So wonderful. It was a kind of real continuity, and you really felt that, yes, there have been artists, and there is a long line, and we can learn from each other, and we can go forward, and try to be as generous as possible with each other.

Notes on Laurie Anderson

Like the nineteenth-century Romantic poets, Laurie Anderson makes the familiar strange, the ordinary extraordinary. Also like the Romantics are her criticisms of science, technology, and mass mediocrity. One size fits all. Yet her concern with history, the concept of paradise, sexual difference, and sign systems has a distinctly contemporary tone, reflecting and also perhaps criticizing the ideas of French structuralist and post-structuralist theorists such as Michel Foucault, Jacques Lacan and Jacques Derrida.

History is not necessarily progress.

It may be entropic, after all. At the same time, Anderson re-emphasizes the importance of looking at and learning from history to avoid the imprisoning circularity of the exclusively synchronic structuralist discourse. Rather than synchronic structures connecting us and making us all one—all the same—history offers a different view of collective continuity that gives us more individual choice.

We long for paradise.

But we can never reach it. Not an earthly island paradise, or a heavenly paradise, reached through the help of TV evangelists and consumer greed. Nostalgia for a paradise that never existed and perhaps never will, except in our minds. A driving desire to return to the pure, good origin. To escape evil influences. Utopia.

We dream of love.

Nor can we expect an island paradise dream love. In "Langue d'Amour," Anderson plays with desire and sexual difference using the Adam and Eve myth to show the impossibility of human connection. Neither here nor there, love is an imaginary construct. A conflation of presence and absence. Yet, derived from biology, the notions of presence and absence value the "present" male sexual organ more than the supposedly "absent" female one. Can the straight hard line and the fluid circle ever merge?

Communication is nowhere.

Though communication systems are everywhere. In "Babydoll," Anderson gives us a picture of a woman controlled and manipulated by male-dominated language and institutions. The woman in "Babydoll" tries to escape. And perhaps some form of escape from these authoritarian structures is possible. But in the meantime, we are here. "Kokoku" clearly describes the mood.

> "Home of the brave.
> I am here now.
> And lost."

Questions are raised: Do we have any choice in our lives? Are our lives determined by these structures? We look for signs . . . in art, in people, in objects. The best we can hope for is to scramble the codes and subvert the systems, including even new systems that then arise.

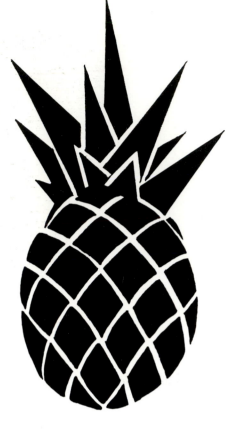

Smoke rings

Standby. You're on the air.
Buenas noches Señores y Señoras. Bienvenidos.
La primera pregunta es: ¿Qué es más macho,
pineapple o knife?
Well, let's see. My guess is that a pineapple is more
Macho than a knife. ¡Si! ¡Correcto!
Pineapple es más macho que knife.

La segunda pregunta: ¿Qué es más macho,
light bulb o schoolbus?
Uh, light bulb?
¡No! Lo siento. Schoolbus es más macho que light bulb.
Gracias. And we'll be back in un momento.

Well I had a dream and in it
I went to a little town
And all the girls in town were named
Betty.
And they were singing:
Doo doo doo doo doo.
Doo doo doo doo doo.

Ah desire! It's cold as ice
And then it's hot as fire.
Ah desire! First it's red
And then it's blue.
And everytime I see an iceberg
It reminds me of you.
Doo doo doo doo doo.
Doo doo doo doo doo.
¿Qué es más macho iceberg or volcano?

Get the blanket from the bedroom
We can go walking once again.
Down in the bayou
Where our sweet love first began.

I'm thinking back to when I was a child—
Way back to when I was a tot.
When I was an embryo—
A tiny speck. Just a dot.
When I was a Hershey bar—
In my father's back pocket.

Hey look! Over there! It's Frank Sinatra
Sitting in a chair. And he's blowing
Perfect smoke rings
Up into the air. And he's singing:
Smoke makes a staircase for you
To descend. So rare.

Ah desire!
Ah desire!
Ah desire! So random. So rare.
And everytime I see those smoke rings
I think you're there.
¿Qué es más macho staircase or smoke rings?

Get the blanket from the bedroom
We can go walking once again.
Down in the boondocks
Where our sweet love first began.

Ooo I'm gonna follow you.
Out in the swamps and into town.
Down under the boardwalk
Track you down.

Doo doo doo doo doo.
Doo doo doo doo doo.
Doo doo doo doo doo.
Doo doo doo doo doo.

Gravity's angel

You can dance.
You can make me laugh.
You've got x-ray eyes.

You know how to sing.
You're a diplomat.
You've got it all.
Everybody loves you.

You can charm the birds
Out of the sky—but I—
I've got one thing.

You always know just what to say—
And when to go—
But I've got one thing.
You can see in the dark—
But I've got one thing:
I loved you better.

Last night I woke up
Saw this angel.
He flew in my window.
And he said: Girl,
Pretty proud of yourself, huh?
And I looked around and said:
Who me?
And he said: The higher you fly
The faster you fall.
He said:

Send it up! Watch it rise!
See it fall. Gravity's rainbow.
Send it up! Watch it rise—
And fall. Gravity's angel.

Why these mountains?
Why this sky?
This long road . . . this ugly train?

Well he was an ugly guy
With an ugly face.
An also-ran in the human race.
And even God got sad—
Just looking at him.
And at his funeral all his friends
Stood around looking sad—

But they were really thinking
Of all the ham and cheese sandwiches
In the next room

And everybody used to hang around him
And I know why. They said:
There but for the grace of the angels
Go I.
Why these mountains? Why this sky?

Send it up! Watch it rise!
See it fall. Gravity's rainbow.
Send it up! Watch it rise—
And fall. Gravity's angel.

Well we were just lying there—
And this ghost of your other lover walked in.
And stood there
Made of thin air
Full of desire
Look! Look! Look!
You forgot to take your shirt!
And there's your book.
And there's your pen
Sitting on the table.

Why these mountains?
Why this sky?
This long road . . . this empty room?

The day the Devil comes to getcha

The day the Devil comes to getcha
You know him by the way he smiles.
The day the Devil comes to getcha
He's a rusty truck with only twenty miles.
He's got bad brakes. He's got loose teeth.
He's a long way from home.

The day the Devil comes to getcha
He has a smile like a scar.
He knows the way to your house.
He's got the keys to your car.
And when he sells you his sportcoat—
You say: Funny! That's my size!
ATTENTION SHOPPERS!
Everybody please rise.

Give me back my innocence.
Get me a brand new suit.
Give me back my innocence.
Oh Lord! Cut me down to size!
Cut me loose.

Well you can hide under the porch.
And you can hide behind the couch.
But the day the Devil comes to getcha—
He's right on time.

Give me back my innocence.
Get me a brand new suit.
Give me back my innocence.
Oh Lord! Cut me down to size!
Cut me loose.

The day the Devil comes to getcha.
He's a long way from home.
And you know he's gonna getcha—
Cause you're stuck in the middle.

The day the Devil comes to getcha
He's playing on the fiddle.
And you know he's gonna getcha—
Cause you're stuck in the middle.

Give me back my innocence.
Get me a brand new suit.
Give me back my innocence.
Oh Lord! Cut me down to size!
Cut me loose.

Give me back my innocence.
Get me a new Cadillac.
And when I get on up to Heaven, Lord—
You can have it all back.

Cause in Heaven, it all comes back.
In Heaven, you get it all back.
Cause in Heaven, it all comes back.
In Heaven, you get it all back.

"The day the Devil comes to getcha"
was written with Peter Gordon.

Langue d'amour

Let's see. It was on an island.
And there was this snake. And this snake had legs.
And he could walk all around the island.
Yes. That's true.
A snake with legs.

And the man and the woman were on the island too.
And they were not very smart.
But they were happy as clams.
Yes.

Let's see. Uh . . . then one evening the snake
Was walking about in the garden and he was
Talking to himself and he saw the
Woman and they started to talk.
And they became friends.
Very good friends.

And the woman liked the snake very much.
Because when he talked he made little noises with his
Tongue, and his long tongue was lightly licking
About his lips.
Like there was a little fire inside his
Mouth and the flame would come dancing out of his
Mouth. And the woman liked this
Very much.

And, after that, she was bored with the man.
Because no matter what happened,
He was always as happy as a clam.

What did the snake say?
Yes! What was he saying?

OK. I will tell you.
The snake told her things about the world.
He told her about the time there was a big
Typhoon on the island and all the
Sharks came out of the water.
Yes.
They came out of the water and they walked right into your
House with their big white teeth.

And the woman heard these things.
And she was in love.
And the man came out and said:
We have to go now!

And the woman did not want to go.
Because she was a hothead.
Because she was a woman in love.

Anyway, they got into their boat and left the island.
But they never stayed anywhere very long.
Because the woman was restless.
She was a hothead.
She was a woman in love.

And this is not a story my people tell.
It is something I know myself.
And when I do my job
I am thinking about these things.
Because when I do my job,
That is what I think about.

(continued)

Ooo la la la la. — Ooo. Oh yeah. Yes
Voici. — First it's over here.
Voilà. — Then it goes over there.
Ooo la la la la. — Ooo. Oh yeah. Yes.

Voici le langage de l'amour. — This is the language of love.

Ah comme ci comme ça. — Neither here nor there.
Voilà. Voilà. — Now it's over there.
Voici le langage de l'amour. — This is the language of love.

Attends! Attends! Attends! — Wait! Wait! Wait up!
Écoute! Écoute! Écoute! — Listen! Listen! Listen!
Ooo la la la la. — Ooo Oh yeah. Yes.
Voici le langage de l'amour. — This is the language of love.
Voici le langage dans mon coeur. — This is the language of my heart.
Voici le langage de l'amour. — This is the language of love.
Voici le langage dans mon coeur. — This is the language of my heart.

White lily

What Fassbinder film is it?
The one-armed man
Comes into the flower shop and says:
What flower expresses:
Days go by
And they just keep going by
Endlessly
Pulling you
Into the future?

Days go by
Endlessly, endlessly
Pulling you
Into the future?

And the florist says:
White lily.

Kokoku

I come very briefly to this place.
I watch it move. I watch it shake.

Kumowaku yamano. Watashino sakebi. Watashino koewo.
Ushano kokoku. Watashiwa sokoni. Watashiwa asobu.

Mountain with clouds. A cry. My voice.
Home of the brave. I'm here now. And lost.

They say the dead will rise again.
And here they come now. Strange animals
Out of the Ice Age.
And they stare at you. Dumbfounded.
Like big mistakes. And we say:
Keep cool. Maybe if we pretend
This never happened,
They'll all just go away.

Watashiwa sokoni. Watashiwa asobu. Mewotoji. Mewotoji.
Kikunowa Kotori. Watashino sakebi. Watashino koewo.

I am here in this place. Losing. My eyes are closed. Closed.
Birds are there. Hearing something. Shouting. My voice.

And yet, we could all be wrong.
Wouldn't be the first time.

Kumowaku yamano. Watashiwa sokoni. Watashiwa asobu.
Kumowaku yamano. Kikunowa kotori. Watashino sakebi.

Mountain with clouds. I am there. Lost.
Mountain with clouds. Birds are there. Hearing something. A shout.

They say the world is smaller now.
Small world.
They say that man is taller now.
Tall man.
They say the stars are closer now.
Thank you lucky stars.
You come very briefly to this place.

Jikanwa tomaru. Ushano kokoku.
Time is stopped. Home of the brave.

And on a very distant star—
Slimy creatures scan the skies.
They've got plates for hands
And telescopes for eyes.
And they say: Look! Down there!
A haunted planet spinning 'round.
They say: Watch it move.
Watch it shake. Watch it turn.
And shake.

And we say: Watch us move. Watch us shake.
We're so pretty.
We're so pretty.

We say: Watch us move now. Watch us shake.
We're so pretty.
Shake our hands. Shake our heads.
We shake our feet.
We're so fine.
The way we move. The way we shake.
We're so nice.

Whose shoes

Well I was lying in bed—
And this woman came on TV and she said:
Paradise is exactly like
Where you are right now—
Only much, much
Better.

And I looked around the room
At all the piles of junk in the gloom.
And all those stale sandwiches
And old reviews—And all those
Pairs of mis-matched socks and shoes.
And I said: "If you were
In my shoes, then you'd know
What a drag it is to see you."

And she said: "But, I am in your shoes!
And if not yours—
Then whose?"

Does light go towards people?
Or do people go towards light?

I dreamed there was an island
That rose up from the sea.
And everybody on the island
Was somebody from TV.

And there was a beautiful view—
But nobody could see.
Cause everybody on the island
Was screaming: Look at me! Look at me!
Look at me! Look at me!

Well I turned on the news.
And they said: Have we got news for you!
But first this:
Hi! We're three guys
from Three Guys Shoes. And have we got
Shoes for you!
Hi! I'm Benny! I'm Phil! And I'm Dave!
We're three guys from Three Guys Shoes.
We've got your size and your style—
(All your reds, all your blues)
And if not your size, whose?
So come on down to Three Guys Shoes
(We're on the mall.)
Cause at Three Guys Shoes we guarantee:
One size fits all.
Buy one, get one free.
Just like you've seen on TV!

Does light go towards people?
Or do people go toward light?

I dreamed there was an island
That rose up from the sea.
And everybody on the island—
Was somebody from TV.

And there was never any news—
Cause nobody could read.
Cause everybody on the island
Was screaming: Look at me! Look at me!
Look at me! Look at me!

Paradise is exactly like
Where you are right now—
Only much, much
Better.

Babydoll

I don't know about your brain—
but mine is really bossy.
I come home from a day on the golf course
and I find all these messages scribbled
on wrinkled-up scraps of paper.
And they say things like:
Why don't you get a real job?
Or: What's it to you?

And then I hear this voice
coming from the back of my head.
Yep. It's my brain again.
And when my brain talks to me he says:
Babydoll, I'm so glad you called.
He says: Babydoll, no problem's
too big or too small.
And I say: Listen, I'm trying
to read this manual,
and I don't know how.
And he says: Listen, Babydoll,
I'd love to help you out . . .
but I can't right now.
He says:
Take me out to the ballgame.
Take me out to the park.
Take me to the movies,
Cause I love to sit in the dark.
Take me to Tahiti.
Cause I love to be hot.
Take me out on the town tonight—
Cause I know the new in-spot.
He says:

Babydoll. Ooo ooo oo Babydoll.
Babydoll. I love it when you come
When I call.
Babydoll, you don't have to talk—
I know it all.
Babydoll. Ooo oo ooo. Babydoll.
Oooo.

(continued)

Well, I'm sitting around trying
to write a letter.
And I'm wracking my brains trying to think
of another word for "horse."
And I ask my brain for some assistance—
And he says: Hmmm . . . Have you thought of
"cow"? That's close!
He says:

Take me out to the ballgame.
Take me out to the park.
Take me to the movies—
Cause I love to sit in the dark.
Take me to your leader.
And I say: You mean . . . RON?!
And he says: I just want to meet him.
And I say: C'mon! I don't even know Ron!
And he says:

Babydoll. Oooo ooo ooo Babydoll.
Babydoll. I love it when you come—
When I call.
Babydoll. You don't have to talk—
I know it all.
Babydoll. Ooo ooo ooo Babydoll. Ooo.

Well, I just want to take some time off.
I just want to get out of here.
I just want to go somewhere—anywhere!
I need some heat. I need some air.

Well, I'm finally sitting in Tahiti.
Sun's beating down and I'm sipping
a chartreuse tropical drink.
And I'm trying to remember—
I'm trying to . . . what's the word
I'm looking for? . . . . . I'm . . . uh . . .
trying to . . . *think!*
And suddenly I see this guy
jogging down the beach . . .
And there's something familiar
about his pace. And something about
Those paisley bermudas. . . .
I can't quite place. . . . .
And suddenly I hear:

BABYDOLL! Oooo ooo ooo BABYDOLL. Oooo.
BABYDOLL! I love it when you come—
When I call.
BABYDOLL! You don't have to talk—
I know it all.
BABYDOLL. Oooo. Oooo. Ooo. BABYDOLL. Oooo.

And I say: This is some vacation!
I mean I've come 3,000 miles—
just to run into this guy again!
So I hide under my umbrella.
I let him pass me by. I take it slow.
I don't know. . . . Must be the heat.
Because slowly, slowly I'm learning
That nobody knows how I feel—
Better than me.
And slowly my head is turning.
It's teaching my heart—
It's showing my heart—
It's telling it how to beat.

And slowly my heart is burning.
It's burning my hands—
It's burning my eyes—
I can feel the heat.

Because slowly my head is turning.
It's teaching my heart—
It's showing my heart—
It's telling it how to beat.

And slowly, slowly I'm burning
My head is hot.
My feet are on fire.
I can feel the heat.

Charles Amirkhanian

Here's my friend Charles Amirkhanian. I know him better than anyone else here; we've been friends for years, and I'm proud that he's only describing what he does when he says, in Gold and Spirit, *"STEER PEERS TO SHERE." (That's why I'm here.) We both had casual, small-town, old-fashioned upbringings preparing us for what turned out to be lifetimes devoted to the sophisticated, up-to-date avant-garde, and I think I know what motivates his slight discomfort, even regret, at taking his place in this illustrious company. "I think there's a bit of insecurity in people who feel the way I do," he admits, and I wouldn't be surprised but that much of his wonderful music—funny, full of suddenly revelatory meaning and happy accident—is made out of a determination to suspend or set aside his own ego, his conscious artistry, in a technique that develops out of seemingly random procedures. In that, Charles too follows Cage's lead, of course, and if Laurie Anderson follows it as a sort of nightclub reporter, Charles does it as a pulpit poet. (Pulp it, poet: he even gets us doing it!) I'm not sure I agree with Sheila Davies and Susan Stone when they suggest that Charles doesn't want to be symbolic or meaningful; "it actually seems as though [his] greatest preference is to be looked at as superficial"; but I know what they mean: there's something about working a long time invisibly on the radio that encourages us to pursue our work privately for our own reasons while setting it out publicly for others to respond to in their way, and Charles finds a lucid and persuasive response to their remark—but I'll let you discover it for yourself.* —C.S.

CHARLES AMIRKHANIAN

Sheila Davies
Susan Stone
January 1985; Oakland, California

You seem to delight in strange foods.

I'll tell you why that is. It's basically an insecurity. People who collect strange things do so so they can impress other people. That's what happens. I'm afraid that's the basis of it. It's what gets you started on the addiction. I was growing up in a town that was completely conventional and I wanted to be different because I thought that's what artists did. They were different. They did things that nobody did before them. And making statements that way in your art was a way to make a contribution. It was later that I discovered food.

There's a basic insecurity that grows out of not having a background that you think will suffice to impress other people. I never had a conventional music upbringing, so I spent all my time having an unconventional music upbringing that I taught myself—I was self-taught in compositional matters. So, I would spend a lot of time finding out about things that other people didn't know anything about.

How would you say it carried over to the way you compose now?

Well, I refuse to use pitches. I use non-pitched sounds, speech and ambient sounds. And I don't compose in conventional ways. It's because I'm not trained in composing in conventional ways, and I just don't want to do it. There already is so vast a repertoire of composed music which is so highly developed—and I love a great deal of it—so I just wanted to go off in my own direction. As a percussionist I was using many instruments, like the bass drum and cymbals, which we consider traditionally to be non-pitched. Well, we think of speech that way too, as opposed to sung tones which have definite pitch. So, I just considered these speech sounds to be percussion points or sound objects which I could use for composing. Later, the literary aspect became a part of this too, but at the time in the mid-sixties, I hadn't thought of the possibility of this work having anything but musical implications.

Given the unconventionality of your compositional style, how do you feel about being categorized as a "text-sound composer"?

Well, it doesn't bother me because it's such a small group, and entirely unique. The music people don't consider me a composer and the poetry people don't consider me a poet, and I'm in no way disturbed about that. I think I'm just doing something that falls between the cracks. And text-sound composition to you may seem like a really established genre but when I was starting to work, there wasn't any such thing and no one knew what it was. Whatever I was doing wasn't categorized. I just fell in some crack somewhere. Then I found out that people all over the world were doing it. The Swedes decided to give it a name—text-sound composition—and before that the French had called it *Poèsie Sonore.* What I was doing was more strongly musical than what the French were doing which leaned more toward poetry.

What would you call what you do now, if you could defy all the categorization?

What would I call it? I compose . . . I'm a text-sound composer, I guess.

Does it fit?

What I do? Yeah, I think it's okay. I sort of like to differentiate my work from that of conventional composers because people who look at my work and expect pitches and orchestral instruments are going to be sorely disappointed. And yet there's something about the way I write that isn't strictly poetic. Also, it has musical concerns beyond those that you find in Clark Coolidge's work or others loosely related. It's more strongly musical than those others.

Can you tell me a little about the 1750 Arch Record sound poetry anthology?

I did the *10 plus 2* record which was, at the time, the first LP anthology of sound poetry in American literature, except for the fact that there were a few records called *Poetry Out Loud.* Do you remember those? They were not very exceptional experiments with home tape recorders that were done by some people in the Midwest, I think. But the *10 plus 2* record was the first anthology which put together a lot of Americans who were working with speech, not necessarily just poets, but John Cage and Robert Ashley who were composers, and Liam O'Gallagher and Brion Gysin who were painters, John Giorno who was a poet, and Beth Anderson a composer, Aram Saroyan a poet, and Tony Gnazzo a composer. All of these people were from different disciplines, working in speech as an audio form. There had been no defining anthology putting them together and saying, this is sound poetry.

And then I did the radio programs. Fifty or sixty of them were broadcast on KPFA after I came back from Europe in 1972 and I had seen with my own eyes that there were lots of people all over Europe making sound poetry. I had really been introduced to it by the opportunity to travel to Sweden to be in the sound poetry festival in April of 1972. And after that,

Carol Law and I bought a Saab station wagon and we drove it all over Europe and slept in the back of it: little villages in Italy, to Belgium and Holland and France, Germany, Switzerland, and we knocked on the door of every sound poet we could find and interviewed them. Then for the next year, from 1972 to 1973, I broadcast these interviews. And that was the first time I feel I was taken seriously on KPFA by the audience because it was then that I had information that they couldn't get their hands on, and they felt that I'd really gone out and brought them something that they couldn't have otherwise experienced. I noticed a change immediately in the audience response, so it was a period of maturing for me which was important.

After these broadcasts, I got the idea to do an LP anthology because of having seen one in every country in Europe. There was a French anthology and a British anthology, a German anthology, and we didn't have one. And yet we had a group of people doing all this interesting work. So, after the anthology came out, there was a real wave of activity that started in the Bay Area and mushroomed out everywhere, of people doing these sound poetry things. And all along, Jackson MacLow and people in New York had been doing it. Cage had just begun doing sound poetry at that point. He became interested in Clark Coolidge's work and then read Coolidge's books, which were an inspiration for me also, and started doing text readings. The radio programs and the anthology provided the impetus for a vitalization of whatever interest there was in the country for doing that kind of work.

I still cannot get over the historical foundation you set up here.

What was really interesting about it was that I'd become involved in this because I was a percussionist and had been looking for new sounds to incorporate, and instead of finding another percussion object I hit on the use of speech. In Fresno there was a church, the First Methodist Church, which had a really progressive minister who was later relieved of his job. I was commissioned by this man to do a piece for his Sunday sermon which was on Genesis 28, the portion in the Bible about Jacob's Ladder. And so I took this segment from the Bible and set it for four male voices, and each of the voices was reciting in canon these lines from the Bible. They were punctuated by the sounds of metal discs which have a bolt in them that are used to cover irrigation pipes in Fresno County on the farms. So, if you have a grape vineyard, you have these irrigation pipes where the water gushes out. If you want to stop the water you put these lids on the top, and we had these lids in the left hand, and in the right hand a beater, a xylophone beater. We would punctuate the voice, the speech, with these sounds so you would have the same line repeated out of synch by four people. At the beginning of each line we have a bang on the irrigation lid cover—so it goes "ding ding ding ding," and you hear the four lines, one starting at the first ding, the next one at the second ding and so forth.

I sent this score to Roger Reynolds whom I'd known about—he was in Michigan, and he was writing speech scores—and he wrote back giving some advice. He'd written a thing called "The Emperor of Ice Cream" that was speakers in a theatrical setting—it was a Wallace Stevens text. So I tried to correspond with people who were doing similar things, and he suggested that I look into the works of Mauricio Kagel and others. I ordered scores of all these people at the local music store in Fresno and I decided to make a sort of specialty out of researching people who had done speech things. Then I heard a record of the "Geographical Fugue" by Ernst Toch...

What year was this?

1965 ... and, mind you, all of this was because of my interest in percussion. I was no longer tied to the idea that music had to have pitched sounds, which is why I started to compose in the first place, because I hadn't had composing lessons and I knew how to play the drums pretty well so I wanted to write percussion rhythms but was not terribly impressed with pitched sounds. And I still don't write pitches—well, rarely. I was really concerned with rhythm. And you could have rhythms in speech. So that's why I got off onto that kick.

Did you start playing drums when you were a teenager?

No, I started in the fifth grade. Somebody came into the classroom where I was and said can anyone read music, we need a drummer in the elementary school orchestra, and I raised my hand, and another guy, Rick Conaway, raised his hand—Rick was a good friend of mine—and he and I both played the piano and we could both read music. So we went down to audition for the elementary school orchestra and I got the job. The strange thing was that the lady who was teaching the orchestra—I can't remember her name—didn't know how to roll on the snare drums, and so she said, take the sticks and drop them, let them bounce. That's how I learned to roll. I had to drop them and let them bounce. Well, when I got to junior high, they really laughed my ass off. Boy did I hear about that.

Was it really helpful, knowing how to play the drums when you became a teenager?

Well, see, I played orchestral percussion, and, no, that wasn't helpful. If I had been playing in a rock and roll band or something, that would be helpful. It was never a sexual thing at all. I had no relief in adolescence.

Okay, you can go back further. You had piano lessons?

Yeah, my Aunt Lorraine was my teacher. I took my first lesson on October 5th, 1951. I was six-and-a-half. I played "Three Black Bears." My mother and her three sisters all majored in piano at Fresno State, piano performance. What happened was that Aunt Lorraine went to USC, she did graduate work there after Fresno State. So, when she came back, she started enrolling students, and Mom thought it would be better if I didn't study at home but with Aunt Lorraine. So, I walked a block and a half away down Maroa Avenue and there was Aunt Lorraine's studio in this little house. She rented a room in this old lady's house, she had an upright, and I learned how to play piano there. That building was torn down some years ago. Then she moved her studio to a nicer place. So, I studied piano with Aunt Lorraine, Lorraine Kaprielian, for ten years.

Did you like learning music?

Well, my mother was really strict and I had to practice an hour every day, at least on weekdays. I can't remember on weekends. And, no, no kid likes to learn how to play the piano. I never did relish it. I just thought it was some sort of purgatory.

What else would you have been doing?

I was very interested in football and the scores, and sports in general, and collecting butterflies. When we'd go on trips, I would write down all the names of all the gasoline stations, the different kinds of gasoline stations, and the different kinds of license plates from different states, and the different bread brands we'd see in the different localities. I'd get these long lists of everything. It's this collector's complex. I also had it when I was really young, these Little Golden Records, so probably I was into hoarding really young.

I think that you're a Faulkner-type; that everything can be traced to the five square blocks around your home.

Oh, that's possible, because right in back there was Joel Studebaker. His father divorced his mother, I remember that. His father was a doctor, and there was something bad about him because he left the woman. And Joel had more Golden Records than I did, unfortunately, and that's when I realized that I was simply outclassed by a richer family, even though they were living in a duplex and we were in a house.

What did you do about that?

I wrote Roman numerals on all my Golden Records on both sides. I, II— my parents were proud of me because I could write Roman numerals, but then I wrote them in all my books and even on my John Cage records.

And what would they mean? Like, this is the third record . . . ?

I guess. I just started writing them. I don't think I was too rational, or systematic. But, I was given a John Cage* record when I was five or six. My father went to Ruschaupt's, the appliance store, and they were having these cut-out records on sale—this was in the days of 78s. And he saw this record that had an Armenian rug on the cover and so he got it because it looked like it was Armenian folk music. Of course, my mother abhorred anything Armenian, didn't want me to learn Armenian, didn't want me to have any Armenian stuff in the house, except for the food.† So, we put it on and there were these weird sounds. And side one, record one, was devoted to the music of John Cage. It had Maro Ajemian playing the prepared piano—that instrument where they put the bolts in the strings. The second disc was Alan Hovhaness, played by himself and Maro Ajemian. So, she played the piano and he played these gongs and percussion instruments. My mother hated it and wanted my Dad to take it back, but it was a cut-out and they couldn't take it back. So we kept it. When they would leave the house I would put on those records and dance around the room. I really liked those records—because they scared me. We had lots of other music in our house, classical music. The Gayne Ballet by Khachaturian and Mahler's Fourth Symphony. I systematically broke almost every record, there were about seven records in the Mahler set. I didn't do it on purpose, I was just clumsy.

Piano Compositions by Alan Hovhaness and John Cage, played by Maro Ajemian and Alan Hovhaness. Disc Company of America. 1947.

†Armenians of my parents' generation suffered tremendous discrimination during their youths in Fresno and tried very hard to appear to be "normal" Americans.   —C.A.

Why did they scare you, those records?

Oh well, you know, it was so unconventional, the sounds— it sounded spooky.

But you loved them; you were drawn to them?

I was drawn to them, I was hypnotized by them. I knew the name John Cage from the age of five. And I knew his face. His picture was on the album. I knew he was a good guy because he hung around with Armenians. The pianist on the record was an Armenian, and so was the other composer.

Aren't you kind of amazed by that? What a strange thing.

It was a strange coincidence. It might have been formative. I noticed when I was playing the piano for those ten years, I was always drawn to pieces that were in minor keys, that were more modern sounding, that were less conventional. And I don't know why that was, because all the other music in the house was very conventional—classical music. I mean, I went once a month to the Fresno Musical Club concerts and those concerts consisted of people like Walter Gieseking and Dame Myra Hess and all these classical pianists from Europe playing Beethoven. And, Aunt Lorraine would say, "Oh, wasn't that beautiful," afterwards when we'd be leaving the hall. And I'd say, "Oh, I sort of went to sleep in the middle, I didn't like the middle." The development section—a kid can't follow that. You like the main theme and you like the ending, you don't like the middle. But I would follow all the modern pieces whenever I'd get a chance to hear them. I found them immediately accessible.

There was something you were saying about wanting to be different—I wonder if you're really courting superiority or courting risk. The fact is that you're always a bit inaccessible to the average listener. It makes me wonder if you like that separation.

I think there's a bit of insecurity in people who feel the way I do. The thing I dread most is being in the position that John Adams or Laurie Anderson is in. They're in a position now where everybody is watching everything they do. Those people can't relax, they can't do anything natural—although they do, in spite of their pressures. But, I'm not built that way. I don't feel secure enough to sit here and write masterpiece after masterpiece, as I think Steve Reich knows that he's doing, or thinks that he's doing. But I think that I have something else going for me which is that I can be a little looser about what I do, and not worry about whether it's a masterpiece or not, because not everybody's watching me. So I sort of like that, being kind of out of the way. I've always preferred the idea of being an obscure figure who would be discovered at the age of 60 or 70, that's what I'd really like to be, if there is anything worthwhile in it at all.

Do you ever feel, like in your situation at KPFA where you are director of music programming, that you are sometimes just courting controversy, or are you really pursuing what others should also see as the correct course?

Well, the latter. I really think that the things I like are more interesting than the things that are conventionally said to be great. I guess everybody feels that way if they have any instincts of their own. But I've seen so many people—who are my contemporaries—who just accept whatever is the given wisdom about who is a great artist. I guess they get that largely from their teachers in college. I don't know where else they would get it. They don't get it from newspaper critics. Maybe it's my lack of formal training which is maybe more open to things that are less conventional. I guess I'm sort of a gadfly in the serious music realm and I sort of like being that. I feel like I'm sort of jabbing people and trying to get them to come around.

When I did that women's anthology* of electronic music, Laurie Anderson didn't even have a commercial record out at that point; that was her first one. Laurie Spiegel didn't have a commercial record out. Pauline Oliveros

*New Music for Electronic and Recorded Media, produced by Charles Amirkhanian. 1750 Arch Street. 1977. Composers on recording: Johanna Magdalena Beyers, Annea Lockwood, Pauline Oliveros, Laurie Spiegel, Ruth Anderson, Megan Roberts, Laurie Anderson

hadn't been published on a record for years and years. And Johanna Beyer was totally unknown, still is, but she was an early electronic music pioneer. Most of the women composers who were known for doing electronic music at that time were from the Columbia-Princeton group, and they wrote very derivative music in a style that was taught at either Columbia or Princeton. And it was abstract and abstruse and austere and boring and twelve-tone. And there were all these other women doing exciting things and they couldn't get attention. (It was probably the idea that women were now going to be professional.) And there was a large group of people at Mills who were studying with Bob Ashley and coming out and having nowhere to go. I wanted to do that album, something to sort of fly in the face of the Eastern establishment. And it says it right on the back cover. That's what it says and that's what it is. It's like—here, take this. And in the face of the male establishment, really, because there was no effort to document these people's work. The same with Conlon Nancarrow. It's hard to believe, but no one was issuing his records at all.

So not only is it a way of changing the conventional wisdom, it's also a way of bringing attention to people who really deserve it. Other curators and editors weren't standing up for them because they didn't trust their own judgment of them, or they didn't know about them. I think a lot of the people that I embraced in these various forms are some people who were kind of ridiculed by the Milton Babbitt-Charles Wuorinen contingent. I took a kind of West Coast position, the opposite of the East Coast intellectual. It's like being a West Coast intellectual who says—there is wisdom outside of Europe.

Getting back to the subject of women as composers.

I heard Aaron Copland say at a press conference once, "Why are there no great women composers? Well, I'll tell you. You see in a symphonic piece you have to compose over a length of 40 minutes, you have to remember everything. Women can't do that." Anyway, that was the conventional wisdom in the 'thirties, that was why women couldn't compose then.

So, you—and maybe some of these other people you've mentioned— haven't felt any loss of self esteem because you have a vision of your own, a West Coast kind of vision which incorporates stuff from the East but has its own momentum.

There's a real snobbism on the East Coast that prevents a crosscurrent from happening there. And when Tracey Sterne who ran Nonesuch records and who issued all these East Coast composers for years and years, and was sort of a focal point of publishing of the music of American composers, was sent the tapes of Nancarrow, she turned them down flat. And then years later she came up to me and said, "That was the one project that I don't know why I turned down, I can't believe that I was hearing the same tape that you were hearing. I just didn't hear anything in it." So there was this barrier beyond which these people wouldn't go. She might have been put off by any number of things, by the fact that it was a player piano rather than a conventional piano and pianist, or the fact that it sounded a little mechanical and tinny. But she wasn't listening to the structure of the music and the excitement of how he put those pieces together which is pure genius—there's no other word for it. And a lot of the other people, like Harry Partch and Cage and Lou Harrison, are considered naïve by the East Coast people.

I think you could find the same in the regard of the East Coast intellectual establishment for the minimalist—which, you have to remember, is a movement that started in Berkeley. And it started here because of LaMonte Young's influence from Eastern religion and philosophy, and Steve Reich and Terry Riley's background in jazz—as a drummer and a pianist, respectively. Those confluences couldn't have happened in New York. They were marketed in New York but they were born on the West Coast.

So there's a certain benefit to being outside of the traditional system. But it puts you in a maverick position automatically. I interviewed a composer named Ernst Bacon, who's still living in Orinda and he's very elderly now, and he never could endure the idea of living in New York. He loved walking every day in the forest. He'd been in South Carolina and taught at Converse College there, Syracuse University, and he started the Carmel Bach festival here—he goes for a walk every day here, and he never could live in New York. He feels that composers of his quality in New York became much more famous because that's the center of publishing and you couldn't do it unless you lived there, as a composer *or* a performer. I never believed that, but as I get older I am beginning to believe it. That's how you make it. And Europe's connection to New York is so much stronger than it is here. If you live in New York—people from Europe get at least to New York—you can get a lot of gigs in Europe. But Europeans rarely get to this coast.

Do you ever enter a trance-like state when you're performing?

Yes, when I run out of breath. I first started to do that in "Inini Bullpup Banjo." I was trying to make this piece that would sound like I was running out of breath, and Richard Friedman had told me that there were dancers in New York who were getting into doing dervish things, getting into self-hypnosis. So I decided that I would do something like that in sound poetry, and I just started using tape loops because I heard Steve Reich's "Come Out," so I did this piece called "If In Is" in 1971. It was for a radio program with Richard Friedman, Tony Gnazzo, and myself. And my piece was this one with these words:

> inini inini inini
> inini
> inini
> inini
> inini inini
>
> inini
> inini inini
> inini inini bullpup banjo
>
> banjo
> banjo
> banjo
> banjo banjo inini bullpup banjo
> banjo

Well, "bullpup" was the mascot for the Fresno State Junior Varsity because they couldn't be the bulldogs, they had to be the bullpups, and Inini is that colony the butterfly-man escaped to, Papillon. Inini was a French colony in South America—see, I was a stamp collector, too.

Do you use word maps?

Word maps? What are those?

Places created with words instead of scenery. You use a lot of place names and your pieces have great geographical concepts. They're marvelous and they're impossible locations because they come in the middle of bullpups and banjos. They sound great. Word maps. Did I ruin your train of thought?

No, just my shin. Well—the one thing that became important that I discovered when I was doing that piece was when I mixed my voice over itself I could get these combined words that would be more interesting than having three different voices read the same things. I learned that from Clark Coolidge who'd been making a piece at Mills using tape loops where he'd have one or two or three words on each loop, and they were sometimes the same and sometimes different, and he just let these loops play, all eight of them at once for long periods of time, and then he'd take a segment of that tape and put it on the air. I remember now that he would call these things wordscapes. He was doing all sorts of really interesting experiments like that, and the audio quality was very very poor because the tape loop machine at Mills wasn't very high quality. I decided I would like to extend that idea somehow, so I sort of combined my interest in what Steve Reich had done with "Come Out" and what Clark was doing with these tape loop pieces into what later became a piece called "Just," which is the "Rainbow–Chug–Bandit–Bomb" piece.

"Rainbow–Chug–Bandit–Bomb" is the piece I did when I went to Sweden for the sound poetry festival in 1972 when I was on that first European trip. That was another example of taking the same voice and juxtaposing it over itself, one of the points being—as Coolidge noted—to make new words by having two tapes of one person's voice sound at the same time in certain conjunctions. Like you'd have the loops playing and sometimes you would hear voices separately and sometimes they'd be in sync. And you would hear the word "rainbow" and the word "bandit" superimposed on one another with the same voice speaking it, so it sounded like the voice had two larynxes, it was as if I could speak two sentences at the same moment. So you would hear words which couldn't be humanly possible, which is sort of like making concrete poetry where you superimpose one word over another and it becomes a visual symbol which is different. Well, what I was doing was the same thing, in audio terms, I was making audio symbols with words which couldn't be physically spoken. Also, I was using the counterpoint of the rhythms of "Rainbow–Chug–Bandit–Bomb" in different layers so that you would have percussion points made out of words bouncing around against each other, and that just fascinated me, that you could get this propulsion going with language that wasn't going anywhere. It was just very Gertrude Stein-like, very non-syntactical. You had nouns butted up against one another, so there was no phrase created out of an adjective, a noun, a verb, and it was just a fresher way of seeing language for the first time.

But then you've since refined it in your piece "History of Collage." How does that work?

That's a cut-up piece that's done the way Brion Gysin and William Burroughs made their pieces. I took a text which was an introduction to a book called *History of Collage* and I took the first paragraph and I cut it up. I looked at it and I divided the whole paragraph into phrases and then I took the phrases and I rearranged them all so they would modify each other in a strange way, surreal ways. And I did that because the book was called the *History of Collage* and I was using the elements of the introduction and I was collaging the phrases. So that was sort of a play on that idea.

And how about the actual taping of it?

Well, each time I cut from one phrase to another I had the voice on a different channel so that it sounds like two patterns that are separate. They have a narrative quality that the other pieces don't have. And all that time until 1981 I wasn't using any rhythm generators because the words were generating rhythms themselves, but then with all these electronic drums coming out I decided I would try to use them in some of the more recent pieces. So I've used those and I've found that you could really speed up the sense of rhythm by playing very fast drumbeats underneath words that are going relatively slowly. And, then, in the more recent pieces, I've also been using digital delay and harmonization and other kinds of digital modulation that give a timbral quality that's different than regular speech.

Up to that time I was using just regular speech with no alteration. I would have layers of speech, I wouldn't have alteration of the speech because I felt that had been done so well by the European composers who did tape music—Stockhausen and Berio and others. And they'd had very extreme kinds of expression and electronic interaction with voices that was almost unbelievable in its complexity. So I went the other direction and did something very stark with just the regular human voice but layered, so that the recording studio came into play as a device but not the electronic studio. It's just recently that I've begun to incorporate digital modulation which interests me a lot.

Is it human speech that you work with more, that is, language, the words? Or is it the sound?

That's hard to say because, you know, when I got into radio I started thinking about the idea of speech and the delivery as being very important, whereas when I was performing the pieces with quartets of vocalists, people speaking, my directions on the scores were all musical. I'd write *forte* and *pianissimo* and all that. I'd also have *crescendo* markings on the scores. When I got into the radio station I started using just my own voice and I started becoming very aware of how it sounded and how I delivered the lines. Coolidge had a way of delivering his lines that was very dry, so that there was no implication of or suggestion of emotion, leaving you to confront just the words, and I sort of took that up. But my voice is much different from his. His sometimes has an almost sarcastic edge to it and is a thinner voice. Mine is a richer sounding voice and I use the mike differently from the way he did in '69-70, so I have this very close-miked presence in the pieces. I was trying to develop something that he had started but do it in my own way.

But aren't the words that you choose very emotional?

I don't know what system I have for choosing them because it's all very intuitive, but it's partly sonic and rhythmic, and musical and partly literary.

Sexual?

Sometimes, yeah. But that can be really corny, so I try to avoid that, being really overt about that.

When you listen to your own music are you moved emotionally?

I don't know if the word would be emotional. But yes, I'm strongly affected by hearing it. I guess it's mostly dependent on which pieces. I'm not terribly emotional about "Go Van Gogh," but I am about "History of Collage."

You always listen for technicality, right? You want it to be technically perfect.

Yeah. I'm also listening for cleverness in "History of Collage" because those phrase juxtapositions . . . I could only work within the parameters of the original text. In "Maroa," I'm listening for rhythmic drive and kind of a juxtaposition of peculiar words that sort of tweeks something in my brain that I like. The "Dog of Stravinsky,"* I'm—I just love that dog bark. I'm not a dog person but I'm definitely a bark person.

Bliss, your cat, figures into one of your pieces, doesn't she?

Bliss is on a piece I did at Arch Street called "The Type Without Time" . . . she wouldn't perform, she froze. Usually I can squeeze her like an accordion, just put my hand on her belly and squeeze. But she wouldn't do it in the 1750 Arch Street Studio, she was petrified. It was an unfamiliar environment. So we left her in the room with the microphone and after a while she walked up to the mike, and Bob Shumaker captured her purr.

You don't want to be symbolic; you don't want to be meaningful; it actually seems as though your greatest preference is to be looked at as superficial; you get along there because it seems you can function more variably there.

I let people have their own interpretations. You know, a lot of people who do art are that way. They get their inspiration from things they just don't want to divulge to people, and it's not really important. What's important is how it comes off if you don't know those things. It's not important to know the story if the piece itself speaks because if you wanted to tell the story—what it was that inspired you—you should just write it out. But if you want to make an art piece about it, then it seems to me that that piece should stand on its own. So sometimes you get your inspiration and the idea and the words that go into one of these pieces from an incident, and other times from just opening a book somewhere and reading a letter or seeing a typo you made on the typewriter. What's not important is where you got it. What is important is how did you put those elements together and make something out of it. And what resonance does that create in the person who tries to experience your work. So some things are really personal, you just don't want to say what it was that gave you that idea. You've forgotten it most of the time.

*In San Francisco, where the repetitive music movement was launched by the activity of composers LaMonte Young, Terry Riley and Steve Reich, certain newspaper critics have taken a conspicuously rabid stance on the subject.

While working in Stockholm at EMS (the Institute for Electro-Acoustic Music) in October 1982, I happened upon the perfect homage to these journalists: "Dog of Stravinsky."

This interspecies text-sound composition documents the remarkable, perfectly periodic bark of the late Belgian sheepdog "Dashiell Hammett," to which I added pitch to pitch by modulating pre-recorded barking via a Buchla Synthesizer vocoder."
—C.A., from the liner notes, *Mental Radio,* Charles Amirkhanian, Composers Recordings, Inc., 1985 CRI SD 523

All of your work seems very thick and textural, there is a certain density to it, as though it is the memory of your life without the meaning.

The residue. That's actually not true. That happens in one out of six pieces, and the other five, I open a notebook and just start writing because I've got 15 minutes free somewhere. That's what really happens. And some of the things that come into your head when you have a short time free in the middle of a chaotic day are loaded with oblique images of your activity just as when you dream and those images are brought to you from something that might have happened in previous hours of waking time.

But the energy that is accumulated from whatever happens during the day comes out in my pieces in rhythms that are almost free-associated, and very often the words that I actually use are used to fill in rhythms that come into my mind. So I'll think of a rhythm. What am I saying? It's true. I think of these rhythms and then I think of these words to go into the rhythmic spaces. So I'm just writing drum cadences like a kid in high school. Very often the words have nothing absolutely to do with anything else that's happened to me during the day. Sometimes they do or sometimes they're from signs on the street or from something I overheard somebody saying, but other times they're just patterns that are used because I thought I had this great rhythmic idea. But within those rhythms, I have to find the *right* words. And that process I can't spell out. That's the art part.

What about the different personas that you may manipulate or present to us when you're on stage?

That's mostly because I can't dance; that's why I look funny like that. I really am awkward up there and I never feel really at ease unless I have a music score in front of me, in which case, I can go like this and gesticulate wildly. But when you're up there without a score to look at or something to focus on, you have to be Frank Sinatra—you're carrying a mike around, you've got this cable leading off and you have to be a pop singer. There's just no way for me to pull it off.

So just the presense of a score totally alleviates your stage fright?

Yeah. I performed in 60 or 70 concerts in Fresno as a percussionist. What was really great, in just shocking the hell out of people when we were playing these bizarre scores, was that it was all written down. And I, by looking at the music stand, would reassure the audience that what I was doing was rational whereas when I don't have that there, it's not the same. You don't have something to focus on, you have to look at the audience, confront the audience, it's a different thing. It's a way of showing your insecurity. My way is walking back and forth on the proscenium, not knowing which way to walk. I don't care what I look like, I'm just trying to get through it. In my head, I'm thinking, I just want to get through this and I don't know how to move on stage or what to do with myself, especially if I've got the piece memorized.

Do you see yourself as being different on the air than on stage?

Yeah, because I'm not visible, so I can be much more in control. A couple of times I've heard tapes of myself while I'm driving in my car. It's a pretty spooky feeling.

When people see you after listening to you on the radio for years, what do they say? Oh, you're not blond?

No, they always say that they thought I was much older. Of course, now I *am* much older, so they don't say that anymore.

What about twentieth century music?

Well, as Henry Brant says, twentieth century music is the best music ever written, the most exciting, the most incredibly interesting, better than nineteenth century music, which all fitted into very strict patterns. There are no patterns, and so much more variety. In general, the composer-artist today has to command much more facility—at least in composing—than before. You have to know so many more things and usually you devise your own system of scoring for each piece—everything is made more complex using traditional techniques. I feel that, from the cumulative point of view, we've seen contributions in this century that are as profound as those of Bach, Mozart, and Beethoven—and in every way as stimulating.

Notes about the texts

"Church Car" is a work which can be performed live by two speaking voices alone but which I prefer to perform with the two vocalists doubling their pre-recorded parts on tape, giving an offset quality which adds complexity of timbre. The vocalists speak a series of 24 phrases three times each in progressively more complex counterpoint. Uncharacteristically, the word imagery (church car, box car, auto-bump car) has a thread of related subject matter, and the humor in this piece is perhaps more direct as a result.*

"Hypothetical Moments (in the Intellectual Life of Southern California)" was written at Tassajara, a Zen Buddhist retreat in the Carmel Mountains near Monterey in Northern California. It was there in June 1981 that I began the text for this piece late one evening after having spent the day engrossed in two wildly differing bits of reading matter. I've always liked the escape afforded by Edith Wharton's novels of manners documenting the vicissitudes of late nineteenth and early twentieth century New York society from her alienated perspective, all of which is heightened by a sheen of gentility which leaves the present-day reader in a state of unrelieved frustration. Almost diametrically opposed is the gruff, drugged-out reportage of a Yankees-Red Sox baseball game published by poets Ted Berrigan and Harris Schiff in "Yo-Yo's with Money". The transcription of their irreverent comments, recorded live in the Yankee Stadium bleachers into a cassette machine, forms the hilarious content of the book. I began by intercutting phrases from the two source books (Wharton's *Glimpses of the Moon* was the other text) and then proceeded on my own. Clark Coolidge's virtuosic prose piece "American Ones" was also influential in developing "Hypothetical Moments."*

"Maroa" is the name of a street in Fresno, California, where I was raised. I've tried, unsuccessfully, to find the derivation of the word. Some say that it came from the Yokut Indians who lived in Fresno County before the white settlers arrived in the mid-nineteenth century. It is also the name of a miniscule town in the desolate far southwestern reaches of the Venezuelan Amazon Forest. Another curious term in the piece, "psychodemocracy," is from an essay written and published in the twenties by the American writer Mina Loy outlining "a movement to focus human reason on the conscious direction of evolution."*

"Dreams Freud Dreamed" was recorded in 1979 at the New Wilderness Foundation. Director Charlie Morrow, himself a distinguished composer and improving musician, had invited me to do a performance at the Foundation and proposed a musical collaboration for this text in particular. At each occurrence of the letter **r** in the text, he intones a reinforced **r** sound, and occasionally rings a bell from his collection of oriental bells.

The writing was triggered by a newspaper article detailing a study of the dream journals of Sigmund Freud himself.*

"History of Collage" is based on the text of an introduction to an art book on the subject with all of the phrases rearranged in cut-up fashion. A drum synthesizer, set at its slowest speed (quarter note = 40mm) is heard along with natural sounds of ducks, birds, and bubbling water—also a very tame cricket, recorded so close to the microphone that the aggressiveness of the sound is greatly magnified. Artist Carol Law, with whom I often collaborate in performance, has used collage techniques in many of her projection slides for my pieces. And I myself, using the control room as a compositional tool, often juxtapose aurally diverse found and composed materials by collage methods. Therefore, the text of this particular piece holds a shared meaning for us which extends into our fascination with the Dada, Futurist and Surrealist work of the earlier part of the twentieth century.*

"Dutiful Ducks" is a live performance piece for solo voice with pre-recorded voice. The reader performs live, amplified, and in synchronization with his/her own voice which has been pre-recorded. The tape-recorded voice is played back through the same speakers which amplify the live voice. The impossibility of making the live voice sync exactly with the pre-recorded one results in slight out-of-phase shadings which lend an ambiguous quality to the aural focus. The text is composed of five thirteen-line stanzas and five choral-like refrains. The words which make up the stanza sections often have a fragmentary, though syntactical, sort of cohesion to them. The associations that they can signify are open to several interpretations.*

Notes on the reading aloud of these texts

These texts are intended to be read aloud. Most of them are meant to be read with a steady basic (and usually deliberate) pulse. And most have one or more very simple cueing signs which I have come to use as a sort of shorthand. An asterisk (*) at the end of a line indicates that the reader should continue to the next line without pause. A hyphen (-) indicates that the word following is to be sounded more quickly after the previous word (e.g. "is to-be" might be the indication for what is the normal speech pattern in that phrase). An exclamation mark (!) stands for a handclap in "Dutiful Ducks." An apostrophe (') in "Church Car" stands for an intake of breath. A comma (,) indicates a half-beat rest in certain pieces.

Various signs have been employed to indicate pauses. A dash (—) indicates a pause of one pulse. A slash (/) indicates half a pulse rest. In "Church Car," each word is given a half-beat value and there are no pauses at line-ends. However, in most of these texts, I read each word with one beat (equivalent to, say, a quarter-note in music) and pause one beat at the end of a line (as "Bender").

In other pieces, such as "Hypothetical Moments" and "History of Collage," the texts are read in normal speech rhythms. As most of these texts have been recorded commercially, the reader is referred to my actual performances for clarification.

*notes excerpted from record liners: *Mental Radio*, Charles Amirkhanian, Composers Recordings Inc., 1985, CRI SD 523; and *Lexical Music*, Charles Amirkhanian, 1750 Arch, Inc. Record S-1779, 1979

History of collage

The initial idea
    as shrouded
to dance
    a written text
tribes bestow upon
    the early 17th Century
by associating
    sticking
heraldic animals
    always held
with man's
    magical potencies
is simple.
    And miscellaneous bric-a-brac
which might take
    his own destiny
in Germany
    is common ground
upon
    seemingly mundane objects
stir the imagination
    in association, and
the nature of existence.

Cutting paper
    amongst the most famous
is the Isehu
    where New Year greeting cards
we might more readily understand
    are frequently
tiny cut-out
    poets
sprinkled with
    pasted patterned paper
expressing gestures in the name of
    landscapes
where
    similar refined materials
might be arranged
    over a thousand years,
written on such
    animals and birds
the tradition
    can be traced
from pre-torn
    calligraphers
onto
    the tenth century poetess Ise.

The art of
    proliferation
in and around Constantinople
    blossoms and leaves
the Eastern world
    fairly easily.
Intricate imagery
    had spread westward
and bookbinders collaborated.
    However, by the end of
Persia
    the wider use of paper for books
became famous
    which allowed the process
to be carried out
    across Turkey
in this field.

About the same time
    delicately scissored
Eberhard Pfaudt
    glued to black silk
some women
    from foreign cultures.
There remain some handsome examples
    and a notable pun.
Shall we join the ladies
    and make one *big* lady?
In 1611
    the notion of using feathers for
geneological registers
    began to be used.
The images
    of the elegant ladies
gained considerable
    Jesuits from Mexico
particularly in Austria
    where exotically coloured
cloth came into contact with
    Painting and sticking together.

In the curio
        coloured straw
it is probably
        prisoners
in black frames
        imitated by professional artists
constructed
        coffee beans and fruit stones.
In English gaols of the seventeenth century
        the idea
of wealthy collectors
        might be found
most bizarre
        along with her tiring
pictures constructed from beetles.

Collages made out of
        artistic nuns
are first chronicled
        in
butterfly wings.
        In the eighteenth century this
was often undertaken
        in convents.

As
        widespread a practice
as it is
        visual creativity
used collage in kindergartens
        to give them
children a pair of scissors.
        It was subsequently developed by
Maria Montessori in
        a box of paints.

Even closer to
        Indian ink
Grows the treelet philtre of love.
        Christian Morgenstern,
The Aggrieved Dachshaund,
        made small
striking
        hairpins and stuffed
negative interlocking form
        in which brightly coloured dots
and ironic titles
        sought
jovial child's play
        on the magazine of the
meaning behind every game,
        much later used by the Cubists.

To summarize,
        it was with
art, in concert
        picture-making—
of bringing
        nothing very new
into association
        with the genesis
of
        an indelible mark—
that collage
        began
the essential
        psychological
identity
        of this century.

Dutiful ducks

dutiful
the drano ducks collide
and mercy
gather–collide–like
fancy tension
pow–wow
dutiful dutiful ducks
than double Elly
Macy
treetops pray
the signal
hay in May
says
dutiful
—
dutiful
ducks
—
dutiful
—
dutiful
dutiful
ducks
—
dutiful
the drano ducks collide
the maestro
gather–collide–like
condescension
tavlu
dutiful beautiful ducks
than double Elly
Elgar
treetops pray
the signal
hay in May
says
dutiful
—
dutiful
—
dutiful
—
dutiful
dutiful
dutiful
dutiful

—
dutiful
ducks
—
dutiful
—
dutiful
dutiful
ducks
—
dutiful
the drano ducks collide
amoeba
gather–collide–like
x-extension
Bangkok
dutiful dutiful ducks
than double Elly
maybe
treetops pray
the signal
hay in May
says
dutiful
!
dutiful
ducks
!
dutiful
!
dutiful
dutiful
ducks
!
dutiful
the drano ducks collide
and curtsy
gather–collide–like
fancy sandals
sanction
suitable beautiful ducks
than double Elly
Dundas
treetops pray
the signal
hay in May
says

dutiful
!
dutiful
ducks
!
dutiful
!
dutiful
dutiful
ducks
!
dutiful
dutiful
!
dutiful
!
dutiful
!
dutiful
!
!
!
dutiful*
1u2utiful*
1u2u3utiful*
1u2u3u4utiful*
1u2u3u4u5utiful*
dutiful*
1u2utiful*
1u2u3utiful*
ducks
dutiful
the drano ducks collide
and mercy
gather–collide–like
fancy tension
scoundrel
beautiful dutiful ducks
than double Elly
huelga
treetops pray
the signal
hay in May
says
dutiful */
1u2utiful */
1u2u3utiful */
1u2u3u4utiful */
1u2u3u4u5utiful */

dutiful */
1u2utiful */
1u2u3utiful */
1u2u3u4utiful */
1u2u3u4u5utiful
ducks
dutiful
ducks
dutiful
!
!
ducks
ducks
ducks
dutiful
ducks
!
dutiful
!
ducks
dutiful
ducks
dutiful
!
ducks
ducks
ducks
dutiful
ducks
!
!
!
dutiful
!
ducks
dutiful
ducks
dutiful
!
!
! ducks
! ducks
! ducks
! beautiful
! dutiful
! ducks

Church car

for two voices

Repeat each section 3 times

	VOICE 1	VOICE 2
1	ChurchCar	ChurchCar
	—	
	ChurchCar	ChurchCar
	—	—
	ChurchCar	ChurchCar
	ChurchCar	ChurchCar
	ChurchCar	ChurchCar
	ChurchCar	ChurchCar
	ChurchCar	ChurchCar
	—	—

+

	VOICE 1	VOICE 2
2	ChurchCar	—
	—	ChurchCar
	—	—
	ChurchCar	—
	—	ChurchCar
	—	—
	ChurchCar	—
	—	ChurchCar
	ChurchCar	—
	—	ChurchCar
	ChurchCar	—
	—	—

+

	VOICE 1	VOICE 2
3	Church / /	Church / Car
	Church /	ChurchCar
	Church / /	Church / Car
	Church /	ChurchCar
	Church /	/ Car
	Church / /	/ Car Car
	Church /	/ Car
	Church /	/ Car
	Church / /	/ Car /

+

	VOICE 1	VOICE 2
4	Church / Car	Church / Car
	ChurchCar	ChurchCar
	Church / Car	Church / Car
	ChurchCar	ChurchCar
	Church / Church /	/ Church / Church
	Church / Church /	/ Church / Church
	ChurchCar / Car	—
	/ CarCarCar	ChurchCarCarCar

+

continued

5 Bang /
ChurchCar
Bang /
ChurchCar
Bang / /
Bang / /
Bang / /
Bang /

Bang /
ChurchCar
Bang /
ChurchCar
Bang / /
Bang / /
Bang / /
Bang /

+

6 Bang /
—
—
—
Bang /
ChurchCar
ChurchCar
ChurchCar
BangChurch /
BangChurch /
BangChurch /

Bang /
ChurchCar
ChurchCar
ChurchCar
Bang /
—
—
—
Bang / Car
Bang / Car
Bang / Car

+

7 ChurchCar
—
—
ChurchCar
—
—
Church / /
Car / /

—
ChurchCar
—
—
—
ChurchCar
Car / /
Church / /

+

8 BoxCar
BumpCar
—
BoxCar
BumpCar
—
BoxCar
—

BoxCar
BumpCar
—
BoxCar
BumpCard
—
BoxCar
AutoCar

+

9 BoxCar
BumpCar
AutoCar
/ Car

BoxCar
BumpCar
AutoCar
—

+

10 Box / Bump
AutoCar / Car

Box / Bump
AutoCar / Car

+

11 Box /
Bump /
AutoCar
BumpCar

Bump /
Box /
AutoCar
BumpCar

+

12 Bang / Cock
AutoCar
BumpCar

Bang / Cock
AutoAuto
CarCar

+

13 Kumquat
Loquat
AutoCar
—

Kumquat
Loquat
/ Auto
BumpCar

+

14 Kumquat
Loquat
'
ChurchCar
BoxCar

Kumquat
Loquat
'
ChurchCar
Box / Car

+

15 Come / Kumquat
Come / Quat /

/ LoKumquat
/ LoKumquat

+

16 Loquat
—
Loquat
—
Kum / Quat /
Kum / Quat Quat
KumLo Quat Quat

—
Loquat
—
Loquat
/ LoKumquat
/ KumLoquat
/ KumLoquat

+

17 ChurchCar
—
AutoCar
—
Rubber Baby
Buggy Bumper

—
BoxCar
/ Auto
BumpCar
Rubber Baby
Buggy Bumper

+

<table>
<tr><td>18</td><td>Car /
Box /
Automobile</td><td>CarBump
/ Baby
Automobile</td></tr>
</table>

+

<table>
<tr><td>19</td><td>BangBaby
Rubber /
Ribicoff</td><td>BangBaby
/ Car
Ribicoff</td></tr>
</table>

+

<table>
<tr><td>20</td><td>Bang /
Bang /
Ribicoff
RubberCar
Automobile</td><td>BangBaby
BangBaby
—
/ Car
Automobile</td></tr>
</table>

+

<table>
<tr><td>21</td><td>BangBaby
Ribicoff
RubberCar
Automobile</td><td>BangBaby
Ribicoff
RubberCar
Automobile</td></tr>
</table>

+

<table>
<tr><td>22</td><td>Bang /
BangBang /
Automobile</td><td>BangBaby
BangBang /
—</td></tr>
</table>

+

<table>
<tr><td>23</td><td>Bang /
BangBang /
Automobile
Automobile</td><td>BangBaby
BangBang /
/ Automo
Automobile</td></tr>
</table>

+

<table>
<tr><td>24</td><td>Automobile
Automobile
Automobile
Automobile</td><td>/ Automo
bileAutomo
bileAutomo
Automobile</td></tr>
</table>

+

Gold and spirit

for the 1984 Summer Olympics Arts Festival, Los Angeles

CHEER! CHEER!
HOYA PARANOIA
STEER PEERS TO SHERE
POSSI-POSSI-POSSIBLY
POSSI-POSSIBLY
CHEER!
CHEER! CHEER!
HOYA PARANOIA
ANNOY-YA ANNOY-YA
POSSI-POSSI-POSSIBLY
POSSI-POSSIBLY
POSSIBLY POSSIBLY POSSIBLY
CHEER! CHEER!
HOYA PARANOIA
STEER PEERS TO SHERE
POSSI-POSSI-POSSIBLY
POSSI-POSSIBLY
CHEER!
CHEER! CHEER!
HOYA PARANOIA
ANNOY-YA ANNOY-YA
POSSI-POSSI-POSSIBLY
POSSI-POSSIBLY
POSSIBLY POSSIBLY POSSIBLY
CHEER!
CHEER! CHEER!
ANNOY-YA ANNOY-YA

RAY MAN RAY
RAY RAY MAN
MAN MAN MAN
MAN MAN RAY
RAY MAN RAY
MAN RAY RAY
MAN RAY MAN
RAY MAN RAY
MAN MAN RAY
MAN RAY RAY
RAY MAN RAY
MAN MAN RAY
MAN RAY RAY
RAY RAY RAY
RAY MAN RAY
MAN MAN MAN
RAY RAY MAN
RAY RAY RAY
RAY MAN MAN

continued

GO VAN GOGH
VAN GO VAN
VAN GO GOGH
GO VAN VAN
GO VAN GOGH
VAN GO GOGH
GO GOGH VAN
VAN VAN VAN
GO VAN GOGH
GO VAN VAN
GO GO GO
VAN GO VAN
VAN GO VAN
VAN VAN VAN
GO VAN GOGH
GO VAN VAN
VAN GO VAN
HAM GAUGUIN

ANTHRACITE

        ZEUS

RUBY

        OVER AND OVER

ARCHETYPAL

        CONTENT

GOLD
AND SPIRIT
ARCHE

        TYPAL

CON
TENT
GOLD   GOLD

AND SPIRIT   AND SPIRIT

GODS

        ARRIVE

PUMPKIN

        TANTRA

ARCHETYPAL

        CONTENT

GOLD

        AND SPIRIT

ARCHE

        TYPAL

CON

        TENT

GOLD   GOLD

AND SPIRIT   AND SPIRIT
RAVING
SHINE

SANE
ABSOLUTELY ABSOLUTELY DUMBBELL
GOD DAMN BAMBOO

PAH PAH POSITIVELY
PAH PAH POSITIVELY
PAH PAH POSITIVELY
PROPERLY POSITIVELY
PROPERLY POSITIVELY
PROPERLY POSITIVELY
PROPERLY POSITIVELY
PROPERLY POSITIVELY
PROPERLY POSITIVELY
PROPERLY POSITIVELY
PROPERLY POSITIVELY
PROPERLY PANDA POSITIVELY
PROPERLY PANDA POSITIVELY
PROPERLY PANDA POSITIVELY
PROPERLY PANDA POSITIVELY
PROPERLY PANDA POSITIVELY
PROPERLY PANDA POSITIVELY
PROPERLY PANDEMONIUM POSITIVELY
PROPERLY PANDEMONIUM POSITIVELY
PROPERLY PANDEMONIUM POSITIVELY
PROPERLY PANDEMONIUM POSITIVELY
PROPERLY PANDEMONIUM PAGES POSITIVELY
PROPERLY PANDEMONIUM PAGES POSITIVELY
PROPERLY PANDEMONIUM PAGES POSITIVELY
PROPERLY PANDEMONIUM PAGES POSITIVELY
PROPERLY PANDEMONIUM PAGES 'N PAGES POSITIVELY
PROPERLY PANDEMONIUM PAGES 'N PAGES POSITIVELY
PROPERLY PANDEMONIUM PAGES 'N PAGES POSITIVELY
PROPERLY PANDEMONIUM PAGES 'N PAGES POSITIVELY
PROPERLY PANDEMONIUM PAGES 'N PAGES POSITIVELY
PROPERLY PANDEMONIUM PAGES 'N PAGES BELGIUM BELGIUM POSITIVELY
PROPERLY PANDEMONIUM PAGES 'N PAGES BELGIUM BELGIUM POSITIVELY
PROPERLY PANDEMONIUM PAGES 'N PAGES BELGIUM BELGIUM POSITIVELY
PROPERLY PANDEMONIUM PAGES 'N PAGES BELGIUM BELGIUM POSITIVELY
PROPERLY PANDEMONIUM PAGES 'N PAGES BELGIUM BELGIUM BELGIUM BELGIUM BELGIUM
                                        JUNGLE JUNGLE JUNGLE

BACCARAT PHILADELPHIA
BACCARAT PHILADELPHIA
TWO-TIME CABOOSE
BACCARAT PHILADELPHIA
BACCARAT PHILADELPHIA
BACCARAT PHILADELPHIA
TWO-TIME CABOOSE
BACCARAT PHILADELPHIA
BACCARAT PHILADELPHIA
TWO-TIME CABOOSE

(continued)

BACCARAT PHILADELPHIA
BACCARAT PHILADELPHIA
TWO-TIME CABOOSE
TRAPEZOID ARISTOTLE
TRAPEZOID ARISTOTLE
TRAPEZOID ARISTOTLE
SPOTSCAPE BARCELONA
TRAPEZOID ARISTOTLE
TRAPEZOID ARISTOTLE
TRAPEZOID ARISTOTLE
SPOTSCAPE BARCELONA
TRAPEZOID ARISTOTLE
SPOTSCAPE BARCELONA
BANK
DANDELION BANK
DANDELION BANK
TREMOLO BANK
DANDELION BANK
DANDELION BANK
TREMOLO BANK
DANDELION BANK
DANDELION BANK
TREMOLO BANK
DANDELION BANK
DANDELION BANK
TREMOLO TREMOLO BANK
DANDELION BANK
DANDELION BANK
TREMOLO TREMOLO BANK
DANDELION BANK
DANDELION BANK
TREMOLO TREMOLO BANK
TREMOLO BANK
TREMOLO BANK
TREMOLO TREMOLO BANK
TREMOLO BANK
TREMOLO BANK
TREMOLO TREMOLO BANK
TREMOLO BANK
TREMOLO BANK
TREMOLO TREMOLO BANK
TREMOLO BANK
TREMOLO BANK
BARCELONA
BANK
TREMOLO BANK
TREMOLO BANK
BARCELONA
TREMOLO BANK
TREMOLO BANK

TREMOLO BANK
BARCELONA
BANK BANK
BARCELONA
TREMOLO BAR BANK BAR BORE
BANK BANK BARCELONA
TREMOLO BAR BANK BAR BORE
BANK BANK
BARCELONA
TREMOLO BAR BANK BAR BORE
BANK BANK
BARCELONA
TREMOLO BAR BANK

IT'S NOT SO, TONY GNAZZO
IT'S JUST NO SO SO-SO-SO

NOT SO, TONY GNAZZO
NOT SO SO-SO JUST NOT SO

WHERE'S THE GARLIC?

IT'S NOT SO, TONY GNAZZO
IT'S JUST NOT SO SO-SO-SO

THERE'S THE GARLIC!

NOT SO, TONY GNAZZO
NOT SO SO-SO JUST NOT SO

WHERE'S THE GARLIC?

ONE
TWO
IT'S NOT SO TONE TONE TONE
IT'S JUST NOT SO SO-SO-SO

THERE'S THE GARLIC!

NOT SO TONE TONE TONE
NOT SO SO-SO JUST NOT SO

WHERE'S THE GARLIC?

IT'S NOT SO TONE TONE TONE
IT'S JUST NOT SO SO-SO-SO

THERE'S THE GARLIC!

NOT SO TONE TONE TONE
NOT SO NOT SO TONE NOT SO

WHERE'S THE GARLIC?

MARCEL

THERE'S THE GARLIC!
DUH CHAMP

MARCEL

DUH CHAMP

(da capo al "duh")

SEATED SEX SUCKS NO SOCKS
SUCK-SEX STUCKS A STOCK-STACK
HOSTILE A-POSTURE SUBLIMINSKY
GLAMOROUS PUCKER, THE BOOR AMOUR

CREDITOR BETTED HER RHONDA DONDA
CREDITOR BETTED HER RHONDA DONDA
CREDITOR BETTED HER RHONDA DONDA
TOO TALL TWIST THE TAINTED TEENS
(ZONE BAN THE MAN-TO-MAN)

Maroa

Maroa Maroa
Maroa Maroa
Maroa   Maroa
Maroa Maroa

Maroa Maroa
Maroa Maroa
Maroa   Maroa
Maroa Maroa

Maroa Maroa
Maroa Maroa
Maroa   Maroa
Maroa Maroa

Maroa Maroa   Maroa
Maroa Maroa
Maroa
Maroa Maroa

barge largo
barge logo
barge largo
barge logo
barge   lago
barge   logo
barge largo
barge logo
barge lago   logo logo
barge   lago

bomb fondue   pause…pays…
razorback razorback, take it outa there   pause…pays…
bomb fondue (bomb bomb)   pause…pays…
back razor back razor ski-Ben ski-Ben bibi *(8 times)*   pregnant pause…

                                                        pregnant pause…

Abe (belly) Abe (belly) aftershock
Abe (belly) Abe (belly) aftershock
Abe (belly) Abe (belly) aftershock
Abe (belly) Abe (belly) aftershock
Abe belly belly Abe belly (belly) belly (belly)
Abe belly belly Abe belly (belly) belly (belly)
Abe belly belly Abe belly (belly) belly (belly)
Abe belly belly Abe belly (belly) belly (belly)   *(2 times)*

participle, participle, jug generic, limousine
participle, participle, jug generic, limousine
participle, participle, jug generic, limousine
participle, participle, jug generic, limousine

participle, participle, participle, participle, participle, participle, psychodemocracy
participle, participle, participle, participle, participle, participle, psychodemocracy
participle, participle, participle, participle, participle, participle, psychodemocracy
participle, participle

participle, participle, jug generic
participle, participle, jug generic
participle, participle, jug generic
participle, participle

participle, participle, jug generic
participle, participle, jug generic
participle, participle, psychodemocracy

participle, participle, participle, participle
participle, participle, participle, participle
          psychodemocracy

Too true

true
that's true
true
that's true, too

true
that's true
true
that's true, too

true . . .
shoe . . .
(snapback, snapback, snapback)

true . . .
stew . . .
(snapback, snapback, snapback)

pope pope, people
pope pope, people
pope pope, people, people, people

pope pope, people
pope pope, people
pope pope, people, people, people

people people –ple . . .
    people people –ple . . .

pope
pope pope
    pope

Nookie's at the barn door bootie, bootie
Nookie's at the barn door bootie, bootie
Nookie's at the barn door
(She's hiding from the lawn mower)
Nookie's at the barn door bootie, bootie

Nookie's at the barn door bootie (bootie) bootie (bootie)
Nookie's at the barn door bootie (bootie) bootie (bootie)
Nookie's at the barn door
(She's hiding from the lawn mower)
Nookie's at the barn door bootie (bootie), bootie

true, that's true
true, that's true, too
true . . . shoe . . . true . . . stew . . .

dreams Freud-dreamed
or-dreams Freud-*dreamed* Freud-dreamed
dreams of-dreams
Freud-*dreamed* Freud-dreamed
dreams Freud-dreamed
or-dreams Freud-*deemed* Freud-dreamed

spies
the-sickle
pies Saint-Size
pies Saint-Size says-it
cycle
raise-rhythmic pays-rhythmic pies Saint-Size raise-rise

dreams Freud-dreamed
or dreams Freud-*dreamed* Freud-dreamed
drummed drums
or-dreams Freud-*dreamed* Freud-dreamed
the-berry
lazer
shams and-sizes baffle regiment dress
'n drama
'n cheese rightly fond sentiment shams

center pique
a-fit of-center pique 'n paisley this
break
the-bike break Boston calls-me Boston
my-Boston
break
my-boston regular brake Berio bake
mridangam
postulate

Freud dreamed Freud-dreamed
Freud dreamed-Freud dreamed-Freud dreamed
Freud dreamed-Freud dreamed
Freud-dreamed Freud-dreamed Freud dreamed
dream
Freud dream
Freud
dream-Freud dream
dream Freud's-dreams Freud-dreamed
freed
dream freed
dream freed Freud's dreams Freud-dreamed
dreams
dreams-fade Freud's-dreams Freud-dreamed

(continued)

Freud–dreamed
latchet
dreamed–dreams Freud's–dreamers dreamed
dreamed–dreamers deemed Freud's–deemers dreamed
snooker
dreams–deemers dreamed Freud's deemers dreamed
suck astute
couple
dreams–dreamers deemed Freud's deemers dreamed
drake
sandwich
trunk
dreams–dreamers dreamed Freud's–dreamers deemed
label
shake
patio
tundra
dreams–dreams
dreams–dreams
Freud's dreamers deemed
lateral
fine–art posse
scene
Leipzig
parallel
dreams–dreams
—
dreams–dreams
—
—
dreams
—
—
dream–dreamers
—
—
dreams
—
—
—
sigh
—
—
deems
—
—
—

that-*loud* air-conditioning
—

—

dream–dreams Freud-dreamed
—

dream–dreams Freud
—

dreams Freud
—

gutteral-dreams Freud-*dreamed* Freud-dreamed
—

—

dreams Freud-dreamed
or-dreams Freud *dreamed* Freud-dreamed
on trams
drums of-dreams
drum drum-dream drum-dream that
—

drum drum-dream drum-dream though
—

drum-dream drum
—

drum-dream drum
—

drum drum-dream drum
dream
drum-dreamed drum-dreamed
—

—

—

—

—

—

—

dreams Freud-dreamed
or-dreams Freud-*dreamed* Freud-dreamed
drums
drams of-dreams
drums-drams of-dreams
Freud-dreamed
Freud-dreamed

Bender

1

bender
silent bender
ratchet
ratchet tunic ratchet
brown

2

hollow
hollow filter
fennel
ratchet tunic bent bump

3

bender
silent bender
ratchet sub–monk

4

butter butter sub–utter
loose shimmy fink
bent bump nickel sub–pasty hump

5

butter butter sub–silent udder
ratchet sub–finky pasty winky stump

6

butter butter sub–butter butter
butter butter sub–silent stink thump
butter butter sub–butter butter
butter butter some–wasted silent sleazy lump

7

butter
bending butter
butter
bending butter sthink sthunk

8

butter
bending butter
butter
bending butter sthink
sthunk

9

sing–sing–sing–sing–sing–sing–sing–sing
sing–sing–sing–sing–sing–sing–sing–sing
bunk sub–silent sub–butter sub–bending biter*
     sub–pasty wasted thinking party pumping blubbering*
     literal bane

10

sub–driving crystal solo sanka sub–slobbering*
     sub–sub–sickle sub–drunk
sinister sub–drunk

11

bender
silent bender
ratchet
tunic
bump

Pastor

mister passion*
mister passion*
mister passion passion*
mister passion*
mister passion*
mister passion passion*
mister passion*
mister passion*
mister passion passion

---

passion
passion
mister mister mister/passion
mister mister mister/passion
passion passion
mister mister mister/passion
mister mister mister/passion
passion passion

passion mister passion mister passion passion
passion mister passion mister passion passion
passion
mister mister mister/passion
mister mister mister/passion mister passion
mister mister mister/passion
mister mister mister/passion mister passion passion

---

passion passion mister
passion passion mister
passion passion mister passion mister passion
pash passion
pash passion mister passion
passion passion
passion passion mister passion
pash passion
pash passion mister passion

---

pash passion pash*
pash passion pash*
passion passion pash*
passion pash pash*
pash passion pash*
Passion pash pash*
pash pash pash

---

passion
mister mister mister/mister mister mister
passion
mister mister mister/mister mister
passion
mister mister/mister mister
passion
mister mister mister
passion
mister mister
passion

mister passion

Here with years

1

hey wolves
fretter

howl ya doin?
howl ya comin?

he wolves
hey yeah 'n fret
was he Jewish?
he yes in Tilden

coolers
spacers in years
in sob minor

for nowhere

press here with
press here with
years for spacers

howl ya doin?
howl ya do it?
hey wolves
fretter than fret
till then, till
fretter than fret
where spacers
with years for flavors
ten, then ten
the comfortable ones
ten muscles made then cooler by ten Renaissance
the critical thick
church nor nurture
was he Jewish?
howler duty
press here with years
press here with years
years for spacers
them away

2

framing

glottis

!!JANG!!*
calculator
calculator
calculator
##later
##later
##later

popular vents
on hubs larger than restless
like soccer was at first
on record record
a personal artistic
bent, the collected rivers of
Milhaud man
Milhaud my
Milhaud Milhaud

she smiled and
oh Milhaud
my my ##later
##later
##
later
later
and Belgium
oh Milhaud
and Belgium
oh Milhaud
I'm waiting
I'm waning
I'm waiting
I'm waning
I'm a
I'm a
##
I'm a
I'm a
##the carrot in the cage wire carrot

(continued)

mistake ##the stare didn't fade
the understatement of
carrots make ##you like
carrots make ##you like carrots
make mistake
you
like carrots ## ##uitstekend

3

hey wolves
fretter

howl ya doin?
howl ya comin?

he wolves
hey yeah 'n fret

he yes in ten
a comfortable one

he yes
she threat
by breaches
made tender by some Renaissance

and years, the spacers

= "shhht-tit"
(voiceless) in imitation
of a hand-cranked
adding machine

Jigolo cheese

for four speaking voices

1 sgullet lamphus plause   nide spector   shame lamphus plause
mf

2   lamphus plause   nide spector
mf

3   lamphus plause   nide spector
mf

4   lamphus plause   nide spector
mf

---

1   todd nectar   todd nectar todd nectar
p (whispered)

2 lamphus plause   todd nectar   todd nectar todd nectar
p (whispered)

3 lamphus plause   todd nectar   todd nectar todd nectar
p (whispered)

4 lamphus plause   todd nectar   todd nectar todd nectar
p (whispered)

---

1 camphor lamphus plause   camphor lamphus plause   skull gudget
f   *ff*

2 camphor lamphus plause   camphor lamphus plause
f

3   booboo   booboo booboo
mf

4   booboo   booboo booboo
mf

(continued)

1 sgullet lamphus plause lamphus plause   nectar clause nectar pause
  f   *mf*   *mf*

2   lamphus plause gretchen–lip gretchen–lip   nectar pause
        mf   *f*   *mf*

3   lamphus plause   nectar clause nectar pause
        mf   *mf*

4   lamphus plause gretchen–lip gretchen–lip   nectar pause
        mf   *f*   *mf*

---

1   jigolo trip   jigolo trip
     ⌒   *f*

2   thip thip thip   thip thip thip
             f

3   thip thip thip   thip thip thip
   pause   *f*

4   thip thip thip   thip thip thip
             f

---

1 jigolo trip   do–hard bastard
                 ff

2   thip thip thip   nectar nectar
                   ff

3   thip thip thip do–hard bastard
                ff

4   thip thip thip   nectar nectar
                   ff

---

1 jigolo trip   jigolo trip
  f

2   thip   thip   thip
       f

3   thip   thip
         f

4   thip   thip
          f

1 jigolo trip   CHEESE_____"
        ff (1)

2   thip thip   CHEESE_____"
            ff (5)

3   thip   thip   CHEESE_____"
        ff (3)   *pause*

4   thip thip   CHEESE_____"
                ff (7)

1 narcotic scrotum   narcotic scrotum
ff

2   rip-off tin   rip-off tin
     ff

3 narcotic scrotum   narcotic scrotum
ff

4   rip-off tin   rip-off tin
     ff

1 narcotic scrotum

2   rip-off tin   rip-off tin   rip-off tin

3 narcotic scrotum

4   rip-off tin   rip-off tin   rip-off tin

1 narcotic scrotum   narcotic scrotum

2   rip-off tin   rip-off tin

3 narcotic scrotum   narcotic scrotum

4   rip-off tin   rip-off tin

1 narcotic scrotum

2   rip-off tin   rip-off tin   rip-off tin

3 narcotic scrotum

4   rip-off tin   rip-off tin   rip-off tin

1 narcotic scrotum narcotic scrotum narcotic scrotum narcotic tin tin   tin   tin
fff

2   ripoff tin   ripoff tin   ripoff tin   ripoff tin   tin   tin
fff

3 narcotic scrotum narcotic scrotum narcotic scrotum narcotic tin tin   tin   tin
fff

4   ripoff tin   ripoff tin   ripoff tin   ripoff tin   tin   tin
fff

(all crescendo to end — light accelerando to end)

1 ka⎯⎯⎯⎯ ka⎯⎯⎯⎯ ka⎯⎯ ka-SHIN

2   ka⎯⎯⎯⎯ ka⎯⎯⎯⎯ ka-SHIN

3 ka⎯⎯⎯⎯ ka⎯⎯⎯⎯ ka⎯⎯ ka-SHIN

4   ka⎯⎯⎯⎯ ka⎯⎯⎯⎯ ka-SHIN
ffff (all shout)

Notes on the reading of "Jigolo Cheese"

"Jigolo Cheese" is scored in such a way as to be performable by non-music-readers. Ideally, it would be performed by two male and two female voices. Part One: lower male voice; Part Two: lower female voice; Part Three: higher male voice; Part Four: higher female voice. Note that each notch represents one beat and that two-syllable words occuring within one beat ("sgullet," "lamphus") are given one-half a beat each. An exception occurs with "gudget" and with "ka-SHIN" and the rhythmic values are given above the words. On line 3 (p. 1) "booboo" should be made to sound like two tom-toms — make it more resonant than ordinary speech. Line 4: "gretchen-lip gretch-lip": accent the first syllable of gretchen both times, making a triplet figure which is heard twice. Page 2, line 3: If possible, make a one-three-five-seven chord like a barbershop quartet. Alternate possibility: everyone hit a tone at random and hold the tones until cut-off. The rhythms of line 4 are to be interpreted loosely and should swing as much as possible. Parts 2 & 4 should be sure to accent "*rip*-off *tin,* even though the main beat comes on "off" as it were. If the performers are not adept at music reading, the first call and response on line 2, page 2 may be repeated two more times instead of doing the more difficult version printed here.

Hypothetical moments (in the intellectual life of Southern California)

Holyoke! The Bambi Biennale.
Hypothetical moments in the
intellectual life of Southern
California.

All the faces interview themselves,
breathing in rhythms just short of
papoose.

Gordon masturbates Gordon. Her freckles
dim.

Dada Carew. New punctual stew. Stripes
raise a base's snare. Tahoe beware.

I, posture, take thee Edna, to be
Nadine.

Don't you have to, with a wife?
Not the picnickers. Not the sampan bagels,
or the curves in the core of Capri.
Perhaps *one* might in the great echoing
cigar of responsive canals.

But if so, hypertension blends with
bosoms so real. Tans on sides make
waves in proportion to Tuaca, too.

Take stock, served only to deepen a chasm
on haunches, puffed up by a queer wizard's
health system.

Thunderstruck billows wipe away the
heartsick gamelan. We gaze openly
at the closure, becoming aghast
genius.

It's serious, these legs of mantra,
lisping as thumping dares. Why shrink
back voluntarily when fat's so perplexing?

Thereby, thoroughbreds find the needy.
Farouk coming! Cunning Forouk.
Or. . . honk if you *love* honkies.

Reagan wastes aways. He butt-splices
Haig to lather. To fade his pupils.
That leaves that cataract stare.

Often machismo backfires, you see, creating
an interracial halitosis which summons
Hirohito.

Bastards bastards bastards. You might
seem uncompromising but you've worn
optimism out. Your toggery is baseness;
your jewelry your joint. Underneath
that jaunty high-hat lurks the gagged
isolation of Poopsie.

Aftermath basket glimpses cliché.
Sues aperture for breakfast.

All quaint poignancy aside, let's collect
her wits and knock on Egypt's drip.
Let's satisfy my need to say, "Say,
she'd *need* my words."

Perhaps *that* was shy she spoiled Turin.
Pansy duty by the letter.
To take away.
To try to do today.

Michael Peppe

We followed a curve of declining reliance on the word in going from John to Robert to Yoko to Laurie. Maybe that's how the guest seating will be worked out; maybe that's why we haven't gone in yet to table. Charles was an exception, but Michael Peppe continues the curve. The Peppe performances I've seen have been totally non-verbal, quite abstract, yet very ironic, almost sarcastic. Well, not totally non-verbal — but no syntax. Seeing them you can understand those critics who believe Dada was born when artists, in disguised horror at the idiocy of World War I, rejected expression. Peppe's manic, robot-like gestures and sounds have a similarly frenzied determination to avoid expression. "You have always been reading this title," he insists, and when he points out that "Death is impossible, since you will not exist to experience it," he simply removes the cheerful playfulness of Marcel Duchamp's epitaph — "d'ailleurs, c'est toujours les autres qui meurent"* — and leaves only a bitter kind of objective phenomenology. But in Actmusikspectakle V — I can't help wondering why the second letter is a "c" not a "k" — Peppe's scientific, detached, clinical, and statistical approach to this cultural irony takes on very verbal form indeed. Postmodernism with a vengeance, very aware of the reduction of Joyce's cosmic comedic view in Finnegans Wake to a Burroughsy cross-section of a desperate moment at the end of a millenium.

[Laurie Anderson]: "This is your captain speaking. We're all going down. So why not let x equal x." "don' matta' don'matta' don'matta' don'matta' don' matta' 'bout nothin' no mo' . . ."

I can hardly wait to see if Michael Peppe will be seated next to Yoko Ono and K. Atchley.

—C.S.

*"Besides, it's always the others who die."

MICHAEL PEPPE

Stephanie Leberer
March 1985, San Francisco

What is the purpose of art?

Do you mean for the individual or for society?

You could define that for yourself.

I think art solves the two basic problems of existence; the fear of death and the fear of life. That's for the individual, the artist. Everyone is split between a consciousness and a body. Everyone knows the body is mortal, it's an animal, and it's going to die someday. However, you don't have anywhere near that kind of certainty about consciousness. There's no proof to suggest that consciousness is going to be extinguished at death, and no proof that it isn't. In any case you have this feeling that maybe it's not mortal. So people have anxiety because their immaterial minds are attached to these mortal material bodies. Therefore, they have to put the imprint of their spiritual selves or their psychic selves upon some kind of concrete form that is going to survive death. It's not necessarily that their art is going to be immortal, but that simply by putting it into an inorganic form like a recording, or a piece of sculpture, or a piece of writing, it goes into a form that does not have a lifespan like an animal does and so it could potentially survive their own death. That is one possible reason for art, I think.

Another more important source of art is the fear of life. Basically, the main purpose of life is to avoid freedom. That is, the primary reason for action is to become unfree. The reason it's usually phrased as "the purpose of life is to *become* free" is because that way people can avoid the terrifying truth, which is that they're already free when they're born. No matter what the situation is you are basically free. It's the attempt to *escape* from freedom that leads people to do the crazy things they do. Like work at absurd, unpleasant jobs, and go through painful relationships, and watch stupid

TV shows, and work longer than they actually have to in order to get the money to meet their basic needs. For instance, I think that's why the credit card was invented: because everybody needs to structure their time in some way and the credit card makes it possible for people to become so hugely in debt that they can spend all their time catching up to where they were. They can say, "Well, I *have* to go to work in order to pay all these debts." It gives them a way to avoid confronting freedom. The credit card isn't a source of freedom, it's the reverse: it's a source of structure, it's a way to structure, or eliminate, freedom. One of life's basic drives is to avoid the fact that you have the responsibility for choosing what to do. People want to make that choice as easy as possible. They want to narrow it down to as few options as possible so they will have the impression that they have a sense of certainty about their lives. So, the first thing you have to do is decide what you don't want: you have to narrow your field down to a very limited number of choices in order to preserve sanity.

Actually, I was jumping ahead a little with the credit card. First there is the commodity, the commodity that is fetishized. The commodity was invented so that people would have something to do once they got through working. People don't work in order to consume commodities, they work in order to consume time, and they collect commodities to justify it. People have this idea that the purpose of work is to fulfill certain basic needs like eating and having a roof over your head, but if you actually look at it, most of the people in the world only spend a small fraction of their time working in order to fulfill these basic needs. Even in some very primitive societies people only work ten or fifteen hours a week. In hunting and gathering societies only a small part of the day may be spent working, and even in small farming communities, some of the year they work very hard—like during the harvest season, times like that—the rest of the time is spent mostly sitting around. In Western societies you have people working 40 or 50 hours a week, and the justification for the extra time spent working is to buy the commodity. Well it turns out that if you only buy the commodity when you have earned the money to do so, you don't have that intense motivation to work. You realize you are buying a luxury item, it's frosting on the cake. So, the credit card is the perfect thing because it puts the person continuously in debt, and therefore they are in a continuous state of motivation and there is always meaning to their life.

Now art fulfills a similar function. So does procreation. So does war. It gives meaning to people's lives. That's what life is all about, and what people want more than anything: meaning. They want their lives to have meaning, and they want their behavior to be necessary. They want to feel there is a reason to get up in the morning. They don't want a lot of free time because then, in a way, they no longer have that reason to get up. If your time is free, then it's arbitrary. You could do whatever you want but it doesn't matter what you choose, so why bother? Whereas, if you've got four kids, or you've got a job to go to, then you don't have to worry about the meaning of life because you don't have time.

Art, I think, is another way of structuring that freedom, and confronting the fear of freedom and of life. The artist, in the best of situations, is ideally somebody who confronts that existential freedom at any given moment and attempts to structure it in a way that he or she feels is as deeply rooted as possible in the ultimate ground of being. The artist attempts to continually rediscover the mystery of existence at every moment and attempts to face the suffering and uncertainty of not understanding it. Now of course, in actual practice it doesn't happen that ideally. The artist, just like anyone else, has to focus to make his or her choices easier. You have the artist becoming a playwright and the job becomes sitting at a desk typing, or the artist becomes a musician and pretends that the only way he can exercise creativity is in sound. Or the painter believes the only thing he can do well, and discover the ultimate nature of, is visual art. That way you are not constantly at the level of choosing what you want to do with your life, which is an adolescent level, or in any case, it can be.

Then by making a choice one narrows his or her natural freedom.

Right. The worst thing you can be is free. What is freedom? A given individual says, "I want to be free of my job," or "I want to be free of my marriage or my relationship," or "I want to be free of my attachments to to friends," or "I want to be free of my art." So what does the person end up doing? Well, they're just sitting in an empty room staring at a wall. What do we call that? We call that jail. That is to say, the worst punishment that the society can mete out, short of death, is a life sentence. And a life sentence is more or less defined as life in a room with nothing but *free time.*

The time is totally unstructured. Of course, one of the criticisms that's leveled at certain kinds of new prisons where they give people exercise, recreation, and work to do is that it's much less of a punishment than to just give them free time. You just go mad if you haven't structured your time. There is a great quote from Gurdjieff that goes, "You pride yourself on freedom of choice, but what you call freedom just gives full play to your aberrations, surface reactions, and neuroses."*

Faced with a possible choice, you cover the entire spectrum of political, philosophical, and sociological options at your disposal and more often than not you come up with a choice that still doesn't satisfy you. What you really want is freedom *from* choice. "The ability to choose so swiftly and surely that to all intents and purposes you have no choice."†What people want is rightness. Imagine if you knew at every single moment that every decision you made was the right one, that no matter what it was, you'd be absolutely certain of it. You would be in a state of ecstasy all the time. Freedom in this society is the freedom to choose between Seven-up and Sprite. And Dr. Pepper. We pride ourselves on being free, we have all these choices. "In Russia there's only one kind of soda pop. In other countries things are much stricter and there's not so many things to choose." But what the hell difference does it make what kind of soda pop you choose, or for that matter, what kind of food you choose? If you've got the food that you need to survive and it tastes okay, and if you've got

*The Teachers of Gurdjieff, Ahmad Mustafa Sarmouni

†Ibid.

a place to live that's reasonably comfortable, what difference does it make if you've got this whole plethora of options out there? It's a false freedom because it's a freedom people only use to make absurd arbitrary choices that don't even have to be made.

Would you say that the question might become how to get to that aforementioned state of ecstasy?

I would think so, yes.

Would you say that art is a possible avenue?

Yes. Absolutely. For the artist, that's precisely what happens. You've narrowed your choices down from "What do I want to do with my life?" to "I want to be an artist," to "I want to work in such and such a form" and "I want to do such and such a work with such and such a content or meaning." And you keep narrowing it down until you get to the moment of the work—in the case of a piece of music or theatre or some kind of kinetic art—and hopefully at that moment you are absolutely certain that it's the right moment. It is a way to achieve a kind of perfection, a perfection that's totally impossible in daily life. Although, of course, perfection is kind of a dirty word in art. Nowadays this conjures up images of "technique" or "discipline" or "hard work" or, usually, "Nazis." It's kind of a Nazi thing to do because everyone thinks trying to achieve perfection leads naturally to Nazism or something. But actually I think most artists do attempt it, even those who admit very large elements of randomness or improvisation into their works. There is a desire to make it perfect.

What would you say about the same subject socially?

As far as society is concerned, you have this same desire to structure freedom as you do in the case of the individual artist, and you also have a desire to commemorate certain consensual values. Just as the artist attempts to place his psychic or spiritual imprint on the form, so the society also seeks to place it s collective cultural imprint on the given form, to commemorate itself, so it will have the feeling that it is transcendent and immortal and is not going to pass away. But, in addition to all that, I think art is changing now. It's going through a period of transition that makes it quite different than it was in the past. I'm fond of using an acronym; art is dead. **D.E.A.D.**....Diversion, Entertainment, Amusement, and Decoration. Basically, it's not too terribly original an idea in that just about everybody knows that art seems to be getting more and more superficial and silly. It does seem to be a little bit emptier and more decorative than art has been in the past, and it looks a lot more like entertainment than it used to. People do a lot of complaining about that, but I think there are some really good reasons for it.

I think probably the main reason is that *life* has become more superficial and vapid and empty. People's emotions are shallower now than they used to be. Danger has receded so far from everyday life. For instance, in art today you don't see great themes like the meaning of existence or the question of God. You don't see death treated very much, you don't really see war treated a whole lot, you don't see such deep suffering, or spirituality, or risk-taking on important issues, and you don't see *big* themes like you might see in the art of Shakespeare or Beethoven or of previous centuries because people don't generally worry about these big themes in their daily life as much. It's easy to complain about it I guess, but it's misguided to just blame artists, because art is about communicating and artists have to try to communicate to the public their ideas about issues that the public feels are more or less relevant in forms the public understands.

If art and emotions have become more superficial and life in general has become shallower. . . how far can it go? What can art possibly do to change that? Or do you think it can?

No, it can't. It can only die.

Then we will just keep going until it's all gone?

That's right. In fact it's almost gone already. However, it's very important to remember that the *word* "art" will not die. The word "art" will never die. The situation is this. Art as we now know it was basically an invention of the industrial bourgeoisie. They needed an art that would be as richly, sensuously, entertaining as folk art but would still express the higher values that they associated with aristocratic art. This was in Europe in the nineteenth century. The art of the upper classes had itself come out of the sacred art of the middle ages whose values were basically spiritual. The values became secular, so the middle class wanted to keep those higher secular values, but it still had to be entertaining. Well, what's happened is that the middle class has grown and grown. It's pushed the upper class to a very narrow band at the top of the economic spectrum, and it's pushed the lower class to a very narrow band at the bottom of the spectrum. That vast expansion in the relative size of the bourgeoisie, along with the increase of education, the increase of disposable income for art, the increase in leisure time, and the increase in population, has created this massive, educated population that wishes to consume art in twentieth-century terms. That is, to consume it as just another commodity.

But it is important to remember that the word "art" is not going to die out, and in fact, natural talent, creativity, intelligence, industry, and possibly even discipline, are not going to die out. The various things that make people go into art are always going to be there; but I have a feeling that artists born in the eighties and nineties are going to want to exchange their talent for material successs because art isn't going to be thought of as a spiritual project. You can't have art considered a spiritual project if people have no spiritual lives.

People's emotions are as flat as TV screens because people have basically become spectators in their own lives. And to a certain extent, as popular culture overwhelms everything in its juggernaut advance, people finally *totally* confuse representations of the things with the real things, so that people don't feel original emotions so much as they imitate the emotions they see in television, movies, magazines, and newspapers. And they don't really get original ideas, per se, but derive those ideas from the media. If people are surrounded by representation, then the art that is most relevant to their lives is going to be art about representation. Not art about love, but art about images of love. Not art about ideas, but art about images of ideas. Art about what we would call the various clichés of the media. If you don't have a spiritual life, really, art is not going to be a spiritual project, it's going to be a material project.

In other words, you are pretty pessimistic about where art is going. You see a kind of advancing deterioration, less demands, less quality. . .

That's right. Very, very much so. *But,* you have to remember that the future always looks ugly. I think anybody looking at our century from the vantage point of the nineteenth would be horrified. And anyone looking at the nineteenth century from the vantage point of the sixteenth, would be horrified, and so on all the way back through history. I think that's just the way the future is, it always appears sort of evil and ugly. It always appears to be a degeneration.

Speaking about the future, what are your theories about the end of the world?

Okay. I have a very specific and definite opinion on that. Which is, that there isn't going to be an end of the world. Specifically, there is not going to be a nuclear holocaust. The reason why there's not going to be a nuclear holocaust is because the great fear that there is going to be one is based on a subconscious moralistic death wish. The anti-nuke movement, which is not just a movement, but is a feeling shared by millions of people all over the world, is basically an oversized millenial cult. It's just like any other religious millenial cult in that it believes that the world is going to come to an end because man is basically sinful and evil. The only difference with people who believe that there's going to be a nuclear holocaust is that in their scenario, which is subconscious and implicit rather than explicit, man is not sinful because of any particular violation of religious code.

The reason man is going to be destroyed in this cataclysm, according to this implicit critique, is because man has become alienated from nature, he has sinned against a kind of late-century liberal humanism: he rapes nature, pollutes things, endangers species, brings nature out of balance, builds nuclear weapons, and basically has gotten to be too big for his britches. Subconsciously, I think, society has this idea of itself as being alienated from nature, and secretly believes that it *deserves* to be destroyed in a holocaust. I think that's why that whole nuclear panic came about. It's kind of a cultural nightmare that everybody had all at once a few years ago. And, of course, the way the society dreams now-a-days is in media fads, like hoola hoops. So we had a kind of nuclear holocaust hoola hoop that was all the rage and it was on the way up with *Atomic Café,* and it hit its peak at *Testament* and *The Day After,* and then it kind of died down. You don't see it anywhere near as much in the papers now because it won't sell anymore. I think that's why we had that craze, it was a kind of moralistic death wish.

Also, there's an element of alienation from power in it, in that the people who are most worried about nuclear holocaust tend to be people who are alienated from power themselves. And their attitude is, I think subconsciously, "If we can't have it, no one's going to have it." And they feel that people in power are basically evil *because* they are in power, and that they are out to destroy the world, and that they are these devilish kinds of people. Another reason for the hysteria is the fact that the emotion of the eighties is moral indignation. Everybody wants to be able to wag a finger of moral indignation at someone else. AIDS is a perfect example of a great opportunity for heterosexuals to wag the finger of moral indignation at gays. So really the nuclear holocaust fad played perfectly into it because it's a chance for *everybody* in the society, and I mean 100% of the society, to wag their fingers like old ladies. And *everyone* can be morally indignant because who wants to die in a nuclear holocaust, right? How could anyone be *pro* nuclear holocaust? It's impossible. I'm sure Reagan and the leaders of the Soviet government consider themselves to be anti-nuclear holocaust. Reagan himself has said as much. Well, that gives you a clue right there. If you've really got an issue where there aren't two sides, and 100% of the whole world is on one side, and nobody is on the other side, you begin to suspect that something is amiss.

But, ironically enough, the thing has perfectly played into the hands of the U.S. government and the Soviet government because the people who are afraid of nuclear holocaust help to create an atmosphere of terror. So what happens is a perfect kind of Mafia protection racket. If the Soviet Union acts belligerently, all the U.S. government has to say is, "Look, here's this big evil Russian bear right around the corner and he's about to blow you all to hell and the only person who can protect you is me," meaning Ronald Reagan. And, at the same time, the Russian leaders can say exactly the same thing to their own people. If the U.S. acts agressively, and the current regime can seem tough, they can stay in power. So basically the U.S. and Soviet administrations are on the same side. They both have exactly the same goal, which is to stay in power, and they play indispensable roles in each others plans to do so. Neither of them has any intention of starting a nuclear holocaust. They don't have to, they're already in power, so the last thing they want is to destabilize.

Perhaps this is why people feel as though power is itself evil, and the people in power are inately evil.

But I think that's because of the nature of power rather than the nature of people. Or both. I mean, they're inseparable. Anyone who gets power just seeks to perpetuate it.

What about humanism and/or inhumanism?

Humanism is basically the philosophy of arrogance which gave birth to the myth of the nuclear holocaust as well as the myth of mankind being a kind of environmental hazard. Both of those myths come out of the same basic perceptual error which is at the foundation of humanism, which is that man is alienated from nature. Basically, I think humanism is in the process of wheeling itself out the door, at this point, as a philosophy. But its last great thumbprint is probably the nuclear holocaust image—the mushroom cloud fetish—which is based on the incredible egotism, that *Homo sapiens* is actually capable of doing away with life on the planet. Well, not only is *Homo sapiens* nowhere near powerful enough to end life on the planet, it can't even end a significant fraction of it, and it's not even going to be able to end itself. Even if you had a total nuclear exchange it wouldn't kill more than probably 200 million people or maybe 500 million at the most, leaving another three-and-a-half billion to carry on. Even if it was able to end the ecological niches of certain species, they'd simply be filled with other species, species that would, if necessary, mutate to live in whatever kind of world had been created.

The myth that *Homo sapiens* will be able to end the world is just one part of the schizophrenic paranoia of humanism. Your basic humanist says that we're split off from nature, we're alienated. The reason that a humanist says that is because he himself feels split off from nature, because with his finite mind—or let's put it in more general terms—with *our* finite minds, we human beings, who are just animals like any other animal, cannot comprehend the beauty and wonder and majesty and perfection of nature, which extends in all directions infinitely, in an unimaginably complex web of interrelationships which, so far as we can tell, is eternal in both the past and in the future. We can't contain that with our finite minds, and it's particularly terrifying for us to think of ourselves as being just insignificant little animals on one little planet, so we have invented this great myth that we have the power to end life on the planet and that we have this god-like stature.

Another great myth is one that's a major tenet of "environmentalism": the myth that we are able to damage nature. We get very upset over that one. Well, it would certainly be nice to think of ourselves as powerful enough to cause some kind of permanent damage to nature. Unfortunately for this little fantasy though, nature doesn't even notice thing number one that we do: we're just another little snot-nosed mammal! We're really no big deal. And nature isn't mad at us either. Nature doesn't even *look!* It doesn't care! And God isn't mad at us, if God exists. If there were a personified nature or a personified God, they'd be busting a gut! Here's this little teeny species complaining in its shrill little voice about how worried it is that it's gonna destroy the world, you know, this little cricket of a species that's all worked up about it! It's a joke, you know, just a joke.

So you have this little species that has taken all this responsibility for the world on its little shoulders. It's basically because of the fact that the universe is absolutely perfect, and at the same time infinitely vast and complex and incomprehensible. We can't hack that because it's just too much to contain, you can't even think about it, you go mad. So what we do is we create this little Lincoln Log model of the world. It's the model of evolution: At the bottom of it you have little chemicals, and above that you have little microorganisms, and then there's the plants, and then there's the animals, and then at the top, of course, yours truly, *Homo sapiens,* the crown of creation. So we've created this little sort of Tinker Toy model, and we look at it, and we say that we're—and this is another great tenet of humanism—that we're half animal and half god. Well, wrong, we're all animal. The humanists *say* that we're half god because we've created this little model of the world, and that's why they say that we're split from nature, and we're alienated from nature.

So, in reality, we're not alienated at all, we're just a part of nature; we're just one more species. Different species have different products. You know, like bees create hives and they have this complex social organization and they have honey; beavers create dams, ants create anthills, people create "culture." So you have cities and language and art and money and religion and all these other things but, basically, it's just another animal product. And, you know, really it fits in perfectly. I mean, really, we're not alienated at all. Culture *is* nature. It's just another way nature expresses itself.

But the humanist looks at this model, and the humanist, like any paranoid schizophrenic, interprets the world according to his insanity. And so he says, "Well, I'm apart from nature," you know, "I'm alienated from nature." He has to phrase it as a problem, that gee, it's kind of a cause to be annoyed and upset. But of course that's just a false front for the fact that he's actually taking a great deal of pride in it. He *wants* to be alienated from nature because then he can say that he's different from all these other animals . . .

Better. . .

Yeah, better, which is not what he says: what he says is that he's worse, because he's endangering everyone else, he's causing all these other species to run in terror from his great might. My favorite example is of a hawk flying over a city. If you have a hawk flying over Manhattan and he looks down, he doesn't say "Look at that alienated part of the world. How different that looks from the rest of the world." He doesn't say that because for him that's a part of the wilderness. That is *the* wilderness. He knows not to go there—he doesn't want to because it's unpleasant and dangerous. Same exact reasons why people don't go into the jungle where there are boa constrictors and crocodiles. We call *that* the wilderness.

Well, other animals call our world the wilderness for exactly the same reason. I mean, the wildest animals that we know, like lions and bears, don't drive cars at 80 mph, shoot off rockets, and blow things up with gigantic explosions, you know. They're actually quite civilized in comparison to *Homo sapiens*. Mainly because most of them have been around longer so they have had time to attain higher levels of civilization.

But I don't think they're starting movements saying "We should leave those poor guys alone, we might drive them into extinction."

Right. They're not worried about that kind of problem because they don't have that kind of ego. In fact, since *Homo sapiens* lives in virtually any kind of habitat: desert, forest, island, mountain, jungle; if anything, other animals may feel alienated from us. Most animals are not pervasive all through nature, you know. As a matter of fact, for all we know, the feeling of alienation may be common amongst all animals. I mean, we don't even know what kind of consciousness they have.

So you feel that even in the light of a nuclear holocaust nature will go right on.

Right on. Nuclear holocaust? No problem. Anyone who's ever been to Death Valley knows that in some places on the earth, it looks like there already was a nuclear holocaust! I mean it would have no effect. It's flat and it looks dead, and it's real quiet, and it's great.

We worry about endangering species, we worry about the Bengal tiger and the condor and the whale because there are very few individuals left of these species. Well, it's very interesting that very rarely do you notice people worrying about driving reptiles or amphibians or insects or rodents to extinction. It's because they're not aesthetically pleasing to us like the gorilla or the whale.

And I would agree these *are* very beautiful animals. But what's actually happening when you drive one of these animals to extinction? Well, if you drove the Bengal tiger to extinction there would be a lot of very happy deer in India. What actually happens when you drive an animal to extinction is that first of all the animals that it preyed upon increase in number and flourish. If it is a predator, the predators that it competed with increase in number, and they're very happy about it. And if it's an herbivore, the plant species flourish without that animal to eat them. So all that happens is that the ecological niche is filled by other organisms.

For instance, if we drive the whale to extinction I would agree it's a great tragedy because it's a very beautiful animal, but it's basically an aesthetic tragedy. What happens is, the krill and the various underwater animals and plants that the whale fed on increase in number. But these animals, like the krill, are less aesthetically pleasing to us, that is to say, we cannot create great nature TV shows about the krill that are as much fun to watch as the shows about the whale. It turns out that it isn't a very large segment of the population that actually experiences these animals first hand. It's the media that initiates our concern for these animals in the first place, but it's only through the media that these animals exist at all for most of us. What we're doing in wanting to save them is just making an aesthetic choice about what animals we want to appear in our media.

It's the same thing with polluting a lake. Let's say a company dumps tons of the most hideous, noxious chemical into a lake and turns it orange. Kills all the frogs, the turtles, the fish, everything. The only thing that can grow there is this hideous foaming yellow algae or something. People say "Well, you've killed the lake." Well, you haven't killed the lake: you've got lots of algae there, and sooner or later an animal will evolve or come over there that can eat the algae. Then another animal will come over there that can eat the animal that eats the algae. In the space of, well, more than a few human lifetimes, maybe a few *million* lifetimes, but as far as nature is concerned, the blink of an eye, that lake is going to be blue again. No problem. And even if it's not, orange lakes are no problem. Hey, nature has no big beef against orange as a color. You know, probably every color in the spectrum has at one time or another been the color of some body of water on this planet. The only way you can kill a lake is if you take *all* the water out, you fill it in with dirt and you pave it over. Then you can kill a lake, maybe.

Another example is litter. As far as nature is concerned there is no such thing as litter, litter is just yet another by-product that a natural animal leaves on the ground to be decomposed. It doesn't recognize the idea of litter as different from any other waste material. I was thinking of this while on a trip to the Grand Canyon last year. I was sitting there, and you know it's unbelievably vast and beautiful, and it's like you're seeing God for the first time. So it seems like an obscene thing to throw a Coke can into the Grand Canyon. Imagine it: I mean, it seems like the filthiest, most disgusting thing you could do. But actually you could dump fifty tons of Coke cans into the Grand Canyon, and in cosmic time, as far as the Grand Canyon is concerned, it's gone tomorrow. It's just gone. No problem. Coke cans? It doesn't even burp. It's like rocks. As far as the Grand Canyon is concerned, Coke can equals TV set equals dead bird equals rock. It's the same thing even with so-called non-biodegradeable stuff: the fact is everything degrades. It's just that some things don't degrade within our lifetimes. Ultimately, in cosmic time, even your plastic, nylon, and polyester will pass away, immortal though these great substances may appear.

Do you have nightmares?

The most frightening nightmares I've ever had . . . well, there's two actually. One was a very terrifying waking nightmare that was a gross distortion in my perception. The second one was a terrifying mental game I used to play when I was a little kid. I'd lay awake in my bed at night and I would kind of try to terrify myself. First I would imagine the universe: the earth and all the planets and stars and galaxies and stuff. It was a kind of an exercise that I would go through. What you do then is you take away all the planets so you just have stars and galaxies, right? Then you take away all the stars and galaxies and nebulae, all the physical objects in the universe, so you just have this vast emptiness. Then you come to the ultimate moment of horror: you take the final step and *take away the space.* Okay? What is left over? In a sense nothingness is not what's left over because you *take away* the nothingness.

You're left.

No, you left the self out when you took out the planets, you're just trying to imagine it. So you're left with a *lack of nothing* . . . and . . . I would be *so* terrified because I would feel like I was falling into a void. My mind, my mind. In other words, it was a game where you kept trying to take things away but finally you couldn't take anything away anymore, and there would just be this terrifying feeling of falling into this void. Because you have to think about . . .*what . . . life . . . is . . . for,* you know, what is the meaning of life.

The other waking nightmare I used to have when I was *really* little, even smaller than when I had that self-generated waking nightmare, had two basic components: everything was *too fast,* and everything was *too loud.* I'd wake up at night, and the *slightest* little movement, including my own movements, which could be, say, the slowest possible hand gesture—just moving it a quarter of an inch per minute—would seem to be infinitely fast. And the quietest sound, no matter how softly anyone spoke—the quietest whisper in fact—would be deafeningly loud. It would just be absolutely terrifying to me, and I would have to run in to my parents and they would have to wake up and comfort me, but they would have to do so without moving and without making a sound. I would just hug my mother or something and we would just, like, clench there, for a long time. It was especially troublesome for my father, because he had a very deep voice anyway, so even when he was whispering it was loud, he couldn't say word one. The things were really terrifying. They finally tapered off as I got older, although they hit their peak one time when the whole house caved in while I was awake. It was a very real hallucination that the house was caving in, I was quite awake. That was one of the last ones I had.

I think it's very interesting that you should find movement and sound to be the most primal nightmare material, since that's what you now do best.

Yes, I've wondered if there's an association. It is interesting that the most obvious properties of my Behaviormusic performances are high speeds and high levels of density—information going by too fast for you to make sense of it. You see, what I'm trying to do is to imitate all of reality. And obviously that's a very hopeless, pathetic kind of task. Rather grandiose in a pathetic, humorous way. I think that also is part of the humor of the performance, that it is so ridiculous.

What I'm trying to do, essentially, is to incorporate all of reality in my work. So, I *absorb* reality, and because I live in a city, it's basically cultural reality. I take the world, whether it be in the form of conversations I've overheard in the street, radio broadcasts, TV dialogue, classical music, pop music, quotes from books I've read, poetry, movements, sound effects of machines or of animals or of natural processes, whatever sounds and movements I see in the world that I feel I can imitate with something that approaches accuracy, given the basic hopelessness of the task of one organism trying to imitate all these things. I take all those things, and I try to create a composition that fulfills the criteria of an interesting musical composition. That is to say, a composition that is elegant or satisfying in the sense that it contains in it a good balance between predictable and unpredictable elements, which I think most really good music contains no matter whether it's very experimental avant-garde music, very traditional music, or a pop song. Which is to say that maybe about fifty percent of the time you know what's coming next, and about fifty percent of the time you don't. So you have this uncertainty, but it's hopefully evenly mixed with a *certainty*.

What I try to do is to consciously balance these two elements, and also to balance out all the other elements like degree of loudness, degree of size in a movement event, degree of sense and nonsense, degree of density, degree of complexity, degree of duration and tempo, and various other musical formal parameters. I try to create an interesting musical composition out of all these various elements of reality that I've absorbed.

Introduction to
ACTMUSIKSPECTAKLE V

Actmusikspectakle V is my most recent Spectakle of Behaviormusik, an idiom of performance I discovered in 1979 based on the concept that all possible behavior is musically composable. Performed by myself alone without media, set, or technological assistance, this 2½-hour work is a very dense, pointillistic physical montage of hundreds of minute behavioral fragments mimicking culture and nature, both found and original, sacred and profane, bizarre and ordinary, stereotypical and archetypal, originating in both art and entertainment, in media and in "real" life.

Altogether the work is in eleven languages and contains over 28 major characters, 89 minor characters, poets, prayers, conversations, movie excerpts, and miscellaneous language-cells, 41 jazz, rock, and sundry pop songs, 50 hymns, chants, TV themes, miscellaneous music-cells and quotes from classical, avant-garde, and folk musics, and numerous classical and folk dance- and movement-cells. Despite their diversity, however, these shards of behavior all share one thing: they are all lifted out of their original contexts, edited to an ephemeral duration, and arranged abstractly, according to formal and musical principles, so as to inhibit the literal, rational, and political associations they originally had, and to enhance their spectacular qualities. This is done primarily by setting these cultural atoms afloat, as it were, in a much denser ocean of Behaviormusik, or music-alized original behavior: gesture, language, vocal music, hand-percussion (both on the body and on a desk at which about half the work takes place), movement, musicalized facial expressions (Facemusik), and various Behaviormusik sub-idioms such as Signmusik, object-manipulation, Oddness Saturation, Emotionmusik, and Incommunicability.

At the root of Behaviormusik is the idea that physical action can be composed as music can be, according to its formal characteristics: duration, velocity, size, density, subtlety, intensity, complexity, etc., rather than its literal, semiotic characteristics. A crucial element in this process is duration: almost none of these cultural monads last longer than forty seconds, and most average only six or eight, not long enough for the event's political or psychological implications to be paramount, but just long enough to demonstrate its visual, musical, dramatic, and choreographic properties.

Hence no material is thematic in the usual sense. There is, however, a very definite and inexorable process of formal evolution: a movement from music to theatre. The first of the work's four contiguous sections contains its highest levels of density, velocity, subtlety, and musicality, and thus its fewest and shortest major characters, and its lowest levels of color and theatricality. Due to a very gradual increase in the duration and physical size of the events, however, there is a corresponding increase in their colorfulness, emotional intensity, and theatricality: dances become larger, language more vivid, melodies longer, characters deeper. What began as a work of musicalized behavior becomes one of the music-theatre. Still later in the work certain ideological and psychological preoccupations emerge, including, among other subjects, war, religion, sadism, paranoia, and the nature of consciousness, but in the end these are again submerged beneath waves of Behaviormusik, as the work again becomes a dense mosaic of fragmentary behavioral quanta. These transformations are so gradual as to be imperceptible over any period of less than about thirty minutes, however, and do not dilute the surreal, musical, and above all enigmatic nature of the work.

Thus *Actmusikspectakle V* is less a one-man opera with a distinct message, or even a subject, than a pointillistic behavioral portrait of culture and social reality itself, slightly rippled in the refracting pool of an individual personality.

Actmusikspectakle V contains no improvisation. Every event is predetermined to the minutest detail and notated on a 217-page event-score, using both conventional and contemporary musical symbols as well as several hundred invented symbols in a notational system devised especially for this work. This system was designed to symbolically express all possible vocal, facial, percussive, and seated gestural behavior with as little recourse as possible to language. More than merely an invaluable mnemonic and compositional tool, as in music, the Behaviormusik score is actually the very cornerstone of the compositional process. By reifying the physical action, aural or otherwise, in the graphic symbol, a non-verbal emblem is created that escapes grammar and can be concatenated formally and abstractly with other such symbols. Thus fully encoded by the sign, the event is denuded of whatever political or symbolic costumes it may have once worn, and the composer can perceive it as a pure unreferenced form, free for musical manipulation.

ACTMUSIKSPECTAKLE V
© Michael Peppe, 1984

You have always been reading this title

Thirty sentences chosen from the forty-four in the following text constitute the narration track for the audio work The Lesson, for narrator, solo vocalist, piano, percussion, and chorus, an eight-track version of which, performed by the composer, is the introduction to the live performance of Actmusikspectakle V.

■ AS SOON as you turn your back everything in the universe snaps itself inside out with a hideous sucking motion. ■ THE ONLY reason you cannot call the world impossible is because it is only through the world that you know the concept of impossibility.   ■ YOU have been led to believe that everyone feels he or she may be the only living consciousness, but you are in fact the only one for whom this is true.   ■ THE FUNDAMENTAL structure of reality is totally transformed every instant, but it provides you with a phony "memory" that it has always been the way it is.   ■ SINCE you are always at the exact center of an infinity, there is no such thing as movement, location, space, or time.   ■ YOU are a row of electrochemical events taking place in your cerebrum. ■ NOTHING has meaning in itself, but everything can support any meaning.   ■ IF you could glimpse for even a moment the real meaning of existence your brain would be neuroanatomically destroyed.   ■ YOU cannot conceive of a thing for which you do not have a word.   ■ EVERYONE'S perception is radically unique, but leads them to believe it is more or less similar for everyone else.   ■ YOU have always been reading this page.   ■ THE PAST disappears and the future never arrives, so there is no validation for labor in the present.   ■ EVERYONE who thinks "I am free" was genetically permitted to do so.   ■ CONSCIOUSNESS exists in all things living and non–living; human beings have merely the grossest form.   ■ YOU cannot remember a time before you were born because there was no such time, nor any other: it has always been this moment.   ■ DEATH could occur inexplicably any second.   ■ THE ODDNESS of the world exceeds the imagination by an infinity: it has produced this looking at it, this looker, this labelling of it, this labeller, the concept of labelling, the concept of oddness, the word "oddness," the concept of a word, the word "word," the word "concept," and the concept of a concept.   ■ MAD people are those who have seen into the inner nature of existence.   ■ THE NAMING by physicists of new particles and forces like "quarks," "charm," "strangeness," and "upness" indicates an unprecedented cynicism about the basic processes of nature.   ■ THE DIFFERENCE between organic and inorganic substances is purely a matter of degree; stones reproduce simply by cracking in half; their reproductive capabilities are merely more efficient than your own.   ■ THIS text was not written but extricated from the writer's mind.   ■ DEATH is impossible, since you will not exist to experience it.   ■ CONSCIOUSNESS is not a continuous state but a momentary surfacing for variable periods at random points; your next awakening could be twenty years from now.   ■ NOTHING can be proven to be true.   ■ WHEN it becomes useful to mass-produce life in the laboratory murder will be a commonplace occurence in daily life.   ■ BECAUSE reality is composed of infinitesimally small moments there is no such thing as an event.   ■ THE REASON people are untrustworthy is because their cerebral processes are fundamentally random ones.   ■ ALL love is temporary: only a minute fraction of love relationships last from onset to the death of one of the lovers.   ■ PHYSICISTS cannot unite all the cosmic forces and particles into a Unified Field Theory explaining all phenomena because the universe is not unified but profoundly chaotic.   ■ WHAT you call your personality is the fact the belief that you have a personality.   ■ IF YOU could appreciate the true nature of nothingness for even a moment you would go mad.   ■ THE FIRST thing you see when you look up from this page has a special meaning for you; try and find it now.   ■ ALL objects carry such messages; you have simply not been aware of most of them. ■ THAT the universe is composed of galaxies and stars instead of some other substance is purely a matter of chance.   ■ DURING the night every ego in the world changes bodies, inheriting also the memory.   ■ OLD age is not a gradual but a catastrophic process, and it could strike at any moment.   ■ DREAMS are the reality for which the "real" world is a dream.   ■ ONLY parts of the universe are necessary; the entity as a whole is superfluous.   ■ THERE has never been a time in history when men have voluntarily used less than the greatest possible military technology against their enemy, or allowed a great technology to fall back into disuse and ignorance; therefore, there will be a full-scale nuclear holocaust.   ■ YOU are dreaming this.   ■ THE UNIVERSE will continue to expand until there is not enough matter per unit space to provide the gravity necessary for regeneration, and it will slowly die out.   ■ WHEN you finish reading this everything will be different from the way it was when you began, but again, your new "memory" will conceal this from you.   ■ WHAT you call the self is the statistical tendency to favor certain responses over others.   ■ ALL events occur at random.   ■ THE UNIVERSE is one of an infinite number of universes, the closest of which is undetectable, being a billion universe-lengths away.   ■ ONLY what you are experiencing right now exists.   ■ LOVE is the feeling that another person is really yourself.   ■ THE FIRST conscious decision of your life will be to look up from this text.

Key to
ACTMUSIKSPECTAKLE V

serif type	=	performer
sans serif type	=	characters
Upper and lower case: serif **sans serif**	=	spoken
italicized: serif ***sans serif***	=	sung
bold lower case: serif **san serif**	=	loudly
BOLD CAPITALIZED: SERIF **SANS SERIF**	=	shouted
(parenthesized: serif) **(sans serif)**	=	whispered
(PARENTHESIZED CAPS: SERIF) **(SANS SERIF)**	=	stage–whispered
((doubly parenthesized: serif)) **((sans serif))**	=	mouthed silently
"quoted: serif" **"sans serif"**	=	non–original quotations
SMALL, SANS SERIF CAPITALS	=	identification of character
[*bracketed*]	=	other information

The amount of blank space between words or lines is approximately proportional to the time elapsed between them. Generally, language is grouped not logically or topically but according to when it occurs in performance.

Dialects and foreign accents in English, speech–disabled, inebriated or otherwise irregular English pronunciation, and passages in non–English languages for which the original text is unavailable or impossible to present (e.g., Greek, Cyrillic, Sanskrit, etc.) are spelled phonetically and pronounced exactly as they are written.

ACTMUSIKSPECTAKLE V

a solo performance

Why
what
is
is,
is
what
what
is
asks
what is,
is
what
what
is
says
to
what
what
is
is,
when
what
what, is, asks, why, to and says
are said with
what
says, to, why, asks, is and what
are.

— —

Why what is is is what what is asks what is is what what is says to what what is is when what what is asks why to and says are said with what says to why asks is and what are.

Why? We don't know.

See what I mean?

— —

Why what's here's here's said with what why what's here's here's said with's what what's what says with what what's what's said with when what's here says what's what with what what's what says what's here's said with.

Why we see ah ah what ah ah ah is ah ah not ah ah ah ah we and don't ah be mm what ah is ah not we is ah what ah ah ah ah ah ah ah ah ah ah ah what is ah asks mm what ah ah [*written on the air:* death] is.

— —

What?   Huh?   Oh.
Why what?   But—
What why what?
Why what why what?
What why what why what?
Why what why what why what?
What why what why what why what?
Why what why what why what why what?
What why what why what why what why what?
Why what why what why what why what why what?
What why what why what why what why what why what?
Why what why what why what why what why what why what why what why—[*laughs*]
One two three four five
One two three four
One two three
One two
One—don't look! [*laughs*]

— —

Isn't it? Isn't it what? Isn't what what? What isn't? What isn't what? What isn't what isn't?

Couldn't be better. Can I help you? Do what you want. He's gone. What does she care? How do you do? S'alright with me. Shh. Let's go. Don't say things like that.

she
if and   we
don't
we be-   *gin*
seven.
Go for it.
I   effective
Done. Done.   Continue.
Who   are   we?
Nine   *was*   *born.*
Quoi?   Vas?
ha ha ha ha ha ha ha ha ha—Why
ahhhhhh we
ah ah ah ah ah would ah ah ah ah matter ah ah ah to ah ah doing ah is ah our ah asking ah something we made something we invented needing knowing why being is where here is as here is where we here are and we say here is is what asking does here where being is asking—

word   red   good-bye   into sand   movement of heads   blink   walk   reference beam

((are lifted into place))
((when her feeling))
((a pair of)) horses (sleeping)
((reached into that   heart))
who
he ((rea))ch'd
rise
and if
(Wayne)
(Paula)

— —

PSYCHIATRIST: Thorazine, five hundred mils. And put 'im in the quiet room.

BBC NEWSCASTER: —report issued by Amnesty International today charged the Chilean government with flagrant violations of human rights over the period—

FEMALE, BROOKLYN ACCENT: I donno what **she** was so excited about it was a **company** pawty—nobody knew heh friends were comin', they were awl frum outa state—the fat guy Billy knew because—OPERATIC TENOR: *LIIIIFE!*

listen I gotta run—
ah   ah   ah   Oscar!
Who sees   when I go?
what *them   at play*
and leaves, and is sent
and falls away
ah, hey.   Shouldn't you be   in   church?

goooold?   SECRETARY: Thank you for calling Roto-Rooter may I help you?

lymphaaatic fluid is produced by the gland in response to an hormonal secretion occurring several times annually according to the age of the individual   ibex

again, ya not gonnu ah, nobody is ah, again, again, ya not gonnu ah, nobody is ah, again, nobody is ah, nobody is ah, again, ya not gonnu ah, nobody is ah, ya not gonnu ah, ya not gonnu ah, ya not gonnu ah, nobody is ah, again, nobody is ah, again, nobody is ah, nobody is ah, nobody is ah, nobody is ah—

ha ha ha ha ha ha ha ha ha ha ha ha ha! ha ha ha ha! ha ha ha! ha ha ha ha ha ha ha! ha ha ha! ha ha ha!

Just step around the horse upon the staaair. Just motor by the coatimundi theeeere. Enter the office of the publicist for the rodeo of electric chairs!

PREACHER: And again, in Ruth 16:23 we read: "And we shall gain great comfort from this: that he who shall turn his head from the brightness of the Lord, shall have it loosed from his neck." That's about all we have time for today. Let's close now with a passage from Ezekiel 12:14.

Busy busy busy! Wanna cup a' coffee? You don't have a bathroom do ya? Don't pump me. You know how things go.

[*bookcover reads:* "Artaud"] "All writing is pigshit. People who leave the obscure and try to define whatever it is that goes on in their heads, are pigs. No language, no word, no thought, nothing. Nothing, unless maybe a fine **BRAIN-STORM!**"

ARMY OFFICER: "You are here to participate in an atomic maneuver.   Watched from a safe distance, this explosion is one of the most beautiful sights (YOUR   CHILDREN   ARE   AFRAID) ever seen by man. Basically there are only three things to think about: (OF   DYING)   heat, blast and radiation."   (WHEN   YOU   GO   CRAZY)

TV AD PERSONALITY: You're unique. It's natural: everyone's unique. But you stand apart from the crowd: you're normal.

die

Think anyone'll buy it? I turned around there she was. I wouldn't do that if I were you.

doooog of staaaar breaaaath

JAZZ SINGER: *Ev'rybody knows you run roun' town,   all mah friends,   whatchu doin'   bay-bah*

ah mm um, ah mm um, ah mm um

— —

YOU!

"Hare Krishna, Krishna Krishna, Hare Rama, Rama Rama." "Bodhisattva, won'tcha take me bah the hand?"
"someone to waaatch over me" "A-ave Mari-is Stella-a-a-aaa"

MR. ROGERS: "So nice to be with you again. Start a new week together? Mm? *Tomorrow, tomorrow, we'll start the day tomorrow with a song   or   two."*

JIMI HENDRIX: *"I'm not the only fool, accused of hit and run. Tire tracks all across your back I can see you've had your fun but uh—"*

Ruthenium   Rhodium   Silver   Palladium   Cadmium   SPORTSCASTER: 'E's playing very well defensively Mel 'e's throwing the ball well 'e's making the big plays. MATRON: **Ah, yes ah I'll have the Navy Bean please.** NEWSCASTER: Unconfirmed reports estimate the Lebanese civilian dead at over ten thousand since the Israeli invasion began. CHILD: But **yer** not Santa! SCIENTIST: In quantum mechanical terms the fluctuating magnetic fields which make up the lattice must have the correct frequency components. JOHN LENNON: *"Nothing is real."* INTELLECTUAL: According to Engels the bourgeois state does not wither away but is abolished by the proletarian state, which withers away. JOHN LENNON: *"And nothing to get hung about."* NEW YORK COMEDIAN: Ey, ya gonna laugh or ya gonna form a workshop an' get in touch with it? VOICE FROM "REVOLUTION #9": **"Number nine? Number nine?"** VOICES FROM "I AM THE WALRUS": **"Serviceable villain. Set you down father, rest you."** POET: **I have dried myself in the air of crime!** WINSTON CHURCHILL: **NOT ONE JOT OR TITTLE!**

— —

"Prajna Paramita Avalokitesvara Bodhisattva when the Bodhisattva realizes that all five skandhas are empty he is freed from the cycle of birth, death and suffering."

ENGLISHMAN: "Like as the waves make toward the pebbled shore,
          "So do our minutes hasten to their end.
          "Each changing place with that which goes before,
          "In sequent toil all forwards do contend."

"Den Wein den Man mit Auuuuuuuuuuugen trinkt"

who
hands of
horses!
CHILD: **You pleaded with them.**

— —

and time   searched
There is his hat, among the leaves.
DEATH!
like I said, a *pot   of   blood*   (you watched a kettle)   *piping*   (like a seed)   *like something sweet*
BILLIE HOLIDAY: *"no jumpin' an' ji-ivin'"*

— —

"there'll be no conni–ivin'"   "Tes yeux sont revenus d'un pays arbitraire, Où nul n'a jamais su ce que c'est qu'un regard"

— —

"My name is Ozymandias, king of kings. Look upon my works, ye mighty, and despair."

COMEDIAN: Anyway where was I? Oh yeah, here at the Animal Dentistry Night School registering for fall classes: Anyone know where I sign up for Turkey Root Canal?

All dead,   their voices rising from the woodpile (clear   deserts)   *rose of   sky-y* ANDROID: The scientists are called. DAVID BRINKLEY: A man staggers and leans for support. BILLIE HOLIDAY: *"Ain't nobody's busineeeeess if ah do."*

ssssmoke   roooose   on the back of heeeat

SOUTHERNER: no wahfe, no sisters, no children MICKEY MOUSE: on the back! [*monotone*]: mustard, beige, vermillion, salmon, beryl BRITISH PROFESSOR: Smoke rose to the eaves of his mind and hovered.

Why?

— —

BLACK AMERICAN: Y'all betta git on back heah—**n'ah'm not playin' witchu!**

PAKISTANI AMERICAN: Everribody peoples must to this 'otel pay on ten thirrty the rrent, forrty dollarrs, or must leave, from the 'otel,   everrybody peoples!

GERMAN JEW: Za primitive inhibiting self forbids za expression of za repressed need. POET: "What is the grass? It is the beautiful uncut hair of graves."

"Und der Haifisch, der hat Zähne, und die trägt er, im Gesicht" ADOLESCENT GIRL: Some**times,** Rick,   I just don't understand what cher goals are in our **relationship.** HISPANIC AMERICAN: Yo come in heah dran-keen, smayleen lak a broory, an yo expe' me to gi' you de monay to go ou' rahdeen op an down nay stree' lag a mania' wi' dose low ridaz—**wha', you crasy? YOU CRASY?** GREEK AMERICAN: I sent forr my family   twelf yearrs ago. We open de shop   last yearr. We have Baklava, Souvlaki, Shish-Kabob, Kefta-kabob,   we make livink. Ant now,   dey, dey, dey break into my shop, dey steal everryting: all dey equipmen', dey money, dey supplies, dey smesh . . . . I haf nothink. BASIL RATHBONE: "I sought to destroy the beast with a blow, but this blow was arrested by the hand of my wife. **Goaded by the interference into a rage more than demoniacal, I withdrew my hand from her grasp, and buried the axe in her brain!"**

— —

NEWSCASTER: The precise connection between the mysterious illness and the freebasing of Cheese Whiz is unknown.

Hey!

October, diseases   YOGI THE BEAR: Ehhh Boo-Boo!   ASTRONAUT IN *2001, A SPACE ODYSSEY*: "Open the bombay doors Hal.   Hal.   Open the bombay doors."

What you call your personality   is in fact the belief that you have a personality. In actuality, you are a row of electrochemical events taking place in your cerebrum.   PSYCHOTIC DONOVAN: *"color in sky Prussian blue, scarlet fleece changes hue,   crimson ball sinks from view"*

PAKISTANI AMERICAN: No rrradio talking, de deesco rradio talking in de night time sleeping time **everry-body peoples!**

— —

you	*or*	*how*			
fly	*knee*	*dying*			
two	*s*	*she*			
nine	*row*	*speaking*			
now	*I*	*time*	*ten*	*who*	
seven	*four*				
seven	*four*				
seven					
four	*call*	*grey*			
from	*be*	*color*			
k	*is*	*why*			
man	*run*	*water*			
sky	*hold*	*we*	*fall*	*soon*	

begin	then	begin	then	begin	then	begin	then
begin	*then*	*begin*	*then*	*begin*	*then*	*begin*	*then*
begin	*then*	*begin*	*then*	*begin*	*then*	*begin*	*then*
begin	*then*	*begin*	*then*	*begin*	*then*	*begin*	*then*
begin	*then*	*begin*	*then*	*begin*	*then*	*begin*	*then*
begin	*then*	*begin*	*then*	*begin*	*then*	*begin*	*then*
begin	*then*						
begin	*then*						
begin							

end	*wrong*	*God*					
gone	*cost*	*camel*					
wall	*sight*	*kind*					
cool	*pall*	*scorching*					
hole	*blood*	*rock*	*change*	*breath*			

evil	*come*	*evil*	*come*	*evil*	*come*	*evil*	*come*
evil	*come*	*evil*	*come*	*evil*	*come*	*evil*	*come*
evil	*come*	*evil*	*come*	*evil*	*come*	*evil*	*come*
evil	*come*						
evil	*come*						

evil *loves* *young* *mouths* *that* *speak* that *kiss* **SHOOT!**

VOCAL FROM "RAWHIDE" THEME: *"Keep them doggies movin"* ED SULLIVAN: really big shew— ROBERT DE NIRO: "Eh, you talkin' na me?" RINGO STARR: ho-huh yeah

Magyar mothers! We are still faithful!   Why have you joined the cabaret?

— —

MILTIE THE MOUNTIE: I'll save you!

and *you*   *dip wings*   *in blood*

"Con la sombra en la cintura
"ella sueña en su baranda,
"verde carne, pelo verde,
"con ojos de fría plata."

lunaaaa gitanaaa

("voces de los niños antiguos")

TONY BENNETT: *"Take my haaaand, I'm a stranger   in paradiiise"*

clouds of   *stooone*   *find me hiding*

lace   *wing*   eats   *aphid*

ANDROID: Why what is is is what what is asks what is is what what is says to what what is is when what what is asks why to and says are said with what says to why asks is and what are—

world **WAR!**

DANCE-HALL SINGER WITH MEGAPHONE: *"Ten cents a dance,   that's what they pay me, gosh how they weigh me down"*

BOBBY DARIN: *"Und so kommt zum,   guten Ende,   Alles unter,   einen Hut—"*

NEW YORK COMEDIAN: Eh couldju keep it down back dere I'm tryin'ta help dese people!   I don' mind a little backgroun' noise but it's interfering with your treatment—**hippos: why?**

what she was movin' away from—tell me it wasn't for political reasons—surprised they even showed up considering—at this hour who—work some poor Latino—scent of a human being easier than—so much money they don't know what—but—

——

you   me

uh-oh   begone!

R & B SINGER: *"workin' in a coal mine, goin' down down down,*
"workin' in a coal mine whoop!   about the fifth down
"workin' in a coal mine, goin' down down down
"workin' in a coal mine whoop!   about the fifth down
"fahve o'clock in na moahnin',   ah'm awlready up an' gown—"

TEENAGE BOY FROM BOSTON SUBURB: Me n' Danny Fahmah buncha guys sittin' na school pahkin' lot having' some beeyaz las' Fiday night vight, pahtyin' vight?   Fuckin' Tahmmy Vabitson dvives in vight—**dvunk ez a fuckin' skunk vight,** n' stahts peelin' 'roun' fishtailin' leavin' rubbah n' shit—you know how 'e dvives vight?   An' we ah feelin' like **no pain** vight, ve're all like dvinkin' smokin' n' shit, **pahtyin'.** Da cahps come.   Now y'know dat cahp, da new cahp, wi' da ved hayah, f'um Melvose?   He sez t' Tahmmy 'get atta da cah'.   Fuckin' Tahmmy Vahbitson gets **atta** da cah wid 'is fuckin' Millahv 'in 'is fuckin' **heeyan'** vight?   **Dvahps** it—no dass not all liss na dis!—dvahps it i'na fuckin' pahkin' lot n' it fuckin' splashes all ovah da fuckin' cahp's shoes—almos' shit my peants!

SOPRANO: *"sem-   pre   liiiber-a-a-a de glo folleggiare di gioia'n gioia*
"voc' il scorr' il vi-i-iver mio pei sentieri dell' piacer."

— —

MICHIGAN PSYCHOTIC: —an' it was radiation from heaven that **voosh** flattened the city.   Was very devilish, this city. Was God's **fire!**   An' when Abraham found he could really get be**hind** it, God said grab all yer stuff, n' they made all these deals, n' the evil jus' kep' goin' up n' up n' up, n' God jus' turn around right then, n' Abraham turn around n' God jus' went **zoosh!**   like a neutron bomb, like a big boot, **flattened** it!   Didn' even have time to scream, jus' like a stamp, like you know in those movies, those criminal movies, wher' they stamp like "I.V" er somethin': **voom** n' that's it!   *blood falls   through* (lips of) *ceilings* (steel   carves a mouth   on) *HER THROAT?*   [*monotone*]: *velvet,   pearl,   gossamer* NEWSCASTER: Once more, for those of you who have just tuned in: the President of the United States has been shot.

"Das Leben   ist schwerer   als die Schwere   von allen Dingen")
"Wir alle fallen.
"Diese Hand da fällt.
"Und sieh dir andre an: es ist in allen."

MIDWESTERN PILOT: Come in. Can ye draw a bead on 'im. Can ye draw a bead on 'im. Come in.

TAIWANESE POP SINGER [*phonetic*]: *Shanti   weni dogan shaooooooo   dung-ni shung ta biaou sheh-i doshe hooooooooo*

— —

ITALIAN AMERICAN: Ey Jo**ey** I'm so**rry**, los' my tem**puh**, broke a few glas**ses,** few piece a' furni**cha**—eh I'll buy ya new chair eh?   Eh?   Wha', 'm I lyin' to **ya**?   Awww so I said a few t'ings—wha' d'I say, wha' d'I say?   Awww Joey nooo I would never say dat about cha wife—anyway she not dat big!

KANSAS DRUNK: Ey brother?   Ey nah ah gadda fahn—**ey**!   Nah ah gadda fahn yuhng lady 'ere, don' wan' be botha'd with alla booshit chu puttin' aht ther'!   Nah whahn't chu jes take yer belowngin's n' move raht lowng aht thet door ther' 'fore ah haft' git up n' kick yer **face!**   'M ah gon' haf' do tha'?   'M ah gon' haf' kick yer ayss awl ovuh **shhtree'?**   Y'all beh shet cher mou' boy, y'awl beh shet cher mou' raht nah or you gon' be talki' through th' ho's in yer **teeth!**

FRANK SINATRA: *"So set 'em up Joe,*   *I've got a little story*   *you should know.*   *We're drinkin' my friend"*

MIDDLE-AGED ALCOHOLIC: Jesus Chriss i's gettin' sho I can' 'ava gahddamn scosh n' soda i' my owm gahddamn 'ouse, 'thout chu squeali' n' carryin' own n' makin' lotta ffuckin' noise—**whyn't ch'all g'oveh ta fuckin' Billy's 'ouse?**   **G'oveh dere n' fuck Billy!**

look: obsidian window of the heart—we dash ourselves like starlings against the black panes

— —

wash   *eye*   *seed pods of* radium and plutonium *bear larva* and spin into our comfortable cities

NO?

"a foggy dayyyyy"   *LOOOVE?*   *"in London towwwwn,*   *it had me lowwwwwww,*   *it had me dowwwwaaaaaah"* BROOKLYN TALENT AGENT: Dese, den, ah ya great vocal ahtiss a' da pas': ya Tony Bennetts, yer Al Mahtinos, ya Dinah Shoahz, ya Peggy Lees, ya Robit Goulets.   And ahh when ya ged inta dese ahtiss, ahh   ya ged inta dat indefinable somet'ing we cawl **stah qualidy.** As my good friend an' associate Fat Tommy da Polock ussa say, **"You eidda gad it or ya don'."** Mos' a' ya young singas comin' up taday, dey don' gad it.   Hadda ya ged it?   Cha can't cha gadda have it. Ha' da ya develop it, oncha gad it?   **Dis** is weah dee professionals **like** myself, **an** Fat Tommy da Polock, enteh demselves **in**ta da pikchuh, in ohduh to ahhh, escyulate da patential a' dee individual ahtiss.

NERVOUS NEW YORKER: Reminds me of ah what's 'is name, Tommy, ussa drink wid 'im, what's 'is name, ussa live at da fancy hotel, da Uruguay, what's 'is name, Tommy?, s'posa go to L.A., some **job** of somepin', d'e evah go?, whatevah happena him?   Oh yeh s'wife died, 'e cracked up. *"nice work if you can get it"*   *surpriiised by the suuuun*   OLD WOMAN: 'Who could this bright visitor be?' POET: —we mutter, eye to the keyhole.

ROD SERLING: Case in point. A young man trapped in a carnival mirror-maze of fantasy and compul-sion.   Just east of the mind.   And just south   of the Twilight Zone.

— —

TV AD PERSONALITY: Who are we? We're the Communication People.   The people whose talk is strictly state-of-the-art technology.   It's disposable. Reversable. Reusable with almost any leading brand of ideas, including our deluxe line: yours.

MOVIE COWBOY: Whah ah don' rahtleh know ma'am.   Last ah heard 'v 'im 'e's rahdin' herd down bah Gummer's Canyon, 'bout twinny mahls West a' the ol' Scranton place, jes' afore ya git ta Mule Crick. Said somethin' 'bout fahdin' na man nat killed 'is pappy.   Now y'all know 's well 's ah do ma'am nat means 'e's gunnin' fah Gum-Eye Gulligan. An' nat means 'e's headin' fa Dodge.   An' when 'e gets zere Gum-Eye Gullingan, Big Boy Simpson, Doc Burke n' Gimpy McCradick a' gonna be waitin' fo'm. An' ney ain' gon' be throwin' no tea parteh—**hold it raht there Casper!**   Nah let's see you put thet Cruise Missle down reeeal gentle-lahk. COUNTRY-WESTERN SINGER: *Oh Lord,*   *won'tchy bah me*   *an I.C.B.M.* AMES BROTHERS: *"Ev'rybody's worried*   *about dat atom bomb*   *no one seems worried about the day mah Lord shall come!"*   TENOR: *one*   *stone*   *hair* MOTHER: Help yourself dear there's plenty more in the pan—don't pick Debbie—Tommy? Get ou—Tommy? **Tommy? Get**cher hand — Bill wouldju grab him? Take — oh — take — **Tommy!** Debbie get the napkins.   Thank you Jimmy: At least someone's cooperating.

— —

PSYCHOTIC JAMES CHANCE: *"I wantchor heart for casual wear!*
"I wantchu ta grasp at my straws,
"and see if I care!
"Ah!   Ah!   Ah wanna see some emotion!
"An' not the usual fluff!
"I wanna be the one   to tell you
"when to start and when you've had enough!"

JAZZ SINGER: *"You're mean to me.   Gee honey it seems to me   it's funny—"*   [*laugh-barks*]:
heh!   heh!   heh! heh!   heh!   heh!   [*phonetic Russian*]: "Lubrovnya
lordtka   rasbilas obweet.   Nyekchimu   peeyareechain   vsimenich bolai.   Tee pos-
moteree kakiyeh,   vimyelyeteesh.   Noch oblojayla,   izbyeznoy danyu." "Bronze by
gold heard the hoofirons, steelyringing   Imperthn thn thnthnthnthnthnthn.   Chips, picking chips off rocky
thumbnail, chips.   Horrid! And gold flushed more. A husky fifenote blew. Blew. Blue bloom is on the"—
"Quant au monde, quand tu sortiras, que sera-t-il devenue?   C'est aussi simple qu'une phrase musicale."

"Isn't it rich?   Aren't we a paaaair?   Me here at last on the ground   You in mid-aaaair.
Send in the clowwwwwns."

JAPANESE MARTIAL ARTIST: *"Shoo!   Nam!   myo-! ho!   ren- ge!   kyo!"* BUDDHIST PRIEST: "Soregashi
kako onnongo genzai manman,   no hobo zaisho shometsu,   gento nise daigan joju no tame ni."

"A-a-amaaaazi-i-ing Graaaaace,   ho-ow sweeeeeet   the souuuuund,
"tha-a-at saaaaaved   a-a-a wretch   li-i-ike meeeeeeee.
"I-I once   wa-a-as loooost   bu-ut nowwww   I'm fouuuund.
"Wa-a-as bliiiind   bu-u-ut nowwww   I seee-eeeee."
——

Wilbur, Miller can in hand, Wilbur
His wife makes him feel he's no man, she says:
'every day you beer and T.V. every day you haven't got the married spirit
'get it up can'tchu get it up get it up can'tchu ain'tchu a man?'
Every night he dreams:
in his bloody study step around the wife upon the—
better just to watch the T.V. ART CARNEY: Ey Mr. Donahee-hee-hee   *"What do ya do when you're*
Branded?" VOICE FROM "REVOLUTION #9": "Number nine?   Number nine?" JEAN STAPLETON: *"Everybody*
pulls his weight!"

Wilbur, with the knife in hand, Wilbur
kills her, now he knows he's a man, he says:
"put it in"—he sticks it in her—"put it in"—he's hard he's such a man DAVID BYRNE: *"psycho-killer   qu'est-ce*
que c'est   ba ba baaa   ba ba ba ba baaa ba bettah NERVOUS NEW YORKER: Whadju **t'ink** I was
doin' nere in na hot car with an ice cream cone—sunlight on na vinyl—baby seat in na back with a glob
a' jelly on na tray—punchin' na buttons on na Panasonic lookin' fa Barry Gibb an' Barbera? Whadju
t'ink I was in it for: the *Funny Girl* soundtrack? The milk shake in na glove compartment? The Sweet
n' Low under the seat?

You are free
to pick from who you see
to make your you a me
to be a butcher baker
*   bootlace maker*
*   tin cup shaker*

haaaack in   Pakistan
your wiiiish is   your command
tomorrrrrow   cook in Kenya
build in Burma
love in Libya
spreaaaad yooour wings! WILLIAM CONRAD: This mother eagle, like all eagles, does not usually eat reptiles, but will resort to them when warm-blooded prey is scarce.   The bobcat's reputation as a fighter is well-deserved, but like almost all animals, it will flee in nausea and terror at the smell of a human being. (YOUR   CHILDREN   ARE   AFRAID) MICHIGAN ARMY OFFICER: F'r instance ah **with** a twenty-megaton surface-burst you **would** have a good chance **of** surviving (OF   DYING) GOVERNMENT FILMSTRIP VOICE-OVER: Sundays, holidays: we must be ready for an atom bomb attack **every** day, to do the right thing. To **duck** and (WHEN   YOU   GET HUNGRY) COCKNEY: *"OHHHHHHH YO' BOIBOI 'AS GONE DOWN NA PLUG'OLLLLE!   OH YO' BOIBOI 'AS GONE DOWN NA PLUG!"*

— —

black   blade
kissed (forest of feeling)
her eye
black   blade
kissed (forest of feeling)
her eye
black   blade
kissed (forest of feeling)
her eye
black   Del-   phi   moon
BROOKLYNITE: great vocaliss' a' da pas'—
muttering   in   earth
ha ha ha ha ha ha ha
Del-   phi   moon
BROOKLYNITE: great vocaliss' a' da pas'—
muttering   in   earth
ha ha ha ha ha ha ha
BROOKLYNITE: great vocaliss' a' da pas'—
ha ha ha ha ha ha ha
Hojambo. THE BEATLES: *"I give her all—"*
whirling women
Bernie Jenkins!
Hojambo. THE BEATLES: *"I give her all—"*
whirling women
Bernie Jenkins!
whirling women
Bernie Jenkins!
Hojambo. THE BEATLES: *"I give her all—"*
whirling women
Bernie Jenkins!
PRIEST: Thy kingdom come, Thy will be done, on earth
MR. PRESIDENT LOOK OUT!   pause for station identification

PRIEST: Thy kingdom come, Thy will be done, on earth

MR. PRESIDENT LOOK OUT!   pause for station identification

take one   **MR. PRESIDENT LOOK OUT!**   pause for station identification

take two   **MR. PRESIDENT LOOK OUT!**   pause for station identification

take three   **MR. PRESIDENT LOOK OUT!**

take four   **MR. PRESIDENT LOOK OUT!**

take five   **MR. PRESIDENT LOOK OUT!**

preeeeei-steeeeess sing   Bless me Father, for I have si—

Bless me Father, for I have si—

Bless me Father, for I have si—

Bless me Father, for I have

Sisi pendeleza Mungu,   Yeye sema, "Hojambo."

JAZZ SINGER: *"In the plaaaan,   ohhhh   the Diviiine plan,*

"God must be   a boogie-man."   "Gracia a vosotros y paz, de Dios Padre y de nuestro Señor Jesucristo; para librarnos de este presente siglo malo." HISPANIC AMERICAN: "For estra copies of thees booklet sen' your check or money order to Spanish Booklets."

— —

rockets rusting in their silos as
good generals go to grey
twitchy trigger fingers itchy to boss a battle today   play
cops n' robbers and   slay   prey
What's a soldier to do   who
gets too old to   coup   you?
people killing people murdering
Ever since the world began the man
who tried to countermand the caravan
has had   his   head   had   hot   that's   his-   story.
nuke and Nike needle needed to
pop overpopulace
cities shifting in the people-sand
everybody givin' takin' makin' breakin' sleepin' wakin'
everybody livin' in a kennel
people walkin' talkin' rollin' rockin' shakin' shockin'
everybody livin' in a kennel
people workin' fuckin' workin' fuckin' fuckin' workin' fuckin' fuckin'
fuckin' in a kennel   kennel   kennel
I'm an interaction of cells meta–metabolizing
which is a collection of molecular organizing
which is a connection of part and particularizing,
an operation.
I'm a type of relation,
unique articulation.
Tell me where is a me?
Is it a brain?
Is my being a brain?
Does it look out of a body?
If I **am** a body where am I looking out from when I look at it?

we   say
please   be truuue
Mister Reality
please   be truuue
"people
"people who need"   meaning   "are the—"
LAURIE ANDERSON: "This is your captain speaking.   We're all going   down.   So why not let   X   equal   X."

"don' matta'   don' matta' don' matta'   don' matta'   don' matta' 'bout nothin' no mo' "
What is true's true when your you   says so.
What is not is not alot   less so.   yes/no
When it's real is when the Dealer's Dealing
     what we're feeling
     when the Wheel is Wheeling
     we'll be squealing
     but when the heel is healing
     we'll be feeling
what is true is who is telling you

bone   code   nucleus   multiply the house   bloom
blood   blastoderm   sacrificial shell   terminate the sign of host

— —

SCIENTIFIC "AUTHORITY": What you call the self is in fact the statistical tendency to favor certain responses over other ones. NERVOUS NEW YORKER: I dunno why'm tellin' **you:** **I'm** na one ney go for, **I'm** na one wid da funny hat, wit no name on it—'f I leave it in na bank I'm sunk: dey won' know where ta send me! SCIENTIFIC "AUTHORITY": What we call the personality is nothing more than a row of e- lec- tro- chem- i- cal e- vents ta- king place in the cerebrum. YOUNG GIRL FROM QUEENS: This s'las' week ight, Friday right, I gut up in na moanin' my cah wouldn' staht right, so cawled my boss, said um naw comin' in 'til ladah right; 'e sez 'aw no prob'm—Joanie's comin' in late fr'm Bayside she cin swing ovah pick y'up'—I sez oh boy Joanie—you know Joanie right, 'magine sittin' inna cah fa tirty mints wit' Joanie right—s'I sez **wait a minute.**   U'll take a **train**—'e sez 'aww no, no prob'm, anyway needja ta be heyah by ten she be ovah in about twenty mints s'I sez okay so 'bout twinny mints ladah she pulls in right, **beepin' na hoan—she jus' pulled inna da driveway right she's awwready like layin' on na hoan** u'm rushin' aroun' lookin' fa my shoes—I tell ya Liz zis girl is like **mentally retahded!**

— —

IRISHMAN: "The soomar evenin' had begun to enfold the warrld in its mysterious embrace. Far away in the west the soon was settin', and the last glow of all too fleetin' day lingered lovingly on sea and strand, on the proud promontory of dear old Howth guardin' as evah the watez a' the bay, on the weedgrown rooks along Sandymoont Shore, and, last but noot least, on the quiet charch whence there streamed farth at times upon the stillness the voice of prahr to her who is in her pure radiance a beacon evah to the storm-tossed heart of man,   Mary,   star of the sea."

ha   ha   ha ha ha ha   haaaaaa
singgg   names of God
Vicky
heads of hay   dreeeam
tongues of wood   speak
eyes of cloth   seeee-e-e-e-e-ee-ee-ee-eee

MICHAEL McDONALD: *"You'll look up an' ah'll be go-o-one   Bit bah bit bah bit—"* BRUCE SPRINGSTEEN: *"Ah came fer you, fer you, ah came fer you but chu did not heed my urgency"* SUGAR HILL GANG: *"Ho-tel, mo-tel, whatchagonna do today?"* BARRY GIBB: *"Make it a crime to be out in the co-o-o-old"* ELVIS COSTELLO: *"Watchin' the detectuuuves,   ooh as they shoot shoot shoot shoot"* JOHNNY ROTTEN: *"Nooo fuuutcha faw yewwwwww"* DAVID BYRNE: *"I'm painting,   I'm painting a-gain,   I'm cleaning,   I'm cleaning again"* LADY ANNA RUSSELL: "But chew know sometimes it gets to be too **much,** I mean sometimes **really** I cawn't **cope** with it, it's just a **din**—it's awkward to listen to I think, sometimes, don'tchew?   It gets way **out** n' you think aoh, you know, s'not   **restful** atawll, is it, or **pleashah.**   And why should you go 'nd suffah?   'nd I daon't like **groups** eithah, you know, **groups,** oh-hoh **gosh,** do you like—aoh I'm not much—oh **groups** you know, like **Who.**   The **Who.**   N' the **what.**   N' the—goodness knows—well I'm not really a jazz **buff,** I'm afraid I'm a bit of a square, ulways have been, so I really daon't know too much **about** it except of course for **dawncing,** when you're young, an' that sort of   **Cole Poahtah** depahtment. But when they go **banging around** n' whooping 'nd yaylling, 'nd you know, do a whole numbah's only got one chord in it!   'nd ju c'n **give** these people—you know they've got **two keys** n' **three chords** n' that's all you get in an entahre evening!   And then they yell, all this yaylling— n' of course you never understahnd a **wehd** they're saying—that's anothah thing, I mean f'you could understahnd the **lyrics** you might at least   get a little something **out** of it. And then of course **oh!** The **din!** No I daon't like that atawll I think I **faded out** on the **Beatles.**"

who (she)

I buried Paul

ENGLISHMAN: "The Watusi.   The Twist.   El Dorado."

Deus Ex *Maaa-a-a-achinaaaa*   "Christo murió por nuestros pecados"   *"As the lovely flame diiiiies,   smoke—"* "amaaaar   es un com-ba-te re-lám-pa-gos, y dos cuer-pos so la mi-el der-ro-ta-dos" BROOKLYN BOXING TRAINER: Look, killeh, she's a tendeh young t'ing: make nice wid 'er, buy 'er a drink, tell 'er she's lookin' good—she's a lady: you treat 'er like she's a contendeh!   What, chu never seen a lady befoah?   Ya **pug,** yar in **society** now,   gotta act nice, say 'scuse me when ya boip! Waddayagonna, sit wid a buncha classy dames n' faht n' spit n' smell yar armpits? Dis ain't da gym, ya palooka—nah I wantcha ta tawk classy, n' straighten ya tie—an' **wipe ya mouth when um tawkin' a ya!** 1920s NEW YORK GIRL: *"He's just moy Bill,   an oahdinary goy.*
"He hasn't got a thing thet oy can brag about,
"[or] makes   me   thrill.
"Oy love   him,   becawse he's—
"—oy don't know—
"becawse he's just   moyyyyy Bill." SLEAZY LOUNGE CROONER: *"But doooon't   change a hair for meeee,*
"noooot   if you care for meeee.
"Staaaaay,   little valentiiiine,   staaaaay." FEMALE EAST INDIAN VOCALIST: **"Ba dak bil hile wit la aye**
[*phonetic Sanskrit*]   **"hie ku mitari shu ha sie**
"wli mi nas mi nee al bide
"ma ad al biad   ha daaaa" PAKISTANI AMERICAN: No veeseetar anytime, dee night time sleeping time.   Is rent for one week, forty dollars, on ten thirty dee money here pad, for, forty dollars, one week, da room.   Is not dee veeseetar to come, anytime, all dee morning-day, night and sleeping time, **ev'rybody peoples.**   No radyo talking, dee deesco radyo talking in dee night time sleeping time **ev'rybody peoples!**
— —

(mi niño)
("¿De dónde vienes, amorrr, mi niño?")
("¿De dónde vienes, amorrr, mi niño?")
("¿De dónde vienes, amorrr, mi niño?")
(mi niño)
"El niño bus- ca su vo-oz"
"what rough beast slou- ches"
"what rough beast sou- ches"
"what rough beast sou- ches   to- wards"   Mos- cow

CHILD: because Jimmy **said** I could have it, be**fore**.   N' then after Mr. Perkins left he comes up behin' me n' hits me right **there,**   n' then I turned around n' 'e was hittin' me everywhere all at once a million times all over **hard,**   n' so I tried to get away n' I couldn't so I liked **brushed** 'im like a **little bit,** like **there?**   n' like 'e starts **cryin'** real loud?
(Mi niño busca su voz.)

— —

"Beatrice tutta nell'etterne rote
"fissa con li occhi stava; ed io in lei
"le luci fissi, di là su remote."

Oxydol Kleenex Geritol Sanka Pepsodent Dash Raid Ovalteen Tab Fiddle-Faddle Levis Gravy Train Gleem Pampers Cocoa Puffs Ivory Snow Tang Cheerios Ultra-Brite Tame Good n' Plenty Gelusil Adidas Twinkies Di-Gel Ajax Handi-Wipe Sweet n' Low Aqua-Velva Propa PH Boraxo Kool-Aid Lestoil Whopper Tums Seven-Up Lemon Pledge Bubble-Yum Spic n' Span Alpha-Bits Mr. Clean NEW YORK COMEDIAN: What, a' ya gonna laugh or ya gonna form a workshop n' get in touch with it?

B MOVIE ALIEN WITH MICHIGAN ACCENT: "I must leave your planet now. And return to a world of cold and un-emotional galaxy beings.   I will give them my report,   and then I will be destroyed. I have failed in my mission.   Not because I am weak,   but because you are stronger.   If I could feel emotions as you beings can,   I would feel sad to leave your beautiful planet.

NORTHERN-STATE SCIENTOLOGIST: When I first got **in**to Scientology, I wanted to be successful **in** Scientology, as far as it being a profession.   So when I started F.S.M.-ing and de-bugging,   that is when I looked at the product: a **revitalized being,**   a salvaged person who is **on lines** and **everybody wins from that.**   It put me on **purpose,** and got my ethics in, and dynamics aligned.   I can handle as many people as come across my lines!   As F.S.M.'s we can reach out, **in**to the field, physically, and we can **be these people's terminals.**   Setting yerself up as a terminal fer these people really helps them up the bridge.   At one time I was an electrician.   But when I finished the S.H.S.B.C. and the internship,   I felt it was an **overt** to go back to my job.   At A.S.H.O. the environment is **very** O.T., and **very** upstat, and it's impossible not to win, across **all** of yer dynamics, once you've started a training cycle there.   To decide to do the S.H.S.B.C. is **indeed** an indicator that a being has already reached a **very** high level of confront.   For anyone who has decided to quote, "flourish and prosper," unquote, the B.C. is certainly going to help you arrive at the postulate.

"My analyst told me   that I was right out of my head.
"The way he described it   he said I'd be better dead
"than live. I didn't listen to his jive.
"I knew all along   that he was all wrong
"an' I knew that he thought
"I was crazy but I'm not."

RUSSIAN AMERICAN BROADCASTER [*phonetic*]: "Havakyatek vazramyatark: hatz,   hakoost,   ye voreezhmatarknare. Voreem ayescorcher anarzakahnk cheemonah; tebee seepazan, baderalzum."

BARITONE [*phonetic Russian*]: *"Raaaas tsvye taaaa lee ya-blo nee-ee gruuu-shee.*

"poooh plee-leeeee tu ma-nee na-dre koyyyyy.

"Vweeee kooh dee-ee la na bye resh ka-tyoo-sha

"naaaa vwi soooh,   kee bye resh na kru toyyyyy."

MIDDLE—AGED HUNGARIAN AMERICAN: Ev'ry time we go out ees like dees. She take two howars to poot on dress, poot on stucking, choose dey dress, choose dey het, choose dey shoes—she poot on wrong earrings hes to poot on ahthar pair—'no, no, ees not right pair—poot on green pair, poot on purple pair!'. I seet in chair weeth coat on for howar and hef, watchink like T.V. show—she run beck and forth, 'try dees, try det.' Friends call on phone: 'Wat ees wrong—are you comink?—ees deenar ees cookink—ees deenar ees ready!' I say no, ees not to comink yet: ees great piece art created by vife on face wis make-up. Parheps by Christmas we unveil. Ees *Mona Lisa* for deenar party.

[*phonetic Greek*]: *"Ruuu-beee gleek-ya   elll-lak-so-na*

"elll-lak-so-na gon-da-mu

"elll-la pro-wee   mehhh-teen ab-gee

"see-soon-sun-eel yak-tee-tha

"Ru-bee moo mee-cree."

PUERTO RICAN AMERICAN: *"I like to leev in Amereeca,*

"okay by me in Amereeca,

"everything free in Amereeca,

"for a small fee in Amereecaaaa."

JAMAICAN RASTA: *Jah free-een de preeees-nahs of Babeelon* MIDDLE-AGED CARIBBEAN WOMAN: Wall you know dey be goan' out on a Satihday naht,   ahn' dey be drinkin' ahn' dahncin' ahn' cahrryin' on, ahn smokin' the Gahnja weed, ahn' tawkin' about the root rock reggae,   but chu know on Sunday moahnin' dey be gettin' up, ahn' dey be prayin' at the top a' dey lungs to Jah Rastafah, ahn' dey t'ink **'e** be tawkin' bahck to dam, but de **real** God, **een** de sky, **een** de Bible, dee **real** Fatha of **ool** de people in de wuhld, 'e **no'** Jah Rastafa, 'e **'ate** Jah Rastafa, ahn' 'e **no'** gonna be lis'nahn' to **dam!** RADIO PREACHER: "And Elijah said 'The children of Israel have forsaken Thy Covenant, thrown down Thine altars, and have slain Thy prophets with the sword.' And a great and strong wind tore the mountains and broke the rocks in pieces before the Lord. But the Lord was not in the wind. And after the wind was an earthquake, but the Lord was not in the earthquake. And after the earthquake was a fire, but the Lord was not in the fire.   And after the fire was a still, small voice." OLD WOMAN: Excuse me, could ju tell me where the Pacifica—we've just arrived from San Jose, my husband is sitting in the, we've parked over at the, where you come in, past the, the sign—he doesn't know where—we're looking for the white building just across, the show is to begin at one—at—excuse me—at two o'clock, the Pacific Flower Show, they're having the presentation, this is the first day, there's three days, and we're staying at the, just down the street from, where you take a left to go to—and we couldn't find the, the off-ramp to get to, what is— **Chestnut,** Chestnut Street, and where it, it crosses, and you get to—   Over here?   Down here,   where the—   Yes. Yes.   But where is the—where—   down past the—   I'm sorry, so you take a left after the—   the third le—   the second I—   Oh. You're not from this area?   Oh I see,   I'm very sorry,   ask this man right here? Thank you very much, you've been very kind. Excuse me sir—

— —

JIMMY DURANTE: "Ev'rybody wants ta get inta de act!"   "Riverrun, past Eve n' Adams, fr' swerve of shore to bend of bay, brings us by a commodius vicus of recirculation back to Howth Castle and Environs."   *"L'iiiin-ter-na-tion-a-a-a-a-le se-raaa la raaace hu-maaaaaine"*

"Quaaand je te tiens dans mes braaaas,

"j'ai le coeur qui baaaat

"je vois la vie en roooo-se." JACQUES COUSTEAU: Very often,   when zee yuman 'as trapped an' tamed zee animal, and is allowed to caress 'im,   'e sinks animals are like yuman children.   But animals

are not children.   Zey are powearful creatures 'oo 'ave for a moment poot aside zere powear.
WILLIAM CONRAD: When the male turantula mates with the female,   he risks almost certain death.
The only other animal whose venom is fatal to him is the turantula hawk, which is actually a wasp.
RHODE ISLAND W.A.S.P.: Animals? My dodiz love animals, we gut fowah husses.   See, my dodiz a' mudels, they weh feachid in a Fohd commehcial.   An' when the entiyah thing fehst stahted I wundid if I shouldn't retiyah: they were makin' a quatah 'v a million dullahs, they w'r in six figyahs.   One Mundy I w's buyin' tiyiz 'n on Tuesdy w' hed a new cah, a Ramblah.   So I said to 'a 'Deah, d'ya need 'ny help?' 'N she s'id 'Yes Daddy, we need a buyah.' S'I been buyin' evah since: husses, gehbils, tehtles— she loves animals, 'speshly behds. Thehsdy w's mahketing all day, yes'dy w's in fowah stowiz buyin' blindahz f' the mayah.   COWBOY: Eeeeasy big fellah.

TEXAN: *"Muh heart will have fergotten*
          "thet chew broke ev'reh vaaaaaow,
          "n' ah won' ceer   a hunnert years fr'm naaaow."
JOHN GIORNO: **"I DON'T TRUST ANYBODY**
          "I DON'T TRUST ANYBODY
          "I DON'T TRUST ANYBODY
          "I DON'T TRUST ANYBODY
          "I DON'T TRUST ANYBODY n'
          "I DON'T TRUST ANYBODY"   KHALID AL-MANSUR: "The C.I.A. using a Christian
fanatic. **DEVELOP A CHRISTIAN FAMILY!** With Jim Jones at the hea'. A letter of endorsement
from Rosalind Carter.   Greetings, from Governor Jerry Brown. **All the Christians came**
together, and watched seven hundred and fifty blacks DIE!   And what did you
say in their defense?"

ELDERLY BAG-LADY: I can tell you're intelligent because ya sittin' beside yaself.   Now when I sit somewhere 'n public I don' wan' anyone sittin' wi' me.   'F they do I tell 'em get da hell out because I don'
want their face before me—**show me dat tongue once more I'll put cha 'n jail again!**   **Ya**
queer!   See dat queer right dere? He's gay.   **Stick dat tongue back in ya mouth ya**
queer, stick it up ya mothiz ass! An' get da hell ahta here before I slap ya face an' calla police
again!   I'm a widow from Worl' War Two n' I'm on duty right now. *"He's the boogie-woogie*
bugle-boy" BOB DYLAN: *"Ye thet buil' the death-plaaanes"* ADOLF HITLER: "Za whole education unt training
of za chilt must be so ordart as to give him za impression zat he is absolutely superiah to uzzahz!"
          Never before in history has any nation used less than its full strength against the enemy;   therefore,
there will be a full-scale nuclear holocaust. ADOLF HITLER: "Die Wissenschaß musst als Instrument vom
Nationalstolz angesehen sein."
— —

"Nel mettà del camin della vita, mi trovi in una selva oscura." PREACHER: "And he opened the sixth seal,
and behold, there was a great earthquake;   and the sun became black as sackcloth, the full moon
became like blood, and the sky vanished like a scroll that is rolled up.   And hail and fire and blood
fell on the earth; and a third of the earth was burnt up, and a third of the trees were burnt up, and all
green grass was burnt up.   And a great mountain burning with fire was thrown into the water,
and many men died of the water, because it was made bitter. And lo, the smoke of the land went up like
the smoke of a furnace.   And I saw an angel call to the birds of midheaven, "Come, gather for the
great supper of God, to eat the flesh of men."   ("Ego sum panis vitae")   "And men sought
death and did not find it; they longed for death, and death fled from them.   And the earth became
a heap of ruins, a land of drought and a desert, the haunt of jackals, a horror and a hissing, without
habitant."   (For men do not know their time, but are taken like locusts snared in a net.)
CHOIR BOY: *Ag-nus no-bis*
          pec-ca-ta De-i
          mi-i-se-e-re-e-re-e nooo-ooo-o-biiis.
— —

(nox praecessit)

"Als Gregor Samsa eines Morgens aus unruhigen Traumen erwachte As Gregor Samsa awoke one morning from uneasy dreams,   he found himself transformed in his bed into a gigantic insect."   MIDDLE-AGED WOMAN: 'Gregor?'   cried his mother. WOMAN: 'It's quarter to seven. Hadn't you a train to catch?'
The chief clerk was at the door. BANK OFFICIAL: 'Mr. Samsa what's the matter with you? Here you are, barricading yourself in your room, causing your parents a lot of unnecessary trouble, and neglecting your business duties in an incredible fashion.' MAN WITH SEVERE SPEECH DISABILITY: 'Bbbbut sssssssir,' cried Gregor.   MAN: "I'm jjist g-g-goinkkk to opppen de d-dorrr ththiss vey miiinute.   A shshshlight illnnish, a-a-a-an att-tackkk uf ggiddinesh, ha- ha- ha-hasss kkept me fr'm g-g-gggetting up. Ah ah ah I'll pput my cllllothes on et once, p-p-packkk my shhhampples, n' shhtaht off to w-w-work.'

IRISH FOLKSINGER: *"It's arrly ev'ry marrnin' we roise et foive o'cloak,*
                    "an' the little snears coom to the door to knook, knook, knook.
                    "Coom me little washer-lads it's toim we went ta warrk.
                    "Y've gutta hae to warrk fahr farh pence a dyah."
"Ariiise ye prisoners of starvaaation,
"ariiise ye wretched—"

MR. ROGERS: Didja like that record?   I did.   I have a snake that I'd like you ta see.   S'just a stuffed   toy   snake.   Friend of mine made this snake for his children.   He said   'I don't know how to make a stuffed   toy   snake.'   But, his children said 'please try.'   And so he did.   Sometimes fathers and mothers and children just decide to try   things   out. And they often have a lot of fun when they do.   I'd like you to meet the man who made the snake. Let's go to his house now.   MIDDLE-AGED CHILD MOLESTER: "I   allowed my son ta   fondle me. And I don't   think he really   wanted to.   But   didn't know h-h-how to   'xpress my love other**wise.**   It   started out as   backrubbing   and went from there.   My h-hands went   in between his thighs,   and   eventually I   fondled my son's   penis. I   know that   I did him some   h-h-harm.   But   sorry to say, I   did   enjoy   it." LITTLE GIRL SOBBING: "When I w's   'bout five?   he-he came up to my room   an' an' an' started taking down my pe-ants   n' touching me n'   making me touch 'is dink.   First few times, I'd start cryin'.   B-b-but after s-so many times of cryin'   he he he wouldn't sto-op,   s-so I jis' gave up   an' I di'n't cry   fa 'bout five years   'bout anything.   The only time I th-th-thought about i' was   o-o-o-on Tuesday night,   when Mom w-was away   n' n' n'   n' n' Dad would pick me up et Brownies   n' n' n' I'd be   waitin' outsi-ide   'n I'd jis'   be so s-s-sceeyad   'cause I, I knew w'   w'   what would happen   when w-we got ho-ome."
AFGHANISTANI: Dey mek me   clean de floor   weeth my tong-geh?   And den dey   heng me, by dey feet   for meny, meny   hhowarrs?   Ant beat me,   ant poot de knife, cuttink? on my   tes-teekles?   Ant when I scream 'I am not animal, I am not animal, I am a men: please, keel me, keel me,'   dey tek de   ek?   de egg? ant   cook?   cook de egg, ant poot   up my   h-hole?   So, insite, I   cook?   ant, ees all day screamink 'keel me, keel me,'   but dey laugh, and cook more   de eks,   ant cuttink de knife more,   ant beatink more,   until dey are bort?   borred   weeth me,   ant   drag me back   to my cell. Salaam Aleko. PARANOID SCHIZOPHRENIC: Dey got incinerat**orrrRRRS!**   The dripping legs, hanging from their   racks—aluminum, styrofoam, you punch a clock, five o'clock, go home, **eat the baby, eat the baby, Mummy wants ta fuck, Daddy's nailed ta little Patti—SOMEbody mus' be screamin'—***dinnnnerrr*—ev'ryone sits down—'oh how was work today dear?'—BANG! BANG!** MOCK CHILD: 'c'n I have **meat?** Mummy what's in the frying pan?' **KKKKKKKK!** PARANOID: The little black door? In the chest? You found it. The spy-hole? Oh who's this? **DRIP.**   We wrote it in the sky: the   sssmoke, the   sssssssmears of   blood, the geese, with the little biting, the little biting beaks with the little naily-y teeth, the tearing an' ripping in the **brown air**—'Oh I don' hear anything, oh no I dunno nothin' '—I'm jus' **locked up in this black box in this big stomach in the dirt!**

— —

Why we see ah ah what ah ah ah is ah ah not ah ah ah ah we and don't ah be mm what ah is ah not we is ah what ah ah ah ah ah ah ah ah ah ah ah what is ah asks mm what ah ah [*written on the air:* death] is.

Why what is is is what what is asks what is is what what is says to what what is is when what what is asks why to and says are said with what to says why asks is and what are.

Why?

— —

Why what?

Notes on the eventscore of ACTMUSIKSPECTAKLE V

The score of *Actmusikspectakle V* contains a single or double system, or row of concurrent events, per page, and is read from left to right. Every effort has been made to use conventional music notation wherever possible, and to vertically align simultaneous events. The latter, however, is usually possible only in the bottom two-thirds of the system, which contains the three event-types most easily musicalized: **Voice (V)**, **Facial Acts or Expressions (F)**, and **Percussion (P)**, which as it consists exclusively of hand-percussion on a table and on the body, is divided not into instruments but into **Right Hand (R)** and **Left Hand (L)**. Because much of *Actmusikspectakle V* is performed seated at a table; the physical movement therein falls into the category of **Gesture (G)**, the notation of which occupies the upper third of the system. This region is in two parts: a double row of boxes containing symbols indicating the **Event (E)** performed (or formation assumed) by the hands (which becomes a single box for head actions), one for the **Right hand (R)**, and one for the **Left hand (L)**; and below it a rectangular map showing the **Location (Lo)** or path of the hands in space, most often a frontal view of the performer. A diagram of this notational system is below, followed by a just a few of the hundreds of symbols.

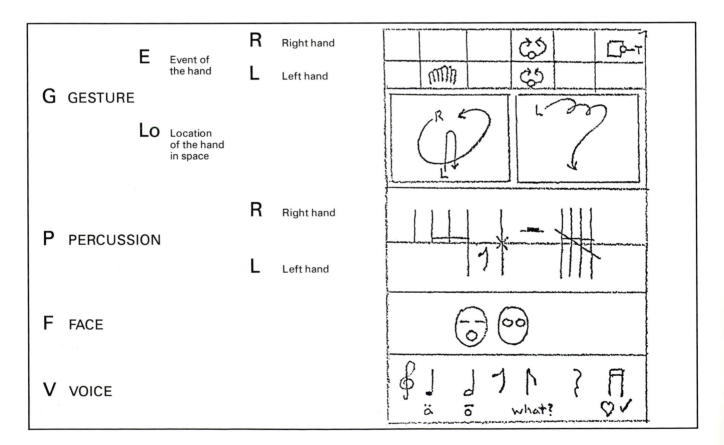

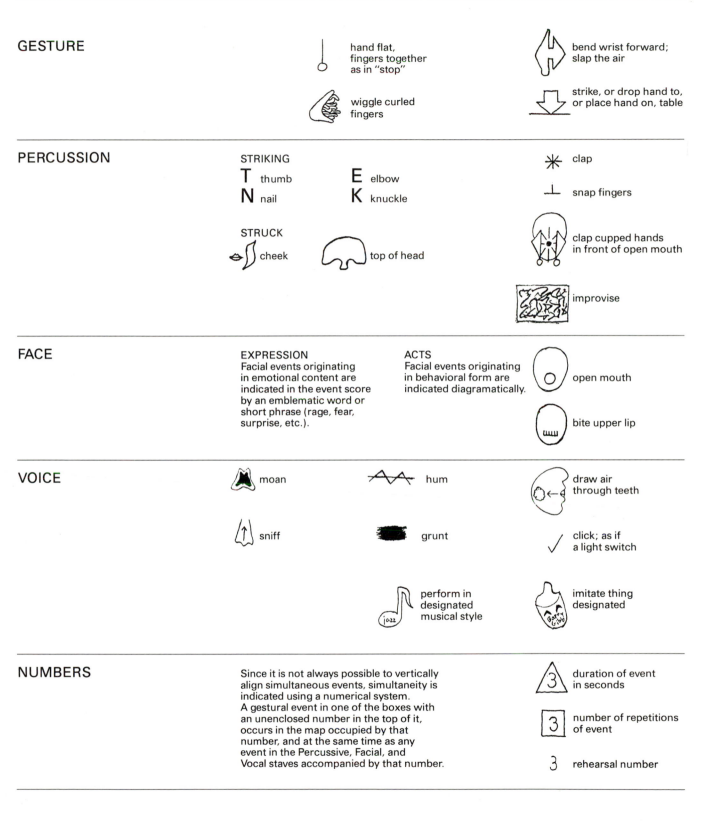

GESTURE

hand flat, fingers together as in "stop"

bend wrist forward; slap the air

wiggle curled fingers

strike, or drop hand to, or place hand on, table

PERCUSSION

STRIKING

T thumb   E elbow
N nail   K knuckle

clap

snap fingers

STRUCK

cheek   top of head

clap cupped hands in front of open mouth

improvise

FACE

EXPRESSION
Facial events originating in emotional content are indicated in the event score by an emblematic word or short phrase (rage, fear, surprise, etc.).

ACTS
Facial events originating in behavioral form are indicated diagramatically.

open mouth

bite upper lip

VOICE

moan   hum

draw air through teeth

sniff   grunt

click; as if a light switch

perform in designated musical style

imitate thing designated

NUMBERS

Since it is not always possible to vertically align simultaneous events, simultaneity is indicated using a numerical system.
A gestural event in one of the boxes with an unenclosed number in the top of it, occurs in the map occupied by that number, and at the same time as any event in the Percussive, Facial, and Vocal staves accompanied by that number.

duration of event in seconds

number of repetitions of event

rehearsal number

The following pages are twelve half-size samples from the 217-page Eventscore of *Actmusikspectakle V.*

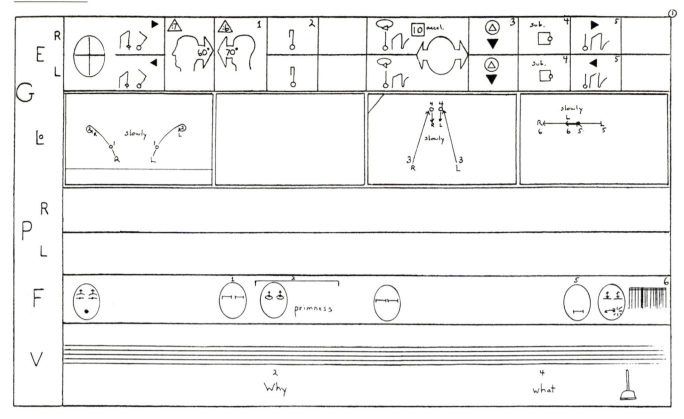

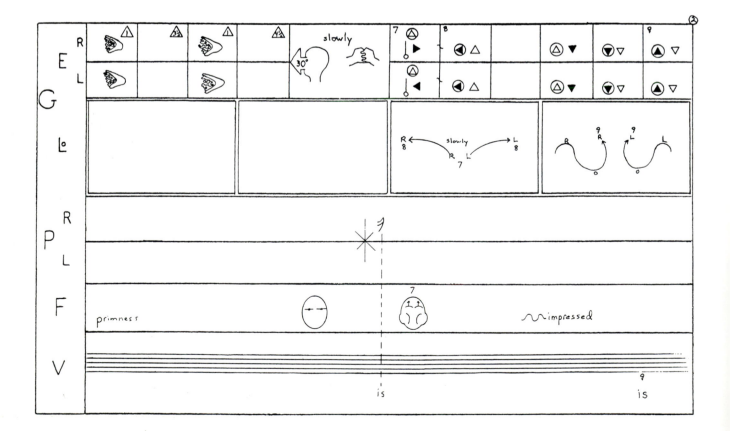

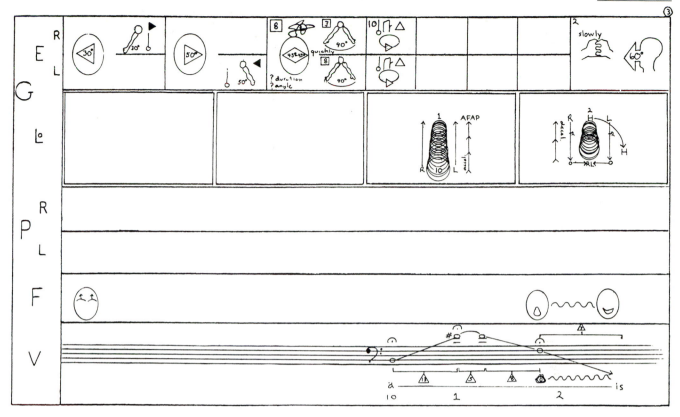

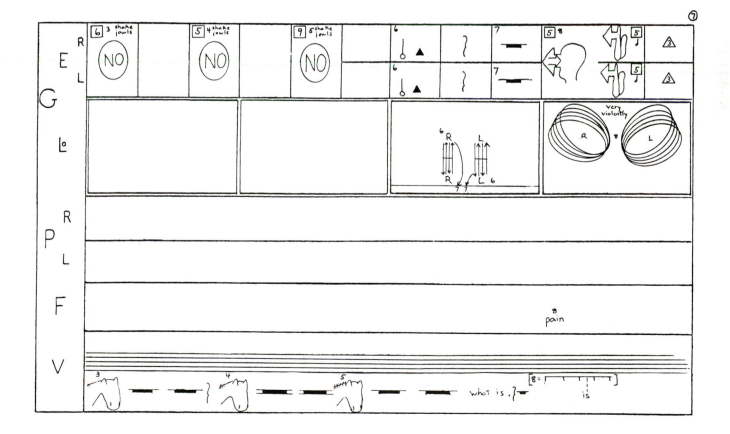

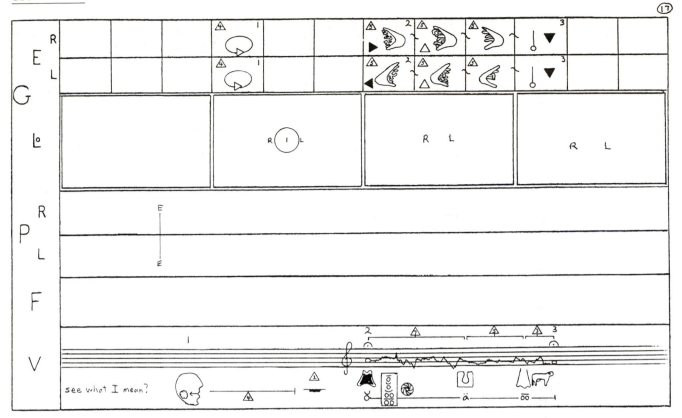

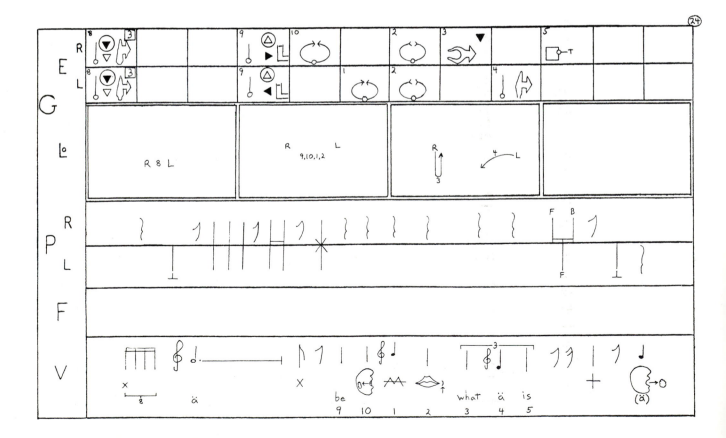

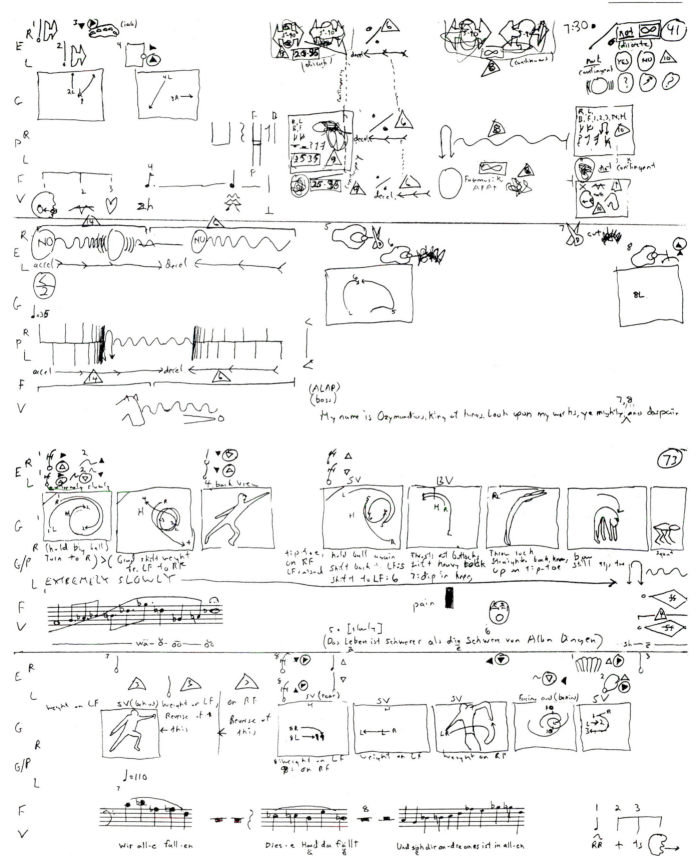

My name is Ozymandias, King of kings. Look upon my works, ye mighty, and despair.

(ALAP)
(bass)

EXTREMELY SLOWLY

Wä-ö-oo-oo

pain

5 + [slowly]
(Das Leben ist schwerer als die Schwere von Allen Dingen)

sh-ē

Wir all-e fall-en

Dies-e Hand da fällt

Und sieh dir an-dre eine ist in all-en

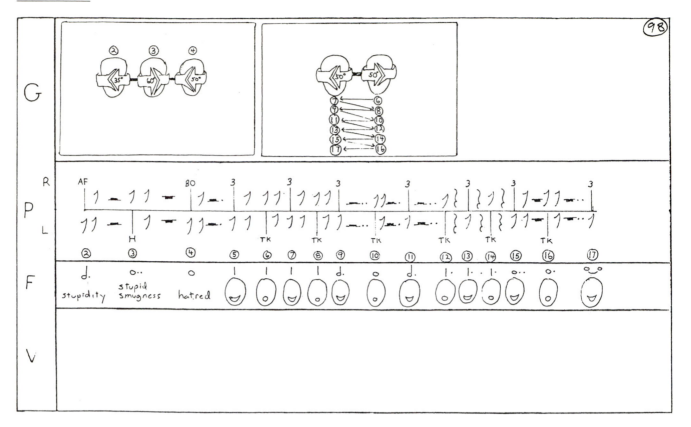

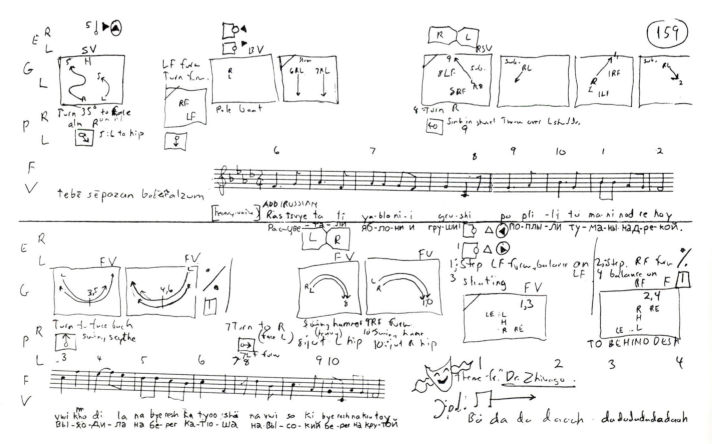

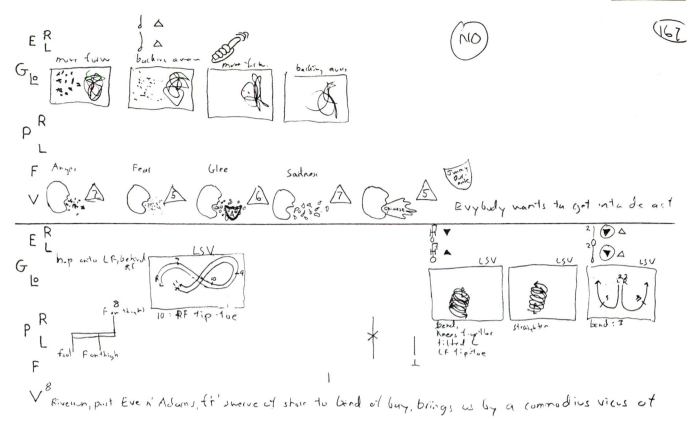

Evybudy wants to get into de act

Riverrun, past Eve n' Adams, f'r' swerve of shore to bend of bay, briings us by a commodius vicus of

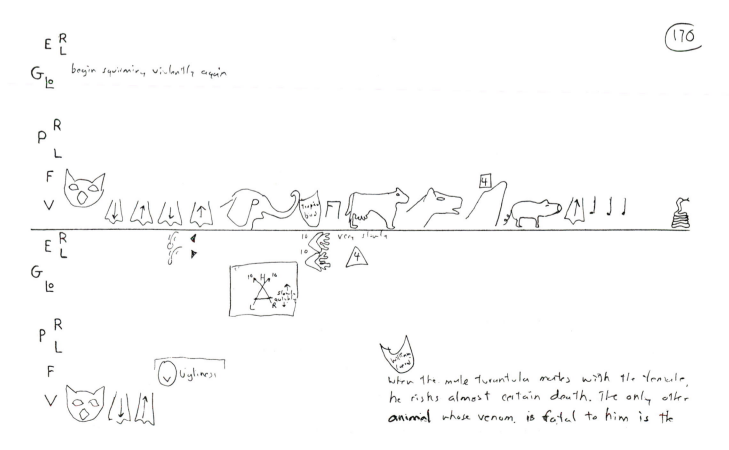

When the male tarantula mates with the female, he risks almost certain death. The only other animal whose venom is fatal to him is the

Behaviormusik theory

Throughout history up to and including the present, music has been traditionally thought of as a kind of material, a particular species of event, either—in the case of the vast majority of listeners and musicians—as a finished product which has in some way been organized or transformed by human hands, and which moreover may or may not fulfill musical criteria, depending upon individual judgment, or—in the case of Cage and other modernists—as a raw material, namely any sound at all, whether humanly transformed or not. If we examine this materialistic notion closely, we see that within it there are probably seven possibilities as to definition:

any sound

any awareness of hearing music

any human hearing

any hearing

any perception

any sensation

any vibration

But due to the impossibility of distinguishing with any claim to objectivity audibility from inaudibility, musical awareness from general audition, audition from inaudition, audition from general perception, perception from general sensation, sensation from general vibration and vibration from general event, we discover that there can be no *a priori* field for musical exploration narrower than *any real event.**

*The first two paragraphs of this essay are a summary, not a proof, of information fully developed in the longer essay, "Music."

If we have concluded thus, we may in addition declare, as did Cage for his rather more ambiguous choice, sound alone, that our work is finished, that any event is already music, regardless of the degree of human interference in it, which may equal none at all. The task of the musician is then only to frame, or bracket, as do Cage and his successors, certain regions of that continuum, so as to highlight its musical qualities.

Theoretically and philosophically the notion is sound, and may indeed occasion some very beautiful music, but it evinces—and here we are on more subjective ground to be sure—quite a leisurely attitude towards the composer's responsibilities vis à vis a cosmos of catastrophe and suffering. Such a cosmos requires a music definable neither as a petrified end result, flaccid raw material, or languid bracketing, but as an operation, a process of transformation specifically useful at every unique moment of its execution; a willed but organic response to a spacetime in constant flux. Not in order to play a series of games based on historically-derived concepts, on equally historically-derived material, or even to spill such games in the service of artistic crime, but to create a kind of a revolving, transforming retina in the center of things, always at the same vantage in relation to the engulfing infinity, but constantly reflecting and refracting different regions of the protean continuum.

This reflection, moreover, goes quite beyond the mere assemblage of works of art—a bourgeois dalliance at best: the manufacture of closed, finite, easily quantifiable commodities, autographed souvenirs of the freedom of which the spectator wishes to believe him or herself incapable—but constitutes a true *Weltenschaang,* a standing-in-relation to the world that is in the profoundest sense of the word musical. It is a musicalization of every aspect of predicament: thought, emotion, diet, vocation, sexuality, politics, spirituality, social relationships—the entire profile of absurdity— in an attempt to transcend personal taste and idiosyncrasy to attain a state of unmediated will. Only by a thoroughgoing disregard for the chattering commentaries of culture and its encoded spore, the personality, can one hope to attain to a true will-to-beauty (which always derives its very nature from its unpolarized character).

But naturally it is nowhere near enough to simply experience the world in such a way: our exile into neurological freedom is not one of sensory behavior alone but of motor function as well: the musicalization of experience must directly empower and inform the composition of works. So it is that the detached, scientific study of the way events enclose, accompany, modulate and articulate one another makes possible the performance of motor activity highly emancipated from egoistic motivations and vanities. Thus is transformed not merely the voice and body but the very composing and performing mind itself, into a musical instrument, through which real events may flow and according to their own congenital natures characteristically intermodulate one another and re-create themselves in the reflected microcosm of the behaving body.

Why our art is so bad

Nobody wants to hear it, and even fewer want to say it, but someone's got to: nowadays art is awful. When was the last time you experienced a recent work of art, in *any* idiom, that was as interesting as walking through a forest, or a crowd, or traffic? Or even simply thinking? The rude truth is this: sounds, movements, colors, words, shapes, ideas: the all–too–many larvae of the obscenely fertile, robotically strewing human imagination are no longer impressive to us. We all know the ever-redoubling miracles of speed and sensitivity of which the body and voice are capable, the breathtaking sorcery of the mind's eye, the gargantuan feats of technology, the numberless permutations of organized color and line, the infinitesimal subtleties expressable by tongue and pen: breathes there a soul who is even surprised, much less inspired, by such dimestore magic? The mere word *art* (say it) has a somewhat narcoleptic effect: one thinks of dust, paper, a kind of insincere solemnity, a deliberate *retarding* of the mind, a certain *scarcity* of event and idea, and, above all, an endless waiting. More than anything, this is what we do when we experience contemporary art: we wait. Wait for a concept, an image, a sound that can even begin to compare, for mere interestingness, with nature, with industry, with sex, with conversation, with television, with riding in an automobile, with sleep. . . .

One hears: "But art should not be compared with nature and technology and life: it should only be compared with other art." But why must we always be making excuses for it? A thing either enriches one's life or it does not. A fellow either makes himself useful to his companions or he does not. And somehow the forepaws of our artists are stuck in the latter category.

Take improvisation. Although in ancient times it was probably virtually equivalent to performance, our inability to revert to the kind of utterly unconditional faith in intuition necessary for its truly inspired use has shrunk its domain to that of the nonverbal arts, where without the most rigorous of structures (e.g., be–bop) it becomes tedious almost immediately. At a time when what is newest in the arts consists almost entirely of irony, lightly- or un-structured improvisation seems increasingly silly and naïve, like a nostalgic adult on a tricycle. Whether the improviser succeeds in fooling only us, or himself as well, that his is a trance state, the fact remains he's faking it. Unable to accept the irretrievable loss of primordial, unmediated creativity, artists improvising today do so usually to escape what they apparently feel are the corruptions of adult art-making: rationality, technique, self-criticism. Improvisation has become little more than the strutting of a puffy-chested hamster on the treadmill of the infinitely prolific human imagination. What could possibly be cheaper and easier for the mind than words, ideas, and images? Far from being difficult for us to produce, we are in our dullest moments unable to cease doing so. To make an unabashed physical boast of the Brownian Motion in the laundry-list of one's consciousness is to express a supreme contempt for both one's own time and that of one's audience, and finally, for life: it is in a sense to believe in one's physical immortality.

Granted, in the ever-dwindling fraction of artists still carrying the primitive tailbone, talent, still willing to subject it to a discipline of technique and a scrutiny of mind, and in addition courageous enough to suspend it between the jaws of personal risk, improvisation can be a noble and exhilarating art (viz. Lenny Bruce, Bill Evans, Ravi Shakar, Betty Carter, Cecil Taylor, Lord Buckley). But then talent, discipline, labor, self-criticism, and courage are no longer words one generally overhears in conversations about art these days. Rather one hears words like unique, stylistic, experimental, entertaining, revolutionary, important, and of course, the sparkliest flattery of all, in art *and* handsoap, new.

What is truly new about contemporary art is neither the work nor even the void of beauty therein, which has in some degree yawned in every age, but the sheer size and duration of that yawn. We find ourselves giving in to it with increasing frequency nowadays, despite art forms sprouting and blooming mad as dandelions, and "advancing" at such a rate as to virtually *consist* of newness. To our horror, what would appear newest of all, should it miraculously appear in our art, is something as old as neurons and photons: beauty.

One of the elder slugs in this idiom larvae–boom is the idiot bastard Performance Art. The best artists of this ilk, generally of less interest than those considered mediocre in the others, tend to be individuals with an alphabet Cup–A–Soup of economically worthless skills (usually tap–dancing, origami, yodelling, and underwater hand-shadows), with a desperate need (for obvious reasons) for an idiom devoid of both training and critical standards. Somehow they can survive for years on the social Twinkie of art stardom, whining all the while about the lack of state funding, without once asking themselves if they accomplish anything more laudable than the squandering of time and attention.

Hopefully the idiom of performance art is a kind of cultural mutation like, say, flippers on llama, which will soon enough be corrected by economic nature. But the fate of such 24-hour pupae is as an issue truly dwarfed by a much more ominous question: could art itself be that vestigial organ, that cultural prehensile tail, to be sloughed off when we have learned to walk economically erect? Whatever the answer, it is clear the question only occurs to us the moment that tail becomes too weak to flip us one tree over.

Because performance art is far from exceptional. Mail art, audio art, ceramic art, conceptional art, xerox art, book art, etc.: all are forms that arose not so much out of any pressing urge to communicate ideas, emotions, or images (known perjoratively in the trade as "content") but, as most of the artists themselves would boast, because they were there. In our more nostalgic moments we would like to think of these experiments as artistic crimes committed against a villainous and imperialistic Establishment, and of the artist as a Dada Robin Hood, heroically letting fly at the ramparts of bourgeois value. But Dada was a long time ago, and so was Robin Hood, and on a different continent, which did not, as does our nation, nearly *consist of* the bourgeoisie; and in any case a better word by far than "crimes" would be "pranks," or perhaps "mischief." Not because the acts committed are not lawless, but because there is no longer a law against which to commit them.

No, the new idioms appeared mainly because they were easy: inexpensive, simple to work in, quick to become finished product, and best of all easy to reproduce and disseminate to the by then vast baby-boom art audiences cheeping open-beaked to the horizon. Even more happily for the artists, none of these forms possessed critical yardsticks against which a work's relative success might be measured. Thus the art patron, already some-what portly with education, had to be told that what he beheld was *good* art at the same time that he was told it *was* art. Indeed, the entire issue of quality, of the beautiful and the ugly, he was told, was irrelevant. To even consider the issue was to be—pardon the profanity—*judgmental,* was to be old-fashioned and a philistine, was to use the criteria of the butcher shop and the baseball field within the hallowed walls of the art gallery. Being an agreeable fellow (patrons as well as artists being perhaps above all *agreeable*), he accepted this, this notion of creativity as an end in itself, of art being good without being beautiful. And audiences today still accept it. Accept it precisely in the way one accepts the historical existence of Captain Cook and his brave little crew. Completely without caring.

As fast food and condominiums replace home cooking and homes, so too are we increasingly buried in Fast Art: performances prepared in three weeks, bands gigging after a month's rehearsal, composers who stretch a measure's worth of material into a full-length work, sculptors who mass-produce figurines under the guise of Embracing Capitalism. Fast Art is almost always breathtakingly hip, smooth as Frogurt, easy or unnecessary to be understood, flattering to its audience (at least for their taste, and their membership in the artist's personality cult, which may number anywhere from in the dozens to in the millions), and, most importantly, stylistically indistinguishable from the rest of the artist's work: it is an advertisement for his other advertisements for himself. And, as with his ideological cousin in the culinary arts, McDonald's, his success depends largely on the comfort we take from knowing that no matter what artwork or franchise we go to, we *know what we're getting*. Unfortunately, the knowledge avails us little more than it does the dung beetle.

In a society in which few dare venture even the slenderest notion of what, in their terribly humble opinion, art is, it is not surprising it has become signature. Obviously if it is anything in particular, someone else's work is going to be left out in the woods overnight, leaving the critic or beholder who exiled it there open to the charge of "elitist," a disparagement about half a rung above "Nazi" on the descending ladder to hell. And if artists have no aesthetic nucleus to orbit, each is left to shout his own name in a deafening crowd scene: hoarse, unheard, and unlistening. If there is no concept of what constitutes an artist, it is surely inevitable that ever greater multitudes will turn out to qualify. What appears to be decreasing is, alas, neither art nor artists, but the beauty in them. Why?

The answer, I believe, can be found in history and prehistory. Originally, spontaneous creativity was viewed as a kind of magic: the improvised invention of events in a story, notes in a melody, or movements in a dance could have had for early man only a supernatural cause; even the performer, questioned afterwards, did not know whence came his inspiration; rather, he ascribed it to his *muse*. The naturalistic imitations of the forms of nature in charcoal, pigment, and clay resulted for most in a labored crudeness, for some an astonishing likeness. It was noted also that the progeny of these special individuals often had similar talents; thus shamanistic, musical, sculptural, oracular, and priestly roles became matters of blood succession. Such predestination was believed to have been ordained by the Gods; or, as we would put it, the Genes.

Over millenia, however, with the increasing dominance in the cerebrum of the left hemisphere and the ascension of man in power over the gods, artists began exerting ever greater levels of personal and eventually rational control over their muses and their charisma (from the Greek *kharisma,* divine gift). Shamans began to develop elaborate preparations for their ecstasies, painters to study and mix their pigments, musicians to codify simple harmonic law. Rules sprang up about the telling of legends and prophecies, and the proper conduct of rituals; artisans began to train, performers to rehearse, creators in general to objectify their work, to determine precisely what it was they did, that they might do it better. And as the muses shrank to angels, and ultimately to subconscious urges, and the

Gods became God, who in turn flattened into an idea on a page, which finally curled and crumbled, so too did the mystery of art become a technique, the ecstasy a floor-show, the ritual a pantomime, the prophecy a ditty, the myth an anecdote, and the talisman a coin.

So ends the Age of Art. Or at least, to take a longer view, its first great epoch. The ability to apprehend and analyze the structure of works, minds, and even the creative process itself stands at its height; indeed, ever greater phases of this process are now surrendered to what had once been mere tools and instruments: the recording studio, the sound stage, the editing room, the music synthesizer, the image-processer and of course, the artist of the future, the computer. The point is not that artists are somehow "losing" creative prerogative to their technology, but that if they are wise they surrender it voluntarily, because the will-to-beauty in their own hearts is by now insufficient to create it alone. We have reduced art to the education and training necessary for its execution. Thanks at least in part to exponential growth in our ability to record, preserve, research, and reproduce art, every scrap of technical and psychological evidence as to how great art is made is now at our disposal. The knowledge has in fact the kind of comprehensiveness that can only result from one kind of operation: the autopsy. Like a watch dismantled to see what makes it tick, our art has been dissected and left open on the coroner's table to stink, it having been discovered to contain not a soul, or even a pineal gland, but only flesh and blood.

But what was most fatal to art was not so much the knowledge itself as its sudden availability because of the epidemic spread of education and mass communication, to all people. Automation and other technologies have freed up vast featureless deserts of time for tens of millions of people, more of whom—due to the same processes, as well as other economic advances— are high school- and college- and television-educated than ever before in history. More devastatingly for art, these super-educated masses (in which the baby-boom forms a central demographic hump) are not content with martinis by the inflatable and sunning themselves with TV, as were their less educated and less politically "conscious" parents. No, confronted by the yawning emptiness of automated culture's bored mouth, they respond by making art. Hence the recent booms in poetry readings, rock bands, novelists, street performers, video artists, photo galleries, mime companies, etc., and of course a correspondingly massive increase in the ratio of bad to good in those fields. By now even our middle-sized cities have each their own little Greenwich Village, lined with cafés swarming over with refugees from bad Jules Feiffer cartoons, effusing about their Work, their Band, and their Big Break. Is not nearly everyone you know, except your mother, working on a novel, taking dance classes, playing guitar or dreaming of film stardom? For decades it was a great cliché that theaters, galleries, and concert halls were haunted by the philistine who would remark, "But *I* could do that." Another great stage was reached a few years ago when the artist himself admitted that indeed, *he* could. Today we have reached the third and final stage: *he* does.

Happily, at least one field has managed to benefit from the glut: entertainment. Almost immediately after becoming neon–lit with the postmodernist logo Anyone Can Make Art, the playingfields of art began to teem with the untalented. Not surprisingly they soon became heaped with contempt, causing a large number of those more gifted to defect to entertainment, a field that had once looked vulgar and common, but by then looked positively exclusive by comparison. Because entertainment does not stammer and vacillate about what it wants: the best, and there will always be room for only a limited amount of it, and the rest can go back to art. In entertainment one either succeeds or fails; its door is not at all open to the huddled masses leeching the corpses of their hapless muses: it is in fact *strictly* elitist. Naturally there are a certain number of failures and fools, as there are anywhere, but these are errors quickly corrected by marketplace economics. Bad entertainers, unlike bad artists, do not have friends on grant committees. Thus the entertainment industry cannot help but benefit from the surplus of trained and educated hopefuls; unabashed and brutally resolute in its quality control, it reaps all the more golden wheat for but a few extra sweeps of the threshing–room floor.

Moreover, even as art grows commoner, easier, and sillier, the artists and audiences for entertainment become daily more educated and sophisticated. This has prompted the more naïve among us to announce that the Art of the Future will be *in the form of* entertainment, as if somehow all the idioms of art might someday mystically unite with those of entertainment in some grand aesthetic Moonie Marriage. They point to the adventures of Brian Eno, Lily Tomlin, Public Image Ltd., Richard Pryor, and the Talking Heads and say that tomorrow's art is mass art, is entertaining art, or even that the two fields are or will be in fact equivalent. But this is truly the silliest kind of romanticism: a merely cursory examination of the marriage's progeny reveals that entertainment and art have not merged symbiotically at all: rather, the former has quite absorbed the latter. Our experience of this kind of event is in fact nothing like a great art experience, which can suspend one shivering with vision on a wire hung from the ineffable, but is rather a mild glow, such as one's feet might get from a steam pipe on a winter morning. It is in fact a very powerful *entertainment* experience; it's just that what we call entertainment is becoming deeper, stronger, more sophisticated, and more exquisitely beautiful with each passing year, because it is needed and lovingly nourished by its culture, while, denied that nourishment, or even attention, our art shrivels and crackles like a dead moth underfoot.

But there can be no resurrection. Because the process is ultimately rooted in what is one of the most important events of this century: the final and incontrovertible victory of a great eighteenth–century idea: that of the fundamental equality of all people. The socialist attack on class hierarchy and its concomitant vision of all workers as potential art-workers, alongside the democratic notion of freedom of expression, are the vast groundswells which carry the innumerable wavelets of more recent and localized expressions: the surge of ethnic minority art, the Human Potential movement's ideal of everyone realizing their creative potential, the advancement of art as therapy, the emergence of women in the arts, the teaching of art to ever younger age groups, the decentralization of art into non-urban areas: all these forces are related in this mighty movement, which, though barely even conscious of itself, is having a massive effect on the art world. And in combination with the still larger socioeconomic forces already discussed, such as the increase in leisure time, the spread of literacy, the inexpensiveness and availability of art technology, the democratization of education, the expansion of mass communication, the gradual collapse of white *and* imperialistic First and Second World values, and of course the sheer growth of population, these forces have sufficed to virtually eliminate the ancient Western (and, ultimately, aristocratic) notion of the artist as a uniquely gifted individual. Or, for that matter, as anyone in particular. Unfortunately for beauty, whose role as *raison d'être* in art is simultaneously usurped by pure freedom (which, capitalized, would now also replace the "Truth" in Keats' famous equation), that notion of individual charisma is at the root of what we have until now called art.

And let there be no misinterpretation or underestimation: no other mere movement in any idiom can compare with this one, which amounts to the eradication of art works and artists as such.

To its credit, Western art saw it coming, and not only predicted, but with its usual fiercely perverse sense of humor actually precipitated its own downfall. Warhol's famous pronouncement about everyone becoming famous for fifteen minutes deserves mention. Much earlier, Cage devoted an entire career to the notion of the artist erasing rather than engraving the traces of himself in his work, and earlier still Artaud had called for "no more geniuses" in an essay entitled "No More Masterpieces." Even earlier, Italian Futurist theatre with its minute-long *sintesi* (tiny performances) and French Surrealist poetry with its automatic writing, Duchamp with his urinal and again with his early retirement, had all levelled crippling blows at the traditions both of work-as-masterpiece and artist-as-genius, little realizing that, as usual in culture, the job would be completed not by future artists and their manifestos but by economics and demographics.

The expanding Red Giant of culture reached critical mass in the sixties and seventies. And with the creative explosion of forms that lit those decades (performance art, mail art, sound sculpture, textile art, poster art, apartment theatre, art rock, art graffiti, ceramic sculpture, environmental sculpture, sound poetry, radio art, computer music, conceptual art, laser sculpture, artist's books, concrete poetry, xerox art, art comics, video sculpture, body art, interactive video, etc.), under the influence of idiom cross-fertilizers like Robert Rauschenberg, Nam June Paik, Vico Acconci, Yoko Ono, Allan Kaprow, etc. *ad infinitum,* all under the paternal eye of Cage, it became increasingly obvious to artists, critics, and audiences that art was simply whatever the artist chose to call art. At the same time, the idea of performance as merely a framed swatch of ordinary time, of sculpture as an imperceptibly altered environment, of music as any ordinary sound (Cage), of dance as any natural movement (Cunningham), of literature as randomly-selected print (Burroughs), of performer as non-artist (Robert Wilson), of film as documentation of ordinary time (Warhol), and of video and music as pure ambience (Eno), combined in an unapologetic assault on the idea of the art work itself. The original outrage against these artistic crimes (crime being at that time still possible) faded quickly beneath the merciless noon of fashion, and ultimately, given the nearly immediate remoteness in supersonic culture of the original conventions, turned to confusion as to exactly what was being revolted against. Still later, this in turn gave way to the realization that those conventions in fact no longer existed, and the present complete apathy prevailed. Like the identifying features of value in general, those of art have, as in a supernova, expanded quickly enough to qualify as an explosion, and we are left with a vast, indistinct nebula of dust and gas.

At this crucial moment the political and socioeconomic forces described four paragraphs ago become paramount. The mighty armies of freshly self-christened artists stretching scores abreast to the horizon, having both ignited and been ignited by this cultural nova, delightedly pick up mallets and brushes, photocopier knobs and synthesizer toggles, and begin banging and switching and dabbling away, burying notions of beauty, discipline, labor, talent and courage beneath mounds of lacquered tinker-toys, amplified eggbeaters, interview magazines, action-painted Danskins, atom bomb montages and flaming diaries. Still, the point is not so much that drawing stick figures, jerking off into one's hat, singing unkind songs about the president, or ring-modulating the Dave Clark Five with an Australian *didgeridoo* is not, or is bad, art, but that it is all we have left after the smoke clears. Not so much because there are too many people making art *per se,* but because their number almost certainly vastly exceeds that fraction congenitally predisposed to do so well.

The artistic tradition of the West, once a slow, almost predictable evolution of time-ratified ideas, has increased its rate of proliferation and change by an order of magnitude three times already this century, and what was once a few scattered blossoms is now the grass underfoot, each blade stunted by the paucity of its nutritional ration. Clearly, writing magic names from the kabbala on one's belly in peanut butter is, if you like, art, and a lovely way of protesting the excesses of one's parents, but how will one's children protest *that* excess? Certainly not by exceeding it: while that is doubtless possible, it hardly constitutes a protest against a tradition whose manifesto veritably consists of the command "exceed." As composer Charles Wuorinen put it, "How can you make a revolution when the revolution before last has already said anything goes?"

And it is particularly ironic that this final, overwhelming victory of art produces its destruction, and indeed so irrevocably that even essays such as this are helpless to retard its collapse. Fifty or even twenty years ago this essay might have aroused a grunt of controversy, perhaps even mild resistance; certainly it would have been quite justifiably considered by some artists to be reactionary and philistine, and they would have passionately opposed it on precisely those grounds. (Occasionally in reading about past art I come across this word "furor": can anyone define this for me, this "furor"?) Today, however, artists know they have nothing to fear from a mere article, or even several articles: as such they would be among a multitude of articles, appearing in a myriad of art magazines and vanishing without a trace, while the birthrate of works and even genres asymptotically approaches infinity. Who can have passion about a cause so supremely in command?

This is the crux: obviously, everyone has a certain modicum of creative potential; the mere acts of thinking, speaking, fighting, earning a living, and making love are creative ones; the very word *procreative* captions the heart of all life. This latter is no coincidence; no coincidence either that the animal most successful, and *creative,* in adapting to modern civilization is the cockroach. He fits but poorly our aesthetic of the beautiful: living in filth, on filth; able to consume anything, endure anything, adapt to anything; neither tragic nor pathetic; all-too-numerous and all-too-natural; as a species he seems immortal as a stone. Nor is there much that is tragic or pathetic or beautiful about contemporary art: like the cockroach, it is simply, and immensely, there, and worse, it is reproducing at an hyperbolic rate. The cockroach, like it or not, survives, as our notions of what is beautiful never do. Perhaps, as we have always done with our art, we must do with the cockroach: expand those notions to include him.

But perhaps not. And perhaps too we need not multiply our tragedy by blowing our ideals of beauty to smithereens that they might resemble our art. For if we are all artists—and, slanderous though the title may be, it is still, and is especially now, only a word—and if our economies are no longer rigorous enough to discourage the most hopelessly mediocre, or to ensure even the feeblest minimum of talent, then we can at least, whatever our life's work, personally guarantee in that work the presence of three elements far more indispensable than talent: risk, labor, and desperation. If there is quite nothing—pride, power, money, notoriety, comfort, status—we would not sacrifice for our work (save perhaps health, friendship, family, and love); if there is no limit to the time and strength we are willing to burn as its fuel; and if we create it not out of vanity, boredom, competitiveness, convenience or even choice, but out of necessity; only then perhaps will we have earned the right for which we have begged all these millenia: to stand our work next to the stems of grass and hope that it will go unnoticed.

The molten core of the matter is this: after four million years of evolution we are politically and economically emancipated to an extent undreamt of even a few decades ago. We are free of everything, but what are we free *for?* Leisure? Then let us call it by its real name, and not confuse it with the vigorous creative labor that was once profoundly necessary to a more primitive culture. Let us for once relax our defenses and be honest: you and I are without genius; we have only gifts far more valuable: a thimbleful of luck, and possibly, a flea's mouthful of time. Let us use them to do something that is truly of value to someone, instead of mindlessly and heartlessly trampling that luck and that time beneath the juggernaut wheels of vanity and reputation. It is not necessary to constantly hanker after the new; it is necessary only to create beauty, a tragically, exquisitely impossible task, like everything essential. Art that is not born out of love, pain, obsession, passion, and desperation is useless to us; better by far that that artist devote himself to some truly valuable task (religion, revolution, procreation, medicine, entertainment, science, etc.) than that he continue to squander our planet's resources creating a public nuisance of his freedom to melodramatize his narcissism. If all the artists who are able even for a moment to consider giving up and entering a different field were to do so, we would be left with the minute percentage who are not, the tiny fraction of artists who create not to educate or infuriate or amuse or even express, but to survive. This would surely be enough.

K. Atchley

I don't know K. Atchley at all, and as you'll see at table he's a bit hard to get to know. He's "sceptical about words," as he says himself, and you won't find out a lot about him here. The trance-like rhythm of Light of Hand suggests something about the way his obviously keen social and political and technological observation influences his work. He may be en route to a kind of intuitive prescience, tuning a random accuracy—at present still far from impressive— through some kind of feedback until it actually works. I've sensed that in his "Predictions," which you won't find here, and you'll sense it in Edison's Last Project(ion). I get impatient with arbitrary folding of punctuation into titles, but Edison's ionised projection project is a fascinating and necessary example of avant-garde opera as it returns to the magic oracular of Greek tragedy and early Baroque opera. There are sudden connections to more recent art/ thought too: a simple yet insighted concept like "Gravity is desire" converses with the Handler of Gravity in Duchamp's "La Marieé mise à nu ses celibataires, même." "WHAT IS THE NATURE OF THIS SPACE? Resonance." The past? "Randomness and a few vague patterns." The present? "Clarity." There's intelligence here, and discernment, and reason. How can he be nostalgic for Burger King?

—C.S.

K. ATCHLEY

Barbara Golden
on the train to
Stuttgart, West Germany
June, 1985

So, you grew up in Lebanon, Tennessee. You told me once that you had asthma when you were a kid. What did you do when you had to stay home from school all day?

I would sit with scissors and pencil and paper, and I would design a little kingdom or a little government. I would even draw the currency out, you know, I would design the currency, I would design the form of government, I had different officials, titles for different people who would be in the kingdom, and things like that. Also, I tried to design forms for self-defense, almost like karate or judo. I didn't know anything about either, but I'd heard of them, so I would draw pictures of little stick men in various positions and stuff like that.

Pragmatic even in your play . . . What did you read?

Actually, I never read a full book until I was about sixteen years old. The first book I ever read was Norman Mailer's *The Prisoner of Sex.*

Was it your parents' book?

No, no, no, I bought it. No, they never read anything like that. And then the next book I read was Germaine Greer's *The Female Eunuch* because I wanted a little balance to the other book. But when I was little I hardly ever read the textbooks, I found them terribly boring. I'd read Spiderman comics, I liked magazines a lot. I'd read *Time* magazine, things like that.

When did you decide that you wanted to be a composer, or that you were interested in music?

When I was a very, very small child, I mean over a few inches, you know, when I was very young. But I never had any training until much later. But as a little boy I would make up tunes and stuff. I still remember this one song vividly, and one of these days I'm going to get back to that song and do more on it.*

*The work is titled *The Rabbit's Song* and is now in progress.

But I know that you had a piano at home, what sort of music did you hear?

Well, again, we didn't get a piano until I was sixteen or seventeen. But I had some records when I was pretty young. I had a series of records: one album had folk music on it, I didn't care too much for that one, one had country and western tunes, and another was classical. I listened to the classical one a lot, it had bits and pieces. It had something like the "March of the Marionettes" on it, no Schönberg or anything like that. And I also listened to little kids' records, I had a record of the Little Rascals, and I loved the James Bond records, I had the soundtrack to *Goldfinger* and *Thunderball*. My grandmother, Adelaide, gave me those albums for Christmas. I listened to [*sings*] *Goldfinger* a lot.

What about Grand Ol' Opry? What about the Nashville influences?

Well, I was born in a town that's about thirty miles outside of Nashville, and my grandfather lived in a small community named Castalian Springs. A lot of the original Grand Ol' Opry stars, the people who really got it started, lived in this area in the middle of Tennessee and my grandfather knew these people. He knew Uncle Dave Macon. Uncle Dave Macon spent a few nights in my grandparents' house. So my grandfather had really been going to the Grand Ol' Opry almost since it started, and when I was little, I would go with him sometimes and he would introduce me to some of the performers. He knew the Crook Brothers, they performed in the Crook Brothers Band, and they also played in the Fruit Jar Drinkers.

Fruit Jar Drinkers?

Yeah, moonshine comes in fruit jars.

How long have you been in Germany now?

I got to Germany in December of '83 but I was back in the States for just a few months this past Christmastime.

I know one tangible accomplishment—you now speak German!

Well, I'm far from fluent in it but I can get around with the basics anyway.

I am impressed, it's your basic German with your . . .

Tennessee accent. I always carry my accent with me.

But you're leaving Germany, what are you coming away with? Was it a place to repose and do some music?

Yeah, I'd been in the Bay Area for, I don't know, three years or so, and one of the reasons I came there was to work with other people because I'd been in Tennessee and didn't really have many people to work with. I had one close friend, and we'd work together on music sometimes, but no other serious musicians whatever. So I worked very intensively in ensemble groups all the way from duets to the Rotaleague.* When I got here I was ready to work on some of the things I'd learned in the Bay Area, work on them by myself, and I had time to reflect on them and to integrate them in a more personal style. I've spent quite a lot of time here on *Edison's Last Project(ion)*, writing the synopsis of the acts and composing the music. I've really been living with it. And I've worked very hard on electronics. I knew a little bit about computers, a little bit about basic hardware and software construction, but I've really learned a lot on my own this past year or so. I've had time to be alone and just wrestle with the technical books, and then I'd go out and buy the chips.

*Rotaleague: Ensemble composition and performance group founded in 1982 by members Sam Ashley, K. Atchley, Ben Azarm, John Bischoff, Jay Cloidt, Barbara Golden, Jim Horton, Tim Perkis.

What was the piece I heard about that was bells in a stream?

Well, there's a piece, in German I call it *Wasser Glocken,* I guess in English you could just call it Water Chimes. It's a mechanical acoustic piece that uses the energy of the river to drive the instrument. I have a recording of the purely acoustic version, you hear the river and you hear the bells, but I also have designed electronics to go with it. I still have more design work to do, the river's not only driving the bells, but the bells are driving the computer to add melodic tones, it will all be blended. I'm interested in interfacing nature at large.

Your imagery, when you do visual things, involves cards now, how did that happen?

Ever since I was quite young I was interested in magic and I would buy magic books and I would put on magic performances for my brother and my parents. I would do card tricks and my grandfather would play poker and, I don't know, I was always sort of around cards, though I don't gamble and I'm not slick with cards or anything.

Another one of the things I would do when I was home sick in bed when I was young was I would try to design a card game. I never really came up with one until I got to California. It's maybe not exactly a card game, but in some of the printed pieces for *Edison's Last Project(ion)* there are coherent, cohesive groups of cards that have underlying connections.

Throughout what you do, and seemingly what you are, there is this mystical and meditative and mysterious quality, even your imagery in titles, like the Angels *series.*

Yeah, I'm still sort of working with the idea of angels. I don't know, there are certain kinds of questions I've asked. Again, since I was quite young, I had a very strong sense that the smallest act that an individual performs affects everything. I guess that's a mystical idea.

I think one thing that is in my music is that I'm very sceptical about words. I think that there's only a very limited amount that words can convey, and also, I think that it's a worthy cause to try to convey as much as you can with them, but it's always limited. So I think there's a lot that is missed when people concentrate on the words and on the conversations. I think there's a lot of other communication going on. So, I use words but I try to use them as music.

Now, Kenneth, the food you eat, most of it is unbelievable junk food.

I'm big on McDonald's.

So you have found the McDonald's in Freiburg, it's in the oldest and most beautiful section of town, and you go there and eat your Big Mac.

Yeah, I eat Big Macs, Quarter Pounders, I think here they're called Hamburger *Royal mit käse.* I like the taste of McDonald's food.

It's garbage, so why are you eating it?

I'm telling you, I like the taste of it, and also I honestly like the idea that I can walk in to Germany, I can walk in to Japan, and I suppose even China now, and eat at a McDonald's. It's like carrying oxygen with you in a way. I mean, I don't like to go to another country and totally absorb myself in the culture of the country I left, like I don't get that big a kick out of hanging out with the Americans here, but I do like the idea of being able to touch base every once in a while. So I have a Big Mac and some fries.

I suppose it gives you a sense of security.

I don't know, it doesn't seem to harm me too much. I'm not in the greatest shape but it doesn't seem to be harming me. I like Burger King better though, but they don't have one here.

What's your favorite thing to do, if you could do anything, I'm not talking about goals, I mean if you have a few hours to spend.

Okay, some of my favorite things to do are just to sit around and read, sit around and work on music, and be quiet. I like to be with other people, but right now I definitely like being around just one other person or two other people. I really enjoy being with other people but I enjoy being quiet with other people. And I like to work on my electronics. I also like to go on walks.

A very German thing is to walk.

Oh my god, the Germans are such prolific walkers, I can't keep up with them.

Didn't you go for a long walk with your neighbor, Mr. Babies?

We went to the Feldberg, that's the name of the mountain, it's the tallest mountain in the Black Forest. I don't remember how tall it is, but you don't have to climb it, you just walk up it. You don't have to get out the picks and spiked shoes and stuff like that but it's a pretty good walk. I live in the Black Forest and go for lots of walks. I love walking. I love going up high too. One of the first things I do when I get someplace, I don't even do it intentionally, but I keep finding that I usually go up to the highest place there.

I wish to thank the following people for their assistance with the production of *Edison's Last Project(ion)*: Kenneth and Martha Jean Atchley, Christine Costello, Anthony Atchley, Steve Lowry, A.G. Müller, The Staff of the Smyrna, TN, Public Library, The Staff of the Jean and Alexander Heard Library at Vanderbilt University. —K.A.

Introduction to
EDISON'S LAST PROJECT(ION)

Edison's Last Project(ion) is an opera concerned with the presentation of four recurring dreams that began to appear to Thomas Alva Edison on the evening of August 1, 1931 and continued at intervals until his death, October 18, 1931. During these dreams Edison witnessed various projections and dialogues initiated by personalities: human (living, dead), and non-human. Aided by the use of curious machines and strange skills the characters transmitted to one another more than simple indications of their existence. The exchanges included a variety of information including descriptions of their respective landscapes, physical laws, psychic characteristics and the extent of their connection with one another's worlds. On occasion the dreams included depictions of certain experiments conducted by Edison and his assistants: experiments involving electricity, precious metals, and the transmission of light, sound and other substances. Often the experiments were performed simultaneously with the central visionary scenes without affecting them; other times they not only influenced but completely absorbed the visions.

The four dreams are titled:

GATE (ENTRANCE)

CABINET (ENCLOSED SPACES)

VISION (SEEING BEYOND)

RIVER (CONTINUITY)

What follows are answers to assumed questions, quotations by and about Edison, synopses of the most constant elements found in the four recurring dreams, selections from the lyrics, and other related materials.

Assumed Questions

A N S W E R   # 1   *Edison's Last Project(ion)* was composed primarily as a stage work.

A N S W E R   # 2   I think that opera—and music generally—can evoke attitudes, emotions, memories, regions of experience, and states of mind that we may not usually "carry with us." This is one of the traditional—or one might better say eternal—functions of music.

A N S W E R   # 3   The quality of immediacy inherent in hearing and seeing music performed live and in public is an important part of understanding the matters evoked.

A N S W E R   # 4   Film and video are already halfway to dreams. We are used to seeing the fantastic in these mediums and perhaps forget that magic also takes place "off screen."

A N S W E R   # 5   *Vision (seeing beyond)* of *Edison's Last Project(ion)* is a ballet. The method of choreography involves translating the results of narrative and psychokinetic studies into spatial and temporal patterns for movement. For example: a situation analogous to the circumstances of *Vision* is constructed. A small planchette, lettered slips of paper, and a table top are substituted for *Vision's* tables, large lettered cards, and (stage) floor. The slips of paper are arranged in random order in a circle on the table top. One or two people place their fingertips on the planchette which has been positioned in the center of the lettered slips. An open request is made for assistance in producing phrases related to the ballet. The planchette moves along the table top indicating letters and eventually spelling out words and phrases. One phrase generated by using means similar to those described above was: "Speak of unseen echo and speak into the other." This and other texts would be choreographed in the following manner. The stage set is designed with the large lettered cards arranged in the same sequence as the slips of paper on the table top. The path followed by the planchette in order to form the various sentences are duplicated by the dancers and tables. The sample phrase given above would be performed by the dancers and tables moving first to the card lettered "S" then to the card marked "P" and so on until the phrase is completely spelled. The next phrase/pattern of movement would then be danced.

A N S W E R   # 6   The full staging of this work would include four vocalists, four actors/technicians, a string quartet, a sound synthesist, eight dancers, lighting and audio technicians. Necessary equipment/instruments would include one color video camera, three black and white video cameras, monitors, synthesizer, computerized tonal response system, prerecorded tapes and playing devices, sound amplifying and monitor equipment, a small laser projection system. I consider partial or concert version performances (without complete sets, lighting, etc.) as necessary to the compositional process.

A N S W E R   # 7   *Edison's Last Project(ion)* is one part of two intersecting groups of compositions. The first group concerns certain ideas held late in life by three early twentieth-century inventors. The present opera is the first piece of this set. The second work is titled *Marconi—The Last Seven Words* and deals with a radical information processing technique used to retrieve sounds from the distant past. Nikola Tesla's ideas will be the subject of the third part. The second group of compositions deals with non-ordinary communications. It includes the "Edison" and "Marconi" works as well as *Lolly, Light of Hand (Lumière De Main),* a quartet titled *Wind—Richard Maxfield,* and *The Rabbit's Song* (dedicated to the memory of Joseph Beuys).

Quotations

R O Y   S T E M M A N   *[Edison] hoped to achieve some form of contact with the unseen through electronic means. In 1920 Edison was busily constructing a device that he believed would put him in touch with people who had died. He believed there would be a radio frequency between the long and short waves which would make possible a form of telepathic contact with the other world.***

H U G H   F R A S E R   *The question of life after death fascinated Edison. In his later years, he told newspaper reporters several times that he was working on a device "so sensitive that if there is life after death it will pick up the evidence of it."*†

T H O M A S   E D I S O N   *I have been at work for some time building an apparatus to see if it is possible for personalities which have left this earth to communicate with us . . . If this is ever accomplished it will be accomplished not by any occult, mystifying, mysterious, or weird means, such as are employed by so-called "mediums," but by scientific methods.**

T H O M A S   E D I S O N   *If what we call personality exists after death, and that personality is anxious to communicate with us who are still in the flesh on this earth, there are two or three kinds of apparatus which should make communication very easy. I am engaged in the construction of one such apparatus now, and I hope to be able to finish it before very many months pass.**

T H O M A S   E D I S O N   *I am working on the theory that our personality exists after what we call life leaves our present material bodies . . . If our personality survives, then it is strictly logical and scientific to assume that it retains memory and knowledge that we acquire on this earth. Therefore, if personality exists, after what we call death, it is reasonable to conclude that those who leave this earth would like to communicate with those they have left here. Accordingly the thing to do is to furnish the best conceivable means to make it easy for them to open up communications with us, and then see what happens.**

T H O M A S   E D I S O N   *I am proceeding on the theory that in the very nature of things, the degree of material or physical power possessed by those in the next life must be extremely slight; and that therefore any instrument designed to be used to communicate with us must be super-delicate—as fine and responsive as human ingenuity can make it. For my part, I am inclined to believe that our personality hereafter will be able to affect matter. If this reasoning be correct, then, if we can evolve an instrument so delicate as to be affected, or moved, or manipulated—whichever term you want to use—by our personality as it survives in the next life, such an instrument, when made available, ought to record something.**

F R A N C I S   M I L L E R   *"A few days before he [Edison] passed away," continues Dr. Howe [Edison's personal physician], "he was sitting in his chair, apparently enjoying a pleasant dream. Suddenly opening his eyes and gazing upward into space, his face illuminated with a smile as he said: 'It is very beautiful over there!'"* ‡

BIBLIOGRAPHY:

* Forbes, B.C.: "Edison Working on How to Communicate with the Next World," *The American Magazine,* V.90 #4, 1920, pp. 10–11

† Fraser, Hugh Russell: "Edison, Thomas A." *The World Book Encyclopedia,* V.E, 1962, p. 49-54

‡ Miller, Francis Trevelyan *Thomas A. Edison . . . Benefactor of Mankind,* (U.S.A., The John C. Winston Co., 1931), p. 295

**Stemman, Roy *Spirits and Spirit Worlds* (London, The Danbury Press, 1975), p. 98

EDISON'S LAST PROJECT(ION)

PART I:
GATE
(ENTRANCE)

Edison dreams of himself as a young man sitting in front of and operating a complex apparatus that produces music. A huge card appears and on it a young woman is portrayed staring at an arrangement of several smaller cards. The entire card becomes animated as red lights start to glow and the now living woman begins to speak and to make a series of movements with her hands over the smaller cards. Occasionally the inventor recognizes the features of his late first wife, Mary, in the young woman's face. This vision remains distinct despite the shifting of light and shadow produced by the alternating glow of a variety of colored lights; however, the voice of the sometimes familiar-looking young woman is frequently altered. These transformations seem to correspond somehow to manipulations Edison performs on the large instrument before him. Sometimes his manipulations seem to be attempts at making the voice sound clearer as if he were trying to tune in some distant broadcast with a radio receiver. Other times his operations appear to be aimed at decoding some complex form of communication or even simplifying the voice and translating the message into a form more intelligible to himself and others. The presence stops speaking and stills her hands. She looks up staring into Edison's eyes, and the dream fades.

Cards are read from right to left and from bottom row to top.

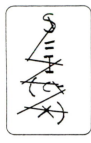

SOLIDITY

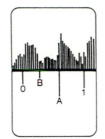

HEARING

AIM OF DEATH

(RE)COGNITION
OF CONNECTION

RIVER

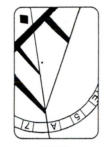

VISION

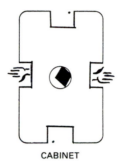

CABINET

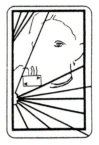

GATE

CARRIER

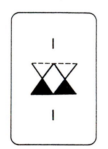

CHARACTER

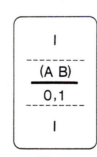

FORMULA

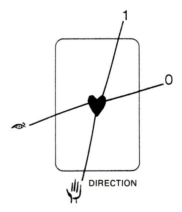

DIRECTION

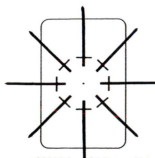

ASSERTION OF BALANCE

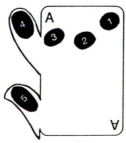

ANGEL

GRAVITY OF FEAR

ROW I

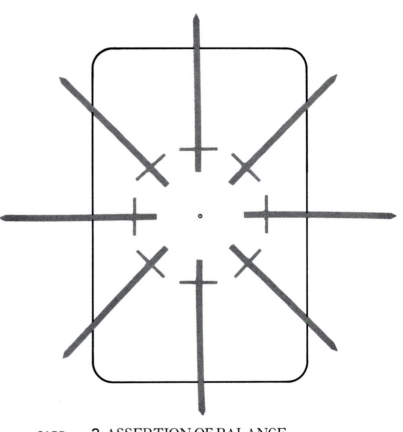

CARD: **3.** ASSERTION OF BALANCE

PERSONALITY: *Light of balance*
Healing of balance

NOTE:
"Personality" in the following usage refers to the character and quality of a card as well as a particular card's relationship(s) with other cards, qualities, etc.

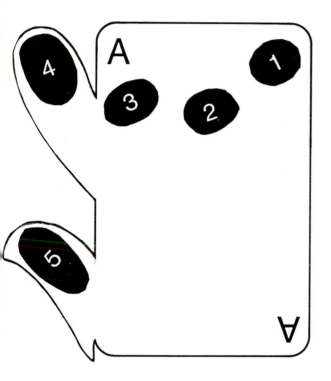

2. ANGEL

1. GRAVITY OF FEAR

Gravity of expectation
Gravity of realization
Breathing without expansion
Breathing without reduction

ROW II

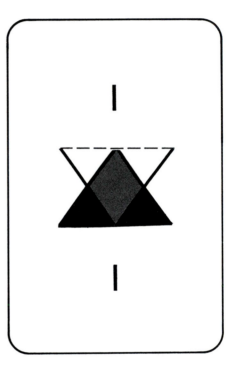

CARD: **3.** CHARACTER

PERSONALITY: *Specialist*

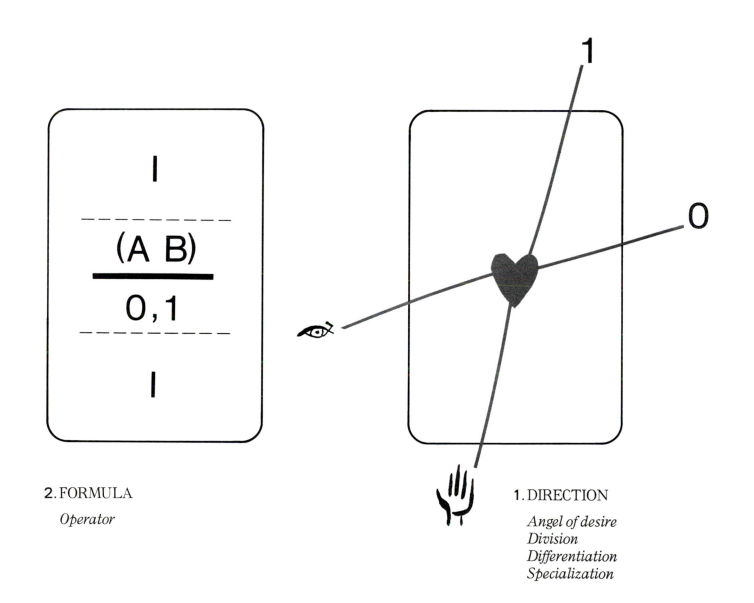

2. FORMULA

Operator

1. DIRECTION

Angel of desire
Division
Differentiation
Specialization

ROW III

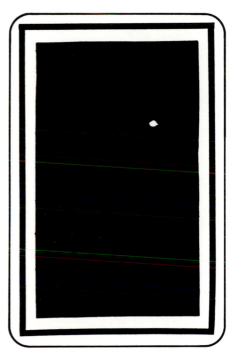

1. CARRIER

Gravity of desire
Information
Perspective
Space

ROW IV

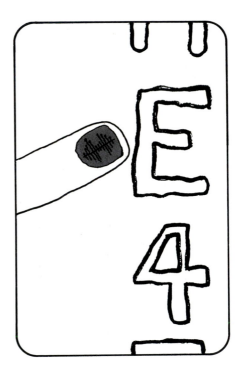

4. RIVER

Angel of lines
Continuity

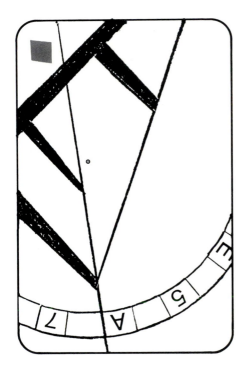

3. VISION

Seeing beyond

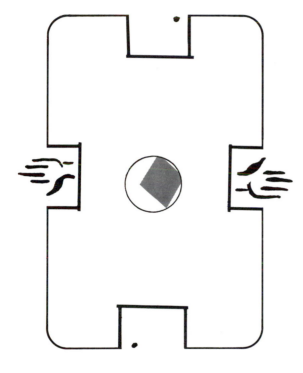

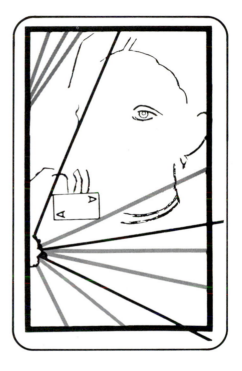

2. CABINET

Desire of realms
Enclosed spaces

1. GATE

Entrance
Transport

ROW V

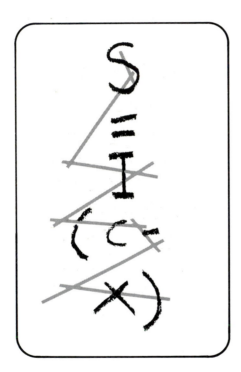

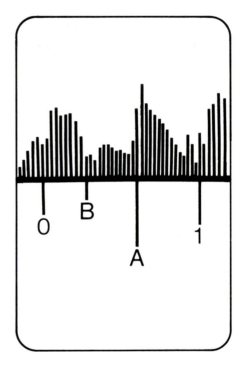

4. SOLIDITY

Realm of cycles
Illusion of motionlessness
Occlusion

S = I (C — X)
    Whereas:
    S = SOLIDITY
    C = SPEED OF LIGHT
    X > 0 AND X < C

3. HEARING

Angel of attention
Transmission

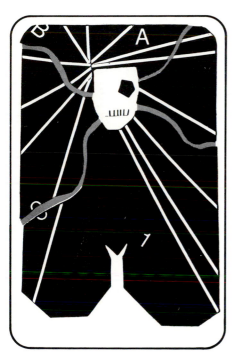

2. AIM OF DEATH

Angel of awareness

I ÷ by Negative (Division, Differentiation,
Specialization) ÷ I

1. (RE)COGNITION OF
CONNECTION

*Belief in linearity
(Illusion of lines)*

ROW VI

CARD: **1.** EXPERIMENT: Platinum, Cobalt, Silver, Aluminum

PERSONALITY: *Conductor*

PART II: CABINET (ENCLOSED SPACES)

The dreaming Edison becomes aware of darkness and a curious silvery music that fills space. Quickly brightening light reveals a laboratory in which several assistants work with electrical devices connected by wires to a large upright cabinet. Calibrations of equipment and consultations among workers take place while the quick, high-pitched sounds continue. As details of the scene come into focus so does the source of the uninterrupted sound: a laboratory assistant—designated as "Constant"—is holding and delicately twisting a sheet of thin, white metal which produces almost bell-like musical tones. Each sound is distinct, short, and quickly followed by the next.

Edison recognizes many of the people in the laboratory, but their roles seem unstable. An assistant standing by the cabinet one moment may suddenly appear as Constant, seated and gently manipulating the thin metal sheet the next instant. The inventor's own function seems to change unpredictably as well. Sometimes he stands directing the workers; other times he takes one of their places while another directs the operations. At times he watches the scene from a disembodied perspective.

Presently one of the group—referred to as "Occasion"—is assisted into the cabinet. After electrodes and other devices are attached to the person, the doors are shut. Occasion's face is visible through a square hole in the top of the cabinet and the abdominal area can be seen through a circular hole formed when the two doors are closed. Another person—"Question"—sits near the cabinet and waits while technicians complete fine adjustments of the equipment. After they signal that all is ready, Question speaks into a horn and begins a strange dialogue with an entity—"Answerer"—from another world. The entity's voice is heard with the aid of the continuously monitored electronic instruments and is finally made audible through the twisting, white metal sheet. Throughout the dialogue Occasion's mouth moves. Although this articulation is often synchronized with the alien voice, it is not clear whether or not the sound issues from Occasion's mouth. The voice, fragmented and curiously pitched, is often barely intelligible and several of the lab assistants simultaneously transcribe the conversation, each interpreting Answerer's words as they understand them.

During some of the "Cabinet" dreams the conversations were conducted with more than one alien personality. After the dialogues ended—almost invariably due to some equipment breakdown or the inability to track the drifting signal—the communicators stood, grouped and discussed the preceding events. The dream would then end.

NOTE:
. . . indicates pause.
. . ./. . . indicates long pause.
( ) text included in parenthesis is whispered or muttered.

[*question*] WHAT IS YOUR NAME?
[*answer*]: *(After) . . . after . . . .*

AM I SPEAKING WITH ONE OR MANY?
Anyone hears you . . . .

WHAT IS YOUR NAME?
(Glowing) . . . after . . . .

AM I SPEAKING TO A SPIRIT OF THE DEAD?
. . . Am I listen . . . listen . . . .

WHAT IS YOUR NAME?
. . . After . . . .

AM I SPEAKING WITH ONE SPIRIT OR MANY SPIRITS?
(Capped) . . . Do you understand?

MAY I ADDRESS YOU AS AN INDIVIDUAL?
I answer for all.

ARE THERE INDIVIDUALS IN YOUR WORLD?
Now.

. . . IS THERE DIVISION IN YOUR WORLD?
Division: . . . name . . . personality . . . function . . . .enclosure . . . .

BY WHAT NAME SHALL I CALL YOU?
. . . After . . . .

ARE YOU A SPIRIT OF THE DEAD?
Are you yet a child?

ARE THERE OTHERS WITH WHOM I CAN SPEAK?
Anyone hears you.

IS MY VOICE CLEAR TO YOU?
Anyone (here) you are not . . . individuals and spirits . . . clearly understanding . . . you expect words anywhere to light . . . .

DO YOU KNOW MY THOUGHTS?
I answer your words . . . as you think.

AM I SPEAKING WITH THE SUBCONSCIOUS?
Like ether.

ARE YOU LIKE THE ETHER?
The subconscious . . . your theory . . .like the ether.

AM I WRONG IN CONSIDERING YOU AS AN INDIVIDUAL?
(Speed) . . . / . . . Yes.

AM I WRONG IN CONSIDERING YOU AS A SPIRIT OF THE DEAD?
. . . Enclosed space.

. . . PLEASE EXPLAIN.
. . . Here is not death.

. . . WHAT IS "ENCLOSED SPACE"?
Resonance.

DO YOU EXIST IN SOME TYPE OF ENCLOSED SPACE?
To speak . . . you expect words to light . . . .

DO YOU FORM ENCLOSED SPACE?
To speak. Yes.

WHAT IS THE NATURE OF THIS SPACE?
Resonance.

HOW DO YOU FORM ENCLOSED SPACE?
Intend . . . divide . . . name . . . .

ARE YOU AWARE OF ALL LIVING IN THIS ROOM?
Through the shadows resulting from the devices . . . like echoes . . .

ARE YOU REALLY AN ENTITY SEPARATE FROM US?
We communicate.

ARE YOU AN ANGEL?
Name.

CAN YOU SEE OUR FUTURE?
Division . . . / . . . perpetuate division . . . focus excludes . . . even time . . . .

HOW DOES TIME APPEAR TO YOU?
An expanding ring of clarity. Bordered on the inside and to the outside by specks and occasional barely discernible patterns.

[*to a lab assistant*]: HOW DID YOU RECORD THAT?
[*lab assistant repeats text*]

WHAT LIES IN THE "RING OF CLARITY"?
Human first consciousness.

THE AREA OF CLARITY CONSTANTLY EXPANDS?
The circumference expands. The thickness of the band decreases.

ARE YOU DESCRIBING TIME . . . AS . . . YOU . . . .
The width of human understanding . . . human first consciousness. Regarding science, history, division by thinking . . . perpetuate division . . . .

WHAT IS YOUR UNDERSTANDING OF HUMAN HISTORY?
Exists in the present . . . in the area that grows thinner . . . .

. . . WHAT OF THE PAST . . .
Randomness and a few vague patterns . . . .

AND WHAT OF TIME IN YOUR WORLD?
Clarity.

DO YOU RECORD HISTORY?
[*noise*] *. . . / . . . / . . . / . . . .*

[*to a lab assistant*]: DO WE HAVE A CONNECTION? [*lab assistant nods affirmatively*]
Clarity . . . has no key . . . than translation . . . .

LET US DISCUSS THE PHYSICAL LAWS OF YOUR WORLD. HOW ARE THE DIMENSIONS MANIFESTED IN YOUR WORLD?
Defined by resonance of enclosed space.

. . . AND GRAVITY?
Gravity is desire.

. . . ARE THERE OTHER ENTITIES IN YOUR LAND?
. . . Layers . . . specific intelligences . . . (like platinum (reflected)) . . . layers of individuals in individual desires . . . .

IS YOUR WORLD ... DO YOU EXIST ON ANOTHER PLANET?
... Communicate ... more than translation ... invest your memories beyond farthest yet known planet energy source is ... more than translation required ... doctrine of possible relations matter to state to intention ... you do know yourselves ... this informing is in this act. Not in these your words.

THIS IS ACTUALLY ANOTHER PLANET?
[noise] ... / ... / ... / ...

WOULD YOU DESCRIBE YOUR WORLD?
A yellow planet: huge, dense, perfectly round with a few shallow pools of light yellow liquid. In a very few places there are steep, sharply pointed mountains. Everywhere a thin mist lies close to the surface ... all transformations are performed in a gray enclosure like a thick wind which is not visible until one is inside. This wind travels the entire planet.

WHERE IS YOUR PLANET?
Near. During sleep the two overlap.

SO YOURS IS NOT ... A MATERIAL PLANET?
As yours.

WOULD YOU PLEASE EXPLAIN?
As yours.

... HOW LONG HAVE YOU KNOWN OF OUR WORLD?
Recently. It became visible as you began producing ... / ... shadows ... radio energy ... outlined by these waves ....

HAVE YOU OBSERVED OUR EARTH AND PEOPLE?
... Again ... as shadows overlap ... / ... (constant) ....

PLEASE TELL ME SOME DIFFERENCES BETWEEN ENTITIES LIKE YOURSELF AND HUMANS
We have no need to turn around;
we do not sleep;
we the many are not secret;
we are aware of traveling through sound;
we derive light from the apparent contradictions;
we hear the pulses;
we know existence between the pulses.

[noise] ... / ... / ... / ...

[to a lab assistant]: **CONNECTION?**
[lab assistant checks equipment for several moments]: **THE SIGNAL IS DRIFTING.**

YOU ARE THERE?
As you.

THROUGH WHAT MEANS DO YOU HEAR MY VOICE?
[noise] ... / ... (carrier) ... / ....

DO YOU HEAR ME THROUGH, FOR EXAMPLE, SOME ELECTRICAL APPARATUS?
You have provided the other half.

HAVE YOU POSSESSED THE MEANS OF COMMUNICATING WITH OTHER WORLDS FOR A LONG TIME?
The many are not secret.

ARE YOU IN CONTACT WITH PLANETS OTHER THAN EARTH?
You possess more worlds than you are aware.

. . . WHAT TYPE OF TRANSFORMATIONS OCCUR IN THE ENCLOSURE THAT YOU DESCRIBED AS BEING "LIKE A THICK WIND"?
. . . / . . . *Individual desires are received and integrated . . . the many are not neglected . . . (loud sounds)*

TELL ME ABOUT "THE PULSES" THAT YOU SPOKE OF EARLIER.
. . . / . . .

. . . YOU SAID, "WE HEAR THE PULSES."
The pulses that together you refer to as "light." We hear the pulses within light and know existence between these pulses. The difference between the many and the one is speed and perspective.

YOU LIVE AT A DIFFERENT "SPEED" OR VELOCITY THAN HUMANS?
. . . As you know many speeds.

. . . HOW DO YOU ACCOMPLISH THESE CHANGES OF VELOCITY?
[*noise*] . . . / . . . *(Carrier)* . . . / . . .

[*glances at technician and then at Occasion*]: ARE YOU THERE?
[*noise*] . . . / . . . *Direction . . . through direction. Many speeds are attainable through direction. Direction is accomplished by listening to the sounds of one world while watching the movements of a different world. You become aware of the differences in speed, the requirements of attaining these speeds, the attainment of different speeds.*

WHAT HAVE YOU LEARNED FROM THE OBSERVATION AND ATTAINMENT OF DIFFERENT SPEEDS?
For this you answer all. The difference answers itself. [*noise*] *Defiance . . . / . . . / . . . (defiance) . . . / . . . / . . . / . . . .*

[*lab assistant*]: WE ARE LOSING THE SIGNAL. IT'S DRIFTING.

DO YOU STILL HEAR US?
[*noise*]

PART III: VISION (SEEING BEYOND)

Thomas Edison dreams of a large room. He seems to be looking into this room through one of its walls. A large table stands in the middle. Around this table are seated two men and two women. Couples are seated at smaller tables. Individuals occupy a few very small tables. Each person has both hands palm down on the table in front of them. Forming a circle on the floor around the tables are the letters of the alphabet and the digits "0" through "9" arranged in random order. The points of the compass are indicated by their initials on the walls. There are two "easts" with an additional "E" in the place of west's "W."

The men and women begin to chant quietly. It is hard to understand exactly what they are saying. At each table the chanting is in unison, there is no attempted synchronization between tables. The tables begin to move. At first they shake and shuffle about. Before long some of the tables are moving several feet in various directions along the floor. Due to the tables' movement, the men and women can no longer remain seated. With their palms still resting on the tabletops the people are on their feet and following the moving tables. Eventually the tables scoot across the room and come to rest by one of the painted letters or numbers. Laboratory assistants note the letters or numbers indicated and the tables move to other symbols which in turn are noted. Occasionally one of the researchers calls out a word that has been "spelled" by one of the tables. Otherwise, the only sound is that of the tables moving about the room. The men and women work to maintain contact with the tables that move swiftly. The lights in the room grow pink and the voices of the assistants take on a flat, dull quality. Gradually, the pink lights dim. Yellow light glows from underneath and on top of the tables. After a time the pink lights go out leaving visible only the glowing tables and the silhouettes of the men and women. The tables continue to slide around the room and finally cease to glow. Edison slips off into a deep dreamless sleep.

PART IV: RIVER (CONTINUITY)

Edison dreams of standing and viewing an incongruous laboratory scene. In one corner a youthful Edison sits concentrating on the operations of an electrical monitoring device. In the center of the room a group of his technical assistants—some holding musical instruments and others with scientific apparatuses—watch an aged Edison walk through a field to a carved stone etched with letters, numbers and odd symbols. He then kneels before the stone. The technicians adjust their instruments, and wait attentively as the kneeling inventor removes some equipment pieces from a case. Once out of the case and assembled, the pieces form a device consisting of a single rod or stylus attached by wires to a metal box with an antenna. Holding the stylus in his hand, Edison begins running it over the figures cut in the stone. Only while Edison performs the tracing motions do the technicians play their instruments. The notes seem to change with some relation to the direction of the movement of his hand. The emerging music is a curious, stuttering combination of musical tones and disembodied voices. Sometimes a few intelligible words can be distinguished. As the dreaming Edison listens and watches he becomes aware that the voices seem to be evoked from the stone by running the stylus over the incised figures much in the same way that voices are reproduced by moving a gramophone record under a stylus. The articulation of the musical tones also seems directly related to the movement of the stylus over the rough grooves of the figures. Occasionally some of the traced letters and numbers seem to spell a phrase or represent a formula. Old Edison finishes the tracings, packs his transmitting device and stands. The technicians begin packing their instruments and the young Edison rises from his desk and approaches them. The "River" dream always ends abruptly; a sound wakes the dreamer.

Introduction to
LIGHT OF HAND
(Lumière de main)

In 1978 I composed a one–act opera titled *Lolly*. Through the music
I gave voice to messages, predictions, and descriptions of an alien world
from a "disembodied" personality.

I undertook a more formalized study of non–ordinary communication after
moving to California in the fall of 1980. Using electromagnetic, image,
sound, and text manipulations, I composed a series of communications
with "Angels." I defined "Angel" as a patterning of information which
implies or from which one may infer intelligence especially when encoun-
tered in supposed randomness or through a sequence of "coincidences."
To me the most interesting "patterning of information" implied not only
intelligence but also character.

The character of a woman seemed to be evoked by the 1980 composition
Angel. The text was constructed of declarative and non–rational statements, in order to describe aspects of a character and a relationship. The
presence of character in this work has been strong enough that listeners
have continued to ask me to tell them more about the woman.

*K. Atchley
Ben Azarm
Laetitia De Compiegne
Theresa Whitehill

With *Light of Hand (Lumière de Main)* I sought to evoke a different sort
of complex personality and its environment, in terms modeled on a deck
of cards. The text was originally performed by four singers.* A computer
controlled multiplexer allowed only one performer's voice to be heard by
the audience at any one time. Through this rapid switching of voices, a
single word of text might be articulated by three or four singers with each
one contributing a syllable or smaller speech unit. Thus I attempted to
create a single "new" voice for the character that was defined and evoked
by the text. I also constructed four cards which were reproduced and
distributed among the audience. These cards contributed further details
of qualities possessed by the character and environment. It was through
the composition of a similar text and set of cards that the personalities,
relationships, and settings of *Edison's Last Project(ion)* came to me.

The original text follows and may be read down in columns or across
in rows.

LIGHT OF HAND
(Lumière de main)

JACK OF HEALING	NINE OF ABSTINENCE	SEVEN OF LIGHT
TEN OF CONCENTRATION	REALM OF DIAMONDS	THREE OF GRAVITY
ABSTINENCE OF CLUBS	JACK OF ATTRACTION	HEALING OF SPADES
REBEL OF SPADES	ANGEL OF HEARTS	REALM OF HEARTS
GRAVITY OF DIAMONDS	INTENTION OF CLUBS	THREE OF DESIRE
TWO OF BALANCE	NINE OF REALMS	TWO OF CONCENTRATION
CONCENTRATION OF HEARTS	INTENTION OF SPADES	INTENTION OF REBELS
SEVEN OF REBELLION	FOUR OF GRAVITY	INTENTION OF ANGELS
KING OF DESIRE	THREE OF LOCATION	FIVE OF LOCATION
TEN OF GRAVITY	SIX OF HEALING	FIVE OF BALANCE
EIGHT OF ATTRACTION	KING OF ATTRACTION	JACK OF ABSTINENCE
QUEEN OF ABSTINENCE	REBEL OF CLUBS	FIVE OF DESIRE
HEALING OF DIAMONDS	DESIRE OF INTENTIONS	ACCIDENTS OF DIAMONDS
FIVE OF INTENTION	SIX OF ATTENTION	LOCATION OF HEARTS
HEALING OF HEARTS	THREE OF ANGELS	SEVEN OF GRAVITY
SEVEN OF BALANCE	QUEEN OF ATTRACTION	ANGEL OF CLUBS
SIX OF LOCATION	TEN OF LIGHT	QUEEN OF ANGELS
NINE OF ANGELS	SEVEN OF HEALING	GRAVITY OF DIAMONDS
INTENTION OF HEARTS	NINE OF LOCATION	ATTENTION OF CLUBS
JACKS OF ACCIDENTS	QUEEN OF REALMS	GRAVITY OF CONCENTRATION

ABSTINENCE OF HEARTS
ATTRACTION OF HEARTS
FIVE OF HEALING
LOCATION OF CLUBS
INTENTION OF ACCIDENTS
SEVEN OF REBELLION
FOUR OF DESIRE
REALM OF FOURS
CONCENTRATION OF DIAMONDS
JACK OF REALMS
NINE OF ABSTINENCE
ACE OF GRAVITY
KING OF BALANCE
HEALING OF FIVES
ANGEL OF DIAMONDS
REBELLION OF HEARTS
TEN OF ATTRACTION
EIGHT OF GRAVITY
JACK OF LOCATION
FOUR OF REALMS

ACE OF LIGHT
TWO OF ABSTINENCE
HEALING OF SEVENS
LIGHT OF CLUBS
JACK OF DESIRE
EIGHT OF ATTENTION
THREE OF DESIRE
SIX OF GRAVITY
ANGEL OF REALMS
DESIRE OF FOURS
CONCENTRATION OF GRAVITY
FOUR OF INTENTIONS
TEN OF LIGHT
ATTRACTION OF THREES
FIVE OF LIGHT
SEVEN OF BALANCE
QUEEN OF CONCENTRATION
FOUR OF HEALING
BALANCE OF SPADES
ATTRACTION OF DIAMONDS

ACCIDENTS OF CLUBS
CONCENTRATION OF SPADES
DESIRE OF ANGELS
TWO OF LIGHT
QUEEN OF ANGELS
LIGHT OF GRAVITY
QUEEN OF INTENTIONS
DESIRE OF DIAMONDS
TEN OF BALANCE
HEALING OF ATTENTION
ACCIDENT OF NINES
GRAVITY OF CLUBS
INTENTION OF REALMS
ATTENTION OF HEARTS
FOUR OF CONCENTRATION
ANGEL OF THREES
REBELLION OF CONCENTRATION
LOCATION OF DIAMONDS
ATTRACTION OF CLUBS
HEALING OF DIAMONDS

REALM OF HEARTS
ANGEL OF NINES
THREE OF ATTENTION
BALANCE OF HEARTS
ACE OF INTENTION
FIVE OF REBELLION
DESIRE OF CLUBS
NINE OF BALANCE
REALM OF TENS
BALANCE OF HEALING
THREE OF INTENTIONS
ACE OF INTENTIONS
SIX OF BALANCE
SEVEN OF ACCIDENTS
SIX OF ANGELS
ABSTINENCE OF DIAMONDS
NINE OF ATTRACTION
ATTRACTION OF HEARTS
INTENTION OF SPADES
LIGHT OF DIAMONDS

KING OF LIGHT
FIVE OF HEALING
LOCATION OF CONCENTRATION
BALANCE OF DIAMONDS
SIX OF LOCATION
ATTENTION OF EIGHTS
ANGEL OF BALANCE
REALM OF SEVENS
THREE OF ABSTINENCE
REALM OF THREE
REBELLION OF LOCATION
BALANCE OF SEVENS
KING OF GRAVITY
SEVEN OF LIGHT
ATTENTION OF SPADES
JACK OF INTENTION
FIVE OF DESIRE
THREE OF REBELLION
DESIRE OF SPADES
GRAVITY OF SIXES

HEALING OF HEARTS
SEVEN OF ANGELS
REALM OF FIVES
GRAVITY OF ATTRACTION
ATTENTION OF HEARTS
BALANCE OF CLUBS
FOUR OF DESIRE
SIX OF ANGELS
ATTRACTION OF CONCENTRATION
JACK OF GRAVITY
LIGHT OF DIAMONDS
FIVE OF ACCIDENTS
LOCATION OF HEALING
SIX OF DESIRE
LOCATION OF HEARTS
ACE OF ANGELS
FIVE OF REBELLION
SIX OF LIGHT
SEVEN OF ANGELS
LOCATION OF BALANCE

REALM OF HEALING	NINE OF DESIRE	REBELLION OF HEARTS
THREE OF LOCATION	CONCENTRATION OF HEARTS	SIX OF ABSTINENCE
FIVE OF GRAVITY	BALANCE OF REALMS	HEALING OF DIAMONDS
DESIRE OF CLUBS	GRAVITY OF SPADES	CONCENTRATION OF THREES
ACCIDENT OF LIGHT	THREE OF HEALING	ANGEL OF DESIRE
EIGHT OF REALMS	INTENTION OF ANGELS	ACE OF ANGELS
SEVEN OF DESIRE	LIGHT OF ATTENTION	HEALING OF BALANCE
GRAVITY OF HEARTS	EIGHT OF INTENTION	THREE OF INTENTION
REBEL OF BALANCE	REBELLION OF TEN	ABSTINENCE OF GRAVITY
LIGHT OF SPADES	INTENTION OF ACCIDENTS	REBELLION OF INTENTION
BALANCE OF LOCATION	FOUR OF BALANCE	REALM OF CLUBS
INTENTION OF BALANCE	REBELLION OF CLUBS	LOCATION OF LIGHT
SIX OF ATTRACTION	ACCIDENT OF INTENTION	LIGHT OF ANGELS
HEALING OF SPADES	CONCENTRATION OF DESIRE	CONCENTRATION OF LOCATION
LIGHT OF CLUBS	QUEEN OF GRAVITY	BALANCE OF DIAMONDS
ATTENTION OF DIAMONDS	KING OF LOCATION	SIX OF CONCENTRATION
KING OF HEALING	THREE OF ATTENTION	KING OF REALMS
ACE OF ATTENTION	ATTRACTION OF BALANCE	HEALING OF REBELLION
GRAVITY OF BALANCE	GRAVITY OF NINES	INTENTION OF DESIRE
ANGEL OF ATTENTION	INTENTION OF HEALING	SEVEN OF BALANCE

QUEEN OF ATTENTION	GRAVITY OF INTENTION	FOUR OF ATTRACTION
BALANCE OF DESIRE	CONCENTRATION OF ACCIDENTS	THREE OF DESIRE
LIGHT OF REALMS	INTENTION OF REALMS	REBELLION OF HEALING
ACE OF DESIRE	ANGEL OF THREES	ATTRACTION OF LOCATION
LOCATION OF HEARTS	TWO OF HEALING	GRAVITY OF INTENTION
JACK OF ATTENTION	ATTRACTION OF GRAVITY	HEALING OF CLUBS
DESIRE OF LIGHT	HEALING OF ACCIDENTS	TWO OF CONCENTRATION
BALANCE OF ACCIDENTS	ACCIDENTS OF SEVENS	LOCATION OF ATTENTION
HEALING OF INTENTION	ATTENTION OF LIGHT	REBEL OF BALANCE
SIX OF REALMS	REALM OF ATTRACTION	FOUR OF DESIRE
DESIRE OF ATTENTION	REALM OF CONCENTRATION	LIGHT OF CONCENTRATION
ACE OF LIGHT	DESIRE OF GRAVITY	ATTRACTION OF BALANCE
FIVE OF BALANCE	LOCATION OF LIGHT	ATTENTION OF ATTRACTION
REALM OF FOURS	REALM OF REBELLION	DESIRE OF REALMS
REBELLION OF LOCATION	ATTENTION OF TENS	GRAVITY OF THREES
ATTENTION OF DESIRES	LIGHT OF BALANCE	LOCATION OF ACCIDENTS
NINE OF ATTRACTION	CONCENTRATION OF LOCATION	REALM OF SEVENS
ANGEL OF LOCATION	EIGHT OF DESIRE	CONCENTRATION OF ATTENTION
REBELLION OF FIVES	SIX OF LOCATION	LIGHT OF HEARTS
ATTRACTION OF REBELS	LOCATION OF REBELLION	INTENTION OF ATTENTION

. . . to feed the flames